Failed imagination?

MANCHESTER
UNIVERSITY PRESS

Failed imagination?

New world orders
of the twentieth century

Andrew Williams

Manchester University Press
Manchester and New York

distributed exclusively in the USA by St. Martin's Press

Published by Manchester University Press
Oxford Road, Manchester M13 9NR, UK
and Room 400, 175 Fifth Avenue, New York, NY 10010, USA
http://www.man.ac.uk/mup

Distributed exclusively in the USA by
St. Martin's Press, Inc., 175 Fifth Avenue, New York,
NY 10010, USA

Distributed exclusively in Canada by
UBC Press, University of British Columbia, 6344 Memorial Road,
Vancouver, BC, Canada V6T 1Z2

British Library Cataloguing-in-Publication Data
A catalogue record for this book is available from the British Library

Library of Congress Cataloging-in-Publication Data applied for

ISBN 0 7190 4786 2 *hardback*
    0 7190 4787 0 *paperback*

First published 1998

05   04   03   02   01   00   99   98   10 9 8 7 6 5 4 3 2 1

Typset in Sabon with Gill Sans display
by Koinonia, Manchester
Printed in Great Britain
by Bell & Bain Ltd, Glasgow

To Jane, Nicholas and Rebecca

Contents

Acknowledgements

The debts incurred in writing this book were immense. I would like to thank the following libraries for extending me every courtesy: in Britain the British Library, London, the Bodleian Library, Oxford, the Librarians at the Royal Institute of International Affairs, London and, of course, the Public Record Office in Kew; in the United States the Library of Congress in Washington, the Seeley H. Mudd Library at Princeton University and the Roosevelt Presidential Library at Hyde Park, New York; in France the Archives Nationales and the Ministère des Affaires Etrangères Library on the Quai d'Orsay, Frédéric Cepède and his colleagues at the Office Universitaire de Recherche Socialiste and the Archives d'histoire contemporaine and, especially, Mme Odile Gaultier-Voituriez.

Individual and special thanks go to those who have read chapter drafts or papers based on this book – in particular, Tony Booker, Edward Broadbent, Clive Church, George Conyne, Phil Deans, John English, Mervyn Frost, John Groom, Dan Hiester, Charles Jones, Zaki Laïdi, Ian Manners, Michael Nicholson, Brian Porter, Paul Rich, Ann Stevens, Jean-Claude Vatin, Fred Whitemore, Jarrod Wiener and a number of anonymous reviewers from Manchester University Press. Paul Bradbury was most generous in lending me his father's papers. I would also particularly like to thank Marie-Claude Smouts and her colleagues at the CERI in Paris for a most enjoyable month there in May 1996; Robert Scharf for his hospitality when I was in Paris; my old friends Neil and Judy Garrecht-Williams, who put up with me in New York, and Chris and Lois Mitchell who did the same in Washington. I would naturally like to thank the University of Kent at Canterbury for its generous financial help and for the two sabbatical leaves it accorded me to write this book, and my colleagues in the Department of Politics and International Relations. Finally, I would like to thank all at Manchester University Press, especially Richard Purslow, Rebecca Crum and Nicola Viinikka. Last but not least, this book is dedicated to Jane and to my children, Nicholas and Rebecca.

Andrew Williams, Canterbury

Abbreviations

ACNP	American Commission to Negotiate the Peace
ACPWFP	Advisory Committee on Post-War Foreign Policy
AFC	America First Committee
ARA	American Relief Administration
CFFR	Council for Foreign Relations
CI	conservative internationalism
DORA	Defence of the Realm Act
EAC	European Advisory Commission
EBRD	European Bank for Reconstruction and Development
GATT	General Agreement on Tariffs and Trade
IMF	International Monetary Fund
LEP	League to Enforce Peace
LNU	League of Nations Union
LON	League of Nations
MAE	Ministère des Affaires Etrangères
NATO	North Atlantic Treaty Organisation
NESPA	National Economic and Social Planning Association
NWO	new world order
OECD	Organisation for Economic Cooperation and Development
OEEC	Organisation for European Economic Cooperation
PEP	Political and Economic Planning
PI	progressive internationalism
PID	Political Intelligence Department
PWP	post-war planning
RIIA	Royal Institute of International Affairs
SND	Société des Nations
UDC	Union of Democratic Control
UN	United Nations
UNESCO	United Nations Educational, Scientific and Cultural Organisation
UNRRA	United Nations Relief and Rehabiliation Administration

Introduction

Why study new world orders?

In this Introduction the intention is to show the thinking that underlies the genesis of this book. It has emerged from my long-standing conviction that most scholars of international relations have a visceral distrust of the time-consuming processes of historical method. They often prefer instead to write in a rather incestuous fashion about each other's work or to talk about 'processes' that neatly avoid too much spade work in archives. International relations has tended to become more and more self-referential, in the process drawing on an ever smaller number of (usually American) gurus who have little regard for the longer-term currents of world history, even within their own culture. Yet the older traditions of international relations' political and intellectual history are far too precious to be left to moulder away on the shelves of libraries. If this book has one good effect it will be to take the strain off borrowings of international relations theorists of the 1970s and 1980s and to put it back on to, especially, those writing between the 1920s and the 1940s.

But equally I recognise that international historians are often of little use to the student of international relations. It may be true that intensive studies of a short period of history are likely to provide better scholarship, but this is usually of little use to the teacher or student of international relations who wants to see the big picture. I wanted therefore to write a book that would not be too simplistic for the international relations scholar interested in theory and long-term processes but neither too insulting to the detailed needs of the historian. The concept of the 'new world order' (NWO) was chosen as the vehicle of this ambition, for reasons that I hope to make clear in this Introduction and in the book as a whole.

By choosing to show the genealogy of the term since 1914, this book tries to cut the onion of international relations in two ways that should be complementary. The first five chapters are a review of both the diplomatic history and contemporaneous literature about the genesis of the NWOs of the twentieth century. They first examine both the motivations and actions of the principal political actors and groups of decision makers during the periods 1914–19 and 1939–45. This exercise is more difficult to repeat for the period after the declaration of George Bush's NWO in 1990, because the archival material is not open to scrutiny and we are not in a position as yet to say how the Owl of Minerva will judge the present era. The aim of these chapters is therefore to demonstrate how key NWO ideas emerged from certain specific historical circumstances, but also as a result of the development of much deeper and older currents of political thinking.

The remaining three chapters aim to extract what is lasting in terms of an ongoing historical dialogue on a series of key themes that emerged from the policy debates outlined in the first five chapters. The rationale for this choice will be further explained in the text but a central assertion is that there is a continuity of theme that has emerged in all the NWOs of the twentieth century (including the present one since 1989). The main themes that will be developed are that of 'security' (which includes a discussion of the role of international organisation as a functional alternative to war); that of the consideration of economic factors in both conflict and in the often-attempted conversion of this conflict into peaceful competition; and, lastly, the 'self-determination' of peoples as a liberating principle.

All of these themes have been differently constituted in the three attempts at an NWO in the twentieth century, so these last three chapters develop a genealogy of the ideas and how they have related to policy issues. These chapters also bring the debate on the NWO up to the late 1990s. The Conclusion will make some overall comments on the issues raised by the book and ask whether we can indeed talk about a 'failed imagination' of the NWO idea or one that can be deemed 'successful'. This book is thus as much an attempt to answer some fundamental questions about the evolution of international relations in the twentieth century as about attempting a synthetic history of the concept and reality of the NWO agenda since 1914. What it does not attempt is to develop any new grand theories of political philosophy, but rather it tries to show how such debates have been mediated (or not) into the policy processes of, particularly, the Anglo-Saxon powers that have dominated the debate on the NWO in the twentieth century.

The idea that it might be possible to create an NWO that would improve the global political, social and economic environment might be seen as a key *leitmotif* of much political thought since (at least) Kant. The nineteenth century saw a plethora of plans in this direction.[1] In the twentieth century this has taken a different turn as the might of the United States and the growth of the influence of public opinion in the foreign policy process have led to pressure to try and modify the very basis of the international system. The result has been the creation of a world where states maintain their importance, but where international capitalism has assumed an increasing role. These considerations and a wider debate about the conditions and problems of modernity have led to an ever evolving discussion about the causes and cures of war and the conditions that are necessary for peace.

Some of this debate has led to deeply pessimistic predictions about the future of humankind, but it has also led many other thinkers and politicians to try and create the conditions of a 'better' world. The contention of this book is that the nexus of considerations, actions and arguments about the NWO project can shed a great deal of light on both the possibilities and problems inherent in these attempts to make this 'better' world happen.

It has become a commonplace to say that the obsession with 'realism' in international relations after 1945 has stilled the debate about possible alternative ideal futures for humankind within the discipline until very recently.[2] However, since the end of the Cold War an explosion of critical, normative and post-modern thought has gone a long way to correcting, perhaps even over-correcting, this obsession. It has also given us a potentially open-ended possibility for a reconsideration of the historical record of international relations practice and theory from before 1945, so that we can ask whether it still holds some wisdom for us in the late twentieth century and beyond. In this new and welcome spirit of reflection, we can thus reconsider some of the classical antecedents and heritage of our discipline. The ideas that make up the component parts of the NWO are used here as a convenient framework within which to undertake such a reconsideration, faced as we now are with security, economic and identity questions that bear more resemblance to the situation which prevailed earlier in the twentieth century than those of the Cold War period within which many of the assumptions of international relations developed. Perhaps we do indeed need to go 'back to the future'[3] to explain some of the unfamiliar problems with which we are faced but which, for our forebears, would not have been unusual. This is not to say that history is repeating itself, but that it does have lessons to teach us.

The kinds of source that such a book could address are clearly potentially openended and a decision has had to be made about which categories to highlight and which to de-emphasise. The main targets are as follows:

- *The archival traces of the key actors in the main event sequences of the thinking through, or better, the 'imagination' of the NWOs before 1945.* To identify who these 'key actors' are is in itself problematic, although the same names crop up continually and are surprisingly small in number. Occasionally, individuals are included that do not immediately spring to mind but who made some very interesting and possibly influential remarks on the subject. A particular emphasis will be laid on the thinking of key politicians and civil servants in Britain and the United States who played a disproportionate role in developing NWO ideas. The NWO has to be seen as a Western construct, and particularly one that came out of the thinking of the two most powerful states of the last 200 years, Britain and the United States. When Noam Chomsky attacks these two states for using the NWO to push their own interests, he is accurately identifying the major players, if not necessarily the game they are playing.[4]

- *The archival traces of major groups of policy thinkers, particularly, again, in Great Britain and the United States.* 'Think tanks' were active during the First and Second World Wars, which had a significant or insignificant input into the policy process. Examining their impact on the policy process helps to show why some ideas become accepted and others rejected by what might be called the 'forces of history'.

- *The examination of numerous 'key texts' written by significant commentators on international relations during the period under consideration.* A prime, but by no means exclusive, focus will be on some of the 'liberal internationalist' thinkers and activists of the inter-war period, many of whom have been neglected as 'idealists' not worthy of serious consideration. Other texts that will be considered are merely 'forgotten classics', such as Alfred Cobban's *National Self-Determination.*[5] It is also hoped by looking anew at such writings to contribute to the long-overdue reassessment of the wrongly assumed necessary diametric opposition of 'utopian' and 'realist' thinking in international relations, one perpetuated by the inspired polemic of E.H. Carr's *The Twenty Years' Crisis.*[6]

Inevitably this will lead to gaps in the evidence presented and in the interpretation offered. There is a lack of access to some key actors' archives or great silences within them. Much of Roosevelt's thinking was not committed to paper, for example. Soviet thinking on the origins of the Cold War has only now begun to come to light as the archives have creaked open.[7] A chapter on France has had to be omitted for reasons of space.[8] But that cannot be helped, as any book has to be selective, and what we have selected here conveys the heart of what is an essentially 'Anglo-American' body of thought and practice. It also has to accept the criticism that history will always be re-interpreted in the light of present circumstances, which change by definition.

Another obvious criticism of this approach is that I might, first, be accused of assuming that NWO thinking is the same as American, or at least 'Anglo-American', thinking. Clearly this is not the case, but thinkers and policy makers in the United States and Britain have in practice defined much of the debate, partly of course as a result of winning two world wars and the Cold War. However, this process has also often been as a result of a dialogue with other kinds of NWO thinking, especially that of Lenin in 1917, which, for example, had a clear influence on Woodrow Wilson's deliberations. Equally, we cannot entirely neglect the NWO thinking of the Nazis (Hitler's *Neueordnung*) or that of Third World thinkers (in the New International Economic Order of the 1970s, for example). Thus the book aims to look at least at some of these tendencies in parallel with the NWO ideas of the 'West'.

Second, it might be argued, 'where does that leave those who are excluded?' – many by geographical location, the sin of not being American or West European, or because they do not live in consumerist societies? It is hoped that these points will be addressed in the latter parts of the book when I look at the thematic areas of the NWO project. I have no axe to grind with those who feel that the NWO has been unequally beneficial to many of the world's peoples, and indeed I would argue that this is its greatest potential weakness.

History and international relations: the neglected link

Writing history, and international relations, is a literary as much as a scientific pursuit. The distinction between what is 'real' and what is 'imagined' is difficult at the best of times – it becomes most difficult when the very subject matter of the 'real' is the 'imaginary', as in the imagination of the NWO. As Terry Eagleton would say: '[l]iterature, in the meaning of the word we have inherited, *is* an ideology'.[9] Literature, in his meaning, is that of the ideology of the English class system, a form of social control to replace religion in a domestic society. 'Literature', albeit of a different kind, plays an analogous role in the NWO; it is an imagining of a future in an extrapolation of a recent past and a longer experience of failure in an international society. In 1919 and 1945 the failure was that yet another great war had been fought. The purpose of the NWO projects was to propose a vision of a unified approach to the future which would harmonise power and ideology (or what Zaki Laïdi calls 'power and purpose'[10]) to create a fairer, safer and more stable international system. In 1919, but most successfully in 1945, this harmonisation was attempted and brought together many of the essential diplomatic, economic and ideological elements of an NWO (if not for all the peoples of the globe). In 1990 the situation was rather different, in that no war had been necessary for, ostensibly, the NWO agenda to 'win'. The imagination had become reality (hence 'the End of History'), even if many predict that this victory will prove hollow.[11]

The intention of the rest of this Introduction is therefore to ask some key theoretical questions to see if they can generate some useful tools for interrogating the historical source – the classic 'who', 'what' 'why', and 'how' questions. The 'who' refers to the generators of NWO ideas. The 'what' refers to the kinds of category of thinking that they have mainly inspired, or what functions they perform in organising our thinking about international relations. The 'why' is more of an attempt to ask what NWOs tell us about why we need to develop an 'historical imagination', or rather not to forget that we have one. The 'how' is a reflection on the more extreme, but nonetheless over-arching, forms of historical imagination that the NWOs can, should and have provoked.

Who imagines NWOs?

There are clearly moments of history when it 'accelerates', and the pent-up imaginings of the intelligentsia and political elites, but also of the general population, see a brief flowering, like the Dannikil Depression after one of its thirty-year downpours. For a brief instant of history the planners and dreamers get a chance to make a real mark and to suggest ways of improving the lot of humankind for the next period. Such have been the opportunities given to what was a relatively small group of individuals in the periods of (roughly) 1914–20, 1939–47 and 1989–92. They have been allowed to dream out loud, to imagine in private and to engineer in public. They have usually, if not always, paid for their dreaming by being subjected to a lasting criticism and scorn for what are inevitably seen as their over-optimistic visions of the future.

But they are nonetheless immortalised by their participation in such epic events, and have become almost heroic figures. The reception given to Woodrow Wilson in Europe in 1919 by the crowd unnerved the 'old' politicians of Europe. Immense quasi-messianic hopes were put in this frail ex-Professor. Herbert Hoover could still refer after nearly forty years to 'the Ordeal of Woodrow Wilson'.[12] One is struck that even the lesser bit players at the Paris Peace Conference have come down to us with heroic or dastardly reputations. Lloyd George, Clemenceau and Keynes, in particular, have never ceased to intrigue us. The same is true of Roosevelt, Stalin and Churchill since 1945; all deeply embedded in the national and international mythology of the twentieth century. In an 'Age of Extremes',[13] as Hobsbawm has called it, we see these people as architects of our destiny, no matter how much 'common sense' might tell us that they were flotsam in the tide of history.

It could be argued that the latest of our NWOs nonetheless demonstrates the failure of the human agency thesis. The leaders of the West were caught napping by the fall of the Berlin Wall; indeed, some tried Canute-like to make it topple in slower motion (such as French President, François Mitterand). Its main self-proclaimed architects (German Foreign Minister, Hans-Dietrich Genscher, George Bush, Margaret Thatcher, etc.) have not seen their original plans fulfilled. The impersonal forces of 'globalisation' and its dualistic side-kicks liberal democracy or economic autocracy, as well as political or social disintegration are widely touted as having won, not human hopes and aspirations.

However, and simultaneously, if the twentieth century has been marked by the 'great man' (Margaret Thatcher as our token woman might count for the latest NWO), it has also been characterised by another form of acceleration, that of the impact of the masses on the elites. Christopher Coker has remarked that the '20th Century was one in which the ideas of the "salon" escaped into the streets [and] ... was also one in which undigested concepts and ideas entered popular currency, Freud's death-wish and Jung's collective unconscious being two cases in point'.[14] Although Coker's emphasis is on the impact of war on that 'modern consciousness', it is also true that in opening up the Pandora's box of 'Open Diplomacy', Woodrow Wilson allowed the popular consciousness to range freely over an area, that of international relations, from where the populace had hitherto been banned. Wilson's aim had been to mobilise the masses behind the notion of peace, and his early success in mobilising huge crowds in late 1918 showed how powerful the idea could be. His *hubris* led to an almost inevitable democratic *nemesis*, as many of his contemporaries, much more wedded to the idea of negotiations behind firmly closed doors, realised. Indeed, Wilson's own insistence that the Council of Four conduct business at his hotel in Paris with the minimum possible of spectators seems to indicate that he feared any extraneous democratic input until his scheme was complete.

The twentieth century has also seen a voluminous literature reflecting on peace and war, which has been constantly drawn upon by leaders to feed their imaginations and whose hopes and aspirations they hoped to fulfil. Hence H.G. Wells or Norman Angell are as much to be acknowledged as creators of the new world order imaginings of 1918–19 (and their subsequent defeat) as Woodrow Wilson. Equally, it is not only literary individuals that have shaped background sentiment upon which leaders have drawn, it is also ideas developed by 'schools' of commentators and small groups of intellectuals. The 'Velvet Revolution' that was epitomised by the coming down of the Berlin Wall in November 1989 had its prophets in writers such as Milan Kundera, its intellectual icons such as Francis Fukuyama and its emerging prophets of doom – in this postmodern age as likely to be CNN talk-show hosts or Australian news magnates as 'serious-minded' commentators. It also had its Adam Smith Institute, its Heritage Foundation and other key groups of elite commentators. The very concept of the intellectual has now been severely damaged by the over-blown imaginings and/or *engagement* of so many among them, as has that of statesmen because of their failure to deliver their promises of a better world.[15] But they have nonetheless had a determinate impact at moments of key decision.

If we accept that this is the 'People's Century' we have nonetheless to reiterate that 'Open Diplomacy' has been more respected in the breach than in the observance by the political elite. There is a great tradition of critics of the NWO who have attacked those who were 'present at the creation', as Dean Acheson said of his own involvement in the NWO of 1945.[16] These critics have constantly tried to get their opposing views heard, often from positions of some influence within the elite structure of their day and before the latest version of the new order had been cast in tablets of stone. Hence E.H. Carr made many attempts to influence the tone of the post-Second World War debate on the future of international relations, most notably in the *Twenty Years' Crisis*. Sometimes the critical commentator would speak

both from the 'outside' and the 'inside' of the policy debate, as did John
Maynard Keynes over the Treaty of Versailles. But even with this proviso,
the clearest architects of the NWOs of the twentieth century have all been
members of the 'Establishment'. And however rapidly they have become
discredited after the event, their legacy has been the basis on which
subsequent institutions were built, and either failed or succeeded.

The key to analysing whether they were successful or not also has its
analogy in the analysis of literature. Georg Lukács' classic text, *The Historical
Novel*, makes the point that the transformation of Europe at the cusp of the
eighteenth and nineteenth centuries was reflected in the literary endeavours
of the period as in its politics. In the country that was in the greatest throes
of economic transformation, England at that time, history was interpreted
more 'concretely' than elsewhere.[17] In 1914–19 history was grasped most
'concretely' in the United States and Russia, both countries of the future, not
the past. Thus the twentieth century has been largely about their struggle for
supremacy in the domain of ideas, policy and power. This is not to say that
other 'older' states and peoples, especially Britain and Germany, have not
played a role, but they did not, largely speaking, play a *determinate* part in
the debate in the long run. They acted as sounding boards for the bigger,
'world historical', to quote Lukács again, ideas for NWOs.

This book is therefore unashamedly 'elitist' in that it aims to decipher
what were the main influences on the elites, but also tries to show how those
influences were or were not mediated into a (sometimes rather temporary)
policy 'reality'. It goes further in that it posits the crucial role of key
individuals, and has therefore to select among a crowded stage those individuals and, occasionally, groupings that really mattered. In so doing the book
has also to be selective and impressionistic. Some influences must of
necessity remain occult, as the art of the biographer and historian combined
cannot fully comprehend the full complexity of even one of the characters
that will appear in these pages, especially as many of them were masters of
the art of disguise. One defence of this elitism is that all of those involved in
these accelerations of history were aware of the magnitude and importance
of their task. They were self-consciously world historical figures, and
certainly self-important. As Wilson said on 11 February 1918, 'We believe
that our [i.e. the United States'] own desire for new international order,
under which reason and justice and the common interests of mankind shall
prevail, is the desire of enlightened men everywhere.'[18]

What functions do NWOs perform?

In the chapters that follow there will be as detailed and informative a
description of the NWO projects as the author can manage. But a few
organising questions as to what they actually *mean* may be initially useful.

These *rites de passage* in international relations each gave birth to wildly exaggerated hopes and correspondingly exaggerated deceptions. What can we say as initial comments about what their architects meant them to achieve?

The restoration of balance, order and stability

Balance

The Congress of Vienna, which arguably created the most lasting NWO, was successful, suggests Kissinger, because it was 'buttressed by three pillars, each of which was indispensable: a peace of conciliation with France; a balance of power; and a shared sense of legitimacy'.[19] If for 'France' we substitute, for 1918, 1945 and 1990 in turn, 'Germany' (twice) and 'Russia', it is not obvious that any of the attempts of the twentieth century have been anywhere near as successful as that of 1815. The aim of all of these was the restoration of order and, in the mind of at least some of the key protagonists, on an injection of new concepts into what that order should be, to make it more 'just' and 'lasting'.

The great 'balancer' of the Westphalian system has always been trial by war. It has been modified at least four times now (1815, 1918, 1945 and 1990) by attempts to guarantee a superstructure, or at least an institutionalisation of peace. Contemporary writers such as Fussell, Coker and Winter have been right to stress the formative nature of war on our modern collective consciousness,[20] but we could equally refer to the influence of writers about, and attempts at, peace. One cannot exist without the other. However, the problem that has dogged all such discussion and attempts is that many of the institutional frameworks developed to tilt the balance of global politics in favour of peace were deeply flawed. Hence Karl Polanyi drew the conclusion in 1944 that the 'failure' of the Versailles Conference was its 'forestall[ing of] any reconstruction of the balance of power system'. He believed that 'Europe was now without any political system whatsoever'[21] and, incidentally, had put its hopes in the false gods of the market. Thus 1919 plus the 'Crash' of 1929 equalled disaster. Others agreed with Polanyi, but added that the states excluded from consideration at Versailles, notably Russia and Germany, were bound to end up destabilising the agreements reached, as did indeed happen.

Can we say that the current NWO is any more stable than that of 1919? Who has now been excluded, and who will now revolt and upset our new 'balance'? In 1918 it was Germany, in 1945 Russia; now it is arguably the masses of people who have escaped notice or been exploited by the economic miracles of the post-Second World War period. Many writers, like Chomsky, claim that the West has as surely 'failed' these people as Versailles 'failed' the German-speaking peoples of Europe. Does this mean that all attempts to create the conditions of an ideal balance are doomed to failure, as every key constituency cannot possibly be satisfied by the result? Does this in turn mean that a wide-ranging periodic war is an inevitability, or that we might finally discover a 'functional alternative to war', the initial impulse behind the creation of our discipline of international relations?

Order and stability

The mainstream theoretical proposition about the purpose of NWOs has been about the re-imposition of 'order'. The Westphalian Treaties of 1648, Utrecht in 1715, Vienna in 1815 and the NWOs of the twentieth century have often been presented as being the restoration of order in the international system after a major international war. This system in effect became a 'society' based on (until 1815) the norms of *'rex est imperator in regno suo'*, *'cuius regno, ejus religio'* and the balance of power.[22] The architects of disorder have often been recognised and an attempt made to 'punish' them for their misdemeanours. This was particularly true in 1815 when the guilty party, Napoleon, was exiled and in 1919 when the idea of 'war guilt' was built into the Treaty of Versailles. The twentieth century has seen the United States modify this, and try to replace the balance of power (with which the United States has always felt 'uncomfortable' in Kissinger's words[23]) with a more stable system of order, which is in effect the NWO. It might be argued that it has not in fact succeeded in doing so entirely, but it cannot be denied that it has modified the debate considerably.

The school that has probably been most famous in pushing the idea of a balance of power being the best guarantee of order is that known as the 'English School', and its notion of an 'international society', particularly as articulated by Martin Wight and Hedley Bull. It is certainly one that has influenced me. International society is defined as

> a group of states ... which not merely form a system, in the sense that the behaviour of each is a necessary factor in the calculations of the others, but also have established by dialogue and consent common rules and institutions for the conduct of their relations, and recognise their common interest in maintaining these arrangements.[24]

Disturbers of the 'balance' have to be treated with great care and, if necessary, sanction. States are thus seen as the main actors in international politics. For the purposes of this book, their formation into a 'society' that recognises and obeys certain norms, practices and principles bears a great deal of resemblance to the stated aims of virtually all the NWO architects since at least 1648. Hence the famous conferences and their outcomes that form the heart of this book can be seen as 'crystallizations of modern international society'. The idea of a society of states looking for order has the immense advantage that it corresponds to the basic urge of the national policy maker to find rational solutions to practical and moral problems at a state and international level.[25]

Andreas Osiander has developed and extended the idea of society and order to introduce the idea that society strives not for order but for 'stability'. For Osiander, all NWO projects of this and earlier centuries (such as that of Westphalia in 1648 and Vienna in 1815) try to reinforce what he calls the 'structural principles' of international society. This will depend on the number and identity of international actors (states, but also international organisations); their relative status *vis-à-vis* each other; the distribution of population and territories among them; and '[t]he various kinds of institutions or organizations that actors may share among them'.[26] In earlier and more recent times this has translated into questions of 'who decides' and 'on behalf of whom' about global security and other arrangements.[27] Leadership of the NWOs of the twentieth century, in 1919, 1945 and since 1990, has been exercised principally by the major powers, and especially the United States and Britain. Hence the focus of this book is on thinking about international politics within those two states.

The influence of the 'International Society' School in Britain and abroad has been immense, but has come under attack on at least two grounds. The first is based on a growing feeling, especially among students of international political economy, that we are now entering a world where the state is no longer the only, or even the most important, actor in global politics. These commentators also point to the increasing escape from the purview of the state of many of the key regulatory functions over such activity as financial transactions. Geoffrey Underhill uses this observation to ask '[w]hether one [can] characterise … the new situation as order or *disorder* …'.[28] It is also now criticised by those who assert, not without some justification, that order, stability and balance are inevitably to the benefit of those who control the society. There is a very vocal school of critical international relations that points to the 'alienating' nature of a hegemonic society of states based on capitalist principles. This 'Gramscian' critique thus sees NWOs as one expression of the 'hegemonic societies in the dominant countries of the world system'.[29] Neither are such questions the exclusive preserve of the 'left'. Elements of this kind of reflection will be seen as coming through in the most unlikely 'conservative' places in the following chapters.

However, to write off the state as an actor, or even as a potential catalyst of emancipation, seems to me to be premature. What we need to do is to redefine its role in an admittedly changed society and to find what role 'hegemony' might also have played in freeing peoples. We might also ask what kind of 'hegemony' (if indeed such a category can really be said to exist) a non-capitalist hegemonic state or society might have provided for us. Did we really want Lenin's version of an NWO to triumph, rather than the, admittedly flawed, liberal-capitalist Wilsonian version? It is hoped that some of these questions might be given a glimmer of an answer by the processes examined in this book. But it must also be stressed that there is as much danger in attacking such huge and complex categories of human activity as 'hegemonic' capitalism as there is in claiming that it gives us all the answers. A more fruitful approach is to keep an open mind and criticise where such criticism is justified and praise where it is not.

The defining of an intellectual climate

One answer to these dilemmas must be to re-examine the historical record of attempts at a more progressive politics in a more imaginative way than is common with the major run of socialist thinkers or liberal/conservative ideologues. We need to take a cue from the post-modern thinkers, if not from their non-methodology, to rethink where the concept of 'progress' has led us. NWO projects are explicitly about creating the conditions for 'progress' and have thus to be unlocked using what has often been called the 'historical imagination'. The late nineteenth and twentieth centuries have provided us with a number of key thinkers on the question of both the need for an historical imagination and what we might use it for. Many of them see history in terms of cycles, or at least as a dynamic. They seek to avoid the extreme dangers of 'historicism', that is, not to see history as an essential dynamic between classes and economic forces, or of a necessary 'progress', but rather as a battle of ideas made immanent.

Many writers in the twentieth century have seen progress in mixed terms, many elements of which were foreseen by H.G. Wells, for example. He, of course, also changed our view of time and space, and therefore of the certainty of it all, quite literally.[30] Certainly, time and space had been made uncertain categories before they came under fire in the trenches. The experience there for millions of ordinary men was of lifetimes being compressed into minutes. For a number of writers composing just before or during the First World War, it seemed like the end of civilisation as they knew it. Kern points out that Thomas Mann's *Magic Mountain* and Oswald Spengler's *Decline of the West* are almost emblematic of this line of thought in the Western imagination. In the very dynamic of their works, 'pre-' and 'post-' war get inextricably mixed up. Mann's hero even gets cured of TB in order to get properly choked to death in the war, whereas Spengler's tale is 'of a twilight of the Faustian soul'.[31] Having done his deal with the Devil of progress, man must succumb to his awful fate of self-obliteration.

Those who went to Versailles in 1919, or took part in post-war planning during the Second World War or have tried to re-create our world since 1989, may not have had the pessimism of Spengler, but they had his sense of being present at a great moment in history. Even diplomats felt it. Harold Nicolson wrote that '[w]e were journeying to Paris, not merely to liquidate the war, but to found a new order in Europe. We were preparing not Peace only, but Eternal Peace. There was about us the halo of some divine mission. We must be alert, stern, righteous and ascetic. For we were bent on doing great, permanent and noble things.'[32] The 1920s and 1930s were to belong to the pessimists or even to those like Georges Sorel who were advocates of violence as the ultimate 'philosophy of modern history'. Sorel looked forward to a 'great foreign war, which might renew lost energies, and which in any case would doubtless bring into power men with the will to govern'.[33] The NWO project can be seen as the antidote to such pessimism, a continuing belief that 'progress' is still possible and as such a reassertion of the Enlightenment belief that humanity can re-create itself, but not without taking due account of the need to be of universal appeal. As such it fits, in its conceptualisation, Ian Clark's description of a 'Whig' view of historical process, one that believes in the perfectibility of humankind. But it also, in its implementation, draws on Clark's 'Tory' view of history, one where human nature is potentially the worst enemy of progress.[34]

The jolting or the destruction of the historical memory?

Perhaps the most striking element of all NWOs is that they seem to provide a coda to a period of conflict or war. The relationship of past to present is thrown, temporarily at least, into sharp focus by a settling of accounts (as at Paris in 1919 and at Yalta/Potsdam in 1944–45), a redrawing of the map and a building of a new *tabula rasa* upon which new hopes and aspirations can be erected. That this process has now contributed, or even possibly led, to what Eric Hobsbawm says is a death of the 'historical memory' might be construed as a serious problem. Hobsbawm even feels that

> [t]he destruction of the past, or rather of the social mechanisms that link one's contemporary experience to that of earlier generations, is one of the most characteristic and eerie phenomena of the late twentieth century. Most young men and women at the century's end grow up in a sort of permanent present lacking any inorganic relation to the public past of the times they live in.[35]

Perhaps also it is just as well that we have lost our 'historical memory', at least in one respect. Coker points out that one of Nietzsche's great insights was that Europeans suffered from an excess of historical consciousness, but one that most of them did not understand and had perverted. History was not being used to liberate but to enslave. Peoples had gained their own freedom only to want to remove it from others.[36] In addition, Nietzsche himself was deformed, his view of the possibility of 'man' becoming 'superman' changed into the need for Germans to achieve their unique historical destiny. He has been blamed by many in the past fifty years for an encouragement of the 'will to power' of Germans such as Adolf Hitler. He is now trundled out to prove that epistemological anarchy is the only possible answer to a post-modern world. The problem is surely not one of blaming philosophers such as Nietzsche for our deformed historical memory, but one of an essentially metaphysical project being deformed to fit our historical experience.[37]

Is this *fin de siècle* different from its nineteenth-century predecessor in that we have developed a healthy cynicism about history? Whereas H.G. Wells ushered in the twentieth century, Francis Fukuyama and Hobsbawm usher it out. All make extravagant claims about trends – the ultimate triumph of science, or that of capitalism or an undefined angst and fear of war. Reading Hobsbawm, one is struck by how much he wants history to be a titanic struggle, a series of competing and incompatible certainties. We are now stuck, says Hobsbawm, in a terrible 'global fog'. Now we know nothing for certain and nothing is clear. 'Thus, for the first time in two centuries, the world of the 1990s entirely lacked [*sic*] any international system or structure.'[38]

The truth is always subtle and certainly contradictory.[39] At the time of all great changes there have been 'utopians' and Jeremiahs. But, as with the stock market, there have been ideas that briefly flared and died and others that looked promising but eventually went to sleep. Equally, there have been lasting ideas, ones that keep recurring in their essence but in tune with historical conditions. These are the ones on which this book will concentrate, while not ignoring the attempts to postulate alternative agendas, some of which, who knows, will see the light of day again in the future. One idea that this book would like to propose in that, on the contrary, we now have a very well-worked out 'system and structure', that proposed by the NWO theorists and practitioners. We may not like it, and many do not, but it is there. One is tempted to say: 'I have seen the present and it works.'

International relations, as a discipline, has certainly suffered from a death of 'historical memory'. Any proverbial observer from Mars could certainly be forgiven for thinking that international relations has become, or had become, a repository for a reflection on the nature (rise, decline, etc.) of American power in the post-1945 period. The 'inter-paradigm debate' of the 1980s and the earlier 'idealist–realist' debate of the 1940s and 1950s might be summed up as battles in this war. As international relations degenerated into a collective introspective delusion about the parameters of American power, the previous dominance of European concerns was forgotten almost completely, the existence of a world outside a purely conservative maintenance of this power obliterated from the international relations mind-set.[40] Versailles was seen as retaining importance because of the cautionary tale it told 'realists' about even listening to the siren voices of the old world. Summaries of international relations theory would nod in the direction of 'classical theory' in quaint deference to long-dead ancestors.[41] The pity of it is that international relations in the United States certainly seemed to have 'forgotten' history, since 1950 or so, while it was in the concrete struggles of the ideas that American politicians did so much to promote at Versailles and Yalta, and in the then and subsequent opposition to them, that is to be found the warp and weft of much of the history of the twentieth century. The wonder is that the United States, and to some extent Britain as well, have produced such good historical literature that has been seemingly ignored by most of their colleagues in international relations faculties. It is about time that the two sides started to cooperate again.

Consequently, we should not confuse the comfortable amnesia of two generations of American university students, and their teachers, with the end of the 'historical imagination'. I think that we could argue that in fact history is back, and it is not necessarily any more pleasant or unpleasant than the amnesia which largely preceded it in the groves of international relations academe. What could be argued is that the history of large sections of the world's population was effectively downgraded by the process of, particularly, the Cold War and the traditions of writing about international relations that it spawned, particularly in American universities. History was killed off deliberately in the interest of stability in the Cold War struggle. With the end of that struggle, it has begun to come out of its many cocoons and fly again. In international relations this is as evident now as it was hidden before 1989. The huge surge in 'normative theory', better described as a return to the centrality of the study of political theory to international relations, would not have surprised Philip Noel-Baker or E.H. Carr or, for that matter, Hans Morgenthau. The resurgence of the subset of this development known as 'critical theory' is clearly a result of the felt lack of historical depth in international relations. Marx was above all an historian. So is the multifarious phenomenon that we call 'post-modernism', which casts back to the beginnings of the modern era for its demolition of the 'foundations' of the present.

This book is thus a small attempt to continue in this reawakening of what I and many others have called the 'historical imagination'. The need for this is not merely one of intellectual integrity to the past, but is also a question of the basis of future sounder policy foundations. In 1993 the historian John Lewis Gaddis indulged in a splendid polemic against the a-historical nature of Cold War political science (of which international relations was a subset). In it he asked the simple question (paraphrased here): What might we have done better to predict the end of the Cold War given the prevailing approaches to international relations that dominated the field pre-1989? Nothing, says Gaddis, as none of the existing frameworks developed since about 1950 were of any use for the policy maker. His somewhat stark conclusion is to quote Robert Conquest: 'If you are a student, switch from political science to history'. Perhaps, suggests Gaddis, 'theory' (by which he clearly means international relations theory as he sees it) is of no use at all, or at least necessitates a wider number of approaches than those currently in use, not forgetting the need to reinsert philosophy and literature.[42] It would be better for those of us who see a future for international relations as a great multidisciplinary melting pot to start to restress the historical input, clearly the intention of the founders of our discipline after the First World War.

I share Gaddis' feeling that a new dawn has to come to international relations if it is not itself to be consigned to the dustbin of history along with telling the runes and psephology. We do have to answer hard questions about such dominant (even 'hegemonic') frameworks as the NWO, and not necessarily to be negative about the (albeit fragile) nature of the West's 'victory'. We also have to point to the parade of dangerous alternative frameworks (such as bolshevism and fascism) that either represented themselves before 1939, or indeed since 1989 ('ethno-nationalism', for one) or have appeared seemingly, but only 'seemingly', due to our wider historical ignorance, for the first time. We may now have a homogeneous and universal society of states in the West, but this can still be threatened from within and from without. Even though most of the NWO themes upon which this book concentrates have reappeared, as they did in 1918 and 1945, as vibrant as ever, perhaps they have resurfaced, like the drowning man, for the third time, only now to sink beneath the waves for ever.

Notes

1 One classic survey of this thinking can be found in F. H. Hinsley, *Power and the Pursuit of Peace* (Cambridge University Press, 1966). A recent study which has a rather different aim is Andreas Osiander, *The States System of Europe, 1640–1990: Peacemaking and the Conditions of International Stability* (Oxford, Clarendon Press, 1994).

2 Some of the major contributions, in Britain alone, to this major rethinking of international relations theory can be found in A.J.R. Groom and Margot Light (eds), *Contemporary International Relations: A Guide to Theory* (London, Pinter, 1994); Steve Smith, Ken Booth and Marysia Zalewski (eds), *International Theory: Positivism and Beyond* (Cambridge University Press, 1996); John Baylis and Steve Smith, *The Globalization of World Politics: An Introduction to International Relations* (Oxford University Press, 1997); Chris Brown, *International Theory: New Normative Approaches* (Hemel Hempstead, Harvester, 1992) and *Understanding International Relations* (London, Macmillan, 1997); and Ian Clark, *Globalization and Fragmentation: International Relations in the Twentieth Century* (Oxford University Press, 1997).

3 John Mearsheimer, 'Back to the Future', in Sean M. Lynn-Jones, *The Cold War and After: Prospects for Peace* (Cambridge, Mass., MIT Press, 1991).

4 Noam Chomsky, *World Orders, Old and New* (London, Pluto Press, 1994). Chomsky's thoughts will be examined in Chapter 7 and the Conclusion.

5 Salvador de Madariaga, *Disarmament* (Oxford University Press, 1929); Alfred Cobban, *National Self-Determination* (Oxford University Press, 1945).

6 E.H. Carr, *The Twenty Years' Crisis: 1919–1939* (London, Macmillan, 1939); David Long and Peter Wilson (eds), *Thinkers of the Twenty Years' Crisis: Inter-War Idealism Reassessed* (Oxford, Clarendon Press, 1995).

7 Caroline Kennedy-Pipe, *Stalin's Cold War: Soviet Strategies in Europe, 1943 to 1956* (Manchester University Press, 1995).

8 It is hoped that this will be published later in a specialist journal.

9 Terry Eagleton, *Literary Theory: An Introduction* (Oxford, Blackwell, 1983), p. 22.

10 Zaki Laïdi (ed.), *Power and Purpose after the Cold War* (Oxford, Berg, 1994).

11 Francis Fukuyama, *The End of History and the Last Man* (New York, The Free Press, 1992).

12 Herbert Hoover, *The Ordeal of Woodrow Wilson* (London, Museum Press, 1958).

13 Eric Hobsbawm, *The Age of Extremes: The Short Twentieth Century, 1914–1991* (London, Michael Joseph, 1994).

14 Christopher Coker, *War and the 20th Century: The Impact of War on the Modern Consciousness* (London, Brassey's, 1994), p. 2.

15 A particularly astonishing and, it must be said, rather amusing and often well-aimed, example of this demolition of the credibility of the intellectual, which has perhaps gone further in Anglo-Saxon countries than others, can be found in Paul Johnson, *Intellectuals* (London, Weidenfeld and Nicholson, 1988).

16 Dean Acheson, *Present at the Creation: My Years in the State Department* (New York, Norton, 1969).

17 Georg Lukács, *The Historical Novel* (London, Peregrine Books, 1969), p. 17.

18 Wilson, quoted in Osiander, *The States System of Europe*, p. 254.

19 Henry Kissinger, *Diplomacy* (New York, Simon and Schuster, 1994), p. 242.

20 Paul Fussell, *The Great War and Modern Memory* (Oxford University Press, 1975); Coker, *War and the 20th Century*; Jay Winter, *Sites of Memory, Sites of Mourning: The Great War in European Cultural History* (Cambridge University Press, 1995). See also Martin Evans and Ken Lunn (eds), *War and Memory in the Twentieth Century* (Oxford, Berg, 1997).

21 Karl Polanyi, *The Great Transformation: The Political and Economic Origins of Our Time* (New York, Beacon, 1944), p. 21.

22 Robert H. Jackson, 'The Evolution of International Society', in Baylis and Smith, *The Globalization of World Politics*, p. 41.

23 Kissinger, *Diplomacy*, p. 19.

24 Hedley Bull and Adam Watson (eds), *The Expansion of International Society* (Oxford, Clarendon Press, 1984), p. 1.

25 For a convenient summary of the 'International Society' School see Brown, *Understanding International Relations*, pp. 51–54 and Jackson, in Baylis and Smith, *The Globalization of World Politics*, pp. 33–47. The most famous argument in favour of such an approach can be found in Hedley Bull, *The Anarchical Society* (London, Macmillan, 1977, 1995). See also Stanley Hoffmann, 'International Society', in J.D.B. Miller and R.J. Vincent, *Order and Violence: Hedley Bull and International Relations* (Oxford, Clarendon Press, 1990), pp. 13–37.

26 Osiander, *The States System of Europe*, p. 3.

27 Michael Mihalka, 'Building Consensus: The Security Model in the Light of Previous Security Arrangements in Europe', *Helsinki Monitor*, no. 3, 1996, pp. 20–29.

28 See, for example, the work of Susan Strange, *The Retreat of the State: The Diffusion of Power in the World Economy* (Cambridge University Press, 1996) and Geoffrey Underhill (ed.), *The New World Order in International Finance* (London, Macmillan, 1997).

29 Mark Rupert, 'Alienation, Capitalism and the Inter-State System: Towards a Marxian/Gramscian Critique', in Stephen Gill (ed.), *Gramsci, Historical*

Materialism and International Relations (Cambridge University Press, 1993), p. 67 and Robert Cox and Andrew Sinclair, *Approaches to World Order* (Cambridge University Press, 1996), p. 247.

30 For a wider discussion of this see Stephen Kern, *The Culture of Time and Space, 1880–1918* (Cambridge, Mass., Harvard University Press, 1983), pp. 89–108.

31 Kern, *Culture of Time and Space*, p. 106–107.

32 Harold Nicolson, *Peacemaking, 1919* (London, Constable and Co., 1933), p. 32.

33 Georges Sorel, *Reflections on Violence* (New York, Peter Smith, 1941, first published 1915), pp. 43 and 83.

34 Ian Clark, *Reform and Resistance in the International Order* (Cambridge University Press, 1980), pp. 1–10. See also the second edition of the above: *The Hierarchy of States: Reform and Resistance in the International Order* (Cambridge University Press, 1989).

35 Hobsbawm, *Age of Extremes*, p. 3.

36 Coker, *War and the 20th Century*, pp. 33–34.

37 I am indebted for this insight to a reading of Peter Berkowitz, who observes that 'Nietzsche's fundamental concern with ethical and political questions is obscured when scholars make him over into a theorist primarily concerned with how we know rather than how we live': Peter Berkowitz, *Nietzsche: The Ethics of an Immoralist* (Cambridge, Mass., Harvard University Press, 1995), p. 3.

38 Hobsbawm, *Age of Extremes*, p. 559.

39 I have not indulged in any fashionable epistemological debate about historical truth in this book. If pressed, I would refer any reader to the eminently sensible and well argued thought of Richard J. Evans, *In Defence of History* (London, Granta, 1997). What historians have to do, says Evans, is show 'patterns and linkages, causal and otherwise' and to awaken what Evans and Trevelyan also called the 'historical imagination', p. 252.

40 To this extent I would entirely agree with Robert Cox in his famous article, denouncing mere 'problem solving' in international relations theory, 'Social Forces, States and World Orders', now reprinted in Cox and Sinclair, *Approaches to World Order*, pp. 85–123. Where I do not agree with Cox is in his excessive emphasis on 'structures' and his seeming dismissal of the role of the individual thinker and statesman.

41 There are, of course, honourable exceptions to this rule, mainly among British writers. Again, most of these were greatly influenced by the 'International Society' School.

42 John Lewis Gaddis, 'International Relations Theory and the End of the Cold War', *International Security*, vol. 17, no. 3, Winter 1992/93, pp. 5–58.

1

The imagining of the Versailles NWO, 1914–19

Introduction

The First World War has arguably had the longest lasting and deepest effect of all the events of the twentieth century. It started by giving a brief burst of excitement, one even near hysterical acclaim, to millions of people who had come to believe that the world needed a 'good war' to sort out the ills of civilisation. In the enthusiasm, the crowd came into its own for the first time in a distinctly twentieth century form, as Nietzsche, among others, had predicted it might, to find its identity in a new sense of community, the community of those about to die.[1] It ended with many others than Oswald Spengler feeling that Western civilisation had stared into an abyss into which it might now be toppling. 'Faustian Man' had made his compact with the 'Machine' and was now 'the *slave of his creation*'.[2] It was the end of an era, that of the liberal elites and the beginning of that of the 'masses', as was realised by Sir Edward Grey in his statement of August 1914: 'the lights are going out all over Europe; we shall not see them lit again in our lifetime'. The First World War was thus '[a] hideous embarrassment to the prevailing Meliorist myth which had dominated the public consciousness for more than a century'.[3]

At the Versailles Peace Conference in 1919 the leaders of the West (the 'Big Four') – Woodrow Wilson, David Lloyd George, Georges Clemenceau and Vittorio Orlando – had to try and resurrect the phoenix of peace and prosperity from the ashes of war. In this they largely failed. This chapter is therefore about the final attempts of the Western liberal elite to try and make this 'the war to end all wars'. This and subsequent chapters will show how the agenda that they developed during and immediately after the First World War drew on both a new thinking about war and peace and also on a pre-existing current of thought and action through the agency of a relatively small number of people. In a nutshell, this is the debate about 'idealism' versus 'realism' as it developed during 1914–18.

In addition we shall examine the policy-making process as it developed before the Versailles Conference of 1919. It will be argued that there was nowhere near the intellectual and practical preparation for the Conference as there was to be for the series of conferences that marked the end of the Second World War. Nonetheless, some key elements were identified. Those that have attracted the attention of historians are clearly the thinking of President Woodrow Wilson, and discussions that coalesced in Britain under the umbrella of the Union of Democratic Control, the Bryce Group and governmental bodies such as the Phillimore Committee. Other inputs that have been rather neglected, at least by Anglo-Saxon historians, such as the French *Commission Bourgeois*, will also be examined, but it must be admitted in nowhere near the detail given to American and British thinking.

The First World War acted as the catalyst for the emergence of an NWO agenda that has undergone constant evolution ever since while maintaining its basic essence. This process is encapsulated in the various projects developed by official and informal groups on both sides of the Atlantic. This is not to deny that 'structural' considerations also counted, but these had to be interpreted by policy makers and intellectuals. Sense had to be made of the chaos of the trenches through a process of imaginative reflection that is the warp and weft of the intellectual history of international relations this century. This chapter and those that follow it aim to show how this process evolved, and how it dealt with its failures and successes.

Anglo-American thinking on the post-war settlement

Although the United States was the 'senior partner' behind the thinking of what was to become the Versailles Treaty from 1917 onwards, it was the interplay between American and British reflection that can be seen as providing the key intellectual input to both the philosophical basis of the Versailles settlement, and particularly to proposals for a League of Nations (LON). American and, particularly, British 'society' had a long pedigree of producing small groups of intellectuals who put much of their effort into pondering the problems of international relations, intellectuals who were as at ease in the drawing room as in the Cabinet. They went to a small number of schools, married other 'people of quality', and were tied into not only the literary, but also the economic and governmental life of their country. Part of their influence lay in the fact that there was a shared belief system that derived from the vibrant Victorian 'ideology', one that espoused the ideal of parliamentary debate as the *nec plus ultra* of civilised discourse, and the ideals of economic liberalism and rugged individualism as the main vectors for beneficial change.[4] Even though this consensus was under threat before 1914 under the assault of more radical socialist ideas, these were largely declamatory and of minority appeal, even among the working classes. The liberal elites were therefore not only contributors to a debate, they were also, and far more than today, the creators of the background thinking for policy, and often policy makers themselves.

In his famous work, *The Twenty Years' Crisis*, E.H. Carr (who was a member of the British delegation at the Paris Peace Conference) makes a particular point of attacking the 'intellectuals' who supported the call for a change in the nature of international relations before and during the First World War for having injected a damaging note of 'utopianism' into the Anglo-Saxon body politick. He claims that these people, many of whom will shortly be described and whom he mostly singles out for particular criticism, sought to make 'practice conform to theory', whereas a healthier and older tradition, that of the 'bureaucrat' 'eschew[s] the formulation of principles and [is] ... guided on the right course by some intuitive process born of long experience and not of conscious reasoning'. This formulation bears some resemblance to those like Arnold Wolfers who have distinguished between the 'traditionalist' and the 'collectivist' in British foreign policy, again guided respectively by instinct and long practice and aspiration, often to moral improvement.[5]

It would be more accurate to describe Carr's thinking as being part of a well-established 'statist' perspective – one of his key objections to the League of Nations was that it put too much liberal faith in an international society and not in a world of states. Another criticism that will be developed in subsequent chapters (and especially Chapter 7) was his belief that at least some of this faith derived from an erroneous reliance on an economic 'harmony of interests' that was tending to encourage a global interdependence, one which liberals saw as a long-term disincentive to war. As we shall see in the following pages, there were many during the First World War who essentially agreed with his reservations. As we hope to demonstrate in the following pages, he might rather be seen as criticising the result of a process of policy making that tended to ignore the liberal 'cosmopolitan' ethic in favour of one that in fact privileged the 'statist' aims of the main Allied protagonists.

British liberalism and the outbreak of war

The 'Liberal Mind' that dominated British political thinking before 1914 was one that was open but also 'halting, weak, vacillating, divided and concessive', as J.A. Hobson described it.[6] When it was faced with a global, or at least a major, European war, it was faced with a problem that it could not really comprehend or deal with, for 'war in advanced capitalist countries would be unprofitable and therefore unthinkable', as Norman Angell had put it in the *Great Illusion* of 1910.[7] In spite of its awareness of the probable consequences of war, it became obvious that the Liberal Government of Herbert H. Asquith would have to deny its instincts for peace and fight to stop German domination of the continent of Europe, and it was with a heavy heart that it did so. *The Times* realised that intervention was 'not merely a duty of friendship [to Belgium and France]. It is an elementary duty of self-preservation ... We cannot stand alone in a Europe dominated by any single power.'[8] However, it is in the light of the above dominant British liberal mind-set that we must understand the body blow that British society suffered with the onset of the Great War. George Dangerfield saw it in almost apocalyptic terms: 'And now the half light fades away altogether, and on the splendour of Imperial England there falls, at last and forever, an inextinguishable dark'.[9] In 1935, when he wrote those words, this was perhaps more clearly the case; in 1914 there were still those who could reasonably suppose that they could turn the tide.

The war was fought by a coalition Government that was made up of representatives of the three major parties, including Labour. Party political differences were somewhat submerged in a common effort to prosecute the war, and what opposition there was to this principal aim was never significant. The argument about how the peace should be made thus largely proceeded in tandem with, and was informed by, the conduct of the war itself. Opposition to the war became more widespread as the war continued, especially after the carnage at the Battle of the Somme in 1916. Lyn Macdonald sees in the shock of the futile destruction of Lord Kitchener's volunteer army 'the first tremor in the rock-like foundations of British society'.[10] Even if this underestimates the already existing shakiness engendered by the 'Great Unrest' before 1914 (a combination of labour unrest, feminist, 'suffragette' militancy, and bitter argument about Home Rule for Ireland), there can be no doubt of the impact on elite and mass opinion in Britain of the casualty figures of 1 July 1916 and those that followed.

The debate on the post-war settlement and a hoped for improvement in the nature of international relations relied for its increased pace as the war progressed on both the mounting casualty figures and the attendant suffering of the civil populations of all the combatant states, including those of the Axis. It also relied on the outside influences of major developments in Russia, although this is not a central concern of this chapter. It is in particular clear that the thinking of Wilson and House (of which more below and in Chapter 2) was influenced in 1918 and 1919 by the proposals coming from the Bolsheviks with their own version of the 'new diplomacy' and the 'self-determination' of peoples. This led to Walter Lippman postulating that the Paris Peace Conference was about the interplay of 'the reaction [Clemenceau], the reconstruction [Wilson] and the revolution [Lenin]'.[11] But the main impetus lay in the interplay of ideas between political commentators and actors in Britain and the United States who had a liberal bedrock to their thinking, but with a widespread feeling that this would have to be modified greatly. The liberal consensus of 1914 was thus split, in Britain and America, into radical and conservative wings, that corresponds in the United States to 'progressive' and 'conservative' internationalism. This division will form the basis of the analysis in this chapter.

The Bryce Group

The 'Bryce Group' was the first, albeit loosely organised, British liberal group that can be said to have any direct influence on the elaboration of post-war plans. It had a membership that included many pre-war thinkers of note, including G. Lowes Dickinson (who can be said to have initiated its discussions and whose ideas are described in more detail in Chapter 7),[12] Graham Wallas and Arthur Ponsonby. Other key members of the liberal intelligentsia hovered in the circle of this Group, including Professor Gilbert Murray, later a key figure in the League of Nations Union (LNU). It could be argued that through its informal nature the Bryce Group was more directly influential in its contacts with government on both sides of the Atlantic and ultimately on the drafting of the Versailles settlement than more radical anti-war groups such as the Union of Democratic Control (UDC, see below).[13]

Viscount Bryce had been a successful British Ambassador to the USA from 1907 to 1913. As such, he had gained a good, though not warm, rapport with Presidents Theodore Roosevelt and William Howard Taft, as well as much better relations with many prominent academic luminaries such as Charles William Eliot, President of Harvard University from 1869 to 1910. His influence on the Democrat Wilson was less given his closeness to the Republicans, but like his later successor in the post, Lord Lothian, he had an acknowledged influence in the United States.[14] He was also entrusted by Asquith early in the war to preside over a committee investigating allegations of German atrocities in their invasion of Belgium, the invasion of which convinced him to support the war.[15] His findings condemned the actions of the German Government and were published with alacrity in Britain; they had some impact in the United States too, as he was not seen as being anti-German.[16] The new British Ambassador to the USA, Cecil Spring Rice, telegraphed the Foreign Office that '[f]riend [i.e. House or Wilson] says that Bryce is the only man whose opinion would carry universal weight with American public who have been quite convinced by the Belgian Report'.[17] The main contact that the Bryce Group had in America was with the League to Enforce Peace (LEP, see below), a largely Republican-dominated body but one which had a profound effect on Wilson's thinking. It first published the Bryce Group 'Proposals' in the USA, giving them prime billing (the first three pages) in a volume of different proposals in April 1917 in the *League Bulletin*.[18]

The Proposals themselves were modest, in that they wished to make sure that after the war the Allies, within which Bryce included the United States as well as Britain and France, would combine in an alliance to keep the peace. They could and should do this within a 'League' of some kind, but Bryce was keen from the outset that this should be an organisation with a 'realistic' operational structure. He would not countenance some of the wilder suggestions within the Group for an 'International Federal System' or 'Joint European Executive'. Most of all he was not against the use of force to enforce peace: 'Nothing will be adequate which does not provide for some moral and military force to keep peace [and] I am not at all sanguine that this is attainable.' Bryce also felt that some kind of international compulsory arbitration would be essential to try and stop conflict breaking out in the first place. Neither did he apportion blame equally for the outbreak of war – Germany was clearly to blame, and must be defeated and punished. This caused him some disillusion with Wilson's seemingly even-handed apportioning of blame, at least until the USA entered the war.[19]

The output of the group was thus less important than the influence of its leader and what he represented of moderate liberal thinking. The group represented a view that was acceptable to both those who supported the war, and indeed played a significant role in it, as Bryce did in his informal contacts with the Americans, and to those on the left who opposed the war. It can as a consequence be considered as having had a major influence on the thinking of others outside it, such as Lord Robert Cecil, who can be seen as the main architect of British policy towards the League of Nations at Paris and beyond.[20] The Bryce Group 'Proposals' were very tentative because of their date of origin, in early 1915, when there was very little support for a reasoned peace in Britain or France. However, they were an important bedrock for mainstream liberal thinking in both Britain and the United States and provided a first ground for consensus about the possible shape of a post-war settlement.

The UDC

In the context of the politics of 1914–18 in Britain, those who stood out against the war entirely could expect to be little heard, unlike groups and individuals whose voice could be listened to as that of a 'loyal opposition', such as the Bryce Group. Pacifism was widely seen as the equivalent of being pro-German, especially early in the war. Such was the initial fate of the UDC. It nonetheless constituted a vital forum for a continued belief and articulation of the central tenets of both liberal and moderate socialist opinion in Britain during the whole wartime period. H.N. Brailsford, J.A. Hobson, Arthur Henderson (the architect of the Labour Party's 1918 Constitution with Sidney Webb), Bertrand Russell and other luminaries sat on its General Council. Its Executive was made up of Charles Trevelyan, Ramsay MacDonald and E.D. Morel, to name only the most famous, all of whom played a significant role in British politics of the liberal left in the inter-war period. It can be seen as an organisation that provides a direct link between the pre- and post-war British political scene. In the domain of foreign policy it was the natural successor of the Liberal Foreign Affairs Group, which before 1914 grouped more than seventy-five Liberal MPs who wished to see a major re-orientation of British foreign policy. In many ways the distinction between Liberal and (many) Labour politicians, especially

MacDonald, was academic, and summed up in the expression and reality of the 'Lib–Lab' phenomenon of the period.[21]

The key demands of the UDC were contained in a document issued in August 1914 and signed by MacDonald, Trevelyan, Angell and Morel. They said that they were not alone in being 'profoundly dissatisfied with the general course of policy which preceded the war' and particularly the 'old traditions of secret and class diplomacy, the old control of foreign policy by a narrow clique and the power of the armament organisations …'. These had 'henceforth to be combated [*sic*] by a great and conscious and directed effort of the democracy … to secure real parliamentary control over foreign policy …'. This would require, '[w]hen peace returns, to open direct and deliberate negotiations with democratic parties and influences on the Continent, so as to form an International understanding depending on popular parties, rather than on governments'. What they did *not* want was a humiliation of the defeated nations or 'an artificial re-arrangement of frontiers, merely becom[ing] the starting point for … future wars'.[22]

The UDC never quite shook off its 'pro-German' tag, and certainly never its 'pacifist' one, especially given that two of its major support groups were the Quakers and the Independent Labour Party, a maverick wing of the Labour Party that had a number of conscientious objectors within its ranks, notably Fenner Brockway. It was constantly assaulted by the pro-Government press, with wartime censorship making it difficult to reply, especially under the draconian Defence of the Realm Act (DORA) regulations. Physical attacks on its members were quite common, and a repression by the Home Office included imprisoning Morel under the DORA and a six-month prison sentence in late 1917. After the war its beliefs and policies became official Labour Party policy and were at least partly institutionalised in the League of Nations, but during the war it was relatively easy for Lloyd George to ignore it. It was to prove less easy for him to ignore the Labour Party, whose views became more and more akin to those of the UDC, especially after Henderson's resignation from the Cabinet in August 1918 as a result of his desire to attend the Second International's Stockholm Conference where a negotiated peace was to be discussed.[23]

The LNU

The UDC's views would have to wait until after the Versailles settlement for the Labour Party to reap rewards of a widespread disillusion to the Treaty that set in in both Britain and America, as well as among the defeated powers. It was realised, even by the UDC, that if they wished their views to be heard they would need to have a more 'respectable' platform for their propagation. The platform was provided by the almost universal belief that grew up as the war progressed that some form of 'alliance' or 'League' was necessary to try and ensure a better post-war atmosphere in international relations. This was not confined to 'idealist' opinion, and was at least discussed even by those who espoused force as the only rationale for international politics.

A League of Nations Society was set up as early as May 1915 and included Lowes Dickinson, Brailsford and assorted Labour Party foreign policy specialists such as Leonard Woolf. Bryce and others largely held aloof although they agreed with its main aim, that a LON should be set up. America's entry into the war in February 1917 suddenly made the Society much more acceptable, and it then attracted key figures such as Lord Grey (enobled in 1916 and Foreign Secretary under Asquith), Bryce, the Archbishop of Canterbury and, most significant of all, War Cabinet member General Jan Smuts, who was to be Britain's main planner for Paris.[24] In June 1918 the Society was joined by a League of Free Nations Association, which included Gilbert Murray[25] and H.G. Wells, among others. There was some concern, coming for example from Lloyd George's then Parliamentary Private Secretary David Davies,[26] that if the two organisations were to merge they might get tainted by association with the UDC, to which Lowes Dickinson and Woolf were also affiliated. When Grey insisted that he would only become President if the two organisations merged, such differences were papered over and the LNU formed in time to greet President Wilson's arrival in Europe.[27]

The most significant 'Establishment' figure to associate his name with the LNU was Lord Robert Cecil. In the 1920s and 1930s Cecil came to see the promotion of the League idea as his main purpose in life, and collaborated closely with a number of key political figures and intellectuals in this task; in particular with Philip Noel-Baker[28] and Gilbert Murray. As Minister for the Blockade, Cecil would have no truck with pacifism or defeatism of any kind while the fighting continued.[29] As a key drafter of the Covenant he came to embody the LNU, and indeed the spirit of the League of Nations itself throughout the inter-war period.

The official British decision-making process before Versailles

Goldstein is right in saying that Britain only began official planning for the Peace Conference, whenever it might come, in 1916.[30] However, there had been a great deal of thought about the nature of international relations that provided an essential backdrop to the more detailed thinking in the War Cabinet before 1916 and in a more systematic way after 1916 in official committees, especially within the Foreign Office. Some of the early memoranda were considered in response to the ideas being put forward by the UDC and the Bryce Group.

The basic British agenda was already laid down in August 1916, and included a desire to consider the future balance of power in Europe, a consideration of what came to be called 'national self-determination' and what should be done with the vanquished Axis powers by way of indemnity. But Britain was also hamstrung by a 'dual, or even schizophrenic' problem of focusing on where its true interests lay, in Europe or with its global empire,[31] a problem that may be said to have persisted to this day in one form or another. This became particularly apparent in intermittent discussions with the Americans about the concept of the 'Freedom of the Seas'. Wilson made this one of his key Fourteen Points, and it also resurfaced in the Atlantic Charter of 1941. The essential element of the British version of 'Freedom of the Seas' lay in its belief that peace had been kept since 1815 by the ever present threat of force, in the form of the Royal Navy, and that this had prevented rogue nations from posing a serious threat to peace. Consequently, it was considered a mirage to put the fate of the world into an abstract 'idea' that was not backed by a credible threat of force. Wilson's view came to be that this force needed to be in the hands of a multilateral organisation.

The most detailed preparation for the minutiae of the negotiating position of specific areas of the world, and especially of Europe, was done by what came to be called the 'Historical Section' (transferred from the Admiralty in early 1918) and the Political Intelligence Department (PID), both in the Foreign Office. Both were the brainchildren of Foreign Office Permanent Secretary, Lord Hardinge and together they provided the most significant factual and analytical input into the elaboration of the British position. The 'Historical Section' created the series of so-called 'Peace Books', of which 182 were originally envisaged and 174 actually produced. They ranged over a variety of subjects, from history to economics and geography. During the negotiations in Paris, the Books were widely used by officials in the British delegation.[32]

The PID was set up in March 1918 to coordinate the flow of information coming in from many different ministries and to produce reports that would be useful to the negotiators. As Goldstein points out, it was the first real experiment of its type in the area of intelligence, as the Government had until then mainly concerned itself with military intelligence. It also clearly represented a bid by the Foreign Office to reassert its authority over Lloyd George's increasingly personalised 'Garden Suburb' secretariat, upon which he relied to make most of his decisions. PID membership reads like a roll-call of the most distinguished British political commentators of the first half of this century. In the area of Central and Eastern Europe particularly there was a fund of in-house talent, where R.W. Seton-Watson, Lewis Namier, Allen and Rex Leeper were key regional directors, and, for the Middle East, Arnold Toynbee. Alfred Zimmern was the main contributor to thinking on the League of Nations and, from 1919, became the first Woodrow Wilson Chair of International Relations at the University of Aberystwyth.[33] Harold Nicolson and Robert Vansittart of the Foreign Office were given on permanent loan to the PID and played a key role in decisions on South East Europe and the Middle East, respectively. The PID's head was Sir William Tyrrell and under his leadership it produced 175 memoranda, as well as many of the 'Peace Books', all of which were circulated to the War Cabinet on a wide variety of country, regional and organisational issues until the end of the Versailles Conference. They also provided a number of key personnel at Versailles itself, especially Tyrrell, Nicolson, Vansittart and Rex Leeper.

The PID was clearly initially seen as suspect both by the Foreign Office establishment and by the Establishment in the wider sense. This was a group of 'experts', a genre viewed with great suspicion at the time, and moreover a group of sixteen experts who were of a very 'catholic' background. The need for it was nonetheless widely realised by the end of the Conference, and General Smuts, who emerged as a key British negotiator at Paris, relied very heavily on PID briefings. In spite of Lloyd George's dislike of the Foreign Office, it consequently played a key role in the Conference. It is therefore curious, but perhaps very British, that the PID was then abolished after the Versailles Treaty was signed, a victim of Treasury cuts and Hardinge's departure to be Ambassador in Paris.[34]

From reflection to policy, 1915–18

In the early years of the war the bitter reaction to Germany's actions made even the most convinced liberal doubt his faith, in Britain and the United States. As the war went on this attitude started to be modified in both official and non-official circles. This was reflected in the output of many significant individuals and governmental committees. As early as mid-1915, Bryce's modest views on international compulsory arbitration were taken up by Viscount Haldane, Lord Chancellor in the Asquith Government that held office until late 1916. The key idea, about which opinion varied, was that of the usefulness of some kind of league of nations, which the British Cabinet was now prepared to accept, but only if the United States were present. The nature of modern war made it essential that adequate guarantees be provided by a system of alliances or mutual support. But what if the system of alliances of 1914 had in itself been a cause of the present war?

There were many who believed that a League could not provide the necessary security assurances that Britain felt that it and Europe required. This is very clearly expressed in a memorandum by Maurice Hankey of May 1916 which can be seen as a statement both of the views of many in and outside the Cabinet and a startling prophecy of what was actually to happen in the 1930s. It was also significant as Hankey was clearly, as Secretary to the Cabinet for thirty years, a key actor in his own right, as is evidenced by him being the only British Government official present at the 'Big Four' negotiations in Paris (see pp. 59–61).

Hankey's view was that there could be no reliance on international organs, for example to enforce international arbitration, as a reliance on this would 'create a sense of security which is wholly fictitious'. Germany's invasion of Belgium was the proof of this, as Belgium had believed it was 'protected'. Britain believed in the 'sanctity of treaties'; the Germans clearly did not. Having finally defeated Germany, 'financial and economic considerations will force peace on the world for at least a generation'. This would persuade 'the enthusiasts for social reform and anti-war and disarmament people' and 'they will persuade the nation to go to sleep as far as its military preparations go'. The problem was that 'the psychology and the ideals of the German, and possibly the Russian, people were quite different. They would be the loudest to assert their confidence in the new international body while, in reality, they would be seeking how they can turn it to their advantage. They would then create "an incident" … which can always be bought about by the mal-treatment, or alleged mal-treatment of the nationals or co-religionists of one country living under the authority of another, or it may be found in some question of tariffs or colonial boundaries'. The Conference would then give them what they wanted or Germany and her Allies would refuse the deal offered and war would ensue.

Even more accurately, Hankey predicted that the rest of the world would then be 'divided on the question on its merits' and particularly the United States. It

> will most likely as not be on the eve of a Presidential election and unwilling to take a hand. In any case, such a democratic society cannot be relied upon to take any part in European affairs. They are so cosmopolitan and so wedded to the almighty dollar that they cannot be judged even by the comparatively low standard of other nations in regard to matters of national honour … They will not fight well for abstract principles or justice, if they fight at all.

Any scheme that counted on American support or based itself on anything other than 'national interest' was therefore doomed to failure.[35]

Even if Hankey's views represented one extreme view in the Cabinet, and though he was to mellow in his interpretation of them himself by late 1918, they were to remain as one firm pole of British Government thinking throughout the war and Versailles Treaty negotiations. The League idea was never, except in the case of Lord Robert Cecil, to have enthusiastic Government backing, arguably even in the 1920s and 1930s, but came to be seen as a vital lever to ensure American involvement in the war. This was a 'realist' viewpoint and was in effect a modest extension of the Congress system of the nineteenth century to include the Americans. However, should the Americans refuse to enter into the bargain once struck, it was quite clear that the house of cards would collapse.

British Government policy from 1916 was therefore directed at finding out if the Americans could be enticed in on the Allied side and, even during the period of low Anglo-American relations in mid-1916, there were significant contacts between the Asquith Government and Wilson's confidant, Colonel Edward House, culminating in the so-called 'House–Grey Memorandum' of May 1916. By early 1918, it was therefore deemed necessary to have a view on the League of Nations project, if only because President Wilson had made it such a key war aim from his re-election in November 1916.

The Phillimore Committee

The key official British input into the post-war planning process came in early 1918 when the War Cabinet set up a committee to assess the implications of a League of Nations, chaired by Lord Phillimore.[36] The major feature of the final report of July 1918 is its distinctly historical bias. Nearly all of the main report is an analysis of earlier projects for a League of Nations, going back to the seventeenth and eighteenth centuries, at which period the 'development of the national state' was accompanied by 'more or less academic projects for establishing perpetual peace'. There followed a learned discourse on the various plans of this genre, from Abbé St Pierre's 'confederation' ideas to those of Immanuel Kant during the French Revolution, and to those of the nineteenth century and the 'Congress' and 'Concert' systems. A key *leitmotif* of the report is that all this can only work with democratic states, and that 'although the spread of *democratic* nationalism seemed to have paved the way to success', militaristic and absolutist states always prevented hopes of peace through cooperation being realised.

The present war was an object lesson that such forces were still at work. The only new elements that might give cause for hope were that, first, '[t]hese conditions have brought home the actual realities and horrors of war to men and women outnumbering many times those personally affected by military or naval campaigns of former years'. Alone this factor might not prove decisive in changing public perceptions of war but, second, '[a] line of thought and feeling is tending in all countries to assign a paramount place, not merely in political speculation, but in the actual organization of government, to the constitutional principle. In the great majority of nations, the personal conception of the state has by now been definitely superseded.' Russia was one example of it 'for the time at least, [having] been entirely displaced' while it was under attack in all the other continental European empires. There were therefore grounds for hope that 'popular forces [were increasingly] uniformly intolerant of any attempt to substitute the appeal to the sword for the methods of the Council Chamber'. This long preamble is in many ways the most remarkable part of the document in that it shows that the ideals pursued by the Committee, and by extension the Cabinet that approved the report, were not far removed from those of President Wilson.

It is a basic statement of the limits of an 'idealist' view of international relations but also an affirmation of belief in such a view in an ideal world, one which was seen as at least partially actually emerging.[37]

Several writers have criticised the Phillimore Committee for producing a plan for a League of Nations which fell far short of what was needed, as in the main report the Committee mainly concentrated on establishing a negotiating machinery among the Allies, not a forum for the views of all nations, victors and defeated alike, as most members of the UDC and even LNU wanted.[38] However, there is much in the final Covenant of the League that is also in the Phillimore Plan, especially as regards the injunction not to resort to war and about the settlement of international disputes. Nonetheless, its principal historically based models provided mainly for the contingency of Great Power collaboration in the case of a crisis or serious dispute, not for any recurrent meetings.[39] It thus drew much more on the nineteenth century tradition of the diplomacy of the Congress system than on the conference diplomacy envisaged by the supporters of the League, and can also be seen as an essentially 'statist/realist' construct that put its faith in states and alliances.

Grey's Memorandum of 1918

This emphasis was also reflected in the LNU, which, as was outlined above, had by 1918 gathered a good deal of moderate, but 'patriotic', feeling behind a more 'idealist' approach to the settlement. In an echo of the Phillimore Committee's approach, the former Foreign Secretary, Lord Grey felt moved to suggest that although '[t]here are projects that exist in a shady form in an atmosphere of tepid idealism', a clear reference to those of the UDC and earlier projects for a League outlined in the Report, there now had to be another try, for now 'the whole of modern civilisation is at stake'. Only those who had no 'ideals' could believe otherwise.

But his conditions for this were utterly 'realist' as the success of a LON depended, first, on the condition that 'the idea must be adopted with earnestness and conviction by the Executive Heads of States. It must be an essential part of their practical policy.' It was now, for the first time, possible for this condition to be met, because now *Wilson* believed it. He acknowledged that the Germans were not convinced, 'for they can conceive no development and even no security except based solely on force' and they had therefore to be persuaded that the risks and dangers of a 'will to supreme power are outweighed by the benefits of abandoning such a will'. It was up to the Americans to convince them of this as guarantor of the League, for small states would believe in anything that makes them more secure, but Germany must be made to feel secure. It and the United States must therefore be founder members.

A second condition was that states must realise that this 'may entail some inconvenient obligation', both to help other states that were attacked and to use other forms of coercion short of force if necessary, such as economic sanctions. This applied to 'civilised states' and 'less civilised parts of the world', with the example of an African chief complaining that before the arrival of 'civilisation' he used to be able to raid others with impunity and that he did not want to pay taxes to have his people protected. This for Grey illustrated that 'although the analogy between states and individuals ... is not perfect' it was also 'not quite irrelevant'. The next war would be far more horrible than even the present one, and would be upon them in 'twenty or thirty years' unless Wilson's vision of the LON was adopted, a vision 'of a peace of mutual regard between states for the rights of each and a determination to stamp out any attempt at war, as they would a plague that threatened the destruction of all'.[40]

For Grey, and a significant number of people within the Foreign Office, establishing the LON should now therefore be *the* war aim.[41] A major British liberal tenet had been modified. There would no longer be a self-regulating international system based solely on a 'harmony of interests', but a recognition that the nature of modern war, and the existence of 'less civilised' states, even among those that were economically developed, made 'idealism' something that had to be backed up by the use of force, if necessary. It was hoped that the League of Nations, based on a firm Anglo-American understanding, could be the basis of this new international order. Grey thus moved his not inconsiderable influence behind a growing, but still small, group within the Liberal Party in favour of a League as a 'realist' answer to the new problems posed by the war.

Woodrow Wilson and the American debate, 1914–18

Few American Presidents have been the subject of so much hagiography, disdain and misunderstanding as Woodrow Wilson. He still evokes awe by the manner in which he seemed to have changed the way not only that the United States conducted its international relations but the terms in which international relations have been conceived of ever since. The 'Wilson Doctrine' was most famously summed up in the Fourteen Points of January 1918, a document to which we shall refer below. Much of the following section examines how these Points were arrived at.

Henry Kissinger identifies Wilson as one 'idealist' side of the 'hinge' of this century's diplomatic practice, with Theodore Roosevelt as the other 'realist' side. America, for Wilson, has to be 'unselfish' in sharing its benefits and attributes with the rest of the world. Whereas for Roosevelt ('the warrior-statesman') America should be internationalist in its national interest, for Wilson ('the prophet-priest') America should be internationalist in the global interest. For Wilson this meant that an almost unbridled interventionism was necessary and for Kissinger the basis of this lay in his 'recognition that Americans cannot sustain major international engagements that are not justified by their moral faith' and that power must yield to morality. This very emphasis on morality is the factor that has so enraged Wilson's critics, from John Maynard Keynes and Georges Clemenceau at Paris to virtually every other 'statist/realist' ever since.[42]

Progressive and conservative internationalism

It is widely accepted that it was a broad coalition of what is termed the 'progressive internationalism' (PI) of the American centre-left in the Democratic Party and to its left in the socialist movement and the 'conservative internationalism' (CI) of William Howard Taft and the LEP before the First World War that were the main inputs to Wilson's thinking on international relations before Versailles. The differences between them need not be exaggerated – Eliot reported to Bryce that there were 'hundreds of American publicists' thinking over the possible terms of peace as early as October 1914.[43] But the groupings, as with their equivalents in Britain, had differences of emphasis. The dialectic between these two forms of internationalism has played an important role in American foreign policy throughout the century and is often referred to by the shorthand 'liberal internationalism'.

The immediate impetus for PI was a product of the period before the war and up to about four months into US involvement in 1917. It drew in both conventional Democrats and socialists such as John Reed and Max Eastman. So for Wilson's biographer, Thomas J. Knock the American left was 'at once the advance guard of the so-called New Diplomacy and the impassioned [proponent] of an Americanized version of social democracy'.[44] PI had many faces, but the first major potential influence on Wilson from 1915 onwards came through the American Peace Societies, such as the Women's Peace Party, led by Jane Addams, which had a platform very similar to the British UDC and demanded disarmament, the democratic control of foreign policy, the compulsory arbitration of disputes, Freedom of the Seas and a 'Concert of Nations'. Even if initially Wilson is said by Knock to have seen this group as 'well-intentioned, but impractical and naive', by 1918 many of these ideas had made their way into Wilson's Fourteen Points speech, so that Addams' campaign can be seen as having given 'a pioneering American synthesis of the New Diplomacy'.[45]

The LEP was the main American equivalent of, and indeed very close to, the Bryce Group, and much more conservative in its proposals – hence its claim to leadership of CI in the United States. It drew its membership mainly from Republican ranks and was thus not as radical on the economic causes of war, on disarmament, on self-determination or on the democratic control of foreign policy as advocates of PI. From early on in the war its emphasis was for a reinforcement of the legal defences against aggression as well as for a backing of these provisions by force and legal sanction.[46] The LEP was also very openly pro-Ally, not against the war and made a great deal of Bryce's report on the Belgian atrocities as evidence of German guilt. It proclaimed nonetheless a 'patriotism with a cool head' and played an active role in trying to influence Wilson.[47] It also espoused most of the ideals, including what came to be called the 'self-determination' of peoples, equality of states' rights and the need for collective security, that were used explicitly by Wilson in his speeches,[48] such as that of 27 May 1916 at the New Willard Hotel described below. It also urged the principle of universality in a future League and the need not to elaborate an institutional framework until the war was over. Taft had expressed his great satisfaction that by the end of 1917 'the English proposal [i.e. that of Bryce's "Proposals"] and our own are practically identical'.[49] The LEP's move to a more radical stance on the post-war ordering of international relations mirrored that of its British counterparts.

The evolution of Wilson's thought, 1916–18

As the war progressed, Wilson's speeches moved in tandem with events and drew on the developing debates within PI and CI to define a new form of international society that was both a response to stirrings in the United States itself and in Europe calling for a new way of organising inter-state relations and a recognition that the war had inevitably changed the nineteenth century balance of power for ever. Wilson wanted initially to act as a 'mediator' in the European war and, when this failed, to attempt to redefine the war aims of the participants so that such a war could hopefully not reoccur. Wilson was having to decide whether the United States should enter the war in the full knowledge that this was not wanted by much of American public opinion, as Roosevelt was to do during the next global conflict. Wilson tried to steer a middle path between 'preparedness' and not getting involved.

However, events militated against isolation as American citizens were increasingly becoming involved in the war being fought in the Atlantic, the deaths of United States' nationals in the sinking of the *Lusitania* in 1915 being but one celebrated example. It also worked against those still clinging to the idea that 'Freedom of the Seas' could be guaranteed by any navy, no matter how powerful. Wilson certainly wanted the war at least to result in a change of international attitudes, as evidenced by a series of celebrated speeches during 1916 and 1917. Particularly significant were the 'New Willard Hotel' speech of 27 May 1916 and the 'Peace without Victory' address of 22 January 1917.

The New Willard speech first laid down his commitment (he used the word 'creed') that 'every people has a right to choose the sovereignty under which they shall live', which was to apply to small as well as large states. It also made a plea for a right of the world to be 'free from every disturbance of its peace that has its origins in aggression and disregard of the rights of peoples and nations'. This 'creed' was given an institutional framework in the 'Peace without Victory' speech: '[t]here must be, not a balance of power, but a community of power; not organized rivalries, but an organized common peace'. This was to be guaranteed by the New Diplomacy, an equality of rights between nations, and government only by the consent of the governed. There was also to be 'Freedom of the Seas' and equality of armaments as part of this commonly enforced peace.[50]

All of these points could be seen as in stark contrast to the aims of any putative Allies. Britain had fought the United States in 1812 over a disputed formulation of the 'Freedom of the Seas', and it saw immense potential dangers to its Empire in the notion of self-determination. Hankey was so incensed by Wilson's speech that he wrote to Lloyd George that such an 'American Peace ... [would be] more dangerous to the British Empire than a German war'. Lloyd George largely shared these sentiments, writing to Spring Rice in Washington that, 'I know the American politician. He has no intellectual conscience. He thinks of nothing but the ticket, and he has not given the least thought to the effect of his action upon European affairs.'[51] British and French official policy from late 1916 on was to try and manipulate Wilson's ideas into a form that would suit their national interests. In this they were in the short run successful; in the longer term they were forced to accept his initial logic.

Non-American influences on Wilson

One of the major questions that runs through many of the writings on the preparation for Versailles has naturally been what effect British thinking, in particular, had on Wilson. On a *prima facie* level there is some clear similarity in the writings of pre-war writers such as Brailsford and some of the Fourteen Points; for example in H.N. Brailsford's statement of 1914 in the *War of Steel and Gold* that '[t]here can be no science of foreign politics so long as foreign affairs are in the hands of small cliques' and in Brailsford's more general denunciation of balance of power diplomatists.[52] Likewise, the UDC greeted each of Wilson's successive speeches on the post-war settlement with some enthusiasm and can be said to have the nearest 'fit' to his Fourteen Points of any other Allied organisation.[53] However, Lloyd George, in common with his Cabinet, never stopped having the deepest suspicions about Wilson and his sincerity, as did many other British and French politicians, often even those who sympathised with his aims. We have noted that Bryce, and most of the centre in British politics, was also deeply hurt by his equation of all the parties in the war as equally responsible. This alone meant that Wilson's reception within the British Establishment was bound to be cooler than might otherwise have been the case.

Other evidence of the unreceptive frame of mind with which Wilson came to Europe can be found in his refusal to meet Bryce to discuss a common Anglo-American approach as early as 1917.[54] He did meet with LNU leaders in December 1918, notably Gilbert Murray at Buckingham Palace and Asquith and Grey at the American Embassy. But, as Donald Birn describes it, 'LNU leaders remained uneasy about their American champion during the Peace Conference. Wilson had espoused open diplomacy, but now he met Clemenceau and Lloyd George behind closed doors ... League supporters trusted Wilson's intentions but feared that he was managing his case badly.'[55]

One of their worries was that Wilson might be influenced by American public opinion and his own delegation. Liberal (and later Labour) peer, Lord Parmoor told Bryce after a private talk with the American delegation at which Herbert Hoover was present in December 1918: '[t]here is a decided attempt to get rid of President Wilson's Peace Terms and a League of Nations ... The talk had given strong feeling that the United States now wanted to leave Europe. "Their job was done."' Wilson seemed to be impervious to such influence, Parmoor decided: '[h]e holds to his ideas with Scotch Presbyterian obstinacy ... to save civilisation ...'. But if he was rejected by the other Allies he was also likely to say '[v]ery well! I do not want to meddle in your affairs; stew in your own juice!' Hoover had explained to Parmoor later that Wilson was 'a little nervous about his reception here, and ... that he would take his own time and refuse to go into details about which he knows little'.[56] None of this was likely to encourage the LNU and those in favour of a Wilsonian settlement.

Another worry expressed by the LNU and British Government sources alike was that Wilson was simply not properly prepared for the Conference. Sir William Wiseman, a key British diplomatic link with Wilson in Washington and head of British Intelligence in the United States, wrote to Balfour that: 'I do not think that he [Wilson] has any specially cut-and-dried proposals to make regarding any of the important questions at issue, but will rather re-affirm his general principles and expect the Allies to make their definite proposals.'[57] Bryce got the same impression, and told Gilbert Murray that 'I fear Wilson has not got a worked out plan. We tried to press him to have one but he did not appreciate the many difficulties of detail. I trust your Society [i.e. the LNU] has worked these out and is helping Robert Cecil – the only member of the Government who really cares.'[58] All that was clear was that Wilson intended to use the Conference as a powerful platform for his general ideas, laid out in the Fourteen Points; as Wiseman put it: 'Wilson propaganda on a very big scale'. The League of Nations was to be the institutional vehicle for all of this.[59]

The British Government was very clearly warned that negotiating with Wilson, even on his favourite subject, would not be easy. Wilson's attitude also indicated that the secrecy of the American preparations for peace, indicated in the conversation with Wiseman and in the conduct of internal

American investigations such as the 'Inquiry' that is the focus of the next section, was seen by Wilson as essential if there was not to be a premature and possibly disastrous reaction within American public opinion to the whole settlement. Wilson was well aware of the American tradition of resisting any foreign entanglements and he believed, probably rightly, that any hint of collusion with the Allies over this before a peace settlement might severely dampen his chances of a working peace system after the war. The forces of isolationism were never far from the surface, and only quiet now because the war was still not won. After it was there might be created an entirely new set of circumstances, unfavourable to all the Allies' plans.

The 'Inquiry': official American planning for Paris[60]

The very title of the main sustained governmental American effort during the period 1917–18 to plan the peace is an indicator of the fears that Wilson harboured about too 'premature' a public discussion of the peace settlement. Wilson initiated the effort and gave it to Colonel House to coordinate, which he did in a rather half-hearted fashion. Its workings were kept extremely low key and initially hidden away in the New York Public Library, where they called themselves the 'Inquiry' to avert prying eyes. The Inquiry was entirely independent of the State Department, although it included a number of people who were later prominent in the American Commission to Negotiate the Peace (ACNP, as the US delegation to Paris was termed) and also a number of those prominent inside and outside the State Department in the Second World War in the planning of the next NWO, such as Walter Lippman and Isaiah Bowman (see below). Like the PID it produced many reports (about 2,000) of varying usefulness and volume, and a final 'Outline of Tentative Recommendations', known as the 'Black Book', on 21 January 1919.

The State Department was largely excluded from the planning process. As a much more primitive organisation than the Foreign Office in 1918, it was considered by Wilson as not yet up to the task of preparing a documentation analogous to that provided for the British delegation. There was little collaboration between the Inquiry and the Department, and they do not, for example, seem to have had much access to normal diplomatic reporting channels.[61] Wilson did not in any case want to entrust such thinking to anyone he could not fully trust and he naturally inclined to the advice of fellow academics who he felt would give a 'disinterested view of the factual evidence'.[62] Colonel House was therefore asked to coordinate a disparate band of 'experts' led by New York professor, Sidney Mezes, a specialist in the philosophy of religion and ethics. Mezes was soon effectively superseded by Dr Isaiah Bowman of the American Geographical Society, perhaps more appropriate given that boundaries were to prove so controversial at Paris. The upshot of this ignoring of the State Department was that Secretary of State Lansing felt increasingly isolated from the discussions (he was

eventually shown the door of the Oval Office in 1920 and was to write a
vitriolic denunciation of Wilson after the war). He clearly also felt very out
of sympathy with Wilson's more idealist views, famously denouncing self-
determination as often impossible when so many of those who were to
benefit were 'too low in the scale of civilisation to be able to reach an
intelligent decision'.[63]

Everyone who has written about the Inquiry sees it as providing a useful
precedent in that no conference had been prepared in such detail before it
happened, but an unfortunate one as well in that it produced haphazard,
uncoordinated and not very useful material. This was eventually recognised
by Wilson, who disbanded it during the Paris Conference in February 1919
and appended its members to the various sections of the ACNP. Few of its
members can be called experts in the sense that the members of the PID of
the Foreign Office clearly were, and British official documentation which
was sent to the Inquiry was of a generally much higher calibre than either its
American or French equivalents. Colonel House was sent a list of the 'Peace
Books' under preparation on the suggestion of Balfour in March 1918 and
the ACNP was the only delegation to be given copies of the completed
Books, a fact which caused some friction as the Italians and the French were
not.[64] Gelfand also feels that there was far too little consultation of any kind
between the various teams that made up the Inquiry, in spite of sporadic
attempts by members to remedy this.[65]

The Fourteen Points

The most useful document that the Inquiry did help to produce is nonetheless a key one. The 'Fourteen Points' speech of 8 January 1918 can be seen as
the main statement not only of Wilson's NWO, but it also justifies
Kissinger's identification of Wilson as one side of the 'hinge' of American
foreign policy this century. It is one of the most important speeches by any
statesman since 1900 and the key statement of the NWO agenda. But its
reception in the years and months that followed is also an illustration of how
ill-defined Wilson's ideas were as practical politics and how far the United
States had to go to persuade itself and the rest of the world of their relevance.

Wilson had asked the Inquiry through House to prepare a statement of
American war aims, which it did on 22 December 1917. This was the basis
of the territorial, but not the key 'philosophical' suggestions, of the Fourteen
Points speech.[66] The speech was a rallying cry for an NWO to follow the war
based on Wilson's distillation of the main debates that he had been following
in PI and CI circles since 1914. They were not original to him, but he
summed up the moment as no one else had. Point I, '[O]pen covenants of
peace, openly arrived at, after which there shall be no private international
understandings of any kind but diplomacy shall always proceed always
frankly and in the public view', remains the definitive statement on the 'New

Diplomacy', a cry for a more democratic and accountable approach to international politics. Point II, guaranteeing '[a]bsolute freedom of navigation upon the seas', Point III, 'the removal, so far as possible, of all economic barriers ...' and Point IV, urging the reduction of national armaments, are central to the emerging consensus of the new internationalism. Point V and (most of) Point XIV refer to a settlement of colonial claims and the establishment of the League of Nations. It can be argued that Points VI to XIII, which are mainly concerned with territorial issues, were clearly influenced by the Inquiry, but it is also clear that these are not the points that Wilson thought crucial and for which the world has remembered his speech. The Points not centrally considered by the Inquiry were also the basis of Wilson's supplementary speeches, referred to as the 'Four Principles' of 11 February 1918, which was mainly an elaboration of his views on self-determination, and of 27 September 1918, commonly called the 'Five Particulars', which makes the link between the notion of self-determination and the League of Nations. The Inquiry therefore cannot take much of the blame or the credit for the speech as it emerged and the agenda it embodied. The question has to be to what extent the agenda was addressed at Paris or later, and in the ambiguous answer to this we find the reasons for Wilson's mixed reputation with historians and political commentators alike.

The American 'Jupiter'

In these declarations Wilson was groping towards a new form of foreign policy for the United States, one that allowed it to keep its essential basis in Washington's principle of 'no entangling alliances' while also allowing for a greater role in world affairs. Kissinger has recognised that the United States was, for the first time in its history, 'projected' on to this stage by 'its rapidly expanding power, and the gradual collapse of the international system centered on Europe'. The main question was as to whether the United States took its place as a natural concomitant of the changed balance of power, which was President Theodore Roosevelt's view, or 'spread its principles throughout the world', a 'messianic' view of America's role as espoused by Wilson.[67] For Britain and France there was arguably no *practical* difference between the two conceptions insofar as they both locked the United States into a global security complex. As we shall see in a consideration of what Britain wanted out of the Versailles settlement, one of its key desires was to involve the USA in the affairs of Europe to guarantee the national interests of the democratic powers against the danger of a resurgence of violent anti-democratic forces like those of Wilhelmine Germany or, possibly, Soviet Russia.

So there is a clear logic from the British and French side that until the end of the war '[t]he prescriptions that Wilson advanced differed in some respects from those of Lloyd George, but the variances were glossed over on

both sides of the Atlantic in the interests of wartime unity'. But it is also right
to say that the Allied leaders had little knowledge of each other before the
Paris Conference and that the European Allies were 'disturbed by the
prospect that peacemaking might fall under the control of a man ... who
seemed to be an extreme idealist and maybe even a visionary'.[68] The Allies
had their channels of communication, mainly through their embassies in
Washington, Paris and London, but it is still surprising how little these were
properly used for coordinating major decisions. Wilson was not, for
example, consulted about the terms that were to be presented to the
Germans in the Armistice by the Supreme War Council in October 1918.
Even before he arrived in Paris he was seen as 'isolated and superior. He is
Jupiter' by Clemenceau. To public opinion in general, Walter Lippman of the
Inquiry told Mezes, Wilson appeared 'a figure of mystical properties, of
really incredible power but altogether out of reach'.[69]

The problem was that the blueprint for the discussions at Paris was very
vague and contained in a variety of exploratory documents, none of which
had really been exposed to public debate in a calm atmosphere or even
properly discussed in the Chancelleries of the Allies. The war had naturally
taken up most of their energies and the preparation for the peace had largely
been done in a series of national vacuums with very different presupposi-
tions in place. Wilson's views had been set out in the Fourteen Points and
Five Particulars during the war itself. They were in many ways a design for a
world that would be very different from that of 1914 if they were to be
implemented in full. The strictures in favour of 'Open covenants, openly
arrived at' was in direct contradiction to British and French faith in secret
diplomacy. The demand for 'absolute freedom of the seas' flew in the face of
all British experience of the previous century, where it believed that it was
the *Pax Britannica* that had enabled commerce to flourish and peace to be
kept. The demand for self-determination of peoples could not be counten-
anced for the 'uncivilised' in the British Empire as Wilson seemed to be
suggesting, even if it had been advocated by Britain for years in Europe as a
way of keeping the balance of power. The removal of economic barriers was
something the British could agree to in principle, but not if it meant the
unilateral opening up of Imperial markets, a debate that had raged since the
turn of the century and would continue to rage around the slogans of
'safeguarding' and 'Imperial Preference'.

Of the major British proposals, Wilson had certainly read the Phillimore
Committee proposals and discussed them at length in August 1918 with Sir
William Wiseman. But he did not want them aired in public. Wilson was
clearly worried that any premature decisions on a blueprint for the League
(or 'Association' as deemed in the Fourteen Points)[70] like those contained in
the Committee's proposals, might severely reduce his chances of selling the
League idea to American public opinion and the Senate (especially a group
around Senator Henry Cabot Lodge). He was most adamant in his desire

that it not be published, as each nation would by such a process 'become committed to its own plan and find fundamental objections to the methods favoured by the others'. His views on Phillimore were also coloured by his feeling that '[i]t has no teeth ... I read it to the last page hoping to find something definite, but I could not'. Wiseman asked if he would then set up an American Congressional Committee to consider the same issues as Phillimore; Wilson reiterated that he would not, again because it would stir up American public opinion unfavourable to the idea (no 'public discussions of the scheme now'). At Wiseman's comment that this would make coordination of Allied plans very difficult, Wilson said he was sure he would see eye to eye with Lloyd George, 'who, he felt, would substantially share his views', even though he could see that such a talk was 'impossible' at present.[71]

The dilemma for Wilson was that his attempt to ensure a peace without indemnities and based on the normative innovations of the Fourteen Points ran into increasingly hostile water within the United States itself as the war drew to a close. What had in January 1918 seemed a worthy and lofty set of intentions, into which groups such as the LEP and even the socialists had made their input by October 1918, had run into considerable opposition within the Senate. The reasons for this were partly party political, partly to do with the increasing anger over American casualties (light in early 1918, relatively heavy by October) and partly to do with a growing anti-Bolshevik fervour, which was associated by guilt with Prussian militarism by the Treaty of Brest Litovsk of March 1918. Republican Senator Lodge, Chairman of the Senate Foreign Relations Commmittee, as well as Theodore Roosevelt, now wanted a 'peace of unconditional surrender ... a dictated peace'. Natural supporters of Wilson's Fourteen Points were correspondingly less to be heard or, as Mayer puts it, 'the domestic foundations of Wilsonianism had contracted still further' and even many Democrats felt that he would have to yield to Republican views.[72] Wilson, in short, was losing his mandate to negotiate almost before he arrived in Europe. The October 1918 election result, which returned a Republican Congressional majority, further underlined this point.

Conclusions: were the Allies prepared for Versailles?

The essence of the dilemma for Wilson and his colleagues at Versailles was that there had never been an attempt at a 'worldwide settlement', and indeed there has never been one since. Neither the Congress of Vienna nor the deliberations during and after the Second World War, nor the emerging settlement since 1989, were as ambitious as Versailles.[73] The obsession in the British 'Peace Books' with previous attempts at world order in international conferences is proof of the desire to learn what lessons history might have to offer. The devil unfortunately proved to be in the detail.

Some commentators have written off the influence of the thinking of such groups as the UDC, the Bryce Group and others in Britain, and the LEP in the United States as having had a 'strictly limited' impact.[74] However, it is clear that the liberal elites in Britain and the United States did have both the access and the motive for influencing the Governments of their day. The First World War saw an immense influx of such thinkers into official circles, being recruited, as we have seen, in droves for Government service in think tanks and official bodies such as the Foreign Office and President Wilson's 'Inquiry'. It is of course difficult to show an exact transmission of influence, and it was acknowledged, as for example by Beatrice Webb, that 'permeation' would be a better way to describe the process than direct 'implantation'. The proof of their influence lies in the nature of the debate in international relations ever since.

An examination of the intellectual inputs of divers groups and individuals into the policy-making process that culminated in the Treaty of Versailles has an intrinsic merit as intellectual history, but is also a useful corrective to those who seem to believe that ideas and policy may touch, but do not have an actual demonstrable effect on each other. The thinkers of 1914–18 had a profound medium- and long-term effect, as the decisions taken during 1939–45 in the democracies were to prove. Arguably, they also had at least a 'permeation' effect in the immediate circumstances of the war and the peace settlement, but also in the actual direction of policy. We could also posit that the policies actually pursued by Governments might have been a lot less developed had these thinkers not been putting forward their plans. The mere fact that Wilson called the LEP 'woolgatherers' is not proof that he did not use their fleece for his own purposes. He and the other Allied leaders had to accept their own logic and the logic of an increased role for what Carr called the 'apotheosis of public opinion'.[75] There was also the problem of what to do about Bolshevik Russia (dealt with in the next chapter), one that presented in 1919 at least the dimly perceived outline of a revolutionary approach to international relations, one where peoples seemed to be given priority over governments. Wilson had to be prepared often to act alone and against what proved to be insuperable opposition. In so doing he wore himself out by October 1919 and lost the presidency in November 1920. The following chapters will show how the insights and imperfections of his vision were taken by a second generation of Western thinkers, activists, politicians and officials that essentially agreed with him but wished to make sure that the agreements would stick a second time round. But at Paris, to use Lippman's categories, 'reaction' won, not Wilson's 'reconstruction'.

In this ultimately vain attempt to reconcile the 'reaction', the 'reconstruction' and the 'revolution', one of the key ideas of liberal and socialist thinkers such as Lowes Dickinson, Angell and Brailsford became submerged in considerations of security, power and retribution. After the most devastating war in history, virtually none of the politicians went to Paris thinking about the medium- and long-term *economic* future of Europe, even if many of the officials in the delegations (such as Keynes) did so. The politicians seem to have tacitly assumed that the old system of Gold Standard and free trade would somehow reappear as if by magic or, alternatively, that it would have to be replaced by a security regime to keep Germany down. The reason for this seems clear. It was observed that economic interdependence had not stopped the war, so now the main thrust of the British, French and Italians was for security measures, be they through alliances or the LON. Wilson was not to prove capable of holding back this tide. It took a leader of Roosevelt's stature to do that in 1944–45. As will be shown in the next chapter, there were many Americans in relatively junior positions who observed what happened at Paris and who were prepared to back Roosevelt up in the Second World War, when they were in positions of power, in a way that the threadbare and ill-organised American delegation could not in 1919.

'Idealism' or 'realism' in Allied Government thinking before Versailles?

Given all the above, it might therefore be asked whether Lloyd George and his staff, or indeed Wilson, went to Paris with a broadly 'utopian/idealist' or 'statist/realist' brief for the necessary proceedings to follow. This is obviously a pertinent question, not only to decide on their frame of mind at the time but also to try and make sense of the literature on the theme that has continued ever since, given a notable impulse by E.H. Carr's *Twenty Years' Crisis* of 1939. Two of Carr's main targets were the utopian 'assumptions of nineteenth century liberalism' and its attendant theory of an economic 'harmony of interests', and the newer belief that a League could somehow reinforce this harmony and provide it with a new impetus.[76] Carr, of course, overstates his case, in that many confirmed 'intellectual' liberals were now convinced that Angell and others had been wrong about the Germans being essentially 'pacific' and over-confident in the restraining force of the 'harmony of interests'.

The problem for some of the liberals was not that they thought they had been wrong about the 'harmony of interests' but that Germany had allowed itself to slide into a 'moral catastrophe' and shown the limits of the idea. For Bryce's American friend, Eliot, Britain had not been much better, especially with its espousal of such barbarities as the blockade of Germany. The accolade of 'highest civilisation' could not now be given to either Germany or Britain.[77] The liberals themselves realised that their faith had been built on sand. What was necessary was to rebuild the foundations on more solid ground. But what was this ground to be?

President Wilson's Fourteen Points were to be largely forgotten in the negotiations at Paris. However, the United States Senate, as we shall see, viewed the virtual abandonment of the economic and humanitarian clauses of the Fourteen Points, and the seeming reliance on force as the basis of the LON (albeit called 'collective security'), as the problem with the Treaty.[78] Its critique was that this was a *'realist'* throwback to an institutionalised balance of power and not the 'idealist' economic and humane reform of international relations that President Wilson had engaged to deliver. It wanted him to deliver a revitalisation of its ideals, a demonstration of American moral leadership. The great tragedy is that he did not, but his successors in the 1940s did their best to get it right the second time around. How the second act of this tragedy played out will now be explained by examining some of the factors that caused this to come about at Paris.

Notes

1   Christopher Coker, *War and the 20th Century: The Impact of War on the Modern Consciousness* (London, Brassey's, 1994), pp. 90–94.
2   Oswald Spengler, *The Decline of the West* (2 vols, London, G. Allen and Unwin, 1926), vol. 2, p. 504.
3   George Dangerfield, *The Strange Death of Liberal England* (London, Grenada Publishing, 1970) (first published 1935), p. 372. On the 'meliorist myth' see Robert Fussell, *The Great War and Modern Memory* (Oxford University Press, 1975), p. 8.
4   One of the best descriptions of the Victorian Briton's self-image can be found in George Watson's *The English Ideology: Studies in the Language of Victorian Politics* (London, Allen Lane, 1973). He sums it up as 'Liberty is the English ideology' (p. 10).
5   E.H. Carr, *The Twenty Years' Crisis: 1919–1939* (London, Macmillan, 1939), pp. 13–16; Arnold Wolfers, *Britain and France Between the Two Wars* (Hamden, Connecticut, Archon Books, 1963), especially Chapter 21.
6   Michael Bentley, *The Liberal Mind, 1914–1929* (Cambridge University Press, 1977), p. 13.
7   Michael Bentley, *The Climax of Liberal Politics* (London, Edward Arnold, 1987), p. 121; Norman Angell, *The Great Illusion: A Study of the Relation of Military Power to National Advantage* (London, William Heinemann, 1910).
8   *The Times*, 20 July 1914, quoted by Paul Kennedy, *The Realities Behind Diplomacy* (London, Fontana, 1981), p. 139.
9   Dangerfield, *The Strange Death of Liberal England*, p. 358.
10 Lyn Macdonald, *Somme* (London, Macmillan, 1983), p. xiii. For its enduring appeal, see Fussell, *The Great War*, Chapter 9. For an account of the social impact of the war on Britain, see Arthur Marwick, *The Deluge: British Society and the First World War* (London, Open University Press/ Macmillan, 1973).
11 For a more detailed analysis of this, see in particular the work of Arno J. Mayer, *Political Origins of the New Diplomacy, 1917–1918* (New York, Vintage, 1970), from which Lippman's comment is taken (p. 391) and *Politics and Diplomacy of Peacemaking: Containment and Counterrevolution at Versailles, 1918–1919* (New York, Alfred A. Knopf, 1967). See also Chapter 2, this volume.

12 Donald Birn, *The League of Nations Union, 1918–1945* (Oxford, Clarendon Press, 1981), p. 6.

13 The author of the best book on the UDC is generous in his praise of this body's influence. Due to its membership, 'the Bryce group [had] an especial impact in liberal political and intellectual circles in the United States...[and] [p]erhaps indirectly through the Bryce group more than through its direct appeals, the Union of Democratic Control influenced the American President'. Marvin Swartz, *The Union of Democratic Control in British Politics during the First World War* (Oxford, Clarendon Press, 1971), pp. 97–98.

14 See George Conyne, *Woodrow Wilson: British Perspectives, 1912–21* (London, Macmillan, 1992), pp. 7–15. See also Bradford Perkins, *The Great Rapprochement: England and the United States, 1895–1914* (London, Victor Gollancz, 1969), pp. 276–278, for a rather more lukewarm view of Bryce.

15 Bentley, *The Liberal Mind*, p. 17.

16 To demonstrate this he actively supported those who were campaigning on behalf of German, Austrian and Hungarian nationals stranded in Britain at the outbreak of war. Indeed, he and many of his generation of British intellectuals were clearly very pro-German. As Keith Robbins puts it: 'Hegelianism was not the same as British Liberalism, but both of them were elevating and lofty.' Robbins, 'Lord Bryce and the First World War', *The Historical Journal*, vol. 10, no. 2, 1967, pp. 255–277), p. 255.

17 Spring Rice to Foreign Office, 16 July 1915. Rice asked in this telegram that a 'friend' [probably House] had asked that Bryce should address a letter to an American 'friend' [presumably Wilson] on the subject: Bryce Papers, File 242.

18 Lowes Dickinson gave a three-month lecture tour in 1916 for the LEP (Lowes Dickinson to Bryce, 3 May 1916, Lowes Dickinson Papers, 8/21). Bryce himself was convinced that the LEP was at the forefront of American thinking on the peace: 'Their propaganda is going on like a house on fire, and Wilson has so deeply committed himself to the project [of the LEP] that he may be expected to continue to support it and make an effort to push it through if American opinion favours it, and above all if the French play along': Bryce to Murray, 11 November 1916, Gilbert Murray Papers, Mss. 125. The *League Bulletin* may be found in Bryce Papers, 20 April 1917, Reel 8/90.

19 Bryce to C.W. Eliot, 1 July 1915, Bryce Papers, MS. Bryce, USA 2, quoted by Robbins, 'Lord Bryce', p. 261.

20 For a more detailed analysis of Cecil see p. 26.

21 The best description of the UDC can be found in Swartz, *The Union of Democratic Control*.

22 This document was not published but rather distributed privately, understandable in the atmosphere in the first few weeks of the war. Bryce Papers, File 239, Reel 8/89.

23 For a description of the UDC's problems and its growing closeness with the Labour Party after 1917, see Swartz, *The Union of Democratic Control*, Chapter 6 and Part III, 'The Rise of Labour'.

24 Bryce acted as a key link between the Society and the Government, writing to General Smuts asking for his support, and Smuts did agree to speak to an initial meeting on 14 May 1917. Cf. Robbins, 'Lord Bryce', p. 270.

25 Gilbert Murray was Professor of Greek at Oxford University and a major

proponent and supporter of the LNU in the inter-war years, as well as providing a significant input into the elaboration of the League itself through his friendship with Cecil and others, including Lord Bryce. He and Cecil had a long-standing intellectual debate about the nature of international relations which continued into the 1950s.

26 David (later Lord) Davies was to become one of the most ardent believers in the LON. Extremely rich, he endowed the first ever Chair of International Relations in 1919, named in 1924 the 'Woodrow Wilson Chair', at the University of Aberystwyth which Brian Porter acclaims as a 'brilliant academic innovation'. The best short description of his career can be found in Brian Porter's, 'David Davies and the Enforcement of Peace', in David Long and Peter Wilson (eds), *Thinkers of the Twenty Years' Crisis: Interwar Idealism Reassessed* (Oxford, Clarendon Press, 1995), pp. 58–78.

27 This paragraph is essentially drawn from Birn, *The League of Nations Union*, pp. 6–11.

28 Philip Noel-Baker was a Quaker, Commandant of the Friends Ambulance unit in the First World War. He was later a member of the Foreign Office staff that Cecil took to Paris, where he helped draft the Covenant, then of the League of Nations Secretariat (1919–22). He was the first holder of the Chair of International Relations at the London School of Economics (1924–29), Junior Minister at the Foreign Office (1929–31), Principal Assistant to Arthur Henderson at the League Disarmament Conference (1932–34) and Labour MP for Derby, from 1936 until he retired in 1970. For more details see Lorna Lloyd, 'Philip-Noel Baker and Peace through Law', in Long and Wilson, *Thinkers of the Twenty Years' Crisis*, pp. 25–57.

29 See, for example, his correspondence with Balfour, with whom he was on intimate terms: Balfour Papers, MSS 49738 and Cecil Papers, MSS 51071.

30 Erik Goldstein, *Winning the Peace: British Diplomatic Strategy, Peace Planning, and the Paris Peace Conference, 1916–1920* (Oxford, Clarendon Press, 1991), p. 10.

31 The first two committees were set up as part of the War Cabinet machinery, and the most significant memoranda submitted were by Sir Ralph Paget and Sir William Tyrrell of the Foreign Office which concentrated on the nationality question, and by Arthur Balfour, First Lord of the Admiralty and Foreign Secretary under Lloyd George after 1917, which concentrated on the European settlement: Goldstein, *Winning the Peace*, pp. 3 and 10–13.

32 This section draws extensively on Goldstein, *Winning the Peace*, pp. 30–47.

33 For a good brief summary of Toynbee's career, see Christopher Brewin, 'Arnold Toynbee, Chatham House and Research in a Global Context', pp. 277–301, and for an excellent overview of Zimmern's career, especially after his time with the PID, see Paul Rich, 'Alfred Zimmern's Cautious Idealism: The League of Nations, International Education, and the Commonwealth', pp. 79–99, both in Long and Wilson, *Thinkers of the Twenty Years' Crisis*.

34 Goldstein, *Winning the Peace*, pp. 57–86 and 94–98. This section is in effect a précis of Goldstein's excellent analysis of the PID.

35 Hankey (Committee of Imperial Defence) to Balfour, 25 May 1916, Balfour Papers, MSS 49704.

36 For a copy of the main articles of the Phillimore Committee's report (official title

'The Committee on the League of Nations') see David Miller, *The Drafting of the Covenant* (New York, David Putnam's and Sons, 1928), pp. 4–8.

37 The text of the Final Report of the 'Committee on the League of Nations' (Phillimore Committee), of 3 July 1918, presented to the Foreign Secretary, Arthur Balfour, and that of the Interim Report of 20 March, as well as the correspondence and so on, can be found in FO371/3439 and /3483. A full copy of the Final Report can be found in the Noel-Baker Papers, NBKR 4/436. Other members of the Committee included Sir Eyre Crowe, the main architect of Britain's German policy before the First World War and Permanent Secretary at the Foreign Office, and Sir William Tyrrell, shortly to be head of the PID of the Foreign Office.

38 A point made, for example, by Donald Birn, in *The League of Nations Union*, p. 8.

39 Miller, *The Drafting of the Covenant*, pp. 9–10.

40 Sir Edward Grey, 'The League of Nations'; Bryce Papers, Reel 8/90, File 243, pp. 147–156.

41 See, for example, Esmé Howard (British Ambassador to Norway) to Bryce, 27 April 1918; Bryce Papers, Reel 8/90, File 242.

42 Henry Kissinger, *Diplomacy* (New York, Simon and Schuster, 1994), pp. 47 and 50. The main chronicler of Wilson's life is Arthur J. Link, who has published Wilson's papers in fifty volumes, all with Princeton University Press. Other classical treatments are Mary Stannard Baker, *Woodrow Wilson and the World Settlement* (3 vols, London, Doubleday, 1923) and, by the same author, *Woodrow Wilson: His Life and Letters* (8 vols, London, Doubleday, 1928–29). Other authors who have concentrated on Wilson will be considered below.

43 Eliot to Bryce, 5 October 1914; Ms. Bryce USA 1., Reel 8/68.

44 Thomas J. Knock, *To End All Wars: Woodrow Wilson and the Quest for a New World Order* (New York, Oxford University Press, 1992), pp. viii–ix.

45 By the Spring of 1918 Wilson's Fourteen Points speech had enabled Addams to team up with other PI thinkers such as Paul Kellogg and Felix Frankfurter to set up the League of Free Nations Association, again more in line with the UDC and those to its left than with the mainstream LEP: Knock, *To End All Wars*, pp. 52 and 161.

46 Eliot (prominent in the LEP) to Bryce, 5 October 1914; Bryce Ms. USA 1, Reel 8/68.

47 Knock, *To End All Wars*, pp. 57–62.

48 Lawrence Gelfand, *The Inquiry: American Preparations for Peace, 1917–1919* (New Haven, Yale University Press, 1963), p. xii. Wilson had already envisaged the idea of collective security in discussions about Latin America as early as 1913. Latin America continued to provide a model for such thinking throughout the next fifty years, as in Roosevelt's 'Good Neighbour' policy.

49 Eliot to Bryce, 21 May 1917 and 8 October 1918; Ms. Bryce USA 1, Reel 8/68.

50 Knock, *To End All Wars*, pp. 76–78 and 112–115.

51 Quoted by Conyne, *Woodrow Wilson*, pp. 67 and 76.

52 Henry Noel Brailsford, *The War of Steel and Gold: A Study of the Armed Peace* (London, G. Bell and Sons, 1914), p. 52.

53 See also J.D.B. Miller, *Norman Angell and the Futility of War* (London, Macmillan, 1986), p. 14. For views of Wilson within the UDC, see Swartz, *The Union of Democratic Control*, pp. 132–140.

54 Robbins, 'Lord Bryce', p. 271.

55 Birn, *The League of Nations Union*, pp. 14–15.
56 Parmoor to Bryce, 12 December 1918, Bryce Papers Reel 8/89. For a discussion of Herbert Hoover at Versailles, see Lawrence Gelfand (ed.), *Herbert Hoover, the Great War and its Aftermath, 1914–1923* (University of Iowa Press, 1979) and Frances William O'Brien (ed.), *Two Peacemakers in Paris: The Hoover–Wilson Post-Armistice Letters, 1918–1920* (College Station and London, Texas A and M University Press, 1978).
57 Wiseman to Balfour, 15 December 1918, Balfour Papers, Add. Mss. 49741. Conyne rightly considers Wiseman as the British Government's key link to Wilson's thinking after October 1917: Conyne, *Woodrow Wilson*, pp. 189–193.
58 Bryce to Murray, 8 January 1919; Gilbert Murray Papers, Mss. 125.
59 Wiseman to Balfour, 22 December 1918 and 15 December 1918; Balfour Papers, Add. Mss. 49741.
60 In addition to Gelfand, *The Inquiry*, see also Arthur Walworth, *America's Moment: 1918* (New York, Norton and Co., 1963).
61 Walworth, *America's Moment*, p. 80.
62 Gelfand, *The Inquiry*, p. 33.
63 Lansing, quoted by Walworth, *America's Moment*, p. 152. It might be commented that the eventual 'mandate' system of the League of Nations agreed by Wilson at Paris was a recognition of such prejudices.
64 Goldstein, *Winning the Peace*, pp. 43–45. Goldstein gives a good summary of the British relationship with the Inquiry, pp. 98–103.
65 Walworth, *America's Moment*, pp. 122 and 126–28.
66 For a lengthy discussion of the Inquiry's input into the Fourteen Points see Gelfand, *The Inquiry*, pp. 134–153. It is reproduced in *Foreign Relations of the United States, Paris Peace Conference, 1919* (Washington, Government Printing Office, 1924), vol. 1, pp. 41–53.
67 Kissinger, *Diplomacy*, p. 29.
68 Walworth, *America's Moment*, pp. 7 and 15.
69 Walworth records Jusserand saying that Wilson had been '*très choqué*' about this, in despatches to Paris on 11 and 12 October 1918, and Supreme War Council Minutes of 6 and 7 October 1918; see Walworth, *America's Moment*, p. 21. For a general view of Wilson and House at Versailles, see Inga Floto, *Colonel House in Paris: A Study of American Policy at the Paris Peace Conference* (Princeton University Press, 1973).
70 Miller, *The Drafting of the Covenant*, p. 18.
71 Wiseman to Balfour, copied to Lloyd George and Cecil, 16 August 1918; Balfour Papers Add. Mss. 49741.
72 Speech by Lodge to Congress of 23 August 1918, quoted in Arno J. Mayer, *Politics and Diplomacy of Peacemaking: Containment and Counterrevolution at Versailles, 1918–1919* (New York, Alfred A. Knopf, 1967), pp. 55–62.
73 A point made by Arthur S. Link in the 'Editor's Introduction' to the *Deliberations of the Council of Four (March 24–June 28, 1919)* (2 vols, Princeton University Press, 1992), vol. 1, p. xix.
74 David Armstrong, in a chapter on the 'Origins of the League of Nations', in David Armstrong, Lorna Lloyd and John Redmond, *From Versailles to Maastricht: International Organization in the Twentieth Century* (London, Macmillan, 1996), p. 14.

75 Carr, *Twenty Years' Crisis*, p. 31.
76 Carr, *Twenty Years' Crisis*, p. 40 and *passim*.
77 See, for example, Eliot to Bryce, 17 December 1914, and 25 January, 17 March and 29 April 1915; Bryce Papers, U.S.A. 1.
78 It is admittedly difficult to be categorical about this as the Senate would probably have accepted the League, and indeed the Treaty, if Wilson had not insisted on Article X being included, which insisted on the use of force to uphold the Covenant.

2

The Paris Peace Conference
and the Treaty of Versailles, 1919

Introduction

An extensive literature exists on the 'lessons of Versailles' and particularly on the 'failure' of the League of Nations (LON), one that started even before the signature of the Treaty of Versailles. The first focus of this chapter is an exploration of the process of disillusionment as it comes out in the documentary record. The key areas that have been identified by contemporaries and historians alike are the mismatch between the security- and 'order'-based sections of the Covenant of the LON and in the broader Treaty itself and the ensuing disagreements between the major Allied powers, especially Britain and France, about how they should be implemented; the exclusion (partly as a cause and consequence of this mismatch) of three of the major powers – the United States, Germany and Soviet Russia – from the LON; and many of the clauses of the Treaty, seen as variously too lenient or too savage, depending on who was commentating.

The situation on the eve of the Conference itself is the second main focus of the chapter, in conjunction with an analysis of the relationships that developed among the Allied leaders. Rather than attempting a blow-by-blow account, of which many exist in a number of excellent books on the Treaty process,[1] the aim will be to highlight the major areas of agreement and disagreement among the principal decision makers and to underline the main areas that were to be a cause of future, indeed arguably of continuing and universal, concern to the student of international relations. In particular the contemporary thoughts of some of the key players, as well as lesser participants, will be used to give a view of the intellectual atmosphere at the time.

The third focus is on how the Conference and the LON attempted to frame the immediate problems of the post-war period. The key points among these are the future of international organisations in general, and in particular their security function, and the allied question of how states should be organised. A final focus will be on a brief analysis of the key complaints of enduring relevance about Versailles and the LON, particularly as made by E.H. Carr. In a discussion of the emergence of NWO ideas, the Treaty of Versailles has provided fertile ground for explaining how ideas to 'improve' international relations can be seen as coming into collision with the realities of those relations. Can ideas, in short, emerge 'before' their time, or does the experience of 1919 prove that analysis of projected 'improvements' has to be preceded by a correct assessment of what 'realities' are? How can such an assessment be made, and did the architects and implementers of the Versailles Treaty and the LON indeed believe that they were violating such a principle?

Three areas of obvious and crucial concern at Paris will be dealt with in later thematic chapters, although they are not by any means neglected here. The first of these is the development of the perceived need for a global security regime based on some kind of League, which will be examined in Chapter 6. The second of these is the consideration of the problems and possibilities that exist for economic regeneration and reconstruction after a major war, a problem that arguably first emerged after Versailles and one which will be examined in some detail in Chapter 7. The third is the issue of national self-determination, which had an element that was, initially at least, purely European in scope, and later of course extended to the rest of the planet as decolonisation, which will be analysed in Chapter 8.

British and French attitudes on the eve of the Conference

British war aims, 1918

As we have seen, during the early part of the war the British Government had not elaborated a detailed war aims programme. It had adopted a list of aims through alliance, notably with the Italians and the Secret Treaties of 1915. Lloyd George's Government after 1916, and especially after the losses of 1917, had begun slowly to embrace a more 'Wilsonian' peace, partly as a result of pressure from groups such as the LNU, but mainly because of a perceived need to make common cause with the United States against countries such as Germany that sought to disturb the balance of power in Europe.[2]

An official amended British declaration of war aims was delivered in early 1918 as a result of the need to accommodate Wilson's views on the peace in a speech by Lloyd George to the Trades Union Congress on 5 January, three days before Wilson's Fourteen Points speech. The venue was chosen to underline to the working man, deemed possibly susceptible to the charms of Bolshevism, Britain's conviction that this must be a just peace. In it Lloyd George declared that Britain's war aims were now threefold: the 'sanctity of treaties' had to be reaffirmed; the 'territorial settlement [had to be] based on the right of self-determination or the consent of the governed', although this was to be extended only to all European peoples and those of the ex-German colonies; and there must be 'the creation of some international organisation to limit the burden of armaments and diminish the probability of war'. These were all things with which Wilson agreed, but with many a difference of emphasis.

For example, the constant British preoccupation with its rights of naval search to protect the 'Freedom of the Seas' and its Empire, had both proved to be constant irritants in Anglo-American relations since at least 1812. Balfour had tried to pour oil on other troubled waters in seeming respect of Wilson's first Point – 'Open covenants openly arrived at' – by a declaration in the House of Commons in June 1918 denouncing the Secret Treaties signed with Italy in 1915 (giving them much of the Adriatic Coast of what became Yugoslavia and other territories in the Ottoman Empire) and with the Imperial Russian regime (now defunct).[3] The British Government showed by such signals that it wanted to be seen as sharing the high moral ground occupied by Wilson. The obvious question was whether this was for reasons of pure expediency or due to some Pauline conversion to Wilson's programme.

One of the key roles in preparing the negotiating briefs for the British delegation at the Peace Conference was given to General Jan Christiaan Smuts, that of the establishment of a League of Nations, which was viewed with extreme cynicism in London but accepted as being one of Wilson's key war aims. Smuts was a member of the War Cabinet who had the advantage of being universally respected by all the different schools of thought about the post-war settlement and of being a representative of the Empire. The main lines that he felt needed to be pursued at the Conference were quite well developed in outline by the beginning of December 1918 in 'Our Policy at the Peace Conference' and 'A Practical Suggestion', the latter of which proposed a blueprint for the League of Nations and which made a deep impression on the American delegation in Paris.

The first of these documents is in fact much more interesting than the second for what its says about British attitudes, as it was circulated solely to the War Cabinet. The document reveals that Smuts had no doubt that the world would be very different after the war and that this would have great implications for Imperial policy, strategically and tactically. In the first place, the defeat of Germany and the 'disappearance' of Russia and Austria left 'only three first-class Powers in the arena of world politics – the British Empire, France and the United States of America'. The balance of power must therefore be re-thought in the light of this new reality. For Britain Smuts considered that this meant siding with America, not France. France had been 'a bad neighbour to us in the past ... I am afraid that her arrogant diplomacy may be revived by the great change that has come over her fortunes ... I fear we shall find her a difficult if not an intolerable neighbour', in spite of being 'most generous' over Imperial issues during the war, as evidenced by the Sykes–Picot Agreement to create the 'mandates' of Syria and Lebanon where France was now 'the principal heir to the "Turkish estate"'.

The main implication of this was that Britain should get as close as possible to the United States from the very beginning of the Conference, as both France and Italy would make difficulties for Britain and, in the case of Italy, 'preposterous claims'. Wilson must be courted actively and his League of Nations idea supported, 'and indeed by going further and giving form to his rather nebulous ideas'. It had to be the League that would solve most of the difficult territorial and economic questions after the war, ones left by the collapse of the Empires of Central and Eastern Europe. Smuts' ideas on the League can therefore be seen as part of an overall policy strategy, a charm offensive on Wilson and the United States to persuade them to stay as part of the new balance of power in the nearest thing to an alliance that could be achieved. Since Wilson had decided that this organisation was the key to a post-war settlement he must be accommodated. The real problem for Smuts therefore lay in whether Britain could work with Wilson to contain French and Italian demands while not forcing him to compromise his own 'ideals' and to convert the League into a real working institution, 'the foundation of the new polity of Europe', an idea that of course foreshadows Rooseveltian and federalist ideas of a united Europe. Only this would cement the United States into the new order and enable Britain to get rid of such 'obnoxious agreements' as Sykes–Picot, something that upset not only Smuts but many other imperialists in the Cabinet.[4]

Smuts was therefore able to synthesise what Goldstein sees as the British delegation's three schools of thought at Versailles: 'the balance of power, the New Europe [i.e. essentially the future of Eastern and Central Europe] and imperial expansion'.[5] Goldstein sees this as exemplifying that Britain therefore arrived at Versailles with no clear overall strategic view of what it hoped to achieve. But could there have been any alternative, given that Britain had such a complicated relationship to all three areas of concern, as was also to be the case in the Second World War? These schools, which were not mutually exclusive, did mean that it was often difficult for the British to agree with France, as French views on all three areas were usually at variance with perceived British interests. They indeed reinforce each other, as over how to deal with Germany, where Britain did not essentially want a punitive settlement and the French did, and over the Middle East, where French views on the future of the Ottoman Empire meant inevitable clashes.

This dilemma meant that the only alternative might be a deal with the United States that preserved the Empire and the balance of power in Europe. This was enough to make even Hankey moderate the clear-cut 'realist' views of 1916 described in Chapter 1, although he was still worried that the American version of a League might threaten such British shibboleths as 'Freedom of the Seas'. By mid-1918 he was now suggesting that a League of

Nations could work and even proposing his own version, a somewhat fanciful federated state structure. The key aim of this would still, however, be to create a barrier 'between contending powers'. Nonetheless, he had clearly lost his stomach for a really hard anti-German peace, and criticised Lloyd George for his 'very hard attitude, talking of judgements and penalties. I fear he may over-state our power and miss securing a good peace, if he is not careful'. Now Hankey favoured 'removing the bones of contention'. Lloyd George gave him the task of the organisational side of the Conference, initially in tandem with Hardinge of the Foreign Office but increasingly as the main actor, especially once the Conference opened.[6]

These somewhat cynical tactics seem to have worked, as many of the Americans arriving in Europe, such as David Miller, the main American technical drafter of the Covenant, waxed lyrical about Smuts' 'moving and appealing style; tending indeed to disarm criticism of the text of the Articles suggested'.[7] Basing himself on Phillimore,[8] especially as regards the settlement of disputes, Smuts decided in favour of a General Conference and a Council for the League, the latter made up of the Powers and a rotating membership of middle and smaller states (unlike Cecil's formulation that envisaged the Powers only). The big idea in Smuts' plan was for the system of what became known as 'Mandates' for ex-German and ex-Ottoman territories.[9] One essential factor in such a close partnership with America for Smuts had to lie in locking in the United States as a protector 'willing to administer such peoples as may choose or be assigned to her tutelage', as Smuts had put it in 'Our Policy at the Peace Conference'.

Much to British surprise, this was eagerly accepted by Wilson. It seems clear that although Wilson had the big ideas he had not fleshed them out in any way. By the time concrete ideas for a League were discussed at Versailles, Cecil was convinced that Wilson had no real ideas of his own: 'It is almost entirely Smuts and Phillimore combined, with practically no ideas in it so that his scheme [for the League was] largely the production of others.'[10] When he went to Paris, Miller tells us, Wilson took only three Memoranda with him. The first was, unsurprisingly, on the LON, 'An Association of Nations'; the second a 'Declaration on Open Diplomacy'; and the third on 'Equality of Trade'.[11] The forward planning of the British and (to a lesser extent) the French Governments paid huge dividends as the negotiations at Paris progressed. This certainly helped the British to finalise the Treaty document with Wilson in a rapid way at the Conference, but of course it also resulted in a document that was far from satisfactory to American, or indeed most of world, liberal public opinion.

We must necessarily doubt that Smuts' proposals on the League were really believed in by the rest of the War Cabinet. Cecil was certainly persuaded by the arguments used by Smuts in his desire to see a negotiation of the Covenant of the League and in following his advice to get close to the Americans. But as he commented to Smuts, 'I only trust that other members of the Government take the same view as you do.' Smuts' fellow South African, Botha, is probably more typical of both Cabinet and Imperial feelings in having the contradictory view that 'I shall support the proposal [of a LON], but I do not see how it is to be carried out. Wilson's point as to the freedom of the seas is nonsense, and I hope he will see that it is. Our object must be to bind Britain and America together. That will make for the peace of the world.'[12] Thus by the end of 1918 the Cabinet was reasonably persuaded that showing enthusiasm for the League idea could be used as a way of pursuing moderate reform in international relations in Britain's national and imperial interest. The only questions were how this might develop in tandem with Britain's Allies at Paris and how this might be packaged so as to look as though it was meant to improve the world.

It is difficult to say if Lloyd George himself believed that this would work as a strategy. Lloyd George was capable of the most duplicitous commentary on virtually any subject, the League of Nations being no exception. Even those closest to him, such as Lord Riddell, could quote him as saying that the League was '"deceptive and dangerous" on Saturday and ... "the beginning of a great idea" on the following Wednesday.'[13] He personally does not seem to have cared much for the League idea (Cecil reported 'he takes no interest [in it]'[14]), but neither was he hostile to it. Lloyd George conducted a very personalised negotiation at Paris, as did Wilson and Clemenceau, but he clearly had a 'national interest' frame of mind. The question was how did he, and his Government, now define this elusive concept, except to keep a balance between the three British 'schools' of Balance of Power, New Europe and Empire?

Lloyd George was certainly blamed at the time by many of the liberals and other true believers in the League of Nations as one of its main betrayers as much by what he did as by the way he conducted himself at Versailles. But perhaps it is fairer to say that it was an idea that nearly achieved a working consensus. Hankey was even willing to have himself suggested as its first Secretary General, a measure of the expectations that this most canny observer of British foreign and domestic policy put in the likely outcome of Versailles, although he was to change his opinion by mid-1919 and the dreams evaporated.[15]

French thinking about a post-war settlement

French preparations for the end of the war have been largely ignored so far in this narrative. This is partly because France's almost sole stated desire was to beat Germany and get revenge: Lippman's 'reaction'.[16] The usual line pursued by historians is that a number of Commissions were set up by Clemenceau's Government, but that he largely ignored them all and acted alone at the Conference, advised only by his military commanders. He is shown as having little sympathy with Wilson and only allowing any discussion of theoretical issues such as the League of Nations and self-determination because he knew that Wilson would want to know his opinion. In this he is portrayed as being far closer to Lloyd George than the Americans in that the British were also, in spite of the presence of such men as Cecil, more inclined to a hard peace than Wilson.

The Commission Bourgeois sur la Société des Nations

The French Government set up a number of Commissions to study various aspects of the territorial and economic aspects of a peace treaty: one Bureau d'études économiques under Senator Jean Morel; a Comité d'études under Ernest Lavisse; and one on the mines and industries of the North East. These were to define French demands at Versailles, which were essentially territorial and financial. Several historians accuse the French of not doing nearly enough.[17] It might therefore be argued that France's policy towards the League of Nations idea that was central to Wilson's thinking, and that of most British commentators, was largely reactive. This is rather unfair, as there had also been a Commission de la Société des Nations (SDN), set up and chaired by Léon Bourgeois in September 1917. This was not a hole in the wall affair and took evidence not only from Government ministers but from a wide variety of officials in the Ministère des Affaires Etrangères (MAE, usually referred to as the 'Quai d'Orsay' because of its location).

In his opening speech to what became known as the 'Commission Bourgeois', French Foreign Minister Ribot acknowledged that Wilson's call for a League had provoked the setting up of the Commission, but he also laid emphasis on the French belief that his LON proposal was not entirely new, but had been an integral intended future part of the Hague discussions of 1899 and 1907 and the system of bilateral Arbitration Agreements set up before the war as a result of these talks. The Commission therefore based its legitimacy not only on Allied declarations of faith in a post-war LON, but also on French notions of a long-established need to codify international law better and to supplement this codification with effectively enforced sanctions, as Aristide Briand had told the French Chambre des Députés in May 1916. The emphasis on the need for force to back up this codification is what differentiates the French view of an SDN from that of Wilson. As Ribot said before the Commission was set up: 'le droit sans la force, qu'est-ce que c'est, sinon l'humiliation de la justice par la violence?',[18] about which the French had had a great deal of practical experience in the field. Clemenceau therefore declared just before Versailles that he wanted a defensive alliance against Germany, made up of Britain, France, Belgium and Luxembourg 'and a new state or states consolidated out of the common territory west of the Rhine'.[19]

This obsession with the need for effective sanctions and defensive structures permeates the whole work of the Commission in stark contradiction to the Wilsonian ideal of state 'equality'. Equally, the Commission felt that the SDN (LON) must not be a super-state, it must enhance sovereignty, not deny it, and be 'a union [of states] to keep the peace'.[20] The Commission did therefore accept the implicit Wilsonian idea, that we have also seen in Grey's comments of 1918, that the League must be based on a common notion of standards of 'civilisation', which had, in turn, to be based on respect for the law and the maintenance of peace. But what, as Grey had also asked, if some states were not 'civilised'?

The Commission therefore wanted the League to be a continuation of the wartime alliance, and in consequence set up before the war ended, but not a political secretariat for the world. It was prepared to accept the idea of an 'International Council', but its main role had to be the prevention and resolution of conflicts by all means from arbitration, through sanctions to the use of force.[21] This is of course exactly what happened during the Second World War with the establishment of the Security Council. But it was not a universalist vision. For the members of the Commission, all that had come before, including the Treaty of Vienna of 1815 and the Hague Conferences of 1899 and 1907, were steps on the progress towards civilisation, and those who did not measure up must be excluded.[22]

Many key features of the Bourgeois Commission's discussions were carried forward fully by Clemenceau into the peace talks, especially the need to provide for effective sanctions against breaches of the peace. The features of the wartime experience of alliance that most struck the French as worthy of emulation were the alliance with Britain, which must be the basis of the LON in peace as in war; the use of effective economic sanctions, especially that of blockade (where they saw much to admire in Cecil's management); and the control (or 'freedom') of the sea. There was a constant obsession that such a war should not happen again and a constant preoccupation that it might re-erupt in twenty years or so, as in 'la paix doit être une paix véritable et non une trêve dangereuse'.[23] Once Wilson had made his Fourteen Points speech there was discussion of the need for two peace negotiations and two treaties. The first would have to be to settle the war (an 'Inter-Allied Conference') and its territorial questions, the second 'tendant à l'organisation du monde pacifié'.[24] In effect this is what happened, with the division of the Treaty into punitive and League clauses.

The key to an understanding of the presentation of the French case at Versailles has to be based on their feelings towards Germany and their Allies. France had over 1,364,000 killed, 740,000 permanently disabled and 3,000,000 wounded and seen a huge swathe of its territory devastated. Clemenceau's later war memoirs, and those of many lesser figures, are a litany of despair over the untrustworthiness of Germany and the uselessness of his own country's response to it before, after and, to a certain extent, during the war. His generation 'saw the loss of Alsace-Lorraine, and never could I be consoled for that loss'. They had further seen the 'tightening up of authority to machine drill men with a view to the most violent offensive; with all the easy-going slackness and fatuous reliance on big words'. But Germany had not expressed any guilt for its actions, the Kaiser's utterances had been self-justifying and uncomprehending to the end, and even at Versailles Brockdorff-Rantzau had spoken to him in the language of the 'challenge ... not a whit cured of his insane folly'.[25]

Clemenceau did not want a peace that would destroy Germany, with only the Rhineland as a buffer zone, he instead wanted a peace with 'guarantees' and a 'Europe founded upon right'. Given the devastation his country had suffered he felt that this was only France's due, especially as he was very aware that the 'progress of [the] murder machines of war goes faster than that of organizations of peace'. These were views much as expressed by Lord Grey and others. There must be a solid alliance of the Powers after the war, not a mere 'talky-talk and super-talky-talk of [Wilson's] League of Nations'. There is no evidence that any of the Commissions that he set up felt any differently, or indeed that the British and many of the Americans disagreed with his doubts.[26] But Clemenceau, and many more in French circles, belonged to an older school of thought on diplomacy that put more faith in a coalition of the strongest powers 'holding the lid down on the boiling kettle of European unrest and dissatisfaction', as Wolfers puts it, 'not in a strategy, espoused by the British for pragmatic reasons, and Wilson for philosophical ones, that called for a removal of the causes of revolt in order to eliminate the chances of an explosion'.[27]

However, Clemenceau felt that the British and the Americans, valiant as they had been in the fighting, could not be trusted to give him any kind of satisfactory peace. His constant worry was the time-honoured policy of the British for a balance of power in Europe and the fear that the Americans had not suffered enough (only 54,000 dead in action, as he constantly pointed out) to understand that the threat and reality of force had to underpin the Treaty and, if necessary, the LON. Not that he disagreed with Wilson's desire for self-determination as the guiding principle of the 'Europe founded on right' – 'an achievement far and away nobler than the violences of conquest'. But he was not sure that it 'was the last word of our civilisation. What is the last word in anything?'[28]

Clemenceau felt that he had gone a long way to meet Wilson's demands. However, Wilson did not help the French to bring their more positive ideas to the table before Versailles, and refused two key French ideas out of hand that might ironically have strengthened his hand with the US Senate later on. The first of these was not to allow a wider discussion of the League until the war was finished (his 'prematurity' argument was used on Paris as much as on London) and the second was the refusal of an establishment of the League before the war ended. The French were non-plussed by this 'laissez faire' and they feared that this approach, 'fidèle à la tradition anglo-saxonne', would not work.[29] The French were thus the least enthusiastic about the League idea, and it was wishful thinking for House and Lansing to believe that Clemenceau was 'much more favourable to the idea [of a League] than he had been at first'. Cecil, who was told this by the Americans, had also heard Marshall Foch say that the League was 'a queer Anglo-Saxon fantasy not likely to be of the slightest importance in practice'.[30] As for Clemenceau, his most frank assessment of the proceedings was one overheard by Hankey: 'I sit between two lunatics. One imagines himself Jesus Christ [Wilson], and the other Napoleon [Lloyd George].'[31]

The 'Allies' at Versailles

If there was to be a League, the three key states now all saw their major goal as the maintenance of peace; all foresaw a combination of legal instruments and institutions (international courts or tribunals) as a first port of call to resolve a conflict and all agreed on the need for sanctions in case this did not work. There was at least an agreement in principle about the idea of 'self-determination'. And of course there was a shared agreement that Germany must be made to see the error of its ways. All also agreed to the need to limit armaments in some way. Where they did not agree was: when the League should be set up (Britain and France wanting this before an Armistice, America after it) and about the idea of the League as the first step towards a super-state (Britain and France against, America, or at least Wilson, broadly in favour). As the new *League of Nations Union Journal* of the LNU stressed in its first edition, before Versailles most of the new order was speculative. They felt they had seen 'the beginning, we hope and believe, of a new world era'. They hoped, as Asquith put it on the second page, that the League would have the role of exporting 'civilisation' and the norms of the 'Comity of Nations' to counter 'militarism'.[32]

Relationships

Probably the most influential critic of the Paris Peace Conference has been E.H. Carr (apart from Keynes, whose views are discussed in Chapter 7). Carr's arguments are based on a well-developed critique of 'idealism' as a utopian construct, as we have already seen in the previous chapter. The Covenant of the LON and the Treaty of Versailles, and those who designed and implemented it, form a central part of his overall critique. One way of responding to his critique is obviously to examine how the individuals involved in the elaboration of the Treaty and Covenant actually behaved. As a participant himself, although rather more as one on the sidelines, he must have been aware of the currents that were flowing at Versailles in 1919 and it is reasonable to expect that he was influenced by them.

During the key part of the Versailles Conference, between March and July

1919, the Allied leaders shut themselves away (as the 'Council of Four': Wilson, Lloyd George, Clemenceau and Orlando, with Baron Makino of Japan in occasional attendance) in almost total secrecy, with only an interpreter, Paul Mantoux, for company (who has given us the only accurate account of these deliberations) and Maurice Hankey for most of the time as main note taker, or 'the real master of ceremonies' as Clemenceau dubbed him. Thus was the first of Wilson's Fourteen Points swept aside – in the words of Harold Nicolson: '[o]ur covenants of peace were not openly arrived at: seldom has such secrecy been maintained in any diplomatic gathering'.[33]

There was no formal agenda, but Hankey transcribed the decisions taken. Before that there were three months of largely sterile bickering over the Treaty in the 'Council of Ten', although the Covenant of the League was relatively painlessly drafted, mainly by Cecil by mid-February 1919.[34] One particularly bizarre and revealing account shows how most of the decisions incorporated into the main body of the Treaty were taken. Hankey relates how he entered Wilson's suite and found the Four 'all sat on the floor looking at maps which I dished out to them. Actually Clemenceau was lying on his tummy. They looked very funny.'[35] The Council of Four decided the fate of most of Central and Eastern Europe and much of the rest of the world in like fashion.

But the defining of the details of the Treaty, derided by Carr as 'the drawing of frontiers', was carried out by technical committees galore in which Foreign Office and other Allied officials came into their own, so Carr's 'bureaucrats' presumably carry a degree more of blame than he seems to want to give them. The traces left by these lesser actors at Versailles give an equally Dadaesque tinge to the proceedings. The diary of Allen Leeper of the Foreign Office's PID, who was one of the British experts on Eastern Europe, is full of entries like 'Harold [Nicolson] is just off to Transylvania' and 'frightfully busy map-making' amid a whirl of lunches and dances. Others, like Clemenceau, seem to have been nostalgic for such delights, as when he quoted the Prince de Ligne at the Congress of Vienna: 'The Congress is not moving, it is *dancing.*'[36]

Among the major players, there was general agreement on most issues between the Americans and British, although not necessarily mutual comprehension. Cecil felt that 'though on broad principles we agree with the Americans most of their details seem to us wrong, though a large proportion of them have been taken from our previous suggestions'. As to the French and other 'foreigners' (meaning also the Belgians and Italians), for Cecil their obsession with 'principle and right and other abstractions' got in the way of business. There were dangers in 'talking about abstract justice to Anglo-Saxons', even though he had high regard for a few French delegates, particularly Jean Monnet and Paul Barthou, both later to be French Foreign Ministers. Cecil's relations with the French leadership were very cold, with ample evidence of bullying by him. On one occasion he told them in no uncertain language that if they did not agree to the Anglo-American League they would 'be left without an ally in the world'. The feeling was reciprocated, Clemenceau saying that Cecil had a 'smile like a Chinese dragon to express a stubborn mind banged, barred and bolted against arguments'.[37]

Truth to tell, personal relations between all the delegations were rarely cordial. Cecil had a low opinion of most of the American delegates. 'Their capacity ... for uttering platitudes is really unlimited,' while Wilson was 'a trifle of a bully, and must be dealt with firmly' and was 'a vain man'. Lloyd George and Wilson (at least initially) did not like each other much, but could agree that they both hated the Italians. Even Americans had their doubts about both their Chief and their delegation's competence. Lieutenant Adolf Berle of the American delegation (later an Assistant Secretary of State in 1938–45) felt 'it is obvious that the United States stands as a strange isolated Parsifal among nations, with Wilson as the great idealist. The socialists make of him a messiah ...'. As to the State Department, it 'is making as much of a bungle of this business as is conveniently possible'. He later resigned over American policy towards Russia.[38]

Cecil also reported a 'growing hostility of the Americans for the French [who had] made the impression of being purely materialistic'; Wilson told him that dealing with the French was 'like pressing your finger into an india-rubber ball. You tr[y] to make an impression but as soon as you mov[e] your finger the ball [is] as round as ever'. Towards the Italians the British, French and Americans exhibited almost open contempt. While Cecil, rather improbably, thought the Italians 'an extraordinarily brutal race', he also wanted them to understand that they 'really are at our mercy', even threatening them with a food embargo at one point to get agreement. To give an idea of the atmosphere two anecdotes will suffice. Clemenceau once loudly remarked in the Council of Ten: 'Where is Mr. Sonnino? [Orlando's deputy] If he has gone, we shall have no objections.'[40] When Wilson refused point-blank to recognise Italian claims to Fiume and Dalmatia he caused Orlando to 'sob'. As Balfour related this later to Hankey: 'he ha[d] known of countries fighting, bribing and intriguing their way to Empire, but he ha[d] never before heard of an attempt to sob their way to Empire.'[41]

The square circle of security, balance of power, revenge and reconciliation

If one had to isolate one key problem of the discussions at Versailles, it would thus have to be that of how to recompense the victors, and particularly France, for their appalling losses in the war, while simultaneously not ensuring the creation of a revanchiste Germany and not alienating Allied public opinion, which was clearly split over its hopes from a settlement as were its respective Governments. As Byron Dexter has written, the LON was essentially set up to solve 'Sir Edward Grey's problem' of pre-1914, 'the construction and maintenance of a defensive coalition to meet and discourage the threat of war by a great expansion-minded power'.[42] It was thus also about how to ensure that this could never happen again.

For Melvyn Leffler '[t]here was considerable tension between Wilson's sympathy for France and his desire to reintegrate Germany into a prosperous world order, between his concern for French security and his antipathy toward balance of power politics, and between his desire to preserve Allied unity and his aversion to alliances'.[43] There was also the problem of what to do about Bolshevik Russia (see next section), presenting in 1919 at least the dimly perceived outline of a revolutionary approach to international relations, one where peoples seemed to be given priority over governments. But France was not easy to appease with such rhetoric; it was, as (British Ambassador to Paris) Lord Derby said, 'still in a mortal funk over Germany'.[44] France's main hope was to obtain security 'guarantees' from Britain and the United States and all else was subordinate to this. As William Keylor has put it: [e]conomic recovery from the devastation of the Great War would prove to be a hollow achievement unless accompanied by an iron-clad guarantee against the reappearance of the cause of that destruction'. As to Britain, Wolfers is right in saying that they had little fear of a real security threat in the foreseeable future and wished from 1919 to 'restore peace, normalcy and economic stability'.[45] In this Britain fundamentally disagreed with France which is why Britain became so rapidly embarrassed and infuriated by France's *revanchisme* after 1919.

Wilson's ideal solution was to create an institution, the League of Nations, that could act both as a permanent arbitrator of these heretofore irreconcilable aims and as a creator of new ideas for forging a cooperative atmosphere in Europe in the post-war era. He tried to do this essentially by persuasion, although he was not averse to the use of threats and energetic cajolery. He was also able to rely on a great deal of organised public and some official support for the idea in Britain and France. But he could not overrule the French delegation at Versailles, so he was persuaded to offer Clemenceau an American treaty of guarantee and agreed to a French occupation of the Rhineland and the Saar coalfields for fifteen years. Lloyd George objected on the grounds of cost and practicality, but went along with the compromise reluctantly.[46] But of course Wilson had thereby effectively denied Germany the norm of self-determination, a decision compounded by a cession of the Saar coalfields to France, thus aggravating German feelings even more. The Saar question was to become a running sore in the inter-war period, but it was at the heart of the post-1945 creation of a united Europe – so perhaps we might argue that historical lessons can be properly learnt.[47]

The main ultimate problem for the advocates of a central role for the League was not the other delegations at Paris, but the relative disinterest or even growing hostility among influential American public opinion for the

League project, a disinterest that hardened into a rejection during 1919. Even during the early stages of the Conference, Wiseman was able to inform the British Government that his sources indicated that it was widely felt that the 'safety of America does not need the League' and that although the 'people of America would be glad to help [the] ideal of the League ... they are nervous as to the effect of a treaty on [the] constitution of the U.S.A. or possible entanglement in future wars, revision of Monroe Doctrine etc ...'. Wealthy Americans were in particular worried about being sucked into the balance of power politics of the Old Europe, and considerable opposition to this tendency was beginning to manifest itself in the Senate. A cross-party coalition, centred on Senators Lodge, Knox and Borah, was gaining ground.[48] This was quite apart from the growing disquiet felt about the treatment of Germany, fickle American public opinion having swung back in favour of the defeated to a certain extent, and particularly about the territorial and financial (reparations) clauses of the Treaty. By the end of the Conference it was obvious even to Cecil that there was little hope of Wilson getting Senate acceptance of a combination of the League Covenant, whose Article X invoked force on behalf of LON peace initiatives, and the widely unacceptable territorial and other clauses of the Treaty of Versailles.[49] Without the LON or the US he realised there would be no viable Treaty, and without the US no viable LON.

The problem of Soviet Russia

Herbert Hoover described Russia as 'the Banquo's ghost sitting at every Council table [at Versailles]'. Although not the most determinate immediate factor, which was of course the fate of Germany, the Russian 'Banquo' highlighted a number of key areas and continued to do so for the whole inter-war period. This has been referred to as the 'Russian–German–Bolshevik nexus'.[50] Given the central problem outlined above of French security and German rehabilitation it was rightly seen as crucial, particularly by Wilson and Hoover, not to push Germany into the arms of Russia, thus amplifying France's security problem. Equally, it was clear that a Bolshevik Russia provided a far more serious potential risk to the West than a Czarist version, given its greater propensity to stir up discontent among the Western working class, already disillusioned by experiences in the war and years of socialist propaganda before the war about the links between militarism and capitalism. Lenin had also made it clear that he espoused the cause of self-determination of peoples, with the countries of the Czarist Empire as first candidates, a cynical statement as it turned out, as the only countries given such freedom were those who could successfully fight for it against the Red Army.

During the war itself the Bolshevik Revolution of October 1917 and Lenin's capitulation to Germany had severely embarrassed the Allies during a key period of the 1917 offensives and had later provided an even worse crisis for the Allies once German troops were transferred from the East to the West to take part in the offensive of March 1918, one which took German troops to within striking distance of Paris. The second major challenge to the remaining Allies came with Lenin's attempt to organise a parallel peace process at Zimmerwald in 1915 and Kienthal in 1916, a movement which swelled to a crescendo in May 1917 calling for a 'peace without annexations'. Although partly aimed at destabilising the more traditional socialist attempts of the Second International (or 'International Socialist Bureau') centred on Stockholm, an organisation that Lenin now dubbed the 'Yellow International' for its composite parties' support for war in 1914, it was also aimed at the war aims of the Allies, clearly defined as annexationist by 1916.

Lenin's 'Zimmerwald Manifesto' of 1915 had used a language devoid of euphemism: 'Millions of corpses cover the battlefields. Millions of human beings have been crippled for the rest of their lives. Europe is like a gigantic slaughterhouse.' Lenin had a uni-causal explanation for this carnage, and a solution – 'the International Socialist Bureau has failed … [so the] working class [must] … take up this struggle … for the sacred aims of socialism, for the emancipation of the oppressed nations as well as of the enslaved classes, by means of the irreconcilable class struggle …'.[51] Wilson in particular recognised the strength of Lenin's claims. It has been convincingly demonstrated by Arno Mayer among others that his Fourteen Points speech was at least partly an attempt to outflank Soviet claims to be the advocates of self-determination (although only Poland is mentioned by name in the speech of the previous Czarist territories that must be freed)[52] and the defenders of a peace with justice. To be sure, at the time (late 1917) Wilson had been convinced that the Bolsheviks would not last and would be replaced by the more liberally inclined Constituent Assembly, a view that was reinforced by experts on the 'Inquiry'.[53] In effect, both Lenin and Wilson felt that they could talk over the heads of governments directly to the 'people', not only among the Allies, but also in Germany.

However, not all Allied statesmen saw such statements being made by Lenin in such a relaxed light. Given the ensuing problems that they provided for the Allies in the West, including the eruption of mutinies, which did not directly affect the American armed forces, it is not surprising that they led to differing reactions. Among the most virulent in Britain were those of Winston Churchill, who immediately became, and remained, an advocate of military intervention in Russia. After a dinner with Balfour and Churchill, Cecil wrote: 'he is mad to intervene [i.e. hopes to] in Russia – a foolish proposal, at any rate at this time of day …', and especially absurd as it was obvious to the whole War Cabinet that there were scarce resources for any military adventure, wherever it may be, as Churchill as Minister for War was well aware.[54] There was a limited intervention, mainly in 1919–20 in the Russian Civil War, but troops committed were never numerous. Arguably the only result of this action was to help the Bolshevik cause by making them seem natural defenders of Russian soil against foreigners and to create a long-lasting myth that was exploited by successive Soviet leaders of an ever 'imminent' attack on the Soviet Union.[55]

During the Peace Conference Herbert Hoover was Wilson's main strategist and spokesman on Russia, Secretary of State Lansing being generally ignored by the President. Hoover was convinced that the Allied food blockade was stoking the fires of hatred anew in Germany, as well as in Central and Eastern Europe, and that this might well lead to an upsurge of German sympathy for Bolshevism, a reasonable fear given the Spartacist uprisings of 1919. Hoover acted as a key economic advisor to Wilson at Paris, with the title of 'Director General of Relief and Reconstruction of Europe' and as head of the 'Supreme Council of Supply and Relief'. Several Americans, such as Bernard Baruch and Norman Davis, also served on these bodies and were to see their views on economic reconstruction given greater emphasis after the Second World War. Hoover clashed constantly with Lloyd George and Clemenceau in these roles, as his desire was to create a kind of Department of Commerce for the World: 'for a brief time a kind of economic government, the greatest experiment ever made in the correlation, control and direction in time of peace, of international trade and finance'.[56] But Hoover was essentially alone in seeing economics as the key to a future stability in Europe, other than Keynes, whose views will be explored in detail in Chapter 7.

After the signature of the Treaty of Versailles and the beginning of an opening up of Soviet Russia in mid-1921, Hoover set up the American Relief Administration (ARA) to help solve the Russian famine.[57] This was not out of any desire to help Bolshevism – on the contrary, Hoover felt that it would strengthen the anti-Bolshevik cause by removing some of the sense of despair in Eastern Europe. Wilson and Hoover were acutely aware that Bolshevism would have to be fought as a set of ideas and as an economic ideal structure as much, if not more so, than as a potential military threat. Churchill's posturings and the farcical intervention by the British at Archangel, off which the Soviet Union's leadership lived for years with tales of 'war scares' and British imperialism, were replaced by Wilson with discreet diplomatic feelers to Trotsky and an attempt, through the nascent League of Nations, to institutionalise a liberal economic order.[58] Wilson never hid his distaste for Bolshevism, and particularly for its breaking of solemn treaties and agreements, the basis for any such order, but he and Hoover were acutely aware of where the danger lay in openly confronting Bolshevism while giving out no alternative ideological lifeline.

Hoover's most detailed description of a necessary economic policy towards Bolshevik Russia at Versailles came in a press statement he gave on 25 April 1919. The enemy that the United States had metaphorically and actually engaged in Russia and Eastern Europe was 'anarchy, which is the handmaiden of hunger'. The basis of the revolutions that were feeding on this anarchy, 'while superficially political, is basically economic'. The attraction of Bolshevism 'lay in its seemingly rational and egalitarian approach to economic problems, and [o]ur people who enjoy so great a liberty and general comfort cannot fail to sympathize to some degree with these blind gropings for better social conditions'. But alas, '[t]he communist land of illusion is that he can perfect those human qualities by destroying the basic organization and processes of production and distribution instead of the ideal of democracy that devotion should be given to the stimulation of production and distribution and to securing a better application of the collective profits arising therefrom'.

The results, said Hoover, had been a collapse of the Russian economy, food hoarding and runaway inflation, with the Bolsheviks offering only the panacea of 'propaganda', one that would not only 'do violence to progressive democratic development' but also lead to widespread crime and possibly 'large military crusades'. What Russia needed, said Hoover, was 'food, peace and employment' helped by a generous Europe.[59] This they did not get from Europe, and although the ARA undoubtedly saved millions of lives, it did not stop Bolshevism. Others saw a more cynical motive. Keynes' particularly damning comment on the American attitude referred to Hoover's intention to give bacon supplies to Germany:

> The situation is a curious one. The blockade on fats to neutral countries is being raised and Germany is to receive fats supplies on a very generous scale. Bolshevism is to be defeated and the new era is to begin ... But the underlying motive is Mr. Hoover's abundant stocks of low grade pig products at high prices which must at all costs be unloaded on someone, enemies failing allies.[60]

Notwithstanding Keynes' bile, it seems clear that Wilson and Hoover shared a horror of Bolshevism and that their thinking during the Versailles Conference bears uncanny resemblance to that seen in the establishment of the Marshall Plan after 1945.

The 'lessons' of Versailles

The 'lessons' of Versailles have been differently drawn both by contemporaries and by many writers since. This has varied from those who believe that the LON was an impossible and naive dream, such as Carr and the so-called 'realists', to those who believe that the people involved in the Treaty's design and execution were far from adequate to the task.[61] The Versailles Treaty was to be a grave deception to any who believed that a new spirit of thinking about international relations might be abroad in Europe. The inter-war period saw many in this latter school, from the outright pacifists to those who wanted governments to use the LON for their every foreign policy move, such as the LNU in Britain.[62] There were constant efforts to implement the clauses of the Treaty designed to bring about disarmament both within, as with the League Disarmament Conference of 1929–33, and outside the LON, as with the Washington Conference of 1921 and many others. All saw their hopes dashed by the German invasion of Poland in 1939 and arguably long before, most dating the 'failure' of the LON to the Japanese invasion of Manchuria in 1932.[63] The exact date is not in reality of much importance; the key point is that the failure of the Versailles Treaty and thus of the LON is generally seen as having been overwhelming.

For those who had gone to Versailles expecting the Treaty to incorporate most, if not all, of Wilson's 'idealist' Fourteen Points, the outcome of the Conference was a disaster. One of them, Harold Nicolson, was not wrong to say that only four of Wilson's Fourteen Points were actually incorporated into the Treaty, and only one of these, that about a League of Nations, was significant (the other three being territorial adjustments such as the return of Alsace-Lorraine to France). What was left out in letter or spirit is much more telling. In Nicolson's words: '[f]reedom of the seas was not secured ... [nor was] Free Trade ... National Armaments were not reduced ...The League of Nations has not, in practice, been able to assure political independence to Great and Small nations alike. Provinces and peoples were, in fact, treated as pawns and chattels in a game. Elements of discord and antagonism were in fact perpetuated.' As Arthur Balfour put it during the Conference, '[w]e cannot be popular, our only chance is to be just'. His wish was not to be fulfilled, and he left Versailles a bitter man, as did so many of all the delegations.[64]

Even 'realist' commentators expressed their view that the Treaty must end by provoking another war. Marshall Foch is often quoted as saying that '[t]his is not peace, it is an armistice for twenty years'. Lloyd George pointed out to Wilson that

> I cannot conceive any greater cause for future war than the German people, who have certainly proved themselves one of the most vigourous and powerful peoples in the world, should be surrounded by a number of small states, many of them consisting of people who have never previously set up a stable government for themselves, but each of them containing large masses of Germans clamouring for reunion with the native land.[65]

Self-determination was a concept untried and untested, as will be seen in Chapter 8. The problem was that it was not the only untried and untested concept – a League of Nations was essentially new, as was the collective security concept that it envisaged.

The judgement of historians on the Paris Peace Conference itself has been largely in agreement with Keynes and his strictures in the *Economic Consequences of the Peace*.[66] Some have marvelled that it was not 'more unsatisfactory', given that it was an uneasy compromise between a

Wilsonian and a French peace and that it 'was not exceptionally harsh, considering how thoroughly Germany had lost a long and bitter war',[67] a thesis that mostly appeals to those who sympathise entirely with the French view expressed by Mantoux. The problem with this theory is that Germany was not in fact 'thoroughly' defeated, and there is a case for saying that they would not have surrendered had they not believed in Wilson's influence on the terms and implementation of peace. In 1945 no such ambiguity was possible, but ironically Keynes' view was also followed, with the result of many years of amical Franco-German relations and a better peace.

As so often in history, no 'logic' will suffice when a thesis, right or wrong, is sufficiently believed by those who lived through it. Hence one key reason for the collapse of the LON and the disillusionment with its founding document, the Treaty of Versailles, lay with the despair felt among many of the participants at the Conference. There can rarely have been so rapid a decline in morale among so wide a section of those engaged in drawing up a major international agreement. Partly, even mainly, this was due to the high-handed attitude of the Big Four, with their deliberate policy of excluding everybody but themselves from the most important proceedings. Partly it was due to the way that they put an inordinate emphasis on the punitive side of the Treaty to the exclusion of the more positive aspects such as the LON Covenant, in which most of the delegates, and indeed most of the secretariats, had come to put their faith for a better world. Wilson had inspired, but many felt let down by the implementation of his vision. The insights and imperfections of this vision were taken by a second generation of Western historians, thinkers, activists, politicians and officials that essentially agreed with him, but wished to make sure that the agreements would stick a second time round.

Lasting impressions

Disillusionment about proceedings in Paris among those who felt that they had had most to contribute in Britain had developed even before the Treaty was properly drawn up. They either felt ignored, like Lord Bryce,[68] or callously overruled, like Keynes, or slighted, like Hankey. In the longer term, virtually the entire discussion on the post-war settlement during the Second World War, particularly in the United States, was premised on a need to understand the 'lessons' of the Versailles settlement. Hamilton Fish Armstrong, by the end of the 1930s editor of *Foreign Affairs* and a prominent member of the State Department's Post-War Planning (PWP) Committees that will be described in the next chapter, believed that '[a] critical analysis of the Armistice of 1918 might well be one of the first studies undertaken by the [State Department] Committee [for PWP]'.[69]

The physical presence of so many US personnel at Versailles and their subsequent involvement in Second World War PWP is itself a gauge of the continuity of thinking about the future of international relations and the United States' place in it. Berle, Bowman and many others within the State Department, as well as many others involved in PWP in some way, such as Dulles, were all concerned not to make the same mistakes twice. Dulles considered as late as February 1944 that the Treaty had been 'excessively harsh' on Germany, but all agreed with him that they needed a 'treaty which we can expect will be in force, not for a year or two, but twenty five years after it is made'. They were also concerned, like Dulles, not to allow isolation and power politics of the 'particular kind' practised by the European powers, including Britain and Russia, to prevail: '[t]his time it is up to us to make it clear first because we were the ones who ran out on them last time'.[70]

Within the Roosevelt Administrations after 1933 the received wisdom came to be that 'the mistakes of that Treaty had been mainly economic', especially for Cordell Hull, who dedicated most of his career to righting that omission. There were also a significant number who felt that the United States' absence from the League had played a role in destabilising the world. But it was also agreed that the fault lay with the nature of German 'militarism' and the need to foster a new spirit of democracy in the German soul, although this led to some very difficult discussions about how this should be achieved. Armstrong put particular emphasis on this, as he felt that it was essential 'not to give successive German Governments any legitimate grounds for complaining that the German people had been double-crossed'.[71] As N. Gordon Levin has commented:

> Many who had been associated with Wilson, or who accepted the essentials of his world view, such as Herbert Hoover, Cordell Hull, Franklin Roosevelt or John Foster Dulles, would continue in later periods to identify America's expansive national interest with the maintenance of a rational and peaceful international liberal order. Wilsonian values would have their complete triumph in the bi-partisan Cold War consensus.[72]

The American Senate's later refusal to let the United States join the League of Nations was part of a generalised disgust about the refusal to entertain new ways of conducting international relations that the vengeful document embodied. It was also in no small measure due to Wilson's refusal to compromise on a line of the Treaty he had negotiated with a now hostile Republican Congress.[73] In his account of the Paris negotiations in which he was an active participant, Herbert Hoover, later President himself, bewailed the 'pestilence of [European] emotions' that had brought Wilsonian ideals to their knees. Both European peoples and governments were infected with the 'genes of a thousand years of hate and distrust, bred of racial and religious persecution and domination by other races ... As a historian, Mr. Wilson was no doubt familiar with their age-old background, but he did not seem to realize their dynamism.'[74] There was a bipartisan view in the United States that Wilson had been misled and humiliated by Europe in 1919 and a corresponding desire either to keep out of Europe's wars or, if that could not be achieved, to ensure that America had the leading role in designing the peace.

Lloyd George and Britain's failure?

Given the centrality of Britain to the 'imagining', and indeed the implementation of Versailles, it is tempting to blame Lloyd George and the British delegation for any 'failure'. Keynes found much to blame in the ignorance of British and French statesmen about the economic aspects of the settlement, with some justification. But Britain was largely a toothless lion by 1918. Curzon, Balfour and most of the Cabinet knew that they could ill-afford any more Imperialist ventures, and even Lloyd George was only keen on ensuring that France and America could be kept in some sort of informal alliance, through the LON if needs be. But they never fully succeeded in reconciling the needs of the 'New Europe' group with those of the Empire and the 'balance of power' tendency. The Dominions had played a very independent role at Paris and were to grow into this role in the inter-war years as 'Empire' became more truly 'Commonwealth'. They were behaving far more along Cobban's thesis of a belief in 'small states' and in the 'equality' of such states, usually at the expense of the 'self-determination' of their neighbouring or domestic minorities.[75] They were as much to blame for their prejudices and lack of solidarity as any Great Power.

Arnold Wolfers has emphasised those in British foreign policy circles in the inter-war years (both before and since) who act as what Carr calls 'realists' and Wolfers calls 'traditionalists', who only give consideration to British interests. In this case, they seem to have based themselves largely on Smuts' ideas evoked in the memorandum 'Our Policy at the Peace Conference' explained above. But of course Smuts' other views, expressed in his memo on the LON, owed much to Wolfers' opposing school, that dubbed 'collectivist' by Wolfers and 'utopian' by Carr.[76] Britain wanted to conclude a successful Treaty, both to please Wilson and because they believed that the LON could genuinely help protect, or at least support, British security interests. The presence of the United States in the League was, as we have seen, a crucial part of this belief. Its absence doomed the League in British eyes from the beginning, a feeling confirmed by the timing of Hankey's disillusionment with the job of Secretary General of the League. He saw the writing on the wall as early as March 1919: 'I have definitely chucked [sic] the League of Nations. My visit to London has convinced me that the British Empire is worth a thousand League of Nations … [and is] the sheet anchor of the world. I can do more for the peace of the world there [London] than in Geneva.' However, he was still, even at the end of the Conference, fully aware of what might have been if the Versailles victors had stayed together – as he commented in July 1919: 'Have I not been Secretary to the Cabinet of the world?'[77] But they did not stay together, and Britain was as much to blame for this as any other state.

Conclusion: the defeat of 'idealism'?

Carr was clearly being simplistic in his statement in the Preface of *The Twenty Years' Crisis* where he wrote that '[t]he next peace conference, if it is not to repeat the fiasco of the last will have to concern itself with issues more fundamental than the drawing of frontiers'.[78] The underlying rationale for the peace had been worked out in some detail before the Allied leaders got to Paris and the basic principles that they wished to implement as policy were clearly defined, if not necessarily agreed upon. But his statement still has the ring of truth. Far too many of Wilson's ideals, upon which the peace was supposed to be based, got lost in the translation into reality.

Ironically the peace was more 'realist' than Carr gives it credit for. It is arguable that had there been a real concentration on developing a 'harmony of interest' in the economic sphere, such as was accomplished (at least among the Western Allies) after the Second World War; had there been an attempt to fulfil the desire for self-determination over the narrow national interest of Britain and France; and had the United States assumed the moral and political leadership of the post-war order that it did in 1945, there might have been a viable NWO in 1919. Carr was right about the Powers not being fair about who got what – and equally to question why they should agree not to use violence when effectively excluded from the use of peaceful means of change. This was true of Japan in the 1930s as it is, say, of Iran today. NWOs have to include more than they exclude and extend basic norms without fear or favour.

Carr also gives us a great deal of food for thought about how this process came about in the inter-war years. Arguably his most penetrating critique is of the 'utopian' mind-set that he asserts motivated the architects of the Versailles settlement in his attacks on the moral equivalence made by statesmen of their stated ideals with their venal aims. The 'national interests' of Britain and France in particular were constantly confused in the drafting of the Treaty. This he clearly would not have minded if the statement of intention had been honest, but it clearly often was not. The Treaty was the creation of the victors in the interest of the victors, but the pretence was that it was for the benefit of 'Mankind'.[79]

However, the question surely is rather whether the architects of Versailles felt that they had made a huge leap for international relations. The archival record seems to indicate that they rather felt that they had made a small and very imperfect step. Time after time we read that Smuts told Cecil the Treaty was 'a terrible outcome of all our professions' (his despair was over reparations and the Rhineland) or Balfour (who despaired over self-determination) or Clemenceau (over Germany and his own colleagues) or all the American delegation (about themselves and everyone else). And these were the ones that did not publish books on the 'consequences' of the peace, at least not immediately. In the nearest that they got to the language of utopianism, Cecil himself felt that 'it was enough if we could do something practical to diminish wars, and must hope that in such an atmosphere there would be a better chance for moral growth'.[80]

The main architects of Versailles, and indeed the LON Covenant, were not Carr's favourite target: 'intellectuals'. They were men like Smuts, Clemenceau, Lloyd George, even Hankey and of course Wilson, none of whom can honestly be accused of left-wing sympathy or of excessive 'utopian' leanings. Even Wilson was able to allow his officials to conduct an anti-'red' witch hunt in the United States with no perceivable qualms. Cecil and Balfour were above all Tory aristocrats, Grey a Whig, none of them dedicated to the overthrow of the Establishment, but rather to its continuance. Neither were they happy with the Treaty, Balfour, for example, saying that 'he should not defend it'.[81] They understood that war had changed and that therefore the thinking of peace had to change too.

Equally, those who were sidelined at Versailles, Clemenceau's 'ineffable group of malcontents' such as Keynes, were sidelined precisely because they did believe in the economic 'harmony of interests'. They could see that the basis of a political and moral renewal lay in the development of a healthy European and global economy. It would be much fairer to blame the orthodox fiscal stance of British, French and, above all, American Governments in the 1920s and 1930s for their short-sightedness than those who were able to foresee the benefits of a global economy, and, indeed, to implement it partially after 1945 and more fully after 1989. That was what was to provide the basis for peace in Europe, not economic nationalism.

The LON was a relative failure as a negotiating forum for change. Sometimes this was inevitably due to the personalities involved. In a discussion of Lloyd George's Russian policy, Richard Ullman comments that his presidential style led to 'confused, ill-prepared encounters between heads of government in which a jumble of different political, economic and strategic issues were muddled up and used as counters operating against each other'.[82] Others have blamed the 'illusions' that came out of Versailles, of which a key one 'was the belief in conference diplomacy as a necessary and effective tool of international negotiation',[83] with the great conferences of Washington (1921) Genoa (1922) and Lausanne (1923) as the proof of this. In fact this illustrates that most of the international negotiation was conducted *outside* the League, a tendency that accelerated after the Locarno Pacts of 1925. For Lord Asquith the main factor to blame was just 'the insanity of statesmen', with Lloyd George (naturally enough) as main culprit.[84]

A coherent realist critique cannot in any case avoid the conclusion that what was also wrong in the inter-war period was that American leadership was missing. Certain American writers have claimed, not without some justification, that America did not entirely withdraw into isolation in the inter-war years, that they in fact played a significant role in the economic and political diplomacy of Europe, and even of the LON.[85] But the United States certainly did not provide the lead that the emerging super-power might have been expected to, in spite of Presidents Roosevelt and, arguably, Hoover, feeling that it should – a theme that will be explored in the next chapter.

Notes

1 Many of these books will be noted in the text.
2 Michael L. Dockrill and J. Douglas Gould, *Peace without Promise: Britain and the Peace Conferences, 1919–23* (London, Batsford, 1981), pp. 17–21.
3 Lloyd George, *The Truth About the Peace Treaties* (London, Gollancz, 1938), vol. 1, p. 94, and Balfour, *Hansard*, 20 June 1918, both quoted by Walworth, *America's Moment: 1918* (New York, Norton and Co., 1963), p. 3; also Dockrill and Gould', *Peace without Promise*, p. 20.
4 Jan Christiaan Smuts, 'Our Policy at the Peace Conference', dated 3 December 1918, circulated to the War Cabinet; Cecil Papers, 51076.
5 Erik Goldstein, *Winning the Peace: British Diplomatic Strategy and the Paris Peace Conference, 1916–1920* (Oxford, Clarendon Press, 1991), pp. 229–231.
6 The King had told Hankey that he was also worried about Lloyd George's attitude to the peace and suggested taking Asquith to Versailles 'for the good of the nation, for the good of Lloyd George himself and to make for unity'. Lloyd George had vetoed the idea. Hankey, Manuscript Diary, 26 August, 13 October, 23 and 24 November 1918, HNKY 1/5.
7 David Miller, *The Drafting of the Covenant* (New York, David Putnam's and Sons, 1928), p. 34.
8 Agnes Headlam-Morley's 'Introduction' to James Headlam-Morley, *A Memoir of the Paris Peace Conference, 1919* (London, Methuen, 1972): Smuts 'did not read most of the papers submitted to him', quoted by Goldstein, *Winning the Peace*, pp. 95–97.
9 Miller, *The Drafting of the Covenant*, pp. 34–39.
10 Cecil, Manuscript Diary of the Peace Conference, 11 January 1919; Ms. 51131.
11 Miller, *The Drafting of the Covenant*, pp. 19–20.
12 Cecil to Smuts, 4 December 1918; Cecil Papers, Add. Mss. 51076. Botha's comments were made to Lord Riddell; see *Lord Riddell's Intimate Diary of the Peace Conference and After* (London, Victor Gollancz, 1933), entry for 22 December 1918, p. 5.
13 Lord Riddell in *The Times* of 23 December 1920, quoted by Michael Bentley, *The Liberal Mind, 1914–1929* (Cambridge University Press, 1977), p. 151.
14 Cecil, Manuscript Diary of the Peace Conference, entry for 20 January 1919; Ms. 51131.
15 Lord Hankey, *The Supreme Control at the Paris Peace Conference: A Commentary* (London, G. Allen and Unwin, 1963), pp. 103–5. He toyed with the idea as early as 13 October 1918 according to his Manuscript Diary. His diminishing

enthusiasm *during* Versailles is also clear from his Diary entries of 30 March 1919; HNKY 1/5.

16 D. Stevenson, *French War Aims Against Germany, 1914–1919* (Oxford University Press, 1982).

17 Goldstein says: 'it has been observed that with the end of the war the French Government "received two months grace" in which to prepare its programme of peace aims. It failed to do so.': Goldstein, *Winning the Peace*, p. 104, quoting Christopher M. Andrew and A.S. Kanya-Forstner, *France Overseas: The Great War and the Climax of French Imperial Expansion* (London, Thames and Hudson, 1981).

18 Ribot to the Chambre des Députés, 2 August 1917. These remarks are all drawn from the Opening Session of the Commission Bourgeois, 28 September 1917, French Foreign Ministry Archives (hereafter MAE), SDN 1.

19 Hankey, Manuscript Diary, entry for 5 December 1918; HNKY 1/5.

20 Meeting of 19 December 1917, MAE, SDN 1. Also discussed at meeting of 8 April 1918 at some length. At this meeting it was suggested by Robert Basdevant, a Professor of International Law at Grenoble, that this would also exclude a political secretariat for the SDN, at least initially. Source: Annexe 26 to this meeting, Office Universitaire de Recherche Socialiste (OURS).

21 There are various drafts of this idea, all drawn up by Robert Basdevant, Annexes 26 and 30 to meeting of 29 April 1918 and Annexe 33 to meeting of 7 May 1918, Source: OURS.

22 This theme of 'civilisation' was particularly pushed by Jules Cambon and Fromageot, but met with general approbation; for example, meeting of 21 November 1917, MAE, SDN 1.

23 Commission Bourgeois, meetings of June 1918 (alliance with Britain), 15 December 1918 (sanctions) and 19 December 1917 ('la paix ...'): OURS.

24 Commission Bourgeois, session of 6 February 1918, OURS.

25 Georges Clemenceau, *Grandeur and Misery of Victory* (London, George Harrap, 1930), pp. 14, 30 and 99.

26 Clemenceau, *Grandeur and Misery*, pp. 137–139.

27 Arnold Wolfers, *Britain and France between the Two Wars* (Hamden, Connecticut, Archon Books, 1963), p. 5.

28 Clemenceau, *Grandeur and Misery*, p. 142.

29 The expressions came out constantly in the Commission Bourgeois, here in the session of 13 February 1918; OURS.

30 Robert Cecil, Manuscript Diary of the Peace Conference, 8 January 1919; Ms. 51131.

31 Hankey, Manuscript Diary at the Peace Conference, 2 July 1919; HNKY 1/5.

32 *League of Nations Union Journal*, January 1919, vol. 1, no. 1. The President of the League was still Lord Grey of Fallodon, with Lloyd George, Asquith and Balfour as Vice-Presidents.

33 Harold Nicholson, *Peacemaking 1919* (London, Constable, 1933), p. 43.

34 Paul Mantoux, *The Deliberations of the Council of Four (March 24–June 28, 1919)*, translated and edited by Arthur S. Link (2 vols, Princeton University Press, 1992). Hankey, in his Manuscript Diary, gives a glowing account of his role in the Council of Four, and he does seem to have imposed some order on an otherwise seamless discussion – see Hankey Diary, entries for 26 and 30 March

and 2 July 1919 in particular, HNKY 1/5; Hankey, *The Supreme Control*, p. 11; Clemenceau, *Grandeur and Misery*, p. 141; Cecil, Manuscript Diary at the Peace Conference, entry for 13 February 1919; Ms. 51131.

35 Hankey, Manuscript Diary, 8 May 1919; HNKY 1/5.

36 Allen Leeper, Manuscript Diary, entries for 14 February and 12 March 1919: LEP1/2 1919; Clemenceau, *Grandeur and Misery*, pp. 149–50.

37 Cecil, Manuscript Diary at the Peace Conference, entries for 4, 11 and 28 February 1919, Ms. 51131; Clemenceau, *Grandeur and Misery*, p. 138.

38 Adolf Berle, Manuscript Diary, American Commission to Negotiate the Peace, entries for 8 and 12 December 1918; Berle Papers, Box 1. For an eye-witness American account of Versailles, see Edward Mandell House and Charles Seymour, *What Really Happened at Paris: The Story of the Peace Conference, 1918–1919, by American Delegates* (London, Hodder and Stoughton, 1921). See also Inga Floto, *Colonel House in Paris: A Study of American Policy at the Paris Peace Conference* (Princeton University Press, 1973); and Frances William O'Brien (ed.), *Two Peacemakers at Paris: The Hoover–Wilson Post-Armistice Letters, 1918–1920* (College Station and London, Texas A and M University Press, 1978).

39 Cecil, Manuscript Diary of the Peace Conference, entries for 13, 16 and 19 January, 7 February, 18 March and 2 May 1919. He was still prepared to admit at this stage that 'perhaps I misjudge [Wilson]. I still like House very much'; Ms. 51131.

40 Cecil, Diary, entry for 20 January and 4 and 7 March 1919.

41 Hankey, Manuscript Diary, entry for 20 April 1919; HNKY 1/5.

42 Byron Dexter, *The League of Nations, 1920–1926* (New York, Viking Press, 1967), p. ix.

43 Melvyn Leffler, *The Elusive Quest: America's Pursuit of European Stability and French Security, 1919–1933* (Chapel Hill, University of North Carolina Press, 1979), p. 4.

44 Derby to Curzon, 7 March 1919, quoted by Dockrill and Gould, *Peace without Promise*, p. 37. Their whole chapter on 'The German Settlement' is very instructive on this 'mortal funk'.

45 William Keylor, 'France's Futile Quest for American Military Protection, 1919–22', in Marta Petriciolli (ed.), *A Missed Opportunity? 1922: The Reconstruction of Europe* (Bern, Peter Lang, 1995), pp. 61–80; Wolfers, *Britain and France between Two Wars*, p. 203.

46 Dockrill and Gould, *Peace without Promise*, p. 38.

47 For French disagreements in the 1920s about the Saar question see Clemenceau, *Grandeur and Misery*, Chapter 12. For the post-Second World War solution see Jacques Freymond, *The Saar Conflict, 1945–1955* (London and New York, Stevens/Praeger, 1960).

48 Agent in New York (un-named) to Wiseman, sent to Balfour, 22 February 1919; Balfour Papers, Add. Mss. 49741.

49 Cecil, Diary, entries of 9 May, where he first gets the feeling that the US won't join or help Europe after the war, and his meeting with Morgenthau, 21 April; agreement for his feelings from Smuts 20 May, and his reluctant conclusions, 26 May; Cecil Ms. 51131.

50 Others present at Versailles agreed with Hoover. Ray Stannard Baker, Wilson's

Press Secretary at Versailles, wrote that '[t]he effect of the Russian problem on the Paris Conference … was profound; Paris cannot be understood without Moscow. Without ever being represented at Paris at all, the Bolsheviki and Bolshevism were powerful elements at every turn'. Quoted by John M. Thompson, *Russia, Bolshevism, and the Versailles Peace* (Princeton University Press, 1966), pp. 2, 3 and 11.

51   Quoted by Walter Kendall, *The Revolutionary Movement in Britain, 1900–1921* (London, Weidenfeld and Nicholson, 1968), p. 96. For a detailed analysis of Bolshevik and socialist moves for peace, see Arno J. Mayer, *Political Origins of the New Diplomacy, 1917–18* (New York, Yale University Press, 1959) and Gerhard Schulz, *Revolutions and Peace Treaties, 1917–1920* (London, Methuen, 1967).

52   Point XIII, an observation that I owe to Heater. Heater has an interesting detailed discussion of the parallels and contrasts of Lloyd George's statements and those of Lenin, Trotsky and the Inquiry about Czarist Russian as well as Ottoman and Austro-Hungarian territories: Derek Heater, *National Self-Determination: Woodrow Wilson and his Legacy* (London, Macmillan, 1994), pp. 42–46.

53   Mayer, *Political Origins*, pp. 339–344.

54   Cecil, Manuscript Diary of the Peace Conference, entry for 9 March 1919. See also Cecil on Churchill and Curzon (also in favour of some kind of military action, but not as outspoken as Churchill), 18 May 1919, both Cecil Papers, Ms. 51131. For the military overstretch of British forces see Churchill to Balfour, 12 August 1919, Balfour Papers, Ms. 49694. A 'serious crisis' was feared in Flanders where demobilisation was crucial to prevent mutinies, keeping 40,000 men in Constantinople was 'becoming insupportable', and all 'new' men would have to be used in Ireland, Egypt or India.

55   There is a huge literature on the intervention of 1918–21. Among the best books on this are Richard H. Ullman, *Intervention and the War*, vol. 1 of his *Anglo-Soviet Relations, 1917–1921* (Princeton University Press, 1961); Stephen White, *Britain and the Bolshevik Revolution* (London, Macmillan, 1979) and Anne Hogenhuis-Seliverstoff, *Les relations franco-soviétiques, 1917–1924* (Paris, Editions de la Sorbonne, 1981).

56   O'Brien (ed.), *Two Peacemakers at Paris*, p. xxxi. The words are Mary Stannard Baker's, from *Woodrow Wilson and World Settlement* (New York, Doubleday, 1922–23), vol. 2, p. 335, quoted approvingly by O'Brien.

57   Benjamin Weissman, *Herbert Hoover and Famine Relief to Soviet Russia, 1921–1923* (Stanford University Press, 1974).

58   N. Gordon Levin, *Woodrow Wilson and the Paris Peace Conference* (Lexington, Mass., Heath, 1972), pp. 248–251.

59   Hoover, in O'Brien (ed.), *Two Peacemakers at Paris*, pp. 135–141.

60   John Maynard Keynes, *Collected Writings of … Activities, 1914–19* (London, Macmillan, 1971), p. 394.

61   For an overview of the critical literature on Versailles see Sally Marks, *The Illusion of Peace: International Relations in Europe, 1918–1933* (London, Macmillan, 1976) and David Armstrong, Lorna Lloyd and John Redmond, *From Versailles to Maastricht: International Organization in the Twentieth Century* (London, Macmillan, 1996), especially Chapter 2.

62   Donald S. Birn, 'The League of Nations Union and Collective Security', *Journal*

of Contemporary History, vol. 9, no. 3, July 1974, pp. 131–159 and Birn, *The League of Nations Union* (Oxford, Clarendon Press, 1981).

63 For more details on pacifism and the belief in disarmament in the inter-war years see Chapter 6. For an excellent account of the LON reaction to the Manchurian crisis see Christopher Thorne, *The Limits of Foreign Policy: The West, the League and the Far Eastern Crisis of 1931–1933* (London, Macmillan, 1973).

64 Nicolson, *Peacemaking*, p. 43; Balfour to Curzon, 1 April 1919; Balfour Papers, Mss. 49734.

65 Lloyd George to Wilson, 25 March 1919, quoted by Baker, *Woodrow Wilson and the World Settlement*, vol. 3, p. 450.

66 Which will be considered at some length in Chapter 7.

67 Sally Marks, *The Illusion of Peace*, pp. 15–16. She also says that 'the peacemakers did not recognise the danger inherent in a situation where Germany was no longer surrounded and checked by great empires'.

68 Bryce wrote to Gilbert Murray in early 1919: 'There could be no use writing to [Lloyd George] he does not read letters, any more than answer them. He never answered one which I sent him 18 months ago about the League of Nations signed by 15 of the leading men in Church and State ... (this presumably referred to the League of Nations Society suggestions for a LON of May 1917). Bryce to Murray, 8 January 1919; Gilbert Murray Papers, Mss. 125.

69 Armstrong, Memo to State Department ACPWFP, 13 March 1942; Armstrong Papers, Box 78.

70 Dulles to Professor William E. Hosking of Harvard University, 22 March 1943, and Dulles, 'Memorandum regarding Germany', 8 February 1944, Dulles Papers, Boxes 22 and 24. Dulles consistently used his experience at Versailles as a preface to virtually any remark on the future of the world after the war.

71 Stimson, Diary, 4 April 1944. He recorded that Knox and Hull 'agreed with me', although an argument developed between Stimson and Knox about how Germany should be treated. Stimson was also one of those who believed that the US should have stayed in the League, albeit with some changes to the Covenant to accommodate Senate doubts; Stimson, Diary, 11 March 1941. Armstrong's remarks can be found in his memo to the State Department Advisory Committee on Post-War Foreign Policy of 13 March 1942, Armstrong Papers, Box 78.

72 N. Gordon Levin, Jnr, *Woodrow Wilson and World Politics*, p. 260.

73 See George Conyne, *Woodrow Wilson: British Perspectives, 1912–21* (London, Macmillan, 1992), pp. 183–189.

74 Herbert Hoover, *The Ordeal of Woodrow Wilson* (London, Museum Press, 1958), pp. 75–76.

75 See Chapter 8 for an explanation of this theory.

76 Wolfers, *Britain and France between Two Wars*, pp. 331–343; E.H. Carr, *Twenty Years' Crisis* (London, Macmillan, 1939), *passim*.

77 Hankey, Diary entries for 18 April and 2 July 1919; HNKY 1/5.

78 Carr, *Twenty Years' Crisis*, Preface to 1st edition.

79 Carr, *The Twenty Years' Crisis*, especially Chapter 5, 'The Realist Critique'.

80 Cecil, Diary of the Peace Conference, entries for 17 January (Cecil on his own views) and 20 May 1919 (Smuts); Ms. 51131.

81 Balfour to Cecil, Diary entry of 26 May 1919; Ms. 51131. Cecil was 'very unhappy about [it]'.

82 Ullmann, quoted in Kenneth O. Morgan, *Consensus and Disunity: The Lloyd George Coalition Government, 1918–1922* (Oxford, Clarendon Press, 1979), pp. 42 and 148.

83 Carole Fink, '1922–23 From Illusion to Disillusion', in Petriciolli (ed.), *A Missed Opportunity?*, p. 15.

84 Jon Jacobson, *Locarno Diplomacy: Germany and the West, 1925–1929* (Princeton University Press, 1972); Asquith to Cecil, 19 October 1922, Cecil Papers, Ms. 51073.

85 The most significant writer in this school for our purposes is Michael J. Hogan, whose path-breaking writings on 'corporatism' will be explored further in Chapter 7. His main work on the inter-war period is *Informal Entente: The Private Structure of Cooperation in Anglo-American Economic Diplomacy* (Columbia, University of Missouri Press, 1977). He then compared this period with the post-Second World War period in *The Marshall Plan: America, Britain and the Reconstruction of Europe* (Cambridge University Press, 1987).

3

The United States and the planning of an American NWO, 1939–44

Introduction

The overwhelming initial impression gained from reading the archival record of the post-war planning process in the United States, Britain and France during the period 1939–45 is that virtually all strands of thought in the United States had developed for the first time a truly global vision of what they wanted to see in the peace, and that this vision was, in their view, progressive and moralistic. They wanted no less than to save 'civilisation'. The second impression is that Britain and France, although they had their global vision of kinds, were essentially backward looking, domestically oriented and insular. Whatever the differing views of the future role of the United States in the world that existed side by side in Washington and elsewhere, they were in constant and dynamic conversation with each other. America made the running in 1941–45 in a way that it had not been able to do in 1917–19. The first purpose of this chapter, which will concentrate on thinking in the United States, and the subsequent chapter, which will concentrate on the discussion in Britain, is to explain why and how this came about.

A second purpose of these two linked chapters is to show how the institutional and private thinking that had been such a feature of the preliminaries to the Versailles settlement were replicated during the Second World War and how they were differently articulated, in the United States but also in Britain. As in the First World War one institution dominated: then it was the British Foreign Office, now it was the US State Department. The big difference was that although Wilson had had a very feeble back-up from the Inquiry, so that 'America's Moment' (to quote Walworth) was lost, now there was a high-powered official American contribution from the State Department, and also a very competent private (or non-official) input from groups such as the Council for Foreign Affairs under the leadership of Hamilton Fish Armstrong[1] and from powerful exterior groups such as John Foster Dulles' 'Commission to Study the Bases of a Just and Durable Peace'

and the Republican National Committee that he also dominated in the area
of foreign policy.

A third purpose is to introduce the main issues that were thrown up by
these official and non-official groupings, although many of them will be
developed more fully in subsequent chapters. The issues were of different
orders of criticality. The immediate first-order problems were to do with the
prosecution of the war against Germany, Italy and Japan and their satellites,
and the problems that this provoked in the relationship between the Allies.
This relationship also gave rise to a great deal of thinking that went into how
to deal with the Axis after they had been defeated. A new ordering of Europe
was slowly conceived in a series of inter-Allied and national committees,
with the conscious desire to avoid the problems of the Versailles settlement.
The main complicating factor here was the probable attitude of the other
great 'ally', the Soviet Union. Chapter 5 will return to these themes in some
detail.

What can only with hesitation be called 'second-order' problems will also
be introduced here and developed in subsequent chapters. The key issues
were to do with the failure of political and economic liberalism between
1929 and 1939.[2] These failings were differently interpreted in the democracies, and their attitudes to a post-war economic and political settlement
varied accordingly. Although there were some similarities of vocabulary, as
for example over the idea of 'planning', the solutions to the problems of the
1930s were generally seen in Washington in global, not national, terms and
were extremely wide-ranging. The United States was trying to create an
NWO based on liberal democratic forms of government and capitalist
economic structures. In Britain (and France) thinking went along no less
ambitious lines, and aimed at what can only be called 'embedded socialism',
based on a radical redistribution of wealth, an almost total planning of the
economy and the creation of a welfare state. As will be discussed in Chapter
7, such national planning went against the logic of a global economic
programme. In Britain and France their 'New [post-war] Jerusalem' also
included a belief that they could hold on to the essentials of their Empires,
and resume their position as great powers in almost equality with the United
States. This was to ignore the realities of industrial decline and to over-
estimate the friendship and duty they believed the United States owed to
them. Sentiment certainly played its part in the relations between the three
Western partners, but it was not the driving force.[3] During the war the
Alliance held together because of a common enemy and because the planning for the post-war period could be made to look quite similar. Come the
peace, the strains began to show very quickly indeed.

The results of the Versailles settlement hung like a cloud over Allied
relationships during the Second World War and gave a powerful impetus in
American circles for an attitude of 'never again'. Many in the United States
had been deeply affected by what was perceived as a cynical disregard for

morality in the debates at Versailles, and the institutional arrangements of the 1920s and 1930s. Britain and France's appeasement of the dictators in the 1930s was but one example of this. This was often summed up in the United States as a greater concern among Europeans for the balance of power and an insufficient attention to 'higher values' in international relations. It would be easy, but wrong, to dismiss this as posturing, as the United States had always seen itself as deeply committed to a moral imperative in international relations and this was its greatest moment of truth. If there was going to be an American peace, it would have to be, in Dulles' words, a 'peace without platitudes' and one that implied as many corrections of moral focus for the Allies as for the Axis.

American thinking on the post-war settlement, 1939: Pearl Harbor

It was perfectly clear to all sections of American opinion in the late 1930s that Europe, and very probably Japan, was heading for another war. The question was whether the United States should get involved in it. A powerful section of this opinion opted for a strict neutrality in an American hemisphere sheltered by the Monroe Doctrine and that of 'no entangling alliances'. Many other Americans knew that this could not be a permanent solution if there was a National Socialist takeover in Europe, but did not wish to become directly involved unless it could at all be avoided. A third group espoused a more interventionist role for the United States in its national interest and in the name of 'civilisation'.

Franklin Delano Roosevelt, who had become President in 1933, had the uneasy task of trying to balance these opposing sentiments against a background of economic depression and rising nationalism and an increasingly aggressive attitude by the fascist powers of Germany, Japan and Italy. His own instincts were Liberal Internationalist and Wilsonian. He and his Secretary of State (from 1933 to 1943), Cordell Hull had spent much of the 1930s trying to push the world (including the British Empire) into more open economic structures through such devices as the Reciprocal Trade Acts[4] and through constant exhortation to the fascists to desist from their more rapacious activities, with little or no success.[5] Coupled with the policies of 'appeasement' practised by Britain and France, it came to look as though there was nothing that the democracies would not tolerate. However justly or unjustly these policies have been treated by historians, it was clear that they could not work for ever, and war broke out in September 1939.[6]

Isolationism and neutrality

Neutrality and its extreme handmaiden, isolationism had always been a factor in American foreign policy, but were given reinforcement by the disgust felt by many Americans towards the Versailles settlement. The United States was born out of a rejection of the 'old' world, with its complicated wars and alliances, and hence Americans have always tended to see war in terms of a moral crusade, either to save the 'old' or to redress the unpalatable new, with Wilson as a twentieth-century version of an older model. Neutrality had received a big boost from the observation that the First World War had not sorted out Europe's ills and this had led to the passage of a Neutrality Act in 1935 intended to prevent a repetition of US intervention.[7]

Isolationism (or possibly more accurately, 'anti-interventionism') was not a homogeneous movement and like all other such tendencies had its hawks and doves, but it did strike a chord in virtually every American voter and Roosevelt had constantly to take it into account. Hence his desire in 1941 that Japan should fire the first shot, and that Germany should declare war on the United States, was based on sound political judgement. Within the United States Congress, isolationism had powerful allies, such as Republican Senator William Borah, Chairman of the Senate Foreign Affairs Committee during both the Hoover and Roosevelt Presidencies, and William Randolph Hearst, the newspaper magnate. Roosevelt himself has been described as a 'pacifist' and an 'idealist'. He was also in the quandary that many 'progressive' Republicans, such as Borah, were supporters of his 'New Deal' legislation while not being helpful in foreign affairs.[8]

This was compounded by a belief, held even by some members of the American diplomatic corps, that Britain was not necessarily a worthy ally and could not win a war against Germany. The most prominent persons to hold these views were Joseph Kennedy, American Ambassador to London, and William Bullitt, first US Ambassador to Moscow in 1934 and at the outbreak of war Ambassador to Paris. Even Adolf Berle, Assistant Secretary of State from 1938 until the end of the Roosevelt Administration, was also said to be 'anti-British ... [but] not proNazi'.[9] Part of this dislike, at least for Bullitt and Berle, lay in their experiences at Versailles, where, as Harper puts it, they had agreed with Keynes over the 'Carthaginian Peace'. Partly it lay in a 'Europhobic strain of Wilsonianism', that in Berle and Bullitt translated into violent hostility to Bolshevism, but in Roosevelt (who was not especially anti-Bolshevik) was expressed more in a 'Jeffersonian' need to control Europe's base instincts for war, a theme to which we shall return shortly.[10]

Many other key players in Washington were pro-British and, according to some surveys, American public opinion was solidly behind the Allies as early as October 1939, if not yet willing to go to war for them. This has led one historian to claim that '[n]ot for the first time in history, and certainly not for the last, what linked the two great English-speaking democracies was a genuine community of outlook – "friendship" in the human rather than the diplomatic sense of the word'.[11] The long-term results of what must none-theless be seen as an essential ambiguity in the Anglo-American Alliance were momentous. They also had an impact on PWP, if only to persuade many Americans, even those sympathetic to Britain, that America must take the lead in most matters of importance, which America duly did.

Internationalism

The legacy of the LEP of the Versailles period was still present in American politics, and again in a bipartisan way. Roosevelt's internationalism in the 1930s had manifested itself principally in his desire, ably managed by Cordell Hull through his Reciprocal Trade Act of 1934, to attempt to reopen the international trading system and reverse the worst effects of the economic nationalism epitomised by the Smoot–Hawley Tarriff Act of 1930 and the Ottawa Agreement of 1932. The inter-war period in the United States and elsewhere had damaged those who wished for a more pro-active internationalism, as conference after conference, on subjects from disarmament to economic management, had foundered in disarray and farce.[12] The restoration of trade was a theme that Roosevelt had given as his second priority in his Inaugural Speech of 1933, after that of dealing with the economic 'emergency'.[13] It was in a revival of the moral imperative of free trade so 'that all men in all the lands may live out their lives in freedom from fear and want', as the Atlantic Charter of August 1941 put it, that Roosevelt saw the opportunity for a bipartisan, and indeed trans-Atlantic, revival of internationalism. The Charter, and the final version of the Lend–Lease Agreement between Britain and the United States, explicitly linked an American commitment not to levy punitive war debts from its Allies in exchange for a promise of an open multilateral post-war economic system.[14]

The Atlantic Charter

The 'Atlantic Charter', as it was rapidly dubbed by the press, signed by Roosevelt and Churchill in August 1941, can be seen as the defining 'intellectual moment' of the Anglo-American relationship in the Second World War. The importance of the Atlantic Charter is that it defined the American need to address not only the problems of the enforcement of peace, but also the causes of war. For Roosevelt it was not enough to condemn armaments races (although it was necessary to control them if possible) and duplicity by foreign powers, it was also necessary to address the economic and political causes of discontent. Hence the most important clauses of the Charter are about the need for freedom of commerce and the need to encourage self-determination and decolonisation. Roosevelt wanted to make sure that the international organisations, or whatever mechanism was needed to implement these aims, had to lock in the democracies for the post-war period. His was, in Reynolds' words, a 'realistic Wilsonianism'.[15]

The Atlantic Charter was also, along with the 'Four Freedoms' State of the Nation speech of January 1941, a clear statement of American ideological leadership. As Ellwood puts it, it showed that '[l]ike Wilson, Roosevelt was convinced of the universal significance of the American historical experience'.[16] The reiteration of Wilson's ideal of self-determination in Articles 1–3 of the Charter went further than Wilson in effectively condemning imperialism. The Charter is thus rightly seen as the most powerful statement of the Rooseveltian version of an internationalist ideal, one that he was now, as Wilson had not been, in a position to implement. As Dulles wrote approvingly, the 'lofty ends' were essentially a linking of the political and the economic in a 'universal' framework – 'peace is recognized as an indivisible whole deriving from the spiritual and material welfare of men everywhere'.[17]

The need to fight for 'Western civilisation'

To do this the United States would probably have to join the war. Roosevelt increasingly believed that America would have to fight and was thus looking for ways to persuade Congress and public opinion that this was so without giving any undue ammunition to the isolationists. But as Lord Halifax (then British Ambassador to the United States) put it, Roosevelt's 'perpetual problem was to steer a course between … (1) the wish of 70% of Americans to keep out of a war; (2) the wish of 70% of Americans to do everything to break Hitler, even if it means war'.[18] He was backed up in this by another influential sector of opinion, epitomised by Henry Stimson, Secretary of State under Hoover and Roosevelt's Secretary for War after 1940. Stimson's diary shows how he wanted to invoke the Kellogg Pact of 1928 as early as April 1939 to get America involved in a war with Germany. He thought Borah and his supporters 'a hostile group of cynical-minded men', and by June 1939 he wanted to attack Japan to protect China from 'the barbarity of the Japs'. Stimson had a very clear vision, one of 'defend[ing] the Caucasian civilisation of Europe', and in particular its religion, Christianity, upon which it was 'based'. This was the basis for the definition of 'right and wrong in the dealings between nations'.[19] Stimson's view of 'civilisation' was largely shared by Roosevelt, who used such terminology in many speeches during the war, and was echoed by many Americans across the political spectrum.[20] If there was to be war it had to be a war that would not end in 'failure' as in 1919. The most eloquent advocate of this view was John Foster Dulles, like Stimson a Republican and one of the key architects of US foreign policy in the Cold War. He deeply believed that the moral and ethical aims of the American republic had to be extended, so that the 'real failure today would be for America to expend her treasure and perhaps her blood without thereby pushing forward the frontiers of peace'.[21]

Roosevelt's dilemma was that he was still essentially wedded to Wilson's moral internationalism, but he could not ignore neutralist and isolationist sentiment. Hence he started the war with a Secretary of War and of the Navy who were isolationist and had to fight every inch of the way to change the Neutrality legislation that he had been forced to accept in the mid-1930s. This legislation, which he only managed to get amended in November 1939 and abolished in 1941, made any provision of military, or indeed any, aid to a country in a state of belligerency a very difficult proposition. Roosevelt's description of Lend–Lease to Britain as 'lending your neighbor the garden hose' was a phrase designed to allay fears that he was taking sides in Europe. This state of affairs continued until the Japanese solved his problem for him by attacking Pearl Harbor in December 1941.[22] After this little was heard from the isolationists as Americans pulled together in the war effort, although Roosevelt could not afford to dismiss the importance of their feelings when it came to planning the post-war settlement. This mostly emerged during and after the election campaign of 1944 for Roosevelt's fourth term, and was one of the major causes of the initial post-war dislocation between Britain and the United States.

A 'radical reduction in the weight of Europe'[23]

A final word on this nexus of policy options has to refer briefly to a theme that will be taken up again in Chapter 5: the perceived need to change the organisational principles of Europe in the post-war world. A clear indication of this new movement was the publication and huge popularity of Clarence Streit's *Union Now* in March 1939, which was widely read and quoted in the United States and made a great impact on informed American opinion.[24] Streit's thesis was essentially that the American experience had showed that federalism could work and was infinitely preferable to the alternatives of nationalism as portrayed by the European experience over many centuries. He proposed a union of the 'North Atlantic democracies' (especially the United States, the British Dominions (including Canada), France, the Benelux countries, Switzerland and the Nordic states – fifteen in all) forming a 'Great Republic' to include citizenship, defence, a customs and monetary union, and a common postal and communications system. He set against his ideal union the present 'league' concept, one which was inevitably 'a government by governments' not by the 'people'. In his view this would give more rights to individuals and to nations and conform to the logic of an ever more interdependent world. A first step might be an 'alliance of the democracies', not a league of all states regardless of their political allegiance, the differences of which had brought down the League of Nations by institutionalising nationalist divisions, isolationism in the United States ('the worst alternative') and the balance of power.[25]

These ideas were strongly supported by John Foster Dulles in the Summer of 1939 in a speech delivered to a mixed American and Canadian audience. Dulles set at the centre of his more modest aim of union (which advocated a quasi-federal union of Canada and the United States, with a common monetary policy, moderately controlled migration policies and nearly free trade) the importance of democracy and the 'rule of law'. Dulles claimed that what had made America great was its ability to give 'opportunity to those who are ambitious and energetic, and we do so largely at the expense of those who have lost such qualities', those he deemed 'the status quo', which clearly included the British. For Dulles, what had to be created was an alternative to war as an exciting pursuit and agent for change, and that he identified was essentially capitalism and the pursuit of wealth. With a rigid international system, peace had become identified with the 'status quo' and '[i]n such a world, both war and peace are alternating phases of an inevitable cycle'. His federalism therefore derived from a rejection, like Streit, of the system of state sovereignty, but only went as far as to advocate 'borders [that] become *structurally* porous and elastic'.[26]

Roosevelt's own views on Europe defy easy compression.[27] Roosevelt shared much of the general American impatience with the European way of doing things, which he saw as a constant source of instability. He would not have disagreed with Streit that 'leaving "Europe" to the Europeans', especially Britain and France, had proved disastrous, although he had sympathised with Chamberlain over Munich, which Streit had not. He was not nearly as sceptical of British intentions as Berle and Bullitt, although he was no great fan either, which others in his Cabinet, such as Stimson and Knox, were. Roosevelt held the balance between the different extremes, and kept his own counsel in this as in so much else, which is one reason why he was such a great President. Harper convincingly argues that he had a 'Jeffersonian' view of Europe, that it had to be 'manipulated from afar' but with minimal direct American involvement. So

> FDR's eventual design for Europe consisted of three mutually reinforcing levels of components: a new political and territorial groundwork, two regional pillars bearing direct responsibility for peace, and an overarching structure in which the United States would occupy the position of keystone or *primus inter pares*. The purpose of these arrangements was to bring about a radical reduction in the weight of Europe, in effect to preside over its eventual retirement from the international scene.[28]

The machinery of PWP in the United States

The overall process of planning the peace, both domestically and international-ally, was collectively referred to during 1939–45 in the United States as 'post-war planning', as is evidenced by files under this title that occur in the archives of all the individuals and groups that are the subject of this book. The process by which this was organised is the focus of this section.[29]

When the head of the American pressure group of the US League of

Nations Association, Clark W. Eichelberger, wrote to Roosevelt in April 1941 'suggesting the preparation of plans ... for future world peace', the President replied that he had had such thoughts himself for 'a long time' and had noted '... a growing determination that ways be found for the creation of a system of international relations which would ensure the maintenance of the great freedoms which lie at the foundation of modern civilisation'. Such work of preparation 'for the future has been and is in progress in the appropriate agencies of the Government, and especially in the Department of State', and he hoped that other people would also 'give serious effort to thinking through the problems involved'.[30] On the other hand, Roosevelt did not, at least in the early part of the war, wish the PWP process to be either too public or too definite. To have given the impression that the United States was, for example, carving up the world between the Allies even before its troops had entered the combat could have been very damaging in the eyes of American public opinion. A compromise was thus struck between Wilson's 1918 stance of refusal (except in the low key 'Inquiry') to discuss the future and those, like Eichelberger, who wanted an open and full discussion of it.

One factor which must be understood is that in all the democracies international PWP was seen as going hand in hand with domestic PWP. The focus of this book is on the first of these categories, but the second cannot be ignored. Roosevelt never lost his interest in the New Deal, although it took up far less of his time than before, a fact of which Eleanor Roosevelt never tired of reminding him. Some major New Deal legislation was passed during the war, especially that on social security (i.e. old age pensions). In early 1941 Roosevelt established an Economic Defense Board chaired by Vice-President Henry Wallace (called the 'Board of Economic Warfare' after Pearl Harbor) to coordinate the economic war effort and especially to 'strengthen the international economic relations of the United States', thus explicitly tying in the international to the domestic sphere, and in this capacity giving birth to many of the post-war international economic organisations.[31] The Office of War Mobilization and its 'Advisory Unit for War and Post-War Adjustment Policies', of which future Secretary of State James F. Byrnes was Director and Bernard Baruch Deputy Director, kept Roosevelt informed about all aspects of anticipated domestic adjustment after the war, especially problems of domestic adjustment such as demobilisation, the re-conversion of industries, and so on. Roosevelt's advisors always insisted that he keep Congress fully informed, perhaps in the awful memory of Woodrow Wilson, who often had not.[32]

Roosevelt was always keen to ensure that support for his policies from public opinion was kept high by the knowledge that America would be primarily helping *itself* by setting up the machinery of international peace and reconstruction. In the planning of the post-war world he also had to be aware of a probable backlash against any over-liberal or too generous policies towards European and other states. He took careful note of public opinion polls, by this time extremely sophisticated in both the United States and Britain, and never relaxed his policy of the regular 'fireside chat' on the radio.[33] The evidence is that he thus managed to carry a large majority of American opinion with him on virtually all of his key policy initiatives, both domestic and foreign, unlike his predecessor, Woodrow Wilson. Dr Gallup, one of the founders of the art of polling, also felt that Roosevelt could himself shift opinion and that this was demonstrated by evidence from before and after the President's speeches.[34]

He was helped in this mobilisation of opinion by the growing realisation that whatever happened during or after the war American foreign policy would have to be reoriented. In 1940–41 the awful possibility would have to be faced as to what would happen if Britain were to be defeated. If that should happen, suggested a paper by Pasvolsky of early 1941, the United States would have to decide whether to 'maintain a policy of political, if not economic, isolation from Europe, meanwhile developing the most powerful defenses possible', or to forge an alliance with the rump of the British Empire or to work out with both the Empire and the fascist states 'some new conception of world organization which might ensure peace for the future and promote economic reconstruction'.

There was also a linked agenda of what may be described as the groping towards the need for a 'world order'. An initial formulation of this by Hugh R. Wilson of the State Department in early 1940 was that the United States would have to cooperate with Europe over economic reconstruction, as it had not in 1919, but that it could not contemplate helping the states of Europe 'with their purely political problems' as US public opinion would not countenance that. However, at this point their major focus was still on reinforcing hemispheric solidarity. Wilson agreed with Berle (and Under-Secretary of State, Sumner Welles, who had made this solidarity a key part of Roosevelt's foreign policy agenda) that one basis for a foray into world politics might be through the Pan American Union. Later on, this regional/global dichotomy resurfaced in discussions on the United Nations, as will be explored in Chapter 6.[35]

Once the United States entered the war the feeling grew in the State Department that 'the war has caused a major revolution in American thinking' and that the United States must now reverse its reticence about PWP, and even contemplate membership of international organisations, because 'our peace and security are menaced to a greater or lesser degree by war between other nations anywhere in the world'. Moreover, progress in military science, and especially the growth of air power, had changed the equation: 'Nature no longer provides security by the protection of distance, for distance no longer exists'. But the key problem was one of how to balance the needs of national security with those of national and international economic welfare and justice.[36] These 'determining principles' were endlessly discussed in State Department committees as 1942 and 1943 drew on, and they inspired a slow consensus that the United States would have to act as a 'world policeman', or at least as one of the 'four big policemen' of the world', as Roosevelt informed Chiang Kai-Shek through Owen Lattimore in early 1943,[37] because it had become in the United States' national interest to do so.

PWP within the Administration

The preparation for, and the waging of, war had to take top priority during Roosevelt's last two terms and the strain often showed. As Grenville Clark put it to Stimson in April 1941,

> it is pretty hard to get the average American willing to go into the war until he sees what the next step is after the war, and what will keep us from making another Versailles Treaty failure. He [Roosevelt] suggested that we ought to be thinking of that and of course we ought, but of course at the present time the real trouble is that we are so busy that we don't get time to think.

The constraints of time and organisation did not get any easier and this often resulted in major splits within departments and between departments over and above the usual 'pulling and hauling' that is American politics, especially once the war broke out; indeed, 'it seems to get worse every week'.[38] The only respite from normality was that bipartisan politics tended to prevail in the interests of the war effort, even if they were to re-emerge a little during Roosevelt's re-election campaign of 1944, a period when PWP was at its height.

Like any American president, Roosevelt relied on a few close allies to do his bidding and carry out crucial and difficult tasks within the Administration and outside Washington, but he also liked to be 'his own decision-maker' and often would let internal Cabinet dissension work to his advantage. He liked to set department against department, often in the name of 'coordination', as with the Economic Defense Board briefly described above. The most significant of his close aides throughout the war was Harry Hopkins, a New Deal official, of whom Stimson had to admit, 'there is no one the President trusts as much …'.[39] Hopkins was used as Roosevelt's roving Ambassador to Stalin and Churchill, and helped define most of the President's wartime strategy. Henry Morgenthau Jr, Secretary to the Treasury, was also a major confidant, often used as a foil for Stimson. Within the State Department, Roosevelt relied a great deal on Deputy Secretary of State, Sumner Welles, who was much closer to him than Hull, but relied on the latter to get his ideas through Congress. He would also listen on occasion to iconoclasts such as Averell Harriman and George Kennan. Many were those who believed that they had convinced him, only to find out that they had not, giving rise to accusations of 'deviousness', which Sainsbury rightly dismisses as Roosevelt's necessary caution and a need to 'test the water' of ideas.[40]

The State Department acted as a clearing house for the mass of suggestions, some of them predictably crazy, that flowed into the President's postbag. Most of the material was replied to by Martin H. Macintyre, his secretary, but some was passed on to the State Department, or the FBI if there was an element of threat involved. Roosevelt hesitated about allowing the State Department to do all the work of organising the post-war scenarios, but the Department nonetheless dealt with everything that might be deemed 'political', with the Department of Agriculture, for example, being used to coordinate wheat policy (which was of considerable importance given Vice-President Wallace's obsession with food security).[41] The Department of Commerce was central in planning trade relations and, of course, Henry Morgenthau's Treasury Department in the PWP of financial international organisations (for more detail see Chapter 7).

PWP within the State Department

Roosevelt was more than sure that planning for the post-war period would never be easy. As he remarked to a correspondent: '[i]t will require all our abilities to arrive at a sound solution ...'.[42] In a very real sense such planning had started before the war got under way in Europe, particularly in the thinking of Berle, Hull and Sumner Welles. But there could be no official acknowledgement of this for fear of alienating American public opinion, and Roosevelt only gave a cautious green light for a systematic examination of options in response to a request from Berle in June 1941.[43] The official launching of the process started with Sumner Welles, requesting that he set up a mechanism within the State Department in August 1941 before American entry into the war. The immediate impetus for the establishment of a machinery seems to have been the signature of the Atlantic Charter by the President and Churchill in that month. Roosevelt approved the establishment of an Advisory Committee on Post-War Foreign Policy (ACPWFP) two days before Pearl Harbor, and it was officially up and running by February of 1942. Domestic matters, such as about demobilisation, were discussed by a committee headed by Vice-President Wallace.[44]

The ACPWFP was officially chaired by Hull, but effectively by Welles, and had a membership that included: the President of the Council for Foreign Relations (CFFR), Norman Davis; Deputy President of the CFFR and the editor of *Foreign Affairs*, Hamilton Fish Armstrong; Assistant Secretaries of State, Dean Acheson and Adolf Berle; Isaiah Bowman (who had chaired the 'Inquiry' and was now the President of Johns Hopkins University); Herbert Feis, the State Department's Advisor on International Economic Affairs; Dean Hackworth, its Legal Advisor; and Leo Pasvolsky, Special Assistant to the Secretary of State and Chief of the Department's

Division of Special Research, set up in 1941, who was also its Executive Officer. The stated aims of the ACPWFP were 'to translate into a program of specific policies and measures the broad principles enunciated in the Atlantic declaration and in other official pronouncements on post-war policy'. Roosevelt told Welles that he wanted 'to be able to have on his desk exactly what he needed on post-war problems, while, meantime, he concentrated on the ways and means of winning the war'.[45]

The 'Division of Special Research' was to provide the Committee with appropriate material so that it could 'make recommendations to the President on all phases of post-war foreign relations and planning'.[46] Its main foci were to be (1) post-war political problems, (2) post-war territorial problems, and (3) the problem of general security. This enormous task was exacerbated by a list of supplementary questions, so it had, for example, to ask under (2) which states should be restored, what were their boundaries to be and what should be done about 'dependent areas'? Under (3) they had to consider problems of disarmament (or arms limitation) and international organisation, including whether there should be an international armed force. Their findings were fed into the three main operational subcommittees of the ACPWFP: Political and Territorial Reconstruction (Chairman, Sumner Welles), General Security (Chairman, Norman Davis) and Economic Reconstruction (Chairman, Adolf Berle). These were given allied subcommittees, notably on international organisation. Leo Pasvolsky of the Department of Special Research played the key role in the collation of material for these subcommittees.[47]

The Department's 'Plan of Work' was elaborated during 1941 and 1942 and continued to evolve as the war progressed. However, it effectively started before the US ever got into the war, at least as early as January 1940, initially in discussions with other neutral Powers. The 'principles on which [PWP] should be based' had a very strong, but by no means exclusive, economic bias right from the outset, influenced by Cordell Hull's already established obsession with commercial matters. Pasvolsky was also very committed to the economic route to a more peaceful world.[48] This emphasis on economic questions derived from a widespread belief that it was 'certain fundamental economic forces', such as demographic pressures, and 'wide fluctuations in economic activity' that had caused the tensions of the 1930s. It was also derived from what Assistant Secretary of State Berle called 'the essential thesis', that 'the standard of living of the European ... and the American people shall not deteriorate but that hope and prospect shall be given for revised standards of living in the future'.[49] From the outset it was also recognised that the way that the 1919 economic crisis had been dealt with bureaucratically had been a major problem. It was observed by Armstrong, for example, that the ARA had been largely ignored by the American Peace Conference delegation, in spite of Hoover's presence in Paris and his leadership of the ARA.[50] This was explicitly a Rooseveltian

'New Deal' for the world and as such it was bound to encounter some opposition within the Administration and outside it from those who held differing views of Roosevelt's domestic policies. (Republican) Secretary for War Stimson often referred to the 'starry eyed liberals' in the Department with some contempt, and increasingly felt that they were pushing the post-war agenda too far to the left. It is nonetheless interesting that he also held the view that economic factors had provided the major causes of the present war.[51] This reflected a bipartisan acceptance of the need for global economic reform, although exactly how this was to emerge was the subject of great debate, as we shall see in Chapter 7.

To achieve the ambitious aims of the 'Plan of Work', it was initially suggested, would require an audit of 'America's Economic Resources and Economic Power in the world', possibly by bodies such as the Brookings Institution (although 'under one direction and supervision', that is, the State Department). It also required a distinct but linked examination of the 'Problem of Enduring Peace'. This would require a probing examination of the failures of the League of Nations, the 'balance of armed forces as a means of preserving peace within the framework of unlimited sovereignty, and also gradations of limitation of sovereignty as treaties and international law'. The key caveat was 'not to sow the seeds of another war' and also to take care not to 'build imaginary castles in the air'.[52]

By late 1942 Roosevelt felt confident enough in an Allied victory to announce to the American public what all these committees were doing: 'The foremost task of a country at war is to win that war. Because of this I have thought it well until now not to enter too deeply into the subject of post-war arrangements. We cannot, and do not wish to, escape the harsh realities by day-dreaming about tomorrow's hopes'.[53] By November 1943, Pasvolsky was able to report to Hull that

> [t]he central feature of our work in preparation for the handling of post-war problems has been in the direction of formulating ways of bringing about a system of organized international relations for the maintenance of peace and security, for the creation of better facilities for economic and social progress, and for the improvement of international relations in other respects.[54]

In inaugurating the PWP process in 1941 Roosevelt in effect defied a neat pigeon-holing as a 'realist' or an 'idealist', insofar as he was well aware of the exigencies of power and military strategy but also had a philosophical goal, that of a just and better world.

The CFFR

Initial discussions between the CFFR and the State Department started in the Spring of 1940, when it was suggested that it would be most useful 'suggesting and developing *ideas* and in assembling *background material*' for use in thinking about the 'effects of the war on the United States and the American interest in the eventual peace'. This background material was envisaged as being to elucidate 'I. Past experience; II. Present situation. The second part would perhaps change with the passage of time and can be brought up to date with the issuance of supplements'. The emphasis was yet again overwhelmingly on drawing up economic contingency plans, and a particular importance accorded to questions of commercial policy, with the Ottawa Agreement coming in for its usual execration and the lessons of reconstruction in the 1920s considered to be of vital importance. Given the situation of the war in May 1940, it was also deemed necessary to dwell on the possibility of a German victory, and here again economic considerations dominated this early discussion: how would a German-dominated Europe affect the European economies and United States trade?[55]

By February 1941 a 'War and Peace Studies Project' had been established, with Philip E. Mosely as Rapporteur, Armstrong as Chairman, and including Isaiah Bowman and Arnold Sweetzer of the State Department. They were supposed to work closely with the Department's Division of Special Research. The aim at this stage was to pursue the strictly neutral task of 'throw[ing] light on the German plans for the reconstruction of Europe in accord with German interests', but more widely to 'understand the inter-relation between American interests and European conditions and possibili-ties' and how these might chime in with German and British intentions. It was made clear that America could not stand by and allow a 'complete German victory, which it is the policy of the United States to prevent'. However, it was equally important not to let those who would come up with 'Utopian blueprints for peace' dominate thinking on the post-war configuration of Europe. The result of this might well be to create in America 'disillusionment, spiritual fatigue, and a desire to cut adrift from European troubles'. One way to do this was to examine the 'actual condition and desires of the European peoples' and not to impose such blueprints, by drawing on the expertise not only of American specialists on Europe, but also as wide a variety of Europeans, based in the United States, as possible in a series of one-day meetings that would naturally include a good lunch.

It was also hoped that '[e]ventually much information concerning British peace aims can be obtained through the special channel of contact maintained between the CFFR and Chatham House'.[56] This channel can be seen as a vital one in providing a passage for British thinking on PWP, not only into the CFFR but also into the State Department. The problem of seeming to be too partisan towards Britain before December 1941 was often recognised in the light of Roosevelt's disquiet over isolationism. Even 'informal contacts and exchange of ideas might easily be construed as involvement in British war aims', believed Hugh Wilson during a visit to London in 1940.[57] But such contacts did take place and included on occasion people such as Pasvolsky and Professors John Kenneth Galbraith and Jacob Viner, the major theorist of Customs Unions.[58] Of course, Pearl Harbor was again helpful in displacing such worries, but the CFFR shared a general American, and indeed Rooseveltian, fear of encouraging British war aims that they saw as 'Imperialist' or excessively based on British balance of power considerations. It was acknowledged that British interests had changed and that a major fear for the survival of the 'British way of life' now predominated, with an acknowledgement among all walks of British life that the nature of the Commonwealth and Empire would have to change. This led on occasion to another, contradictory, fear, at least as late as January 1945, that the British had become too 'pessimistic' and obsessed with 'reinsurance' about their relationship with both Russia and the United States.[59] The CFFR did not want its country to be left holding the baby of world peace and security after the war any more than did Roosevelt.

Five sub-groups were also set up within the War and Peace Studies Project on the 'Peace Aims of European Nations', economic and financial, territorial, armaments and political questions. The first of these took up much of the CFFR's efforts initially, with the others slowly assuming more importance as the war went on, especially after Pearl Harbor. A vast amount of testimony on peace aims was taken and a number of summary documents produced over the next two years. The main areas that emerged as being of constant concern were those of territorial and colonial claims, the treatment of minorities, and the feasibility and desirability of regional arrangements, including by September a 'North Atlantic security system'. Overshadowing this was the desire to ensure the viability of both the 'agricultural states of Eastern Europe' (which included Poland, the Baltics and all of Central Europe) and the encouragement of democracy in France, Italy and Germany.[60]

The summary results of the work by the CFFR were collected together in a series of substantial documents that were circulated to the State Department as the CFFR 'Steering Committee Series'[61] from December 1941, updated annually until the Dumbarton Oaks Conference in 1944. They were favourably referred to in committees of the ACPWFP.[62] However, there is clear evidence that friction developed with the State Department over the provision of these documents. Hull complained as late as July 1943 that he was not getting the documents he needed and by April 1944 he was admitting to Under-Secretary Norman Davis that the State Department itself was not helping by under-utilising the CFFR material. The main culprit, according to Davis, was Leo Pasvolsky, whom he was inclined to want Hull to 'let go', but a more likely explanation was the need to reorganise the Department, which was effectively far too overburdened by all its immediate and longer-term tasks.[63] Decisions now had to be made at the level of immediate policy, and most of these were decided at the level of Foreign Minister and above in the great inter-Allied Conferences that will be described in later chapters.

A reorganisation of the State Department took place during 1944, under the urging of staffer George Kennan among others,[64] one of its results being to send Armstrong to the European Advisory Commission (EAC) in London as deputy to American Ambassador Winant, which will be described in the context of the relations between the Allies in Chapter 5. By the beginning of 1944, the CFFR's role of inputting ideas into PWP had essentially ended and the battleground had been transferred to Europe and the practical exigencies of inter-Allied relations thrown up by the liberation in such bodies as the EAC. In assessing the CFFR's main input, Armstrong himself seems to have felt that its work was not really used properly due to the State Department's inability to absorb it. It was further damaged by the Department's men on the ground, such as Winant, being deeply suspicious of intruders such as Armstrong, and fearing that their presence was the harbinger of a replacement of professionals by amateurs.[65] This was essentially a correct view of the future, with the State Department being transformed after 1944 into a much bigger and less elitist organisation, and one more suited to its post-war global role.

Non-official contributions

There were many outside organisations that tried to make an input into the PWP process, to such a point that the Twentieth Century Fund published an *Organizational Directory* of such bodies in February 1943.[66] However, few had the ear of the State Department or, more particularly, the President. One particular organisation could not be ignored, both because it represented the large and influential Federal Council of the Churches of Christ in America, made up of 'WASP' Presbyterian and Anglican Church opinion, and also because it was run by John Foster Dulles, acknowledged as the man most likely to be a Republican President's Secretary of State. The most consistent attending member of the CFFR War and Peace Studies Group (thirteen out of seventeen meetings in 1941, for example),[67] Dulles was a power to be reckoned with, and not without his allies in the war machinery, including his brother, Allen, who was the Office of Strategic Services' representative in Bern, Switzerland. John Foster Dulles was also very prominent as a foreign policy and moral spokesman, a generally keen isolationist in the 1930s. He had had a long experience of peace conferences, especially Versailles, after which he was the main American legal counsel on the Reparations Commission, and had even been a delegate to the Hague Conference of 1907. He was also keenly aware of Will Roger's dictum: 'We have never lost a war and we have never won a conference'.[68]

The Commission to Study the Bases of a Just and Durable Peace

Dulles was also Chairman of the Commission to Study the Bases of a Just and Durable Peace (The Commission), set up by the Federal Council of the Churches of Christ in America in early 1940. In this capacity he entered into discussions with Sumner Welles to see how the Commission might cooperate with the PWP organs then being set up. He did not envisage an initiation of 'technical proposals' but he did think that they '[could] and should develop certain broad moral principles with which concrete plans should conform'.[69] He had already made his mark in that area by the publication of a much noticed article in *Fortune Magazine* entitled 'Peace Without Platitudes'. This piece was strongly supportive of Roosevelt's Atlantic Charter, and especially the link being made between the need for commercial and financial reform after the war and the President's emphasis on 'growth without imperialism' or, as Roosevelt himself put it in Article One of the Charter, against 'aggrandizement', especially if (Article Two) it did 'not accord with the freely expressed wishes of the people concerned'. Dulles explicitly linked the Charter with Wilson's Fourteen Points and considered it an advance on them. He also suggested, as Roosevelt had not yet done, the need for 'an international body dedicated to the general welfare' and the need to 'establish procedures within each country' to ensure progress towards a more open economic system, a clear reference to an international organisation being given teeth to overcome economic sovereignty.[70] It is also clear that his thinking at this time chimed in very well with certain aspects of Roosevelt's and Hull's beliefs and the work being done within the State Department, of which Dulles was no doubt aware through his membership of the CFFR.

Dulles also made himself useful in providing information for the State Department, as in his fascinating insights communicated to Sumner Welles after his visit to England in June and July 1942. On the key topic, for the United States, of the post-war reorganisation of Europe, he found virtually no enthusiasm for any 'general federation'. On international organisation he was similarly disappointed: 'I found virtually no thinking about a revived League of Nations'. He was greatly surprised about the lack of interest in PWP in England, reflecting at least partly, he acknowledged, the dire military and other circumstances in which it had found itself since 1940. He was in particular troubled by the lack of serious contemplation of the Atlantic Charter, except among the Labour ministers Cripps, Bevin and Attlee, and he found himself bombarded by Eden and Lord Crambourne by a need to understand the 'enlightened' nature of British imperialism. He made it clear to them that he could not agree. He was also worried that the British did not seem to be taking the need to reduce trade barriers seriously as a *quid pro quo* for 'Lend–Lease'. In a telling phrase he commented, '[w]e may feel that this implies a right to influence their post-war tarriff and trade treaty policies to a greater degree than they will be prepared to concede'. His greatest strictures were reserved for what he saw as an unhealthy regard for Russia and was worried about the effect of communist propaganda in the long run. On the other hand, he found a similar non-vengeful attitude to Germany that he was still pushing through the Commission and a general affection for the United States, although he saw clouds on the horizon as the number of American troops billeted in Britain increased.[71]

As will be shown in the next chapter, Britain had in fact had to sign itself up for many of the main elements of the Rooseveltian NWO through the Atlantic Charter and Lend–Lease. Dulles' British Conservative interlocutors were either suffering from psychological 'denial' or at least trying to downplay the immensity of the agreements that they were in the process of making. The Labour ministers' attitude reflected their belief in an NWO, but one that was based on premises, such as national planning of the economy, that Dulles would have found difficult to accept at any stage of his career.

The tone of many of Dulles' speeches during this period as Chairman of the Commission was one of deep Christian commitment mixed rather incongruously with very precise policy statements. One typical speech recalled that 'Christ lived at a time when international and social problems existed in an aggravated form ... In the face of that situation, Christ constantly urged the importance of visions that would see clear, minds that would think straight and hearts that comprehend the essential unity and equal worthiness of all human beings'. The Atlantic Charter was presented by Dulles to his audience as a kind of Ten Commandments, to 'proclaim' it, for which was needed 'the true armor of righteousness'.[72] In this discourse there were enemies of God, notably the German and Japanese leaderships, although their followers were usually portrayed as more misled than evil. There was also the important future problem of Russia, often referred to elliptically through 1943, but increasingly openly in 1944.

The key to the future for Dulles was what kind of 'social and economic order ... will benefit mankind', and on this he saw 'a considerable division of opinion'[72] starting to occur, not only within the United States but also between the Allies. There was also the question of what Russia intended to do in Eastern Europe and China. The Commission's major statement of its view of how the NWO might actually turn out emerged after a symposium in early 1943 entitled 'A Righteous Faith for Just and Durable Peace'. The concluding document of this symposium was sent to a number of prominent persons in Britain and the United States, including Roosevelt.[74] The document was entitled 'The Six Pillars of Peace' and launched what Dulles called 'a second phase of our task', the need to put flesh on the bones of a future international organisation. He warned that 'between the four principal allies, there exist great gulfs of differences in outlook, ideology [*sic*] and material standards'. The 'Six Pillars' therefore foresaw regional as well as global collaboration; the recognition of 'interdependence' in the economic and financial fields; 'a standing international body to study the need for change'; 'some form of international organization to promote the ultimate autonomy of subject peoples'; 'international control of armament' and, last but not least, 'the right of spiritual and intellectual liberty'.[75]

Roosevelt's reaction was non-committal, but as he read the document in

Dulles' presence he remarked 'upon the difficulty of coming to agreements in detail and the necessity of adopting a spirit of compromise'. In particular he warned against an excess of 'idealism' in conceding the demands of Eastern Europeans (Poland and Bessarabia were cited expressly) which would 'lead to a rejection of collaboration [by Russia] as a permanent principle'.[76] This 'Christian Message on World Order' can therefore be seen as Dulles' first major public warning that the alliance with Russia, in particular, might well end in tears at a time when adulation for Russia after Stalingrad was at its height on both sides of the Atlantic. It also went contrary to Roosevelt's wish to keep Russia happy at almost any cost and can be seen as one of the first ranging shots of the Cold War. Dulles also expressed the feeling that the emphasis on the Big Four that was emerging in Roosevelt's thinking, and his seeming abandonment of the small states, fell 'far short' of the moral principles that he wished to see being implemented in PWP.[77]

Dulles during the 1944 Presidential election campaign

Dulles' views were even more openly put during the 1944 Presidential campaign which he helped direct as Thomas Dewey's putative Secretary of State. When the Commission launched its 'Six Pillars' in March 1943, Dulles had announced to Sumner Welles that this was because he feared a 'drift towards a policy of isolation and reliance on our own strength alone'. This became a first statement of a severe divide between the Democrats and Republicans on foreign policy in spite of Dulles' stated hope that he would have the backing of the State Department in a 'non-partisan, or, preferably, bi-partisan' approach.[78]

In its search for a definition for the Republican Party in August 1943 of what its post-war foreign policy should be, it is clear that the committee of the Party responsible for foreign policy was not greatly at odds with that espoused by Roosevelt. Hence it wished for a 'stabilized interdependent world', a prosecution of the war to complete victory and 'the participation of the United States in post war cooperation between independent nations to prevent, by any necessary means, the re-occurrence of military aggression', as well as the 'discouragement of the growth of exclusive nationalism and its inevitable consequences; military and economic aggression'. This would involve the United States 'and other Nations' in 'promoting wider inter-national exchange of goods … and in achieving monetary and economic stability'. The differences lay in the emphases put on the importance of 'peace and justice in a free world' and the need to avoid 'world government'.[79]

Other members of the Republican National Committee veered towards an at least partial isolationism or, as at least one prominent member put it, against 'World Federation or "the quart of milk for every hottentot" idea'. Dulles was not at all keen to be seen to be in any way espousing isolationism, which, as he put it, was now a 'false issue'. He also had no desire at this point to be seen to be openly against the USSR: 'while there is much in their conduct we do not like, yet it has the cardinal virtue of being creative'. If anything, he wished the Republicans to be seen as more creative than the Democrats, more willing to think the unthinkable, not to 'primarily be interested in restoring things as they were and then maintaining them as they are'. What he wanted was 'to make our keynote the righteous and creative faith, first of the individual and then of the nation'.[80]

Dulles was made Republican candidate Thomas Dewey's foreign policy spokesman. One problem was how to translate the idea of a 'righteous and creative faith' into policy and a second was how to get round the 'Roosevelt factor', which became increasingly crucial as 1944 wore on and the date of the election approached in November. On the latter point Dulles made the observation that Roosevelt was running the same risk as Wilson had in his increasingly personalised, even secret, diplomacy with the Allies, and thus losing touch with American opinion and jeopardising the peace settlement. Until the present, he had to admit, consultation with the Republican Party had been excellent, but would it continue to be? As to the 'righteous and creative faith', it seemed to Dulles that this was being put more and more in Russia than in the democratic powers of Europe, especially Britain. He also claimed, somewhat disingenuously, that the idea of a universal international organisation had not been Roosevelt's idea, but the Republicans', for had it not been absent in the Atlantic Charter? Succinctly put, '[p]erhaps Mr. Roosevelt handles foreign affairs as well as any President can be expected to do personally. I criticize, above all, the method'. In a ringing conclusion he added, '[n]ational policies cannot safely be made on the slender thread of the life of a single man. Whenever that is attempted, then it is time for a change'.[81]

The problem for both Dulles and Dewey was that while they made small, if ultimately telling, points from the sidelines, Roosevelt was enacting policy. During the election itself, Roosevelt initiated discussions on the United Nations at the Dumbarton Oaks Conference. Dewey could only applaud it, in a statement drafted by Dulles. The Republican Party was arguably experiencing its deepest period of disunity for many years, and the Democrats were riding higher on Roosevelt's increasing stature as the world leader. The one opportunity for 'dirty tricks' he avoided, when he received testimony that Roosevelt had known about the attack on Pearl Harbor before it happened.[82] Dulles even consulted Walter Lippman in an attempt to package his candidate properly as a foreign policy prophet. Lippman's comment was that Dewey and Dulles must concentrate on the future of relations with Germany and Russia, and if they did so, 'you [Dewey] will have done more than any other prominent political figure, but ... if you do less, on account of the public impression that has been created about you, the impression created will be one of negation and of strong tendency towards isolation'. But as Dulles pointed out, this would only really appeal to the Catholic and Polish vote.[83]

Was the Commission for a Just and Durable Peace successful in its attempts to influence American PWP, or Dulles in his capacity as Republican spokesman on foreign affairs? Dulles later suggested to Hull, after he had got the principles of international organisation and religious and intellectual freedom included in the Moscow Declaration of October 1943, that this was a big advance on the Atlantic Charter and a key objective of the 'Six Pillars', and as we have seen he made similar claims in the election campaign of 1944. But he was the first to acknowledge that the 'move from words to functioning institutions infused with the spirit of Christian fellowship remains a political and spiritual task of immense proportions'. He would also have to accept that the NWO was to be based on 'the military alliance of a few'.[84] Dulles also had to accept that the Rooseveltian propaganda machine was more effective than his. Walter Lippman, who was a staunch supporter of the Rooseveltian line and with whom Dulles had a considerable and not unfriendly correspondence at this period, consistently scored points at his expense.[85] To confront a popular incumbent President in a war situation is always difficult; to go against Roosevelt very risky indeed. Dulles' hour was to come, especially his views on Russia, but not until after Roosevelt's death. However, in the meantime, and before Roosevelt's death, the basic building blocks of his NWO were laid. We shall briefly review what these were before examining how they came to be seen as flawed and were greatly modified.

Concluding remarks: what basis for an American NWO?

The 'organisation of peace'

The 'organisation of peace' was endlessly debated in a variety of possible geometries. Until the end of 1941 membership of the United States in world organisation was seen by many as 'practically impossible'. But some sort of 'grouping of leagues' was nevertheless seen as essential. This paralleled Churchill's later 'United States of Europe' idea and his liking for a 'Danubian Federation', discussed at the Conferences of 1943 at Moscow and Teheran. In 1939 and 1940 some commentators in both Britain and America were thinking along these lines, usually explicitly linked to the failures of Versailles. As Berle pointed out in early 1940, even the Germans and the Russians were talking of creating a new 'machinery', in their case a 'universal empire', but one had to presume that this would not prevail.[86] How these discussions developed will be examined in Chapters 5 and 6.

Other big organising questions derived largely from a re-reading of the Versailles settlement early in the process of PWP in the United States and Britain. One of these was the question of which Powers would act as guarantors of a post-war settlement. Should the emphasis be on 'a central Anglo-American relationship? Or on a new "Big Four" consisting of the

United States, Britain, Soviet Russia and China?' Equally, what role could be given to non-powers, when most of these would in fact be dependent on the Big Four for their rehabilitation after the war?[87] Most important of all, how would the American public and Congress react to the need to commit the United States to the use of force to secure the peace and the post-war peace in particular, the issue which had brought down Wilson's dreams for the LON?

For many there was an awful sense of *déjà vu* about all of this. White House aide Oscar Cox commented to Hopkins in late 1942 in an early discussion of relief efforts that would need to be undertaken after the war: 'You will note that a lot of it sounds awfully familiar: History apparently repeats itself...'.[88] PWP in the United States was so thorough because Roosevelt was sure that such feelings as this should not become a widely perceived truth with the American public, however much they figured in cynical asides in the Administration. Roosevelt's aims and approach were summed up by him in a memo to Morris L. Ernst in March 1943. He wrote that if asked for a definition of America's attitude to the future of international relations they should simply say: 'We were wrong in 1920. We believe in international co-operation and the principles of the Atlantic Charter and the Four Freedoms. We propose to back those who show the most diligence and interest in carrying them out'.[89]

Realism or idealism?

The *leitmotif* of all the working parties and discussion groups mentioned above was over the right mix of 'realism' or 'idealism' that should be used in approaching PWP. Both these terms were used by all the major protagonists in a variety of geometries, but it is remarkable that there was no clear disagreement about what was being done by the Administration. Whatever may have been said since, there was overwhelming support within the United States for the basic thrust of Roosevelt's vision of a post-war order, and no obvious accusations during the war that he was anything other than 'realist' in both his aims and in the execution of them.

Roosevelt's handling of the political situation in the United States can take much of the credit for this and demonstrates that an American President that is prepared to give a strong lead can accomplish more than any other democratic leader. His view, the fruit of his meetings with Stalin and Churchill as well as the input from PWP groups and his basic instincts as a Wilsonian internationalist, was that virtually any price must be paid to secure a settlement that would hold and be acceptable to Congress and American public opinion. It is important to stress that there were very few advocates of a return to isolationism, and the input from groups such as Dulles' in no way equated to the Senate opposition to Wilson that developed during 1919–20. Roosevelt's political acumen was such that he always avoided open conflict with Congress, even on occasion sacrificing a prominent advocate of his line in favour of one who was less in tune with his feelings but more in tune with the mood of Congress.[90] His often-quoted 'deviousness' was a sign essentially of his ability to make every key actor in the United States feel that he had taken their views seriously. Most clearly, it was a sign, as Sainsbury says, that he was 'ever aware that politics is the art of the possible',[91] a major failing of Woodrow Wilson.

But he was not without serious enemies whose barbs in the long run hit home. By attacking Roosevelt's Russian policy and his intentions for the United Nations, Dulles was attempting to occupy the moral high ground, a skill that he was to develop further as Secretary of State under Eisenhower. It could easily be argued that in so doing he subverted the essentially 'realist' thinking of Roosevelt that attempted to see what might be obtained that was useful in the Russian alliance, whereas Dulles was taking the classically 'idealist' position of making moral judgements in foreign affairs. Defenders of Dulles would no doubt argue that Roosevelt was naive to put any faith in Russian promises. Whatever is the case, the clear-cut distinction that is often made between 'realist' and 'idealist' positions once again looks rather flimsy. The end result of Dulles' thinking for Roosevelt's NWO after his death was to make it not the inclusive global order that Roosevelt had wished for, but one that was essentially for the 'West'. The criterion for entry to the NWO 'club' of the post-war period was essentially to become one of accepting definitions of 'freedom' and 'justice' that were far more narrow than Roosevelt had intended in the Atlantic Charter. Taken with Dulles' previously mentioned economic ideas, it might be said that in the long run he has had the last laugh, that we now do have a liberal capitalist system with 'borders that [have become] structurally porous and elastic' and based on the kind of values that Dulles would have said he subscribed to.

Expanding the debate on PWP

But Roosevelt and his advisors also realised that a successful post-war settlement also required that the Allies must be completely on side in the elaboration of such a settlement. Until the middle or end of 1942 PWP had been an essentially American affair. As Dulles had commented in July 1942, this was partly because Britain had been so immersed in the problems of survival and taking the burden of the war effort. Once the United States engaged the enemy in the European theatre as well as the Pacific after October 1942 with the American landings in North Africa, America became quite clearly the senior partner over Britain. After this date Roosevelt was in particular convinced that the other senior partner, Russia, must be included in any settlement and that the 'balance of power' and Imperial instincts of his Allies, even Britain and especially France, must be restrained. The uneasy unfolding of the Allied relationship, in particular after early 1943, is evidence of this, and is one of the foci of the next two chapters.

A number of potential or actual issues of dissension with the Allies had emerged as part of the PWP process until the end of 1942 but essentially they were all related to the principal concern of preventing another Versailles and its disastrous aftermath. The thorny question of what to do with the defeated states of Europe, and in particular Germany, was an immediate concern. In a longer perspective all major opinion in the United States was convinced of the need for a longer-term global security arrangement, and although differences of opinion about exactly how this should develop were clearly evident, there was no major dissension from the overall goal. Differences also emerged about what kind of organisational structure was needed to ensure an economically sound basis for the peace, but again, within the United States, there was no real call for a return to economic nationalism. The Atlantic Charter was seen within the United States as a universally acceptable blueprint for both political and economic reform of the international system. The difficulty lay in putting policy decisions in place to implement it that would be acceptable to the Allies and American public opinion.

The actual detail of discussions within the PWP committees in the United States and the discussions between the Allies in the Conference diplomacy of 1943–45 that is the subject of much of the subsequent chapters, consequently show the development of a conscious American leadership in the PWP process, either by putting pressure on Britain and France or by cajoling the Russians. They also show that Britain was willing to be a 'follower', even where its basic instincts told strongly against such following. The Russians were to prove less amenable, despite Roosevelt's extensive charm offensive and his willingness to override publicly dissenting voices such as Dulles and privately dissenting ones such as Kennan and Harriman. But it would be a mistake to think that Roosevelt and his very able advisors were not aware of the gamble involved. The next two chapters will map out this complicated internal and external relationship and how it impacted on the elaboration of PWP.

Notes

1 Founded in 1919 at the same time as the British Royal Institute of International Relations (RIIA, also known as 'Chatham House').
2 This theme will be developed more fully in Chapter 7.
3 See, for example, Keith Sainsbury, *Churchill and Roosevelt at War: The War They Fought and the Peace They Hoped to Make* (London, Macmillan, 1996). See Chapter 5 for a more detailed discussion of this.
4 Henry Stimson, later to be Secretary for War, believed that Hull had become far too 'devot[ed] to specialisations like the passage of the reciprocity legislation' and had let the State Department get a 'little out of hand': Stimson Diary, 8 May 1940. See Chapter 7 for a detailed examination of Hull's views.

5   The best single book on Roosevelt's foreign policy is Robert Dallek, *Franklin D. Roosevelt and American Foreign Policy, 1932–1945* (New York, Oxford University Press, 1979).

6   The literature on appeasement is, of course, vast. Some useful summaries can be found in Martin Gilbert and R. Gott, *The Appeasers* (London, Weidenfeld and Nicholson, 1963); Martin Gilbert, *The Roots of Appeasement* (London, Weidenfeld and Nicholson, 1966); Peter Calvocorressi and Guy Wint, *Total War* (London, Penguin, 1972); R. Henig, *The Origins of the Second World War* (London, Methuen, 1985); A.J. P. Taylor, *The Origins of the Second World War* (London, Penguin, 1960); Gordon Martel (ed.), *The Origins of the Second World War – Reconsidered* (London, Routledge, 1986); W. Rock, *British Appeasement in the 1930s* (London, Edward Arnold, 1977); and D.C. Watt, *How War Came* (London, Heinemann, 1989). It seems fair to say that the jury is still out on the acceptability or intelligence of the policy, with perhaps a slight edge now being given to the 'revisionist' (i.e. pro-appeasement) school at present.

7   Robert Dallek pinpoints Walter Millis' *Road to War, America 1914–1917* of 1935 as a major milestone in this realisation: Dallek, *Franklin D. Roosevelt and American Foreign Policy*, pp. 102–109.

8   Dallek, *Franklin D. Roosevelt and American Foreign Policy*, pp. 16, 70 and *passim*; Justus D. Doenecke (ed.), *In Danger Undaunted: The Anti-Interventionist Movement of 1940–1941, as Revealed in the Papers of the America First Committee* (Stanford, Hoover Institution Press, 1990).

9   Record of conversations between Stimson and Felix Frankfurter and Stimson and Herbert Feis (also State Department), Stimson, Diary, 2 and 8 May 1940, Reel 6. David Reynolds says that Berle 'combined one of the sharpest minds in the State Department with an obsessive suspicion of Britain': Reynolds, *The Creation of the Anglo-American Alliance, 1937–41* (London, Europa, 1981), p. 256. Berle had been present at Versailles and he was adamant that Britain should not get the chance to throw away the peace as he believed it had in 1919, especially when the United States was so obviously better equipped economically and in every other way to do so now.

10 John Lamberton Harper, *American Visions of Europe: Franklin D. Roosevelt, George F. Kennan and Dean G. Acheson* (Cambridge University Press, 1994 and 1996), p. 51. For more on Roosevelt and Europe see this chapter, below, p. 86 and Chapter 6. For a discussion of Allied relations with Russia see Chapter 5.

11 Roy Douglas, *New Alliances, 1940–41* (London, Macmillan, 1982), p. 31.

12 Dallek, *Franklin D. Roosevelt and American Foreign Policy*, pp. 19–20 and Chapter 4, 'Farewell to Internationalism'.

13 Robin Edmonds, *The Big Three: Churchill, Roosevelt and Stalin in Peace and War* (London, Penguin, 1991), p. 92.

14 For more details on this episode see Chapter 4.

15 Reynolds, *The Creation*, p. 261.

16 David W. Ellwood, *Rebuilding Europe: Western Europe, America and Postwar Reconstruction* (London, Longman, 1992), p. 21.

17 John Foster Dulles, 'Peace Without Platitudes', *Fortune*, January 1942, p. 42.

18 Halifax to Churchill, 11 October 1941, PREM 4, 27/9, quoted by Dallek, *Franklin D. Roosevelt and American Foreign Policy*, p. 289.

19 Stimson, Diary, entries for 4 April, June, 23 October 1939, and 29 November 1941, the latter of which records a conversation with Roosevelt: Stimson, Diary, Reel 6.

20 It has been suggested that this view of the world was essentially racist. Such a judgement may have some meaning in the climate of 1998. There has of course also been much discussion in recent years as to whether this made Roosevelt's Administration less willing than it might have been to help the Jews during the war. Quite apart from the fact that Henry Morgenthau, Roosevelt's closest friend and advisor, was a Jew, the judgement of historians is that such accusations are not by any means conclusively proved. See, for example, Verne W. Newton (ed.), *FDR and the Holocaust* (New York, St. Martin's Press, 1996) and Philippe Burrin, *Hitler and the Jews: The Genesis of the Holocaust* (London, Edward Arnold, 1994), which have some references to this debate.

21 Dulles, 'Peace Without Platitudes', pp. 42–43 and 87–90.

22 Hitler declined to receive a message from 'so contemptible a creature as the present President of the United States' in the Reichstag in April 1939: Dallek, *Franklin D. Roosevelt and American Foreign Policy*, Chapter 9 and p. 186.

23 The expression is from Harper, *American Visions of Europe*, p. 79.

24 Clarence K. Streit, *Union Now* (London, Jonathan Cape, 1939).

25 Streit, *Union Now*, pp. 17–38.

26 John Foster Dulles, 'A North American Contribution to World Order', speech of 20 June 1939, delivered at St Lawrence University, New York state. This document was one of the first considered by the Chatham House 'World Order Group', File 9/18.

27 Brilliantly analysed by Harper in *American Visions of Europe*.

28 Harper, *American Visions of Europe*, Chapter 1 and pp. 77–79. For more on this see Chapters 5 and 7.

29 The best published accounts of at least some of this process can be found in Harley Notter (a State Department official who sat on many of the committees), *Post-War Foreign Policy Preparation, 1939–1945* (Washington, US Department of State, 1949) and Robert C. Hildebrand, *Dumbarton Oaks: The Origins of the United Nations and the Search for Post-War Security* (Chapel Hill, University of North Carolina Press, 1990).

30 Eichelberger to Roosevelt, 6 April 1941, and reply, 12 May 1941, drafted for him by Cordell Hull; Roosevelt Official Files, 4351.

31 Roosevelt to Wallace, 9 July 1941; Franklin D. Roosevelt, *F.D.R.: His Personal Letters*, (New York, Duell, Sloane and Pearce, 1950), p. 1181.

32 See, for example, Bernard Baruch and John M. Hancock, 'Report on War and Post-War Adjustment Policies', 15 February 1944, and Oscar Cox (White House Aide) to Hopkins, 10 August 1944; Hopkins Papers, Box 329.

33 See, for example, Lubin (White House Aide) to Harry Hopkins of 6 January 1944, enclosing report by Hadley Cantril and Gerard B. Lambert on 'Suggested Procedure to make Administrations' Post-War Policy acceptable to American Public'. This purported to demonstrate that there was a need to show that international policy was not at the expense of domestic policy and that whenever possible all comments on foreign affairs should be linked to the public's 'self-interest'. Hopkins Papers, Box 329, 'Post-War Planning'.

34 As related to Stimson in his Diary, 4 June 1941.

35 Leo Pasvolsky, 'Reorientation of American Foreign Policy', 28 January 1941, Pasvolsky Papers, Box 7; and Hugh R. Wilson, 'Memorandum on World Order', 22 January 1940, Berle Papers, Box 54.

36 One key document is that entitled 'Preliminary Memorandum on International Organization', 31 July 1942; Welles Papers, Box 189.

37 Letter from Lattimore to Chiang Kai-Shek delivered to Chiang in Chungking in early 1943, quoted by Dallek, *Franklin D. Roosevelt and American Foreign Policy*, p. 390.

38 Stimson, Diary, entries for 8 and 22 April 1941.

39 Stimson, Diary, 15 April 1941.

40 On Roosevelt's death in April 1945, Morgenthau wrote, 'I have lost my best friend'; Morgenthau, Diary, 12 April 1945, Reel 19. Sainsbury says that Cordell Hull was 'retained for so long because of his influence with Congress … But they were never close and Roosevelt preferred to consult and rely on others – Hopkins, who was virtually an additional Secretary of State for long periods [and] Sumner Welles (Roosevelt's man in the State Department) …'; Sainsbury, p. 196. On the charge of 'deviousness', see Sainsbury, *Churchill and Roosevelt at War*, pp. 8–9.

41 For Roosevelt's views on the division of labour on PWP, see Roosevelt to Jesse James, Secretary of Commerce, 16 June 1942; for his delegation of virtually all suggestions on PWP to the State Department, see Roosevelt memo, 22 December 1941, Roosevelt Official File, 4351.

42 Roosevelt to James K. Pollock (Professor of Political Science at the University of Michigan), 9 April 1941; Roosevelt Official File, 4351.

43 Berle to Roosevelt, 21 June, and Roosevelt to Berle, 26 June 1941; Roosevelt President's Secretary's Files 90, quoted by Reynolds, *The Creation*, pp. 257–258 and 363 fn. 20.

44 Welles to Roosevelt and reply, 1 August 1941; Roosevelt to Hull, 5 December 1941 and Hull to Roosevelt, 22 December 1941; Roosevelt Official File, 4351. Minutes of First Meeting (AC-1) of 12 February 1942, Welles Papers, Box 190.

45 Received by the Department of State, 30 June 1942 in its approved form from Roosevelt, Roosevelt Official File, 4351; also in Berle Papers, Box 54. Roosevelt comment to Welles from AC-1 of 12 February 1942, Welles Papers, Box 190.

46 Memo of 16 February 1942; Sumner Welles Papers, Box 190.

47 There were also less important subcommittees on Disarmament (Chairman, Judge Moore) and a Political one, the role of which seems to have been rather vague (Chairman, George Marblee). The list of those on these subcommittees can be found in a number of archives, including those of Sumner Welles and in the Berle Papers, Box 54.

48 See Pasvolsky, 29 January 1940: 'The Basis of an International Economic Program in Connection with a Possible Conference of Neutrals'; Berle Papers, Box 54.

49 Berle to Pasvolsky, 16 January 1940; Berle Papers, Box 54.

50 Hamilton Fish Armstrong (CFFR and ACPWFP), 13 March 1942; Armstrong Papers Box 78.

51 Stimson, Diary, entries for 17 November 1942; and 23 January, 1 February, 28 March and 6 April 1943.

52 Pasvolsky, 'Plan of Work' 1941, no date, and 28 January 1941, 'Reorientation of American Foreign Policy'; Pasvolsky Papers, Box 7.

53 Speech by Roosevelt, Draft of 15 December 1942; Berle Papers, Box 65.
54 'Memorandum for the Secretary: Principal Features of our Post-War Work', 30 November 1943; Pasvolsky Papers, Box 7.
55 Minutes of a meeting between representatives of the CFFR and State Department, 1 May 1940; Armstrong Papers, Box 73.
56 Group on Peace Aims of European Nations – 'Purpose of the Group', Philip E. Mosely, 28 April 1941; Armstrong Papers, Box 73.
57 Winant (London) to Department of State, 29 February 1940; Berle Papers, Box 65.
58 For example, there was a meeting of the National Economic and Social Planning Association (NESPA), which later became the 'National Planning Association', which was addressed by Julian Huxley of Political and Economic Planning (PEP) on 5 December 1939 in Washington, where they were told about Britain's war aims ('What we are fighting for') attended by Pasvolsky, Galbraith, Viner, Berle, Feis and many other State Department officials. For more discussion of this see Chapter 4.
59 See, for example, 'Peace Aims of the United Nations', 27 August 1942 and Armstrong (by then Second in Command to Winant in London) to Stott (State Department), 9 January 1945, Armstrong Papers, Box 78.
60 CFFR Peace Aims Group, 'Digest of Preliminary Views Regarding the Peace Aims of European Nations', 19 December 1941 and 'Suggestions for Group Studies', 1 September 1942; Armstrong Papers, Box 73.
61 All of which can be found in the Armstrong Papers, Box 75.
62 Cf. Minutes of AC-1, 12 February 1942; Welles Papers, Box 190.
63 Hull to Armstrong, 12 July 1943; Joseph C. Green (State Department) to Armstrong, 6 April 1944; Armstrong Papers, Boxes 78 and 79.
64 For a discussion of Kennan's constant urging for State Department reform see David Mayers, *George Kennan and the Dilemmas of US Foreign Policy* (New York, Oxford University Press, 1988, pp. 25 and 58–62. On Kennan see also Wilson D. Miscamble, *George F. Kennan and the Making of American Foreign Policy, 1947–1950* (Princeton University Press, 1982) and Anders Stephanson, *Kennan and the Art of Foreign Policy* (Cambridge, Mass., Harvard University Press, 1989).
65 See, for example, Armstrong (London) to Bowman (Washington), 7 December 1944; Armstrong Papers, Box 79.
66 A copy can be found in the Berle Papers, Box 65.
67 From my analysis of files in the Armstrong Papers, Box 74.
68 Joe D. Hill to Dulles, 5 November 1943; Dulles Papers, Box 23.
69 Dulles to Welles, 19 August 1942; Dulles Papers, Box 21.
70 Dulles, 'Peace Without Platitudes', reprint from *Fortune*, January 1942, first published late 1941; Dulles Papers, Box 21.
71 Dulles, Report of Trip to England, 28 June–25 July 1942, draft dated 30 July. Dulles Papers, Box 21; also in Sumner Welles Papers, Roosevelt Library, Box 190.
72 Dulles, speech to the National Study Conference, Ohio, 3 March 1942; Dulles Papers, Box 21.
73 Dulles to Cameron P. Hall of the Board of Christian Education of the Federal Churches of America, 3 December 1943; Dulles Papers, Box 23.

74 See, for example, Dulles to Viscount Astor, 18 February 1943; Dulles Papers, Box 22.

75 Published in *Christianity and Crisis*, vol. 3, no. 4, 22 March 1943. The press release with Dulles' comments was issued on 18 March 1943; Dulles Papers, Box 22.

76 Dulles' account of interview with Roosevelt, 26 March 1943; Dulles Papers, Box 22.

77 Dulles to Sumner Welles, 6 May 1943; Memo on the Relief and Rehabilitation Agency (later the United Nations Relief and Rehabilitation Agency (UNRRA)) of 27 July 1943; Dulles Papers, Box 22.

78 Dulles to Welles, 26 February 1943; Dulles Papers, Box 22.

79 'Statement by the Republican Post War Advisory Council of the Republican National Committee', draft of August 1943; Dulles Papers, Box 23.

80 Dulles to H. Alexander Smith (Republican National Committee), 10 August 1943, and Smith to Dulles, 13 August 1943; Dulles to Arthur Hays Sulzberger (of the *New York Times*), 21 October 1943: Dulles Papers Box 23.

81 Draft speech by Dulles, 8 October 1944, circulated to Republican Committee; Dulles Papers, Box 23.

82 Dulles to Dewey, 5 October 1944 and suggested press release of same date. On the Pearl Harbor allegations, Dulles received a detailed memo dated 27 June 1944 from General Walter C. Short, in charge of air defence at Pear Harbor in December 1941. This was discussed with Cordell Hull on 24 August 1944 and not used by Dulles in any way: Dulles Papers, Box 23.

83 Dulles to Dewey, 30 March 1944 and 21 August 1944; Dulles Papers, Box 23.

84 Dulles to Hull, 17 November 1943; Dulles Papers, Box 22.

85 See Herbert Hoover to Dulles on Lippman, 30 September 1943 and Dulles' correspondence with Lippman during 1944; Dulles Papers, Boxes 22 and 24.

86 'Preliminary Memorandum on the Bases of an International Economic Program in Connection with a Possible Conference of Neutrals', 29 January 1940; Berle Papers, Box 54.

87 Armstrong's memo to the State Department ACPWFP of 13 March 1942; Armstrong Papers, Box 78.

88 Cox to Hopkins, Memorandum on 'Commitment to Use Force to Secure the Peace', 11 January 1945 and Cox to Hopkins, 31 December 1942; Hopkins Papers, Box 329.

89 Roosevelt to Morris L. Ernst, 8 March 1943, *F.D.R.: His Personal Letters, 1928–1945*, p. 1407.

90 The particular case in point is that of Sumner Welles, who was allowed to resign during the Moscow Conference of October 1943 in favour of Hull, with whom Sumner Welles often disagreed. Roosevelt saw that Hull was a vital ally with Congress: see Chapter 5 for more details.

91 Sainsbury, *Churchill and Roosevelt*, p. 8.

4

The 'first follower' and Roosevelt's NWO: Britain, 1940–43

Introduction

The purpose of this chapter is twofold. The first aim is to show, in a similar fashion to the last chapter, the way in which official and non-official thinking in Britain drew up its agenda for the post-war period during the war. This will be done by examining, in somewhat less detail than for the United States, the machinery, practice and thinking of various key groupings within British official and non-official circles to show how they interacted. A second aim is to show how these processes chimed, or did not so agree, with thinking already described in the United States. Sometimes this process can be described reasonably accurately, as we have documentary evidence; sometimes the usual leaps of imagination will be needed. A pattern of intellectual concern in the thinking of wartime Britain can be identified, particularly the widely felt need to rebuild the post-war economies and social systems in a spirit that took lessons from the inter-war years and from the experience of the war. In so doing Britain developed an approach to the future that was to have elements of harmony, but also elements of discord, with the American NWO. Both of these aspects will be explored in the following pages.

British war and post-war aims came to be developed through a very lop-sided discussion with American power, with a clear lead coming from the United States. Britain emerges in the role of 'first follower'. It has often been said that the British are deeply suspicious of grand designs in politics, that they believe in an organic development based on sound 'realist' or 'pragmatic' principles. A distrust of revolutionary states such as France in the eighteenth century and Russia in the twentieth is certainly ingrained in the national consciousness and probably explains the weak hold that extremist parties have managed to realise in British politics. There is a correspondingly innate belief that grand external designs create internal divisions, a belief that was a key feature of British planning for the post-war world in both world wars. Hence, as in 1914–18, Prime Minister Winston Churchill was more interested in winning the war than in thinking about a hypothetical peace, partly because he did not wish to create even the semblance of disunity within Britain. He and the Government were essentially pushed into such a definition by internal and external pressure, internally especially from the Labour Party and, externally, from the twin impulses of Hitler and the United States. If Britain did not agree with Hitler's New Order, it had to say what it wished in its place. Roosevelt and others in the United States essentially came up with the key answers. It might be asserted that in so doing, the United States acted in an 'imperial' way, as Geir Lundestad seems to be implying in his recent book on European integration, admittedly one that focuses on the post-war period.[1]

The majority of the processes described and analysed in this chapter will concentrate on the period before the major Allied Conferences of 1943–45 in order to elucidate the main strands of thinking within both 'official' British circles and those that can be deemed 'unofficial', although it is realised that in wartime such divisions become difficult, as they did in the United States. This chapter will therefore be succeeded by another that aims to show how the 'imaginings' of the early wartime period were translated into concrete proposals, and particularly into the machinery that launched the plans for post-war Europe, economic reconstruction and the United Nations, as well as into the disillusionment with the 'Grand Alliance' that in turn was converted into the Cold War. Since there have been a number of books on this period of Anglo-American relations, we shall again only delve into great historical detail where this is merited to bring out the central NWO ideas that were emerging during the conflict.

The machinery of PWP in Britain

Britain did not have the luxury of resources and the opportunities of the American PWP planners. Most of its energy, certainly until early 1943, was directed into survival. But there was also a clear realisation in both official and private circles that Hitler's 'New Order' had to be countered by an alternative view of a civilised future. There was almost universal agreement that Hitler could not be allowed to impose his version of the future on the world and growing horror about what was known of Nazi activities in Occupied Europe. As General Smuts put it in 1944, '[y]ou must speak the language of the Old Testament to describe what is happening in Europe today.'[2] The problem was one of how to formulate a better world without destroying British ideals, some of which, such as the maintenance of the Empire, were in total disagreement with the ideas of the United States, upon which Britain increasingly realised it relied. It has also been argued in recent British historiography that there were significant elements in Britain prepared to accept and even accommodate the Nazi victories in Europe in exchange for a kind of independence. This was not fully resolved until after Churchill became Prime Minister in May 1940.[3]

The central thrust of British planning for the peace centred on the social welfare system that so many politicians and commentators wished to establish. It aimed to rebuild a society that had been severely physically damaged in a way not experienced across the Atlantic. Britain had also been emotionally damaged, not, curiously perhaps, by the defeats at Dunkirk and the bombing of the 'Blitz', but by the realisation that it could not stem the German tide as it had in 1914 or even stop the 'yellow hordes' that took Singapore and much of the Empire in the Far East with such consummate ease. It is said that Churchill only truly wept tears of despair when Singapore fell. There was virtually no disagreement among British political parties about the desirability of maintaining the Empire. The British Empire was part of Britain's core identity, instilled in every schoolchild and believed in with an intensity that can now only elicit disbelief in younger generations.

The link between Britain and the United States was initially on the reasonably neutral ground of how to pay for the war and reconstruction. However, this rapidly turned into an arena of disagreement over the emphasis that was needed about what *kind* of politics and economics had to be pursued in order to finance this and what it was to be *for*, not just in the shorter term, but also in the NWO after the fighting had, hopefully, ceased. The United States' view of the desirability of a future open world economy was in seeming contradiction to those in Britain who wanted to retain the Empire and its trading preferences. As we saw in the previous chapter, the American Establishment had already decided that Britain and the world had to change and a great deal of pressure was exerted to effect that change. The image that is sometimes presented of a harmonious Atlantic Alliance is consequently not the whole truth.

While the key expression in the United States during the Second World War was 'post-war planning', in Britain it was 'reconstruction', a process presented as being authentically British and domestically popular, while the more difficult problem of how this was to be paid for could be left until a convenient later date. As Churchill spent most of the war concentrating on the relationship between the Allies and the prosecution of the war, he left most of this process to his Deputy Prime Minister, Clement Attlee. Halifax has often been quoted as saying that Churchill was 'pretty bored by anything except the [conduct] of the actual war'.[4] While Churchill has until recently escaped criticism for his conduct of the war, he has been more effectively criticised for his relative neglect of the post-war settlement in Britain itself. This has led to a rather contradictory revisionist assault on the Churchill myth, either for not doing enough to counter the proposals for a brave new welfare state world of widespread government intervention, seen as the main vehicles of post-war British decline, or for not doing more to defend the British Empire. He has also been accused of racism and being a warmonger.

Churchill's role was the inevitably unhappy one of having often to go cap in hand to the Americans for help in the war effort and in the process having to give up many of the hallowed principles that had been established for Imperial Preference in trade and, indeed, arguably, that of the Empire itself.[5] It took a great man to be able to take such great and difficult decisions. As a great historian he would not have been surprised by the later attacks.

However, it would be foolish to assert that the central ideas of international organisation, including the post-war economic and strategic order and the future of Europe, including that of the defeated states, did not provide for some major British input into the major Conferences and in such bodies as the EAC (see next chapter) based in London. Although the Americans often made their own decisions and then asked the British to accept them, they also listened to what they were being told. The United Kingdom was the junior partner in this NWO and constantly made aware of the fact, and indeed the British seem on occasion to have been only too helpful to the Americans, but it was in the full knowledge that they needed the Americans in Europe after the war ended if any kind of durable peace were to be possible. Often this did not mean that the British were not listened to, but rather that much of their thinking went along parallel lines to those in Washington. Many British statements echoed the American State Department's, Roosevelt's and (particularly but not exclusively) Hull's obsession with both the economic causes of war and the corresponding economic and social cures for conflict. So it is often difficult to say which was the philosophical chicken and which the policy egg. It would be easy to suggest that Churchill was merely being bullied by Roosevelt when he signed the Atlantic Charter, for example, or that he merely deferred to Roosevelt because Harry Hopkins had told London that Roosevelt 'regarded the postwar settlement ... as being his particular reserve'.[6] It would be more accurate to say that he realised that after the war his blend of Imperial vision would have to give way to a more progressive view of the world, especially as hardly anyone in Britain foresaw Britain having entirely to give up its role as a global, and indeed as an Imperial, power.

Even before the United States joined the war there were signs of a developing fellow feeling that augured well for a future collaboration. Julian Huxley of the PEP Group was typical of this when he was asked to address a meeting in Washington in 1939 attended by Pasvolsky, Berle and a number of prominent economists. For Huxley the main problem of the Versailles settlement had been its dependence on purely political and military solutions to conflict. The inter-war period had shown the hollowness of that dependence, and the Nazis had exploited it. The battle was therefore an ideological one, about how governments and states should relate to their peoples' needs. From now on, 'we cannot separate foreign policy from commercial policy ... The only way of marrying the political elements without destroying freedom, is by working out clearly the essentials of a free civilisation and directing according to them, both politics and economics.' But the state alone could not achieve this, it was essential that the choice be realised: it was either 'subjection to the Nazi war machine or a voluntary participation in new forms of international co-operation'. The political corollary of this combined a need to prevent Germany ever repeating its actions of 1914 and 1939 either by a partition of Germany or by creating 'a permanent alliance between the western powers [i.e. Britain and France] and either Russia or the U.S.A.'.[7] This awareness of the necessity of combined political European and global economic solutions chimed increasingly well with the thinking in Washington that was described in Chapter 3.

Cabinet planning

With Churchill mainly intent on winning the war, the majority of the British negotiating input into the big questions of PWP came from the Foreign Office under Anthony Eden and particularly from a few key Foreign Office and Treasury officials, notably John Maynard Keynes, and were by direct contact with the Americans. An early Cabinet committee set up by Neville Chamberlain and chaired by Sir George Schuster to study problems in connection with the peace in early 1940 has left little trace.[8] The Cabinet Committee on War Aims, set up in August 1940 by Churchill, has been more remarked upon. It was chaired by Deputy Prime Minister Clement Attlee, to whom Churchill left many of what he saw as thankless and irrelevant tasks, 'irrelevant' at that stage of the war when survival was by no means assured. Churchill sank the high aspirations of this grouping with a dismissive 'precise aims would be compromising, whereas vague principles would disappoint'.[9]

Churchill was more than aware that to discuss 'principles' could be divisive in a Cabinet made up of ideological foes, only united by the war effort. There is ample evidence that he was right, with the existence of a very active Imperialist lobby, particularly epitomised by Leo Amery, Secretary of State for India. However, twin pressures forced such a discussion to take place. The first of these was the demand of the Labour Party for social reform after the war, of which the Beveridge Report of 1942 was the main symbol. The second is possibly more important for our purposes, but linked to the first. Roosevelt and, especially, Cordell Hull, were adamant that there could be no repeat of an aimless war, as they saw the case to have been in 1914–18 until the Fourteen Points had been issued. The central thrust of this was, as described in Chapter 3, to realise a world view, summed up in the 'Four Freedoms' speech of January 1941, that was inimical to all forms of economic nationalism and linked to democratic ideals as understood by Americans, particularly individual human rights. There is no reason to believe that the majority in Britain or the Empire in any way disagreed with this basic blueprint; indeed Roosevelt is said to have elaborated it in talks with the British Ambassador to Washington, Lord Lothian.[10] The only real problem was how to implement it without making the same compromises as had been made with Wilson's Fourteen Points.

There was also an awareness of the importance of public opinion and how it must be kept solidly behind the Government for the long term, not just for the emotional needs of the moment, as had happened in 1919. What had been called 'the apotheosis of public opinion', the Versailles Peace Conference, had turned into a political nemesis for its architects and, indeed, for the entire settlement. As R.B. McCallum put it in 1944, '[o]ne probable reason for the failure of the [Versailles] peace is that there was such divergence of opinion as to the sentiments on which peace depended and the means by which the coming of war might be stayed'.[11]

Roosevelt's desire not to be seen to be talking prematurely about the peace was thus mirrored in London. But it was also matched by both better information about the content of public opinion and by a desire to use it to support the war effort in a more sophisticated way than had been the case in 1914–18. This was particularly the case in the preparation of British public opinion for the relationship with Russia by the Ministry of Information. The Gallup poll had been instituted in Britain after 1938, the BBC had an Audience Research Department and there was the mass of useful inform-ation provided by 'Mass Observation' as well as Home Intelligence Reports prepared by the Ministry. As we shall see below, this Ministry, especially as led by Brendan Bracken after July 1941, played a major role in pushing Britain into a definition, and defence of, its war aims, those that became the basis of planning for the peace.[12]

Early contacts with the Americans

The Cabinet realised from 1939 on that Britain could not survive without American help and they also knew that this help would be contingent on an agreement on war aims. To cite but one example of this realisation, the Foreign Office drafted a 'statement' that had been requested by American Ambassador to London, Joseph Kennedy, to lay out the probable con-sequences of a British and French defeat. In a document unrivalled during practically the entire war for its hyperbole, it spoke of 'chaos', 'world wide upheaval', entire swathes of the world being 'swept away' and the end of 'intellectual sanity' (France) and 'individual freedom' (Britain). The Treasury was particularly angered by what was a clear putting of all the negotiating cards on the table at once, a complaint that it was to make more than once in the future. Mainly it was irritated by the tone of hysterical hyperbole. Keynes wrote to S.D. Waley in the Treasury that, 'I infer that you see as well as anyone else that the enclosed [the draft of the letter] is feeble and banal' and that it could have been better written by an 'American novelist'. The significance of the statement is that it was deemed a necessary exercise at all and reflects a real sense that America was vital for British survival, a fact which Keynes was not disputing.[13] Britain was having to get used to being the *demandeur*.

After the defeat of France this realisation grew stronger and in July 1940 the Imperial Chiefs of Staff explicitly stated that they hoped the United States would 'give us full economic and financial support, without which we do not think we could continue the war with any chance of success'.[14] Equally, as the Secretary of State for the Dominions put it to Cabinet on 19 July 1940, to persuade the United States Congress to support Britain it was necessary to counter Hitler's intention to 'represent himself as founding a new European economic system which would sweep away customs barriers ..., wastefulness and inefficiency of an anachronistic capitalist system and all other obstacles which have prevented European economic co-ordination ... [within] an all-embracing and benign totalitarian system'. Maybe Congress would be willing to accept Hitler's claim that Britain was 'the sole barrier to this new economic paradise'. He felt that it was necessary for politicians on both sides of the Atlantic to stress the virtues of 'breaking down artificial barriers to trade' but that this could 'only be achieved by free peoples freely negotiating on an individual basis'. The United States must be consulted immediately about how this might be done: 'Let brain trusts be set going to work out an alternative democratic plan ...'[15] Another memorandum, by Duff Cooper, the then Minister of Information, was considered by the Cabinet at this period. The *leitmotif* of all these suggestions is that they all stressed that the British should have the feeling they were fighting for something, 'the future at home' and for a 'Europe united in goodwill and friendship'.[16] It had taken Hitler offering Britain peace terms to underline the necessity of having an answer to him ready.

Although by the end of 1940 it was clearer that Britain might survive, it was also obvious that the earlier apocalyptic visions of 'chaos' might still be realised without solid Anglo-American cooperation. Lothian therefore persuaded Churchill to send a letter to Roosevelt after his re-election in November 1940 setting out help that Britain would welcome. Lord Lothian 'acted entirely off his own bat' and had to persuade Churchill to send a letter laying out Britain's continuing predicament, especially due to shipping losses and financial overstretch.[17] This and other public statements by Lothian in the United States did much to confirm Roosevelt's desire to act in a 'Lincolnesque' way towards Britain, although this was tempered by a desire not to let this be done without some financial and longer-term cost *quid pro quo* from those he was determined to help. As was stressed in the previous chapter, among American public opinion, in the State Department and indeed within Roosevelt's Cabinet, suspicions of British intentions were still very alive.

There is a temptation to see the period between November 1940, when talk of war aims petered out, and the Atlantic Charter in August 1941 as a somewhat dead period in post-war thinking, a temptation to which many historians have yielded. Some of them also portray the period between March 1941, when Lend–Lease was approved by Congress, and the Atlantic Charter as especially dead.[18] Nothing could be further from the truth. The period must be seen as defining the relative future relationship of the United States and Britain after the war, a relationship essentially of 'leader' and 'follower'.

Churchill knew that he had to tie the Americans to Britain's fortunes, but he was not at all sure that he would be given a good hearing in the United States. As we have seen, there were considerable misgivings among some prominent Americans, even Roosevelt and especially Berle, about the desirability of propping up Britain without it agreeing to fundamental changes in its relationship both with the United States and with the world in general, especially as concerned economic matters. As has been stressed, most Americans felt a great deal of suspicion towards Britain in 1939–40, as Duff Cooper and others realised when they visited Washington. Cooper summed it up as '[i]t was to be hoped that the British would win, but it was to be hoped still more that no American boy's life would be thrown away fighting for the British Empire. The United States had won the last war, and had hardly been thanked for it. They had not even been repaid the money they had lent. The United States had been caught once; they were not going to be caught a second time. I think that is not an unfair sketch of moderate American feeling at that time.'[19]

Thus it was entirely logical that Roosevelt and his advisors should want to 'tie in' Britain to their vision of the future. This 'tying in' initially emerged as the policy which became known as 'Lend–Lease', by which Congress agreed to provide Britain with a huge array of military hardware on a use or return basis, most famously fifty ageing destroyers for use as convoy escorts, in exchange for the long-term lease of a number of important naval bases in the Empire.[20] The details of this are less important for our purposes than the commitments made in the informal discussions that came before and after the signing of the Lend–Lease legislation on 11 March 1941, discussions which did much to concentrate minds in both London and Washington about what the post-war era must look like and particularly the principles on which it must be based. These discussions culminated in the joint declarations of the Atlantic Charter in August 1941 at Placentia Bay.

Roosevelt had already decided, arguably with the Chicago 'X' speech of 5 October 1937, that he would have to help Britain in the event of war. One version is that he dreamed up the basic version of Lend–Lease over whisky and cigarettes with King George VI when the two met at Hyde Park

(Roosevelt's home in the Hudson Valley) shortly before war broke out.[21] When in late 1940 Churchill wrote to Roosevelt to congratulate him on a third term in office on Lothian's suggestion, the US Treasury informed Churchill almost immediately that Morgenthau wished a personal envoy to be sent to discuss a Lend–Lease option, with Sir Frederick Philips being suggested as he had already been to Washington earlier that year. The last few crucial pages of Churchill's letter were about the future of the Anglo-American relationship. The most difficult part of this to draft was about the financial aspects of this, or how to pay for American *matériel* without destroying Britain's reserves of gold and foreign currencies. Keynes suggested that these important aspects should be left for a separate letter that should be 'personally presented to the President' and should not be put on the table prematurely. Keynes knew that any agreement with the United States would have to be paid for, either in gold or in some other way – the 'Consideration'. His suggestion was the ceding of British assets in South America, as the alternative might be 'ceding the raw material resources of the British Empire'.

In his comments on the draft of Churchill's letter, Keynes also suggested that financial help for Britain should be explicitly linked to post-war economic planning, in full realisation that the Americans would so link the two issues. He wanted Churchill to stress that America needed a strong and equal British Commonwealth, 'neither of them must be placed in the position of being the suppliant client of the other ... we must be in the full sense of the word comrades'. He also evoked the spectre of 'violent social revolution in England ... [in addition] to the other problems we shall jointly have to shoulder'. Although these dire warnings do not seem to have emerged in the final draft sent to Roosevelt, they are important indicators of the level of awareness that existed in London that the issue of a post-war settlement was almost as grave as the immediate problems of possible defeat by Hitler.[22]

The Lend–Lease agreement was negotiated remarkably swiftly, and benefited greatly, as Reynolds points out, from the desire of the Americans not to re-create the pattern of inter-war Allied debt that had so soured relations and made a common approach to the peace so difficult, although the Americans did insist on the liquidation of many British assets.[23] The draft agreement was brought back by Keynes to London in January 1941. The key concessions made by Britain included a 'statement in very general terms about the desirability of freeing the channels of trade' but also included the caveat that they had to avoid this 'tying us up in undertakings we could not fulfil', and especially a 'possible revision of the Ottawa Agreements' that had established Imperial Preference. A Cabinet Committee on Post War External Economic Problems and Anglo-American Cooperation, which met for the first time on 7 February 1941, had as its main task the discussion of various trade policy options, including a possible phasing out of the Ottawa Agreements.[24]

During the rest of 1941 the American Administration continued to heap pressure on Britain and its Empire to accept this drastic option, and to make it crystal clear that the main 'consideration' for Lend–Lease in the long term would be the end of the Ottawa Agreements. In Washington in April 1941 Cordell Hull spoke to the new British Ambassador, Lord Halifax, to make it quite clear how keen he was on post-war cooperation and of his wishes to keep up the discussion of bilateral trade negotiations. His tactic, as expressed by Halifax and communicated to the British Cabinet by Eden, was that 'we might both be prepared to keep our respective wild-men in order', by which was clearly meant the Imperial lobby in London and the more extreme advocates of enforced British cooperation in Washington. Halifax recounted that Roosevelt had a few days earlier emphasised both economic and security cooperation by the two states and how the discussion had explicitly linked these questions and the granting of Lend–Lease.[25]

Some in London were outraged by this, a Colonial Office official railing against 'flatulent proposals for declarations of economic policy' and stoutly defending the Ottawa Agreements against hypocritical American attack when the United States had 'a skeleton or two in their cupboard on tariff matters'. The biggest opponent was Leo Amery, who bombarded Eden with excoriations of the American position. But the Dominions were on the whole not against the proposal entirely, and the Treasury came round to the belief that the Most-Favoured Nation clauses being proposed by Hull would on balance benefit Imperial interests and certainly not 'produce the millennium as rapidly as Mr. Amery supposes', a view reiterated on a number of occasions. Kingsley Wood also saw this as a 'positive idea to set against Hitler's New Order'. Eden played the role of ignorant innocence to perfection when faced with Amery's fury, pretending not to understand 'technical matters of this sort'.[26]

In June Keynes, again in Washington, was asked if Britain would agree to set up a joint Anglo-American Commission to examine post-war economic cooperation, to which Churchill and the Chancellor initially replied with a request that this should await the 'proper time' and that the proper subject now was 'particular concrete questions', but on being warned by Beaverbrook (Minister of Economic Warfare) that this would just annoy the Americans and make them liable to ask for payment in cash, Churchill agreed to continue consideration of the idea through Keynes. It has been suggested that Churchill was not against the idea of free trade, and this was probably true, but he had to keep a balance between his own views and his 'wild men' while also keeping Roosevelt happy, not an easy task. So Halifax suggested in June the setting up of parallel British and American groups to study such questions and a later meeting 'to compare the results of their labours'.[27]

Keynes played the key role in all of this, in spite of the assertion that he was widely disliked in Washington for his arrogant manner and has been blamed for forcing the Americans to be so explicit about free trade as an essential element of the post-war system: 'The Economic Consequences of Mr. Keynes', as Reynolds puts it.[28] Keynes certainly also disliked the way 'nothing is secret, nothing is confidential. The President laughed when I said that his method of deceiving the enemy was apparently to publish so much vital information that they would not have time to read it.' The important point is that he was taken by the Americans as a heavyweight and that he obviously respected Roosevelt himself, whatever he may have thought of his subordinates.[29] Eric (Later Lord) Roll commented that '[i]t is impossible to imagine how the Lend–Lease settlement or the loan negotiations or the arrangements for the post-war institution would have come out if the guidance of Keynes in the preparation of policy and in actual negotiation had not been available.'[30] Keynes has to be seen as having played a key role in mapping out not only the economic, but also the political, future relationship between Britain and America, the best man for such a delicate task. Those were desperate times when politics could not be separated from economics, if indeed they ever can be. Roosevelt himself took these negotiations from his own Treasury and gave them to the State Department, which, as Keynes telegraphed, was 'on the grounds that it raises political rather than financial issues *which is all to the good*'.[31]

The 'Consideration' that Britain was to pay for Lend–Lease was therefore certainly financial and in kind, such as the bases (which would have to be maintained partly by Britain over several years), the replacement of lost ships, American access to raw materials (especially rubber and tin) and some transfer of assets, although Halifax said that these costs were 'not very objectionable'.[32] But much more importantly it was *political*, as Keynes himself encouraged Roosevelt to think it should be. Keynes was worried, as was the President, that anything, like debt, that 'impaired our post-war buying capacity for American goods' would benefit neither nation.[33] So Keynes signalled that Roosevelt might, for example, be willing to accept post-war British cooperation in an international police force as part of the 'Consideration' for Lend–Lease, after being present at a long discussion with Halifax and the President in early June 1941. Keynes commented to the Chancellor of the Exchequer that '[t]hat sounds to me, at first sight, rather a good idea, but it needs thinking about'. Keynes and Halifax also ranged widely with Roosevelt over a host of other issues, including Russia ('"Now you are making things difficult" ... smiled [Roosevelt]'), unilateral disarmament (for Europe only) and Europe in general, where Britain and America would have to act as the 'policemen'. Roosevelt avoided detail, 'in very much the same terms as our own Prime Minister', as Keynes put it.[34]

The issues raised by Roosevelt demonstrated clearly that he wished to see not only economic but also political global reform after the war on a quite dramatic scale and that Britain would have to help him in this. The letters sent back by Keynes from Washington in June 1941 convey the sense he felt of great ideas and events in the making. He was convinced that '[t]he post-war world will bring such vast changes that we may gain little if we hang on too resolutely to our nineteenth century economic anachronisms ... we shall gain much more than we are likely to be called upon to sacrifice as "consideration." Possibilities of Anglo-American cooperation after the war open up wide, fruitful fields ... But it will all be much better if we do not hang back too much in *details.* [*sic*]'[35]

Churchill was not entirely pleased about the way the discussion was developing and asked Keynes to desist in his more intemperate musings with Roosevelt until the Cabinet had considered them. The Treasury was also alarmed that Keynes was becoming sucked into 'Cordell Hull's ideas about post-war economic policy'. But Halifax continued to insist that it 'was obviously of the first importance not to quarrel with the Americans on this issue', that Britain should just try and fudge the issue for as long as possible.[36] The State Department was well aware, in Berle's words, that the British 'have become increasingly nervous about any step taken here which might bear in any degree on European politics', but also, as he continued in the same memo to Hull, 'even though the step concerned strictly American affairs'.[37]

It should also be noted that Roosevelt also found allies for his economic proposals when he talked to Dominion officials, some of whom were as least as enthusiastic as Keynes. The Australian High Commission in London communicated to the Cabinet its belief that Roosevelt's vision of 'British Empire – American understanding', explicitly linking 'peace and security' and economic and social questions was correct: 'we are likely to see the history of 1919–1939 repeated unless we evolve definite plans for world reconstruction'. Roosevelt's Four Freedoms speech had shown how this might be done, and by linking 'peace and economic security' to create 'social justice' more concretely, 'Freedom from Want' would improve Empire trade, as better diets would help trade in general, but principally trade in agricultural products. The New Zealand contribution to this debate can be summed up by their comment after discussing the matter with Roosevelt himself that although Imperial Preference had been very good for them 'that [is] not to say that it could not be replaced by something better. That depended on the United States.' The President agreed. 'The main objection from the "Imperial camp" came from the London Colonial Office [Lord Moyne] and the India Office [Leo Amery], not from those they purported to represent.'[38]

The Atlantic Charter led to a long period of very detailed collaboration between Britain and the United States on post-war economic cooperation, bringing in Russia after the end of 1941 and culminating in the thirteen-point 'Pasvolsky Agenda'[39] of July 1942, which laid out extensive proposals for post-war trade cooperation between Britain and the United States and seeing to the 'import requirements of the deficit countries', as well as of wider problems of investment, monetary relations, and even shipping and the 'air problem'. Many of these proposals became tied into Vice-President Henry Wallace's ideas about commodity agreements and controls, and especially with his obsession with wheat, and can be seen as the intellectual forerunner of 1960s attempts to set up 'buffer stocks' and the like, all of which have conspicuously failed. What has remained is the idea of international cooperation on economic matters under American leadership, now so taken for granted among the Organisation for Economic Cooperation and Development (OECD) countries that it is difficult to envisage how difficult it was to get the idea accepted even in the depths of the Second World War.

The Atlantic Charter from the British perspective

In the end, the text of the Atlantic Charter did indeed fudge the issue of free trade and that of imperialism for the moment, with Roosevelt accepting that the issues were too delicate for concrete proposals to be forced upon the British, although Hull and Berle, among others, wanted to push both far more. As Acheson put it to Keynes, Roosevelt was more interested in the 'general approach to the economics of the post-war world', not its detail, although when asked by Keynes whether acceptance of Article VII 'would preclude a system of imperial preference' he agreed it probably would. And, as Roosevelt admitted to an Australian visitor in November 1941, the Charter 'meant the end of the Ottawa Agreement, but he believed that target he was working at meant a great deal more for world and for British countries than the limited pre-war bilateralism on the Ottawa model'.[40] The issue was now firmly on the agenda, and its eventual inclusion in subsequent thinking on a post-war settlement was evidence of the American vision being incorporated and Britain being forced to climb down. There is little doubt that any on the British side, in which we also have to include the Dominions, saw the compromises they had made as meaning the eventual end of the British Empire, even though that was to be the result. But the links that were implicitly made in the Charter between a free trading system and self-determination did effectively sound the death knell of the British Empire.

Wider British reaction to the Atlantic Charter was naturally dependent on the opinion of the reactor, but was generally positive, Smuts calling it a 'Magna Charter of the Nations'. He agreed that the war was a 'fight to the death for man's rights and liberties, and for the personal ideals of mans' ethical and spiritual life'. It was also because there had been a realisation that 'certain patent social and economic evils' could only be settled internationally for the 'good of achieving common justice and fair play for all'. And for this the Russians, and most of all the Americans, were necessary allies: 'Not that I deplore Pearl Harbour! From our point of view it was a heavy price but well worth paying for the immense gains accrued.' Very few men could have made so explicit a blending of Imperial and British imagery with the new ideas of the Charter and got away with it. Smuts' role as an Imperial icon meant he could.[41]

Many in Britain, on all sides of the political divide, resented being preached at by Roosevelt. There was not universal acceptance of this American ideological leadership. Attlee summed this up in a speech aptly titled 'The Lion has due the Lion's share', a reflection on the impact of the Charter in Britain written a year later – 'I know there were some of my friends in the Labour Movement who found it difficult to accept the need for force. I know there were many Conservatives who could not have accepted the necessary interdependence of peace and social justice [implicit in the Atlantic Charter].' Although Attlee understood these feelings, he still felt that Sumner Welles, whom he singled out (rightly) as a major architect of the Charter and the Four Freedoms idea, understood the nature of the future world they would have to live in together – the problem would not be 'primarily one of production, for the world can readily produce what mankind requires. The problem is rather of distribution and purchasing power.' Hence he believed that there would be 'differences of view' about how best to solve this problem, but not more than that.[42]

Even Attlee does not seem to have comprehended the depth of American feeling about the British Commonwealth, which for Attlee and most Britons was an incarnation of Rooseveltian ideals; 'an example to the world of something entirely new, a union of free peoples inspired by common ideals where no single partner is dominant over the rest'. Even (indeed especially) India had 'been given more than a century of internal peace and good government, a thing never known in her history …'. Hardly surprisingly perhaps, General Smuts' key speech to the House of Commons harped on the same message: 'One occasionally hears idle words about the decay of this country, about the approaching break up of the great world group we form. What folly and ignorance, what misreading of the real signs of the times!'[43] Even given the excuse of a need, in darkest 1942, to whistle in the dark, this might be seen as quite astonishing self-delusion.

As the war went on the depths of this delusion continued, with the Americans making it increasingly explicit that they expected to see the British Empire at least modified, or at least to help those 'preparing themselves to assume its obligations', as the United States had done in the Philippines and Cuba. As the State Department (most probably authored by Berle) put it in July 1942: 'The Atlantic Charter offers a complete cooperative relation between those who aspire to independence and those who possess it, as the most effective way to gain independence by those who seek it, and to preserve the independence of those now free.'[44] The British continued to prevaricate on the issue whenever it was brought up. When the Americans dropped their insistence on immediate 'independence' for colonial peoples in return for the phrase 'self-government', they were told that such ideas were 'vague and impractical'. When asked for a timetable for self-government in May 1943 the Foreign Office replied that this was an 'impossible goal'. They moreover appealed to American prejudices by stating that 'an enduring security system is not achieved by multiplying completely independent and small political entities all over the world', a point also clearly made by Carr and Cobban, among others, at the same period (see Chapter 8). There was thus some difficulty in coming to a common position on the fate of colonial peoples up to the beginning of discussions on the United Nations Charter in 1944. As Colonel Stanley expressed it to Isaiah Bowman of the State Department, who was accompanying Under-Secretary of State Stettinius to London in April 1944, '[a]ny statement of colonial policy should become part of a section on dependent peoples in the structure of world organization and should not be a joint declaration [by Britain and the United States]'.

This constituted an advance, thought Bowman, on the previous British position, which had been hostile 'towards any form of international control' of colonies. The point on which both sides met was on the need to maintain security in the post-war world, 'a general security system under which both military bases and economic matters may be agreed upon'.[45] But of course at the time most commentators on both sides of the Atlantic would not have included many of the states that did in fact become independent after the war, especially those in Africa and Asia (other than India), in the list of possible candidates for independence. It was thus possible for the United States and Britain to pretend that both fully understood the wishes of the other in this matter, at least while the war continued.

The debate in Britain about 'reconstruction'

As has been stressed, 'reconstruction' was the key word in British PWP. The dispute with the Americans that culminated in the Atlantic Charter was mainly because Britain wanted to be sure that it would have the resources after the war to rebuild prosperity, but not at the cost of the Allied disunity that had characterised the inter-war period. But as there was a rearguard action by the advocates of Imperial Preference, there was a similar attempt, equally doomed, to stop the tidal wave of public and informed opinion that wished to see not only a new world after the war, but also a new *Britain*.

The Labour Party in particular took very seriously the need for the post-war world to be 'fairer', especially in the economic and social spheres. In a May 1942 speech, Stafford Cripps stated that '[t]his war is not a mere struggle for territory or even for economic advantage to be won by this or that nation or class in the world … and [has] the positive aim of all those peoples who are determined to assert and to win their right to a new freedom – above all, freedom from want'.[46] They were very suspicious initially of both the American plans for an NWO as a plot against socialism but persuaded themselves that Roosevelt's commitment to the Atlantic Charter gave them a mandate to transform British society. Thus, as there were those who saw American views on the Empire as somehow 'compatible' with Britain's (which they were not), there were those who wished to see some sort of socialist, planned Britain after the war and who persuaded themselves that the Americans shared their dream.

Attlee's position as Deputy Prime Minister was far more than a titular post. Churchill left most of the 'Home Front' in the war to him while he was on his frequent forays abroad and in his general conduct of the military side of the war. Consequently Attlee and the Labour Party were able to get many of their ideas for the post-war world thoroughly aired and, in many cases, made official Government policy, such as the need for a National Health Service, a new educational system and a new housing policy, all key parts of the 'welfare state'.[47] The Labour Party held a number of key Government ministerial portfolios, with (among many others) Herbert Morrison as Home Secretary, Ernest Bevin as Minister of Labour, and Arthur Greenwood as Minister without Portfolio and, initially, Chairman of the Reconstruction Problems Committee, a post which he gave up to Sir William Jowitt in January 1942.

National or international 'planning' as the answer?

The answer to both national and international problems that many commentators arrived at in Britain was that of the need for some sort of 'planning'. Before the war the PEP Group had served as a focus for a discussion of the need for planning at a national and international level. Set up in 1931 at the height of the Depression, the PEP Group came to act as the focus for a huge amount of reflection during the war and had a great influence on the setting up of the British welfare state after it.[48] During the war itself the idea of PEP became almost sacrosanct and played its part in the thinking that went into Bretton Woods, an important part of the British input into the attempt to create a 'New Deal for the World'.[49]

Some argued vigorously against it. The most extreme of these was Friedrich Hayek, who had taught at the London School of Economics in the inter-war years and had crossed swords repeatedly with Keynes over state intervention in the national economy.[50] Cobban argued against it on the grounds that planning was the other face of 'economic nationalism' and often led to the same neglect of the real interests of the population. Professor David Mitrany took this view further after the war and suggested that planning would inevitably lead to a reduction of individual freedom. In 1941 he had said that '[c]entralized planning and controls, for both production and distribution, are no longer to be avoided' although he accepted that '[l]iberal democracy needs a redefinition of the public and private spheres of action', an idea that echoes Angell's comments in *The Fruits of Victory* of 1921 (which will be further explored in Chapter 7). However,

> [t]he only possible principle of democratic confirmation is that public action should be undertaken only when and insofar as the need for common action becomes evident and is accepted, for the sake of the common good. In that way … social needs might be satisfied as largely and justly as possible, while still leaving as wide a residue as possible for the free choice of the individual. This is fully as true in the international sphere. It is indeed the only way to combine as well as may be international organisation with national freedom.[51]

Later on, in 1942–43, Mitrany, in an echo of Cobban's fears, pointed out to a Fabian Society meeting on post-war organisation that 'national planning' had had the potential to create a 'nationalistic trend' contrary to the international aspirations of the world socialist movement. The next morning Mitrany relates that H.N. Brailsford (still a major luminary of the Labour Party) 'told me that he had been so worried that he had hardly slept that night'.[52]

Cobban and Mitrany had nonetheless to accept that planning in the context of the war could be 'in a sense inevitable' (as Angell had felt after 1919, as will be outlined in Chapter 7) and beneficial if done well. It was doubly inevitable in the context of the Second World War, as Soviet Russia would only accept a global economic system that allowed for central planning and was believed to have won the war because of it. France was also seen to be developing techniques of planning.[53] Many British commentators saw this as a huge lesson that had to be learnt, including Carr, whose interest in the Soviet Union must be seen as at least partly for the lessons that it could teach about planning.[54] American power had thus been merged with rational allocation of resources in such organisations as UNRRA to save the refugees of Europe (see Chapter 7). Such 'bodies will help to prolong this interdependence and regulation far into the inter-war years'. The end of the war did not mean the end of 'the state of emergency'. Even though some controls might be lifted, to remove them too suddenly would mean a return to 'uncontrolled private enterprise' and to 'risk the repetition of old mistakes'.[55] Cobban's warnings were likely to fall on deaf ears in the midst of such enthusiasm, and planning did not really go out of fashion completely until the 1980s.

Corelli Barnett, a virulent critic of all the planning that went on during the Second World War in Britain (and elsewhere), portrays Churchill and the other Conservatives as desperately trying to hold back the tide of these proposals, fed into the Cabinet from Transport House, the Trade Unions and Arnold Toynbee, Director of Studies at Chatham House, 'from his wartime field headquarters in Balliol [College, Oxford]'.[56] The truth is less conspiratorial. The widespread perception about the Beveridge Report and other measures to overhaul British social policy, as expressed by George

Orwell in 1944, was that 'the only discussion that arises is about whether it will be adopted in whole or in part. This blurring of party distinctions is happening in almost all countries ... the drift is towards a planned economy, partly because in an age of power politics national survival is felt to be more important than class warfare.'[57]

Churchill was put under some pressure by the Tory right within Cabinet not to give in to the growing demands for a social new order in Britain after the war, Brendan Bracken and Lord Beaverbrook in particular warning against the proposed new Health Service.[58] Attlee at times found it very difficult to work with Churchill: 'It is not easy to work with a man in the afternoon in the Cabinet room and then in the evening appear to differ from him on the public platform ... our socialist case must be stated with positive vigour.'[59] But there is no great reason to believe that Churchill was *opposed* to social reform, any more than he was opposed to a new kind of Europe. Often the Prime Minister was prepared to entertain more radical domestic and overseas plans than his Conservative counterparts. As will be stressed in Chapter 5, Roosevelt and Churchill shared a penchant for social engineering. So the view expressed by Land, Lowe and Whiteside that 'Churchill personally was hostile to social reform' is not the whole truth. He was, as they agree in any case, 'forced publicly to commit himself to a programme of reform' after the Beveridge Report was published in November 1942, such was its instant popularity. After January 1943 the Reconstruction Priorities Committee pushed the debate forward over the objections of the Treasury and any residual die-hards in the Cabinet.[60]

'Unofficial' thinking on the NWO in Britain, 1939–43

The first outside, and arguably the most important, body really to grasp the nettle of the links between the emerging American PWP and the 'Reconstruction' agenda in Britain was the RIIA (known as 'Chatham House'), the British equivalent of the CFFR in the United States, with which it had reasonably close contacts throughout the war. The establishment of Chatham House was officially suggested at the Paris Peace Conference. It performed the function throughout the inter-war years of serving as focus for the British articulation of foreign policy as well as being renowned as a centre both for academic research and policy development. It continued in this role during the war years in a number of 'Study Groups' which produced many memoranda on a vast array of issues in international relations, many of them country and area studies, the latter of which cannot detain us here. It would not be an exaggeration to say that Chatham House produced the majority of British 'new thinking' on the necessary revised international relations of the post-war period.

The most significant Groups within Chatham House during the Second

World War for our purposes were the 'World Order' Group (Number XIX), also known as the 'Steering Committee on the Problem of a European Settlement' after October 1939 and eventually renamed in February 1941 the 'Committee on Reconstruction', to which reported a number of sub-committees whose work will be outlined below.[61] The original impetus for such a Chatham House Group emerged from the growing crisis in Summer 1939, with its initial membership including Ernest Bevin, Sir Arthur Salter and Lord and David Astor, with Lord Hailey in the Chair, and was intended as a 'Survey of European Problems'. Germans had been included in this group, who somewhat surprisingly perhaps stayed in it after the outbreak of war.[62]

Immediate pre-war thinking in Chatham House

As was noted in Chapters 1 and 2, British thinking on the Versailles settlement had been very mixed from the outset. By the end of the 1930s these feelings were leading to a fundamental re-think about both the nature of international politics in general and Britain's future role in the world in particular. Chatham House was the venue for much of this reflection as it must be remembered that there were few academic centres in Britain for the study of international relations. One major result had been the ongoing dispute about the usefulness of international organisations as a guarantee of peace and the future of the nation state, with, roughly speaking, Alfred Zimmern and Philip Noel-Baker, the first two holders of the founding Chair of international relations at Aberystwyth, holding to what we would now call a 'cosmopolitan' line against E.H. Carr cleaving to a distinctly 'communitarian' line.[63] The most interesting Chatham House output for the purposes of this study in the immediate pre-war period was that of Group XV, 'The Limits of Nationalism'. The bulky report that was produced by Group XV, *Nationalism: Its Nature and Consequences*, was published in November 1939, but mainly written before this. The Chairman of the Group, and what we may call its 'leading theorist', was E.H. Carr, who also wrote the *Twenty Years' Crisis* during the same period, apparently during wet weekends in Aberystwyth.

Nationalism (discussed in more detail in Chapter 8) was contributed to by a wide range of thinkers, some of whom, such as Carr and Georg Schwarzenberger, went on to become the fathers of British 'realism', while others, such as David Mitrany and Alfred Zimmern, were prime advocates of international organisation and must therefore be dubbed 'utopians' after Carr. The two-page Introduction to *Nationalism* is a curious reflection on the difficulty of unravelling the emotional motives for political action, the balance of selfishness and altruism in humankind and the reflection that nationalism could be a dangerous or benevolent force, with words such as 'tentative' and 'incomplete' abounding. These ideas are then elaborated in a series of case studies. The preliminary remarks thus have all the stamp of a widely negotiated text and reflect the differences that existed in the group that wrote the book. They also show that all the contributors could not be sure that altruism would ever triumph in international relations. Carr himself was less tentative and furthermore managed to insert the idea that to go beyond the nation state to a wider organisational structure was certainly possible in a crisis when there was a necessary 'pooling of resources' but that this, as had happened after the Great War, 'rapidly disappeared after the signing of the Armistice'.[64]

Carr thus threw down the gauntlet in 1939 to those of his own profession who believed that 'law' would guarantee peace, when 'natural law ... can just as easily be invoked to incite disobedience to the law as to justify obedience to it'. He countered that law was only respected when it was backed up by power. Those who felt slighted by it, like the Germans after Versailles, could be expected to break it when strong enough to do so, to right their own perceived wrongs. Using Hobbes as his basis, Carr said that law outside a clearly defined political community was a nonsense: 'Law, like politics, is a meeting place for ethics and power.'[65] The place for its exercise had to remain within the boundaries of the nation state.

While not fully agreeing with Carr's 'realism', the memos circulating in Chatham House during that Summer of 1939, especially those relating to the 'Survey of European Problems', and others cited below by Toynbee, Geoffrey Vickers and others, notably that by John Foster Dulles (quoted in Chapter 3), shared much of Dulles' despair about the high hopes that had been put in the international rule of law. As a memo on the aim of the 'Survey' put it, 'the sanctity of international contract has virtually ceased to exist; state boundaries are constantly changed; such economic prosperity as exists is precariously based on abnormal armament expenditure; and the problem of maintaining international trade and financial relations between "free" and "controlled" economies remains unresolved.' The key elements of a post-war settlement were thus clearly defined as both political and economic before the war even began. Much of the thinking in Chatham House, as in the CFFR in the United States and PWP in general, was thus directed towards finding ways of implementing these insights.

Just before war broke out Toynbee circulated an important paper which asked the simple question: 'Why have we let ourselves fall into this pit twice over within 25 years?' Why did the present crisis contrast so awfully with the way that previous dictators, notably French, had been dealt with in the past, having 'the nonsense knocked out of them' over two centuries by an effective balance of power system? His answer was that the system itself had radically changed and that the old balance could no longer be relied upon as a regulatory mechanism. The driving force for potential conflict now lay in two areas: the 'international competition in armaments' and the linked economic, social and political 'competition'. Either there must be social or military collapse in Britain and France or in Italy, Germany and Japan. The most likely result was that it would be in the democracies because only Germany in Europe was now in a position to become predominant. There was no longer a real balance of power because there was no equality between the 'Powers', and even less with the newer, smaller states of Europe. There was thus now a '"post-modern" age' where 'war has become a prohibitively devastating instrument of policy' and there was no possibility of the balance of power saving the day. If such a salvation were to be attempted the result would be 'a series of shattering world wars at short intervals', Britain and France 'overthrown' by a triumphant Germany.

Since 1919, said Toynbee, 'we have been trying half-heartedly to build up a new world order in which the sovereign independence of the local national states was to have been subordinated in some degree to the Covenant of the League of Nations'. This had been alternated with attempts to 'keep up the old international anarchy' with 'momentary coalitions to maintain the balance of power against some particular state', but there had been a 'post-war hesitation between these two policies [which] is calculated to involve us in a series of first-class disasters at intervals of not more than 20 to 25 years'. Neither Britain nor France could alone alter this reality and they would indeed eventually lose their sovereign independence.[66]

The problem was, where were these 'strange and startling' ideas to come from? Toynbee's answers were essentially to look at the federalist writing that had really begun to emerge in the late 1930s, especially in Italy and Britain, and, latterly, with the publication of Clarence Streit's *Union Now* in March 1939 in the United States, which we have seen made a great impact, at least on informed American opinion.[67] Toynbee also took up Carr's challenge very robustly. He effectively agreed with Carr that the present situation was hopeless and that the LON experiment had not worked, or at least had not been properly tried. He was echoing much of the fear of total war voiced by those such as Bryce, Angell and Brailsford during the Great War but agreed with Carr that power and law had to be underwritten by force. The ensuing debate about the nature of international relations and the future of political organisation, Europe and the world has arguably defined the discipline ever since, and certainly had a huge input into both the policies of the Allied Powers during the war and in their planning for the post-war period. One immediate echo of Toynbee's remarks, for example, can be found in Churchill's developing ideas about Europe and in his proclamation of an Anglo-French union in May 1940.

But the notion that the luminaries of Chatham House or of other groups, such as the PEP Group, had any real idea what the war was being fought about, beyond the question of mere survival and until quite a way into the war, should be resisted. As with the Cabinet, members of these groups had to admit in late 1939 that '[w]e know what we are fighting against, but not what we are fighting for'. 'Ideas' such as the defence of 'western civilisation'

were not much use against a 'dynamic and simple creed', they had to
recognise the 'conflict of ideologies' and that this was one of the 'philosophy
of the Sovereign National State carried to its *reductio ad absurdum*' against
that of 'international community'.[68] The battleground was therefore seen as
being between the efficacy of communitarian versus more cosmopolitan
solutions to security problems as posed by Hitler and his allies. Ideas were
the necessary riposte, but they were to prove difficult to arrive at in Britain,
which partly explains why America took the ideological, as well as the
inevitable military, lead.

Chatham House on 'World Order' and 'Reconstruction'

During the war Chatham House acted as a clearing house for the many
groups, including PEP and the British Coordinating Committee for International Studies (the then professional association of international relations
academia), many of which had overlapping memberships.[69] The main forum
for this was in the 'World Order' and 'Reconstruction' Committees. The
World Order Committee's main task was to produce a set of papers selected
by a Publications Committee which comprised nearly all of the few pre-war
Professors of International Relations, notably C.A.W. Manning (London
School of Economics), Sir Alfred Zimmern, C.K. Webster and J.L. Brierley.
The notable absentee was Carr himself (Aberystwyth) whose *Twenty Years'
Crisis* had notably indulged in *ad hominem* attacks on Zimmern and Gilbert
Murray, first incumbent of the Chair Carr now held, and upset a lot of
people in so doing. The Rockefeller Foundation agreed to foot most of the
bill for the publication of this series with an initial £10,000.[70] The original
list of nine proposed papers was dominantly 'idealist', with pan-European
and federalist ideas prominent. There were also volumes on *Christianity and
World Order* from the Archbishop of York and Leonard Woolf's *Towards
International Government* (an update of his First World War volume,
International Government).[71]

There is evidence of a struggle for the 'soul' of Chatham House at this
stage of the war, with Carr cast in the role of 'hard man realist'. His
summary dismissal of all ideas of world government in his draft Preface to
World Order Papers reiterated the findings of *Nationalism*: 'its authors
accept the view that persistence of national sovereignties is a condition
which must be regarded as permanent.' Only by accepting this, urged Carr,
would the application of 'greater precision of thought to this dangerously
vague conception of "World Order", which is now in everyone's mouth' be
possible. *Nationalism* was described by Toynbee as being seen by Lionel
Curtis and others as 'negative or hard boiled' and the suggestion had been
made that Chatham House should now publish the 'True Faith' to counter
it, which seems to have been done with the first series of World Order
Papers.[72] Looking through the first crop of papers prompted Geoffrey

Vickers to write that there was a 'clear divergence of view ... at which our speculations begin'.

First he identified different conceptions of 'Law, Justice, Order [and] Freedom'. Lionel Curtis' view was that 'freedom means the rule of law'. But the rule of law was itself often regarded by sections of any population, even in Britain, as the 'negation of freedom'. The crucial point for him was that 'order' had to be better defined to show both the British people and the Germans what was meant by it (far from clear at present), and this had to begin with the realisation that 'world order begins at home'. War aims thus had to be 'expressed in terms of social and political objectives' not in 'terms of political frontiers or political institutions'. Britain had to create its 'moral authority' to influence, '[w]ithout this we cannot be a force for world order'. Vickers' answer lay in expanding small pockets of 'civilisation' (in Toynbee's sense of the word) but also in recognising that this would be a slow process and the 'boundaries of what ... Toynbee calls civilisations will remain barriers for longer than the mind can foresee ...'.[73] This echoed both Carr's insistence on the basic communitarian unit of the nation state but also the 'purposive' or cosmopolitan desires of the 'idealists'.

This ideological struggle was also linked to fears that Chatham House would lose its intellectual independence, inevitable in the circumstances of war. It would be too much to say that these fears were couched in a Carr (or 'realist') faction versus a previously dominant and still very significant 'idealist' faction, but there were certainly accommodations that were made. There was a belief, expressed in the Preliminary Report of the Committee on Reconstruction, that it had 'taken for granted that the interests of the Council ... are practical and not academic, that they are directed towards focusing on certain fundamental issues, germane to a situation with which a British Government may be faced, the attention first of instructed people and then of a broader public'. The aim should be directed from the 'outset ... towards the question of Britain's relations with Europe, as lying at or very near the centre of the field [of British policy]'.

The main thrust of their work, it continued, had to be on winning the war, but also to 'ponder post-war policy'. This was based on several assumptions, apart from victory over the Axis, which were that the Dominions would continue to co-operate with Britain and that the United States 'does not pursue a policy which will make it impossible for Britain to accept any responsibilities if she wishes to'. This was by no means sure in early 1941, as a later section of this chapter will discuss. Lastly, it assumed that the 'public mind' would be sufficiently united to carry out any such policy 'consistently and effectively'. The main aim, in the event of all this being fulfilled, was the economic regeneration of 'the greater part of Europe west of Russia'. This would be achieved by 'cooperation with non-enemy European countries, rather than by methods of one-sided control ...', it being left to the inquiry to establish whether enemy countries could be so included.

As with the American PWP process, the emphasis here was also on economic regeneration at home and overseas, the two being linked to each other and to political change. Germany's potential for aggressive behaviour must be curbed and 'political arrangements [would] be required for keeping the peace', but the economic had to be given equal weight. Unemployment in Britain and Europe had to be a primary target for material reasons, but also for 'psychological' reasons, 'e.g. the example of British democracy's success or failure in remedying an internal condition'. This had to be a reply to 'Hitler's New Order' but also 'whether we can set before the nations of Europe any non-material idea or purpose more compelling and more acceptable than the name of European unity with which Hitler cloaks the subordination of Europe to the Herrenvolk'.[74]

The problem for the flower of the British intelligentsia ranged within the walls of Balliol College, Oxford and Chatham House was that they were not really sure what they wanted to propose in the international sphere, unlike in the domestic sphere, where they were sure that the Beveridge Report held many nuggets of wisdom for the rest of the world. This was made clear in a number of meetings held at Balliol and elsewhere in 1941. When three members of the State Department led by Benjamin Cohen joined in one of these discussions they started by stating that Britain would have to take its post-war responsibilities for Europe seriously: '[f]ortunately or unfortunately the British Isles cannot be moved to the other side of Ireland'. Zimmern replied rather defensively that '[o]ne thing is clear – there is a very big difference between people's ideas in 1918 and now. [Then it was] Wilsonian ideas; now they think more in terms of social and economic problems.' The problem was, countered Cohen, that 'it is easy to talk in terms of economic and social needs. But the problem of organizing economic action is very difficult. Nationwide economic and social planning or action has not been easy to achieve in the United States, even with the broad powers of our federal government.' What was necessary and 'the really difficult problem' was to look internationally 'to develop workable forms of economic cooperation. How are we to develop instruments for the healthy economic development of Europe? Do we not perforce have to agree upon the political structure of Europe before these economic instruments can be effectively used? Can we look forward to economic growth on the sands of political uncertainty?'[75]

Cohen's (and ultimately Roosevelt's) answer was a strong network of independent states but with 'economic collaboration', possibly in some sort of federation. The British, he was saying, without too much error, were concentrating on the domestic economic and social situation without taking the broader international political and economic framework into account. His academic audience largely agreed with him, especially Professor David Mitrany, who was to become the author of a celebrated work on international cooperation[76] (see below), although he was not a great fan of federal ideas, as most of the others clearly were, especially Professor Paton. Others, notably Professors Manning and Zimmern, preferred to concentrate on the practical details and on the question of whether the United States would lead.[77] The discussion therefore swirled around the dual problems of the 'economic' before or after the 'political' and what organisational features they should have? We have seen that the Cabinet at this point (May 1941) preferred to dodge the issue of both political and economic PWP as long as possible. This discussion served to confirm that the British foreign policy intelligentsia was nearly as paralysed by uncertainty.

The debate continued into 1942 and 1943, with Chatham House at the heart of a network of groups that also included the Nuffield College Social Reconstruction Survey and the Institute of Statistics. Their findings were considered by the Official [Cabinet] Committee on Post-War External Economic Problems and Anglo-American Collaboration. This Committee's research was wide-ranging and did finally accept much of the American logic about the need for international agreements. Mitrany figured prominently in its deliberations, as did Professor G.D.H. Cole, the prominent Labour Party observer of domestic and international planning ideas in the inter-war period. The 'international agencies' they discussed, including new and existing financial and commercial agencies, and the commodity agreements, all Rooseveltian ideas, sat rather uneasily with their ideas about the 'Processes of Industrialisation', especially with regard to what we would now call 'developing countries' ('Japan, Brazil, Turkey and the Succession states (including Jugoslavia)' and, rather ominously, the USSR.)[78] The 1943 meetings of this Cabinet Committee, dominated by such thinking, mainly reflected a desire to avoid international cartels benefiting 'monopoly capitalism'. 'Public' agreements had to replace the 'private' agreements of 'international cartels'. This opened up potential problems of interpretation, especially when a less liberal Presidential Administration came in with Roosevelt's death. Could this extension of national 'planning' into the international arena be compatible with the open world system that eventually emerged?

Conclusion: were there fundamental differences in the British and US visions of the NWO?

The clear evidence is that the American thinking on the NWO had a huge impact in Britain's processes in the same direction. As we have seen, Roosevelt shared a deep suspicion of British motives for the post-war settlement in line with most Americans, and he attributed blame for the inter-war crisis as much to British and French intransigence and balance of power politics at Versailles as to German aggression. He felt, in short, that a new form of international politics was necessary, one that stressed the 'harmony of interests', regional and global cooperation and a blurring of the barrier between nation and international society. But he also believed that any NWO had to be backed up by force. This was not by any means denied in Britain, with Chatham House and most sections of Government in broad agreement with the idea. Even 'realists' such as Carr were able to see the possibilities of the idea.[79]

Carr's ideas, especially his attacks on Wilsonian idealist notions of international organisation and his affirmation that 'national sovereignty is a condition which must be regarded as permanent',[80] were countered by prominent Americans even before the outbreak of war. Dulles' speech of June 1939 postulating union between Canada and the United States, mentioned above, can be seen as part of a growing American reaction to what they saw as a cynical British hyper-realism based on competing nation states, as can Clarence Streit's *Union Now* and other texts. It was this emphasis on the primacy of the state that many Americans felt had created the basis for new conflict. In its place American thinking saw a clear place for regional arrangements, and the breaking down of national borders, either through Dulles' 'structural porosity' or in the global commercial thinking pushed by Hull. The exact nature of what arrangements emerged to try and realise these aims will be explored in Chapters 5 and 6 in a discussion of the future of international organisation, Europe and Germany, and on 'Economic Reconstruction' in Chapter 7.

The potential for Anglo-American difference on the British Empire was huge, and many, like Dulles, would have liked Roosevelt to be more explicit in his views, which were clearly anti-Imperialist. The incredulity of Dulles when faced with such statements as those of Eden and others in the Summer of 1942 (quoted in Chapter 3) is fairly typical of the American reaction. But Roosevelt was not prepared to push the point too hard and preferred to teach by example and by exhortation. The Philippines were duly given their independence in 1945 and, in the words of the Atlantic Charter, 'the right of all peoples to choose the form of government under which they will live' became a norm of international politics in the post-war era.[81]

The Beveridge discussions in Britain had the main advantage for Churchill of not really addressing the key issues of post-war global economic arrangements. This refusal greatly strained the patience of the State Department, although while Roosevelt remained President he was able to maintain the united Anglo-American front. American insistence and patience paid off in the end, as Britain basically accepted the American post-war blueprint, but the decision by Truman to suspend Lend–Lease the day the war ended in August 1945, leaving Britain with $12 billion of debt, may be seen as a sign of a deep-seated American frustration that their Allies did not see the logic of their desire to have a watertight political and economic common front for the post-war period. The pseudo-socialism of Beveridge (as seen from Washington) was thus a useful uniting factor in British domestic politics, but an irritant in transatlantic relations. Truman's decision still rankles today in many British hearts, but it was a sign that Britain would from now on have to dance to America's tune, which, most of the time, it dutifully has ever since.

The post-war dogma of 'realism' in international relations theory was thus not seen as central to the NWO debate during most of the war. Power and its holders were seen as a 'given' and all basically in harmony with each other. What mainly changed this was of course the onset of the Cold War and the shifting attitudes about Russia, epitomised by the rise of Kennan's ideas about 'containment' (see Chapter 5). But there nonetheless clearly persisted in Anglo-American thinking a belief in the usefulness of regional and global organisations and in the 'spillover' of the economic into the political sphere, what Mitrany called 'low' and 'high' politics in his classic *A Working Peace System*. The only difference was that the boundaries within which this Anglo-American vision were seen to be possible were shrunk to within the states that Streit in *Union Now* recognised as his 'fifteen', which did not include Russia, or most of Central and Eastern Europe, or most of the 'developing world' of the post-war period, and all of which became the basis of the OECD (initially the Organisation of European Economic Cooperation) in the 1950s. In the post-war conditions of the Cold War a federalising European logic held much promise. It might be argued that it is now, post-Cold War, too small a vision for a much 'larger' world.

Hence big differences between American and British policy existed, but they were about how most to benefit from the jointly agreed, but largely American promulgated, NWO proposals in the respective national interests of Britain and the United States. Britain wanted to keep its independence of action, and especially its Empire, post war. The more talented, such as Keynes, could only try and make sure that this happened to some extent, and they largely succeeded in getting Britain's voice heard, if not necessarily always to their entire satisfaction. But the Americans were well aware that they needed Britain as one of the Four Policemen and as the arbiter of the NWO, in at least Western Europe, and that the political, normative and economic 'regimes' (as we might now call them) had to be more benevolent than coercive if the peace were to hold.

Ideas had therefore to be the key, it was agreed by all who thought about these matters in both Britain and the United States, but only ideas that were demonstratively linked to concrete proposals, be they international or national, to do with external or internal security. Hitler had provided the impetus by demonstrating in his inimitable fashion that Europe could be made more secure in its dealings with its enemies while simultaneously being made more 'efficient' in its economic organisation, thus doing away with the scourge of unemployment and simultaneously improving the social and industrial infrastructure. The horrifying efficiency of the German military machine thus provided an exact parallel for Germany's industrial and social efficiency, much as Stalin's Russia had appeared to do until the early 1930s.

The reply to this had to be equally transparent and robust. The genius of Roosevelt and his team lay in making his vision clear in a series of statements that are still remembered today. Although they were seen by British cynics and pragmatists (or 'realists') as incomplete, or even as bereft of content, they were nonetheless extremely efficient in mobilising public opinion, as Wilson's more erudite and detailed Fourteen Points had not. Roosevelt's detractors might have had their sweet revenge in the Cold War hangover that succeeded his death, but it will be argued in the rest of this book that many of the key ideas of Roosevelt's vision did indeed see their apotheosis in the post-war period, even if in a more limited way than he had wished, and that they have now been even more widely recognised in the facts of international relations.

Notes

1 Geir Lundestad, *'Empire' by Integration: The United States and European Integration, 1945–1997* (Oxford University Press, 1998). I am afraid that this was published too late for serious consideration in this book. The point of view expressed in the title is of course one with which many, especially on the left, would agree. It might be added that the opinion of the Free French was left even lower down the pecking order of effective influence, and was essentially forced to react to what their more powerful allies were proposing, although this is not to say that they did not develop a particular NWO thinking of their own, even before the liberation year of 1944. This will be explored in an article that is now being prepared for publication elsewhere.

2 General Jan Smuts to Colville, 29 April 1944; Colville, Diary 1/6.

3 For the history of British relations with Germany before 1939 see D.C. Watt, *How War Came: The Immediate Origins of the Second World War, 1938–39* (London, Heinemann, 1989) and A. Lentin, *Lloyd George, Woodrow Wilson and the Guilt of Germany: An Essay in the Pre-history of Appeasement* (Leicester University Press, 1984). For an examination of the most significant sympathisers with Mussolini and Hitler in the 1930s in Britain, see Richard Griffiths, *Fellow Travellers of the Right: British Enthusiasts for Nazi Germany, 1933–9* (Oxford University Press, 1983) and for what happened to some of them (especially in various British fascist parties) see A.W. Brian Simpson, *In the Highest Degree Odious: Detention Without Trial in Wartime Britain* (Oxford, Clarendon Press, 1992).

4 Quoted by David Reynolds, *The Creation of the Anglo-American Alliance, 1937–41* (London, Europa, 1981), p. 272.

5 See, in particular, John Charmley's attacks on Churchill in *Churchill: The End of Glory: A Political Biography* (London, Hodder and Stoughton, 1993) and Corelli Barnett's *Audit of War* (London, Macmillan, 1987). See also Clive Ponting, *Churchill* (London, Sinclair Stevenson, 1994).

6 Both Reynolds, *The Creation*, pp. 253–254 and Harper, *American Visions of Europe* (Cambridge University Press, 1994), p. 79, quote this statement by Hopkins as being of vital importance.

7   At the NESPA meeting, also referred to in Chapter 6, on 5 December 1939 in Washington, Berle Papers, Box 65. The aims of PEP and the notion of 'planning' will be further discussed below.

8   Roosevelt had been informed of this by the British Ambassador to Washington, Lord Lothian, 29 February 1940; Berle Papers, Box 65.

9   Churchill, quoted by Harold Nicolson in Nigel Nicolson (ed.), *Diaries and Letters* (3 vols, London, Collins, 1966–68) vol. 2, and CAB 65/17, 4 October 1940, quoted by Trevor Burridge, *Clement Attlee: A Political Biography* (London, Jonathan Cape, 1985), p. 144. The episode is also referred to in Kenneth Harris, *Attlee* (London, Weidenfeld and Nicholson, 1982), p. 187.

10 Reynolds, *The Creation of the Anglo-American Alliance*, pp. 252–253 and below.

11 The classic statement of this can be found in R.B. McCallum, *Public Opinion and the Last Peace* (London, Oxford University Press, 1944).

12 P.M.H. Bell, *John Bull and the Bear: British Public Opinion, Foreign Policy and the Soviet Union, 1941–1945* (London, Edward Arnold, 1990).

13 'Position of the United States in the Event of the Defeat of France and Britain in the European War', October 1939, and correspondence between J.V.T. Perowne (Foreign Office) and S.D. Waley (Treasury); Keynes to Waley, 16 October 1939; Foreign Office to Lothian (Washington), 2 November 1939, expressing great distrust of Joseph Kennedy: all T 160/1105/16266.

14 'American Cooperation – Memorandum by the Chiefs of Staff Committee', 3 July 1940; CAB 66/ 243.

15 'Peace Proposals by Germany', 19 July 1940, CAB 66/270.

16 'Propaganda for the Future', Memorandum by the Minister of Information, Duff Cooper, 20 July 1940, CAB 66/275.

17 Although Lothian often acted on his own initiative in this and other public statements about Britain's predicament, he provided an extremely important voice in Washington until his tragic and unexpected death in December 1940, and one that Churchill never tried to silence.

18 Roy Douglas, *New Alliances, 1940–41* (London, Macmillan, 1982), p. 117, asserts that '[t]he first meaningful attempt to propound meaningful war aims in the new context arose … at Placentia Bay in August 1941'. Others say much the same, for example Harris: 'no further progress was made until August 1941' (*Attlee*, p. 187). David Reynolds, *The Creation of the Anglo-American Alliance*, does take this period seriously and is the benchmark against which all others can be set.

19 Duff Cooper, *Old Men Forget* (London, Rupert Hart-Davis, 1955), p. 262.

20 See Chapter 3. A good account of this can be found in Reynolds, *The Creation of the Anglo-American Alliance*, Chapter 6.

21 Characteristically, Harper plays down this meeting as one where Roosevelt treated his guest with 'avuncular condescension': Harper, *American Visions*, p. 22. J.M. Wheeler Bennett, *King George VI: His Life and Reign* (New York, St. Martin's Press, 1958), contradicts this.

22 Memo by Keynes referring to Sir Frederick Philipps' visit, 27 October 1940 and note from the Treasury to the Chancellor of the Exchequer, 4 November 1940; both T 160/1105/19422.

23 Reynolds, *The Creation of the Anglo-American Alliance*, pp. 155–159.

24 Cabinet Committee on Post-War External Economic Problems and Anglo-American Cooperation, 7 February 1941, CAB 87/60.
25 Halifax to Eden, 6 May 1941, Confidential Print W 5382/426/49, also T 160/1105/F17660/02/01.
26 G.L.M. Clauson (Colonial Office) to S.D. Waley (Treasury), 28 May 1941; Waley to Sir R. Hopkins (Treasury), 4 June 1941. On Amery's views see Amery to Sir Kingsley Wood, 30 May and 10 June 1941, Amery to Eden, 6 June 1941 and Eden to Amery, 10 June 1941: all T 160/1105/F17660/02/1.
27 Reynolds makes this suggestion, and also that Churchill put particular faith in Sir Kingsley Wood and the Treasury: *The Creation of the Anglo-American Alliance*, p. 272; Beaverbrook to Waley, 13 June 1941 and subsequent drafts and additions by Churchill and Halifax, among others: T 160/1105/F17660/02/1.
28 Reynolds, *The Creation of an Anglo-American Alliance*, p. 276.
29 For a brief overview of the Treasury view of Keynes see G.C. Peden, *Keynes, the Treasury and British Economic Policy* (London, Macmillan/The Economic History Society, 1988). Keynes certainly found the Americans he met either ill ('Three are very old indeed [Roosevelt, Stimson and Hull seem to be the candidates here] ... Hopkins is an invalid ...') and the others not much to his liking, as with 'the very gritty Jewish type perhaps a little too prominent'. But of Roosevelt himself he wrote: 'He still seems to have the quality of thinking in simple terms on broad lines, of choosing his men and trusting them, and, in fact, seeing and handling things in the big way that he should.' Keynes to Kingsley Wood (Chancellor of the Exchequer), 2 June 1941; all T 160/1105/F17660/02/1.
30 Eric Roll, *Crowded Hours* (London, Faber, 1985), p. 43. For more of Roll's views see Chapter 7.
31 Keynes to Treasury and FO, 21 May 1941; T 160/1105/F17660/02/1. The italics are mine.
32 Halifax to Foreign Office, 21 May 1941; T 160/1105/F17660/02/1.
33 The explicit statement of this is in Keynes to Treasury and FO, 21 May 1941; T 160/1105/ F17660/02/1.
34 Keynes to Kingsley Wood, 22 June 1941, recounting a discussion Keynes had had with Roosevelt, also Halifax to Foreign Office 8 July 1941 and Keynes to Kingsley Wood, same date: all T 160/1105/F17660/02/1.
35 Keynes to Kingsley Wood, 22 June 1941; T 160/1105/F17660/02/01.
36 Treasury to Churchill, 12 July 1941, FO to Washington, 14 July 1941, Halifax (Washington) to Foreign Office, 5 August 1941; T 160/1105/F17660/02/1.
37 Berle to Hull, 26 November 1942; Berle Papers, Box 58.
38 Memo by the High Commission of Australia, 11 August 1941; Sir R. Campbell (New Zealand Minister in Washington) to Eden, 10 September 1941, both CAB 87/60. For the last gasp attempt to have clauses on Imperial Preference excluded from the discussions, see Amery to Kingsley Wood, 14 August 1941 and Lord Moyne to Kingsley Wood, 11 August 1941; T 160/ 1105/ F17660/02/1.
39 Official Committee on Post-War External Economic Problems and Anglo-American Cooperation, Meeting U.S.E. (42) 17 of 17 July 1942, CAB 87/60.
40 Memorandum of conversation between Keynes and Acheson, 28 July 1941, T 160/1105/F17660/02/01, and account by the Australian Minister in Washington to London of discussion with Roosevelt, 20 November 1941, CAB 87/60. Harper, in *American Visions*, says that Roosevelt was 'more anxious that

Britain have the strength to help the United States in Europe than it be hustled into a multilateral trading system that would cripple its economy', p. 81.

41 Smuts, speech in the House of Commons, 20 October 1942; Attlee Papers, 6.

42 Attlee, speech of 6 September 1942; Attlee Papers, File 6.

43 Attlee, speech in Aberdeen of 6 September 1942; Attlee Papers, File 6. Smuts to House of Commons, 20 October 1942.

44 Draft of State Department statement, Berle to Hull, 28 July 1942; Berle Papers, Box 58.

45 'Report to the Secretary of State [Hull] on Conversations in London, April 7th to April 29th, 1944' by Stettinius; Berle Papers, Box 70.

46 Speech by Cripps, annotated by Attlee, who wrote a note to Cripps saying 'I like this very much', 3 May 1942; Attlee Papers, Bodleian, File 5.

47 Among the most celebrated wartime statements are (all White Papers), *A National Health Service* (Cmnd 6502, London, HMSO, 1944); *Educational Reconstruction* (Cmnd 6458, London, HMSO, 1943); *Principles of Government in Maintained Secondary Schools* (Cmnd 6523, London, HMSO, 1944); and *Housing Policy* (Cmnd 6609, London, HMSO, 1945). For a documentary examination of the social reform proposals, see Andrew Land, Rodney Lowe and Noel Whiteside, *The Development of the Welfare State, 1939–1951* (London, HMSO, 1992).

48 The group had been set up in the 1930s to instill some rigour into British thinking on the subject. It was led by Sir Basil Blackett, formerly of the Treasury, and taken very seriously even by the Conservatives in Government. See CAB 117; T 161/1461/S52276, quoted in Land, Lowe and Whiteside, *The Development of the Welfare State*, p. 5.

49 One useful summary of the wartime debates on planning can be found in Asa Briggs, 'The World Economy: Interdependence and Planning', in C.L. Mowat (ed.), *New Cambridge History, Vol. XII, 'The Shifting Balance of World Forces, 1898–1945'* (Cambridge University Press, 1968).

50 See Robert Skidelsky, *John Maynard Keynes: The Economist as Saviour, 1920–1937* (London, Macmillan, 1992) for more on this.

51 'A War-time Submission: Territorial, Ideological or Functional International Organization?', drafted for the Foreign Office's 'Foreign Research and Press Service', reprinted in Paul Taylor (ed.), *The Functional Theory of Politics* (London, Martin Robertson, 1975), pp. 105–123.

52 Mitrany, 'The Making of the Functional Theory: A Memoir', in Taylor, *The Functional Theory of Politics*, p. 36 and fn. 51, pp. 78–79.

53 D. Thomson, E. Meyer and A. Briggs, *Patterns of Peacemaking* (London, Kegan, Paul, Trench, Trubner and Co., 1945), p. 29.

54 Carr himself was of course to go on to admire Soviet planning in the early 1930s and to advocate a 'new society' in Britain based on a form of state planning: E.H. Carr, *The Soviet Impact on the Western World* (London, Macmillan, 1946). See also the forthcoming biographies of Carr by Charles Jones and Jonathan Haslam.

55 Thomson, Meyer and Briggs, *Patterns of Peacemaking*, pp. 32–33.

56 Barnett, *Audit of War*, p. 22.

57 Orwell, from an essay entitled 'The English People', quoted by Andrew Shennan, *Rethinking France: Plans for Renewal, 1940–1946* (Oxford,

Clarendon Press, 1989), p. 202. It is significant that he quoted it in the French context, but how much more true it was in the British.

58 John Colville (Churchill's Private Secretary) records many instances of this kind of pressure in his Manuscript Diary; for example, entry for 9 February 1944, Churchill College Archives, File 1/6. See also Colville, *The Fringes of Power, Downing Street Diaries, Volume 1: 1939–October 1941*, and *Volume 2: October 1941–1955* (London, Hodder and Stoughton, 1985 and 1987).

59 Attlee to C.R. Shepherd (National Agent of the Labour Party), 10 March 1943; Attlee Papers, Bodleian Library, Ms. Attlee 7.

60 Land, Lowe and Whiteside, *The Development of the Welfare State*, pp. 4–5.

61 The reports of the Committees on World Order and Reconstruction can be found in the Chatham House Archives in Files 9/18 (World Order) and 9/19 a–j (Reconstruction). The subcommittees are under 9/20 to beyond 9/46. The initial correspondence to decide on a name is in 9/18a.

62 Naturally the outbreak of hostilities led many German intellectuals resident in Britain (mostly refugees) to fear for their future (and most were indeed interned in 1940) and some to wish to be part of making an input into a hoped for settlement, especially a group around David Astor. This seems to have been an unexceptional suggestion at the time, with the Warden of All Souls College, Oxford only suggesting a small initial group 'and to build it of younger men with expert minds rather than of politicians dating from the Weimar regime ...': Toynbee to Ms. H. Harvey (of Chatham House staff), 16 October 1939; 9/18a.

63 For some brief comments on this see, for example, Geoffrey Stern, *The Structure of International Society* (London, Pinter, 1995), pp. 18–21. Stern in particular notes the seminal importance of E.H. Carr's *Twenty Years' Crisis* (see below) and the infighting that had developed between his 'communitarian' views and those of the 'cosmopolitans', Alfred Zimmern and Philip Noel-Baker (see below for more on this).

64 E.H. Carr et al., *Nationalism: A Report by a Study Group of Members of the Royal Institute of International Affairs* (London, Oxford University Press, 1939, reprinted Frank Cass, 2nd edn, 1963), pp. xiii–xv and 1–7.

65 E.H. Carr, *The Twenty Years' Crisis 1919–1939* (London, Macmillan, 1939), pp. 175–78.

66 Arnold J. Toynbee, 'First Thoughts on a Peace Settlement', 26 July 1939; Chatham House, File 9/18f.

67 For more discussion of these thinkers see Chapters 3 and 7.

68 Memo by the PEP Group presented to the National Economic and Social Planning Association by Julian Huxley, 5 December 1939, already cited in Chapter 3 and this chapter. Berle and many State Department and prominent Government officials heard Huxley's speech, which was distributed in the Department: Berle Papers, Box 65.

69 'Preliminary Note on the Work of the Chatham House Steering Committee on Problems of a European Settlement', 4 January 1940, by Miss H. Harvey; File 9/18a.

70 Lionel Curtis to Sir John Fischer Williams, 31 October 1939; File 9/18a.

71 The European papers included an explanation of Coudenhove-Kalergi's proposals, *Pan Europe*, by L.S. Amery; *The United States of Europe*, by H. Wilson Harris; and *Federalism*, by R.T.E. Latham. Cf. First Meeting of 'World

Order Papers Sub-Committee', of 12 January 1940, at Magdalen Street, Oxford; File 9/18a.

72 Toynbee to Margaret Clement, 25 October 1941; File 9/18a.

73 Geoffrey Vickers, 'World Order', paper of 1 November 1939, Chatham House, File 9/18a.

74 Chatham House, 'Preliminary Report of Committee of Reconstruction, March 10 1941', Appendix I of the *Annual Report of the Council, 1940–1941*, to the Annual General Meeting of 4 November 1941, p. 33.

75 Chatham House Research Sub-Committee on International Organization, Balliol College, Oxford, 2 May 1941; Welles Papers, Box 192.

76 David Mitrany, *A Working Peace System* (originally published 1943), reprinted with an Introduction by Hans J. Morgenthau (Chicago, Quadrangle Books, 1966); Mitrany, 'The Progress of International Government' (1932) in Taylor (ed.), *The Functional Theory of Politics*.

77 Chatham House Research Sub-Committee on International Organization, Balliol College, Oxford, 2 May 1941; Welles Papers, Box 192.

78 Official [Cabinet] Committee on Post-War External Economic Problems and Anglo-American Collaboration, USE (42) 27, 10 September 1942; CAB 87/60.

79 Carr, *Twenty Years' Crisis*, Chapter 14.

80 Chatham House, first draft of Preface to the 'World Order Papers' series, Chatham House Archives, File 9/18a.

81 This link was made explicit in the State Department statement of 28 August 1942; Berle Papers, Box 58.

5

Joint Allied proposals for an NWO: relationships and issues, 1941–45

Introduction

In the previous two chapters we have observed what were essentially parallel planning processes in the United States and Britain. To show the way that these processes coincided with or contradicted each other we must examine how the projects got translated into (at least temporary) realities, policies, institutions and norms for action. The ideas that have so far been considered can only be seen as idiosyncratic elements of a fermentation that gave the final 'brew' in 1943–45, once they were discussed and then discarded, adapted or adopted by the Big Four at their Conferences. The main aim of this chapter is to elucidate that policy process, particularly as it applied to the future of Germany and, by extension, the whole of Europe.

A secondary aim of the chapter is to show how the Allies interacted as they went about this policy-making process. The purpose of this is twofold: first to show that the resulting compromises in effect gave rise to tensions that were to be both creative (as in the decisions taken about the United Nations) and negative (as in the disagreements that emerged about Germany in the EAC). Second, the aim is to show how the ideological tensions that became evident prepared the ground for the Cold War confrontation that was to follow Roosevelt's death in April 1945. The onset of the Cold War heralded the creation of what were essentially two 'NWOs' – one under the aegis of the Soviet Union, the other dominated, but not exclusively controlled, by the United States.

This is the last chapter that deals with the mechanisms of the NWO planning process. Subsequent chapters will look at some of the key themes that had emerged from the Versailles process and from the PWP of the Second World War as contentious issues between the Powers; in particular the question of international organisation, that of how economic consid-erations should play a role in the NWO and, finally, how far the principles of self-determination and human rights should be allowed to inform the norms and rules of an emerging international society. We need to examine these creative and destructive tendencies in some detail to show that the vague Wilsonian ideas of 1919 were to be given a much harder norm-creating effect that largely stood the test of the Cold War and provided the bedrock not only for the liberation of Central and Eastern Europe, but for the establishment of norms and practices that are now being universalised in the way that Wilson and Roosevelt wanted but never lived to see.

The historiography of the Allied relationship, 1941–45

A number of bibliographical comments are in order at this point. It is acknowledged that there has been a vast literature on the relations between the 'Big Three', especially from American and British historians and participants at the major Conferences between 1941 and 1945.[1] This book does not wish to go over that ground again in detail, although it will clearly have to draw on existing scholarship to show how PWP input was used in the policy process, or not as the case may be. The main concern here is therefore to identify how Great Power diplomacy interacted with PWP and in particular to bring out the links that it established between the thinking in Britain, the United States and the Soviet Union.

China played as little real a role in the NWO of the 1940s as it did of that of the 1920s. Roosevelt often said that it was essential to include China in any major decision making. Churchill never had the same view, and always felt that 'she was not comparable to the others'.[2] Hamilton Fish Armstrong of the CFFR felt that China 'would seem justified … in claiming an equal voice … in settling all world-wide questions' and, practically speaking, such an inclusion might be a good insurance policy against China 'trying to take the leadership of an awakening Asia against the West'.[3] But there is little evidence that the NWO planners really listened to the Chinese voice. China was included in a parallel process at Bretton Woods, and excluded with France from the main discussions. Neither state was represented at a high level at the Big Three Conferences until Potsdam in 1945.

Third, it is acknowledged that there is a vast literature on relations between the Allies during the Second World War as an explanation of the origins of the Cold War to which we cannot hope to do justice. This literature, be it 'traditionalist' (i.e. blaming the USSR for the Cold War) or 'revisionist' (blaming the USA) or 'post-revisionist' (blaming both or neither) is beyond the scope of this book.[4] The discussion here will therefore attempt a thumbnail sketch of the principal problems facing the Americans and the British in their relations with each other and with France and Russia, and how they impacted on their PWP procedures.

Allied relationships

De Gaulle, the Allies and the French planning process

France was engaged in a battle for survival and had been ignominiously defeated and its new Government, established in Vichy under the hero of Verdun Marshall Philippe Pétain, was recognised by the United States until the end of 1941. *La défaite* of 1940 in a mere six-week campaign was a military blow of huge significance, and followed a long period described by many (especially French) historians as '*la décadence*', a judgement that is now seemingly being revised to show how France could have avoided collapse. As one of these revisionists also admits, however, no Frenchman had felt able to face up to Hitler in the 1930s (any more than most of the British): 'If rulers and ruled had possessed the courage to say *merde* to Hitler before 1939 the story would have had a very different ending.'[5]

Only General Charles de Gaulle so dared in 1940 and, although hardly anyone noticed at the time (his BBC broadcast of June 1940 was not even recorded), he went on to symbolise France's revival in exile. The relationship of the main symbol of French resistance with the British and Americans was famously difficult, both before and after the liberation of France. Roosevelt would probably have excluded even the Free French under de Gaulle from any role in the planning either of the war or of the post-war if he could have avoided it. Roosevelt more than agreed with Churchill's description to him of de Gaulle as 'a cross between Joan of Arc and Clemenceau'.[6] De Gaulle was to a large extent protected from the unrelenting hostility of Roosevelt by Churchill, who saw de Gaulle as the incarnation of a resurgent France, a country for which he had both considerable affection and whose resurrection he saw as essential for world peace. He also saw an Anglo-French alliance as a cornerstone for rebuilding Europe.[7]

But as the war went on into its darkest period of 1941–42 de Gaulle grew increasingly suspicious that France's interests were being subordinated to those of Britain, especially in the Middle East. Syria and Lebanon proved a particular point of contention, as the British strained to prevent an uprising by nationalists supported by the Germans that would have turned their flank in North Africa. At one point de Gaulle actually contemplated military action by the Free French against Britain in Syria, while British troops were engaged against Rommel in Libya and the *Wehrmacht* attacked the Soviet Union. De Gaulle wrote to his right-hand man in London at the time, Réné Pleven, that although he recognised the inevitability of the Franco-British alliance, 'cela n'est concevable que dans l'indépendance et la dignité [The Syrian episode had shaken] ma confiance dans la sincerité des Britanniques en tant qu'alliés'.[8] Each confrontation that followed reinforced the feeling, as Kersaudy puts it, that 'de Gaulle seemed to be perpetually waging a public war against Vichy and the Germans, and a private war against the British

Admiralty [etc.] … the Prime Minister, the State Department and the President of the United States.' Churchill gave as good as he got from de Gaulle and their relationship often resembled a Feydeaux farce, although one with long-term serious implications, for Britain and France in particular.[9]

There were those who saw this hostility with sadness and feared a replay of 1919–39, in particular those who had been at Versailles and involved in the League of Nations, such as Philip Noel-Baker. Pierre Mendès-France in Algiers, signatory of an Anglo-French monetary accord in 1944 before D-Day, wrote to Noel-Baker saying that 'the future of Europe depends to a great extent on the collaboration of France and England after the war'.[10] Churchill saw this clearest of all and devoted the rest of his career to creating a Europe where British and French aspirations might be reconciled. In spite of all that de Gaulle said and did Churchill remained a firm supporter of the General, defending him against the entire American Establishment and most of his own staff, including Eden. But Churchill also recognised that Roosevelt's wishes had to take first priority, which often led him into a mediatory role between de Gaulle and Washington, a role for which de Gaulle gave him scant credit either during or after the war.

Roosevelt also flirted with Vichy until the American entry into the war, and even after it, advocating keeping the Vichy General, Giraud in power in Algiers even after American troops had liberated it in 1942 during Operation Torch.[11] However, it is quite clear that he did not see any long-term possibility of cooperation with Vichy. Hopkins asked Roosevelt by telegram in May 1942 whether he would like to 'nail that wood pussy Laval to your barn door?'. Roosevelt replied that '[y]our suggestion being studied but consensus of opinion is that odor still too strong for family of nations'.[12] De Gaulle and the Free French did have some supporters in Washington, notably Berle, who was outraged when Sumner Welles referred to the 'so-called Free French' in early 1941, a remark which Berle called 'ridiculous and ill-mannered [and] … for Europe, such remarks are extremely dangerous'. Another notable supporter of France in Washington was the distinguished American historian, Crane Brinton, who constantly urged Washington to take the French Resistance more seriously and who argued that a 'middle group in French politics' and most of the right in France would ensure that democracy returned after the war. However, he probably reinforced Roosevelt's scepticism about de Gaulle by advocating at the end of 1942 that no one group (including 'de Gaulle's Fighting French') should be supported by the United States.[13] But Welles' dismissive tone was more the norm. France was largely seen as an irrelevance in Washington.

The dislike was also undoubtedly because many in Washington feared that the French, were they given the chance, might demand a settlement as punitive as Versailles. The State Department was sent information in early 1943 indicating that France would demand reparations from Germany after the war ('their slice of the melon'), especially if other states did. This was in complete disaccord with most views in Washington (although some reference to reparations was included in the Yalta settlement).[14] There was also a fear that the communists were the main force in the French Resistance, a fear that had some truth in it. From de Gaulle's side it was, mainly, because he felt France had become isolated, a view that even France's inclusion in the talks at Potsdam after Roosevelt's death did little to assuage. He never forgave Roosevelt for excluding him from Yalta.

The consequences of this became even more apparent after the end of the war. Jean Lacouture quotes de Gaulle as saying in 1945 that: 'The Allies are betraying us, they're betraying Europe, the bastards. But they'll pay me for it. In fact, they're already beginning to pay for it, especially the British ...'[15] This attitude had hardened into a quasi-paranoia that never quite deserted the General and certainly coloured all subsequent relations between France, Britain and America while de Gaulle lived.

The problem of Russia

In the discussions about the post-war world, relations with Russia figured as one of, if not the, key issue. A principle that guided nearly all American Administration thinking about Russia from America's entry into the war, and even before that (see below), was summed up by Walter Lippman in June 1942: '[n]o international order can be imagined without Russia as one of its main supports ... If there is to be peace in the world, that peace has to be made in full partnership between the English-speaking sea and air powers and the massive land power of Russia.' George Kennan referred to this as the 'emotionally pro-Soviet' school of thought, which he derided as much as the 'emotionally anti-Soviet' school. Where was the 'dispassionate' school he asked, that which recognised that, necessary and welcome as Russia's resistance to nazism had been, collaboration with the United States on 'a post-war settlement is a different [question] entirely'? In truth, such a counter-school took a long time to develop, such was the United States Government's conviction that the Russians had to be included in the NWO.[16]

As Caroline Kennedy-Pipe points out, 'US attitudes towards Moscow were far from fixed in the Spring of 1945'. Roosevelt has been accused of marginalising those such as Kennan who distrusted the Russian Government by staff changes in the State Department from 1932 on.[17] But even Roosevelt's Vice-President, and successor as President, Harry Truman, essentially tried to follow Roosevelt's policy of seeking cooperation with Moscow until it became clear that this was going to be impossible.[18] As Dallek points out, US Ambassador to Moscow, Averill Harriman and Kennan, both sceptical of Russian intentions, got the President's ear at significant moments. It is clear that 'the portrait of him as utterly naive or unrealistic about the Russians ... has been much overdrawn'.[19]

In support of those who have criticised Roosevelt for 'naivety', one piece of ammunition might be that when he heard about the German invasion in June 1941, 'this Russian diversion', he welcomed it: it might mean 'the liberation of Europe from Nazi occupation and at the same time I do not think we need worry about any possibility of Russian domination'.[20] Roosevelt sent his principal confidant, Harry Hopkins, to Moscow not long after with a brief to ascertain what Stalin wanted for the war effort and to try and give him it. Stalin struck just the right note by telling Hopkins right at the beginning of their interview of the 'necessity of there being a minimum moral standard between all nations and without such a minimum moral standard nations could not co-exist ... the present leaders of Germany know no such minimum moral standard'. Roosevelt could not have put it better himself. Hopkins was particularly impressed when Stalin said to him: 'Give us the anti-aircraft guns and the aluminium and we can fight for three or four years.'[21] Roosevelt and Hopkins should probably have been more sceptical, but in the conditions of 1941 a sense of relief at being told what they wanted to hear is understandable.

From then on Roosevelt was convinced that Russia's benefit as an ally far outweighed its disadvantages as a competitor for power in Europe. His aim was to nudge the Russians into a course where 'the minimum moral standards' could be ensured by the Allies, and right until his death he refused to accept Churchill's warnings that this could not be. He was also seen by some as having a 'Presidential partiality towards Stalin' that grew in 1943 in direct proportion to his diminishing feelings for Churchill.[22] Right before his death in April 1945 he told Churchill: 'I would minimise the general Soviet problem as much as possible. These problems seem to arise every day, and most of them straighten out ... We must be firm and our course thus far is correct.'[23] If Russian suspicion could be overcome all would in the end be well.[24]

This attitude, said Kennan, led to a relationship with the Russians based on 'gushing assumptions of chumminess'. It was also one that would be bound to arouse suspicions in the Russians, whose minds were based on the diplomatic assumptions of Byzantium, not those of Washington: 'The Russians sense in our easy-going laxity a threat to the fundamentals of their society.' But even Kennan had to agree that 'It is not an exaggeration to say that the future of all contemporary civilisation, both oriental and occidental, will be deeply affected by the degree to which we and the Russians are able to come together on courses of action which would promote [the] general stability and prosperity of international life.'[25] Thus the United States' attitudes to the Soviet Union can be seen as based on shifting psychological appreciations, a factor implicit in the title of Kennan's article of 1947: 'The Sources of Soviet Conduct'.[26]

The truth of the matter was that the State Department's musings were far more complex than Kennan imagined. As early as January 1940 Berle was saying that any 'machinery' after the war had to be 'constructed' so that both the German New Order (where 'the center is to be Berlin') and the Russian conception of 'a universal empire, with themselves as the center' were avoided – 'the central assumption here is that neither the German nor Russian ideal prevails'. What he did like much more were the ideas of the 'French and the British [who were] discussing a possible federalized Europe in some fashion' (for more on which see below).[27]

Churchill had famously talked in the House of Commons in June 1941 of having to come to the aid of the Soviet Union in the circumstances of that year. Roosevelt went further than this, partly because he suspected that Churchill's actions in 1919 had not helped Russian friendliness to the West ever since. Roosevelt and many others in Washington distrusted British motives over Russia – something which Kennan probably underestimated or discounted. Eleanor Roosevelt sent Roosevelt a typed extract of Churchill's *The World Crisis: The Aftermath* of 1929 in which Churchill boasted of the 'large sums of money and considerable forces … employed by the Allies against the Bolsheviks during the year [1919]'. A memo with it simply stated: '[i]t is not surprising if Mr. Stalin is slow to forget.'[28] There was not much difference in practice in the American and British positions, they were based on *realpolitik* in the circumstances of war and, in Roosevelt's case, a hope that a clear indication of trust towards the USSR would help him implement his NWO ideas. This occasionally meant that he had to appear to favour Moscow over London or to act as a mediator between them, as at the Teheran Conference in 1943.[29] Washington and London were thus stuck in the dilemma of having to deal with the Russians as full allies while not liking their ultimate project.[30]

It is not at all clear that those in the best position to know were clear what Stalin's ultimate project for Europe was, even though Kennan thought he did and was ultimately proved right. Roosevelt was being given advice, as early as January 1943, and by those normally thought of as being in favour of 'containing' Russia, such as William Bullitt, that Stalin might support all Roosevelt's NWO project. As Bullitt wrote:

> although we have little first-hand detailed information about Stalin's views and aims … [m]any people, including President Hoover, have said lately that Stalin has changed his political philosophy. He is said to share your views expressed in the Atlantic Charter, and to favor the Four Freedoms … He is said to want no annexations but to be interested only in security. He is reported to be determined that the Soviet Union evolve in the direction of liberty and democracy, freedom of speech and freedom of religion. We ought to pray God that this is so ….

Bullitt was of the opinion that the United States had no choice but to believe it, but ought not to be surprised if they were wrong, such was the weight of historical evidence against it. In a remarkable piece of foresight, he wrote that Stalin would be more likely to use the Atlantic Charter as an excuse to annex huge sections of Eastern Europe as his armies advanced, as the 'national racial groups of Europe, who are begging me to accept them ... in the supreme and sacred interest of peace'. The United States might well have to stem the 'red amoeba' from taking Germany 'and keep the Bolsheviks from replacing the Nazis as masters of Europe'.[31]

Anglo-American relations

This uncertainty did much to colour Roosevelt's other famous wartime relationship, that with Churchill. The initial presentation of the Anglo-American relationship during the Second World War owed much to Churchill's presentation of his mostly rosy view of the 'Special Relationship' in his various writings on the Second World War.[32] Another view that can be said not entirely to deny the Churchill thesis, but certainly to qualify it, is that distrust between London and Washington was deeply ingrained and had been accentuated by the uneasy inter-war relationship.[33] Even during the war after 1941 there were many occasions on which the main Anglo-Saxon 'Allies' disagreed fundamentally about both how the war should be conducted and how the post-war settlement should be planned.[34] This distrust started from the twin American fears that not only might they be underpinning British Imperial desires but also that they might be left holding the baby of world peace in the post-war period. If they were to do the second, as they increasingly realised they must, then they had to be sure that they did not also do the first.

As Keith Sainsbury points out, there were many levels at which this distrust operated. On a personal level Roosevelt was by nature a liberal internationalist and anti-imperialist and a social reformer, while Churchill was a Tory imperialist and ferocious anti-Bolshevik. Nonetheless Sainsbury also points out that we should not exaggerate these differences: Churchill and Roosevelt were from much the same social background, Churchill had enacted some of the most important British social security legislation during his time as a Liberal minister before the First World War and was also not averse to discussions of further reform during the current war, such as the vital Beveridge Plan.[35] And, as has often been the pattern in the so-called 'Special Relationship', personal feelings of the leaders of Britain and the United States have played a significant role. There seems little doubt that Roosevelt and Churchill, after some initial hesitancy, held each other in high esteem, even friendship. Their first meeting as Allies at the Arcadia Conference in Washington during late December 1941 is often remembered for the incident when Roosevelt surprised a naked Churchill dictating to his secretary, who is reported as saying 'The Prime Minister of Great Britain has nothing to conceal from the President of the United States.'[36]

However, their relationship was always based on a reciprocal knowledge of which state was ultimately the stronger of the two. Both men knew the inherent limits of a friendship between great statesmen in time of war, and we should rather acknowledge the real affection that they felt for each other in spite of the exigencies of national interest and power politics. The differences and potential reasons for friction should therefore rather be sought out in the demands of such wider considerations. As we have seen, before America actually went to war there were many who thought that Britain might be defeated, with some viewing it as an inevitable and perhaps not bad thing and others thinking that this would be a disaster for Western 'civilisation'. Indeed, Stimson, one of the latter, was prepared largely to swallow any of his worries about the intentions of Britain and to concentrate the war on the European theatre in the interests of propping up Anglo-Saxon values. Roosevelt was always looking over his shoulder at the isolationists and could not be openly seen to be planning the post-war world in any way with Britain until the United States joined in the war.

All Americans were agreed that Britain must change after the war, as has also been stressed, and that this should be in effect a hidden American war aim – the disagreement was about how. Pasvolsky summed it up in February 1941 as American public opinion having 'in varying degrees, suspicion and apprehension as to the nature of international economic policies which a victorious Britain might pursue'. Some conservative Americans also felt that they might effectively be landed with the subsidisation of a British 'New Deal', which was to become a major factor behind the abrupt suspension of Lend–Lease under the Truman Administration upon the election of the 1945 Labour Government.[37] During the war this 'subsidy' did not particularly worry the liberals in the State Department, such as Pasvolsky, who felt that such a 'large program of social justice and social progress, of a new order of human welfare' would go well with the kind of international economic commercial and financial order that he and many others in the Department wished to encourage through the United Nations. But, as we saw in the previous chapter, it did have to be sold to Congress and the more conservative elements in the Administration.[38]

The path that was increasingly mapped out by the United States for Britain from 1940 at least was one of a future much closer economic and security role within Europe. This was the basis of Hugh Wilson's previously mentioned 'Memorandum on World Order' of January 1940.[39] It was urged on Chatham House in May 1941 when they were told that it was not enough for the British to want the United States to stay after the war in an 'Anglo-American Alliance'. Britain must also acknowledge that it 'has a stake in a prosperous and peaceful Europe. Fortunately or unfortunately the British Isles cannot be moved to the other side of Ireland.'[40] But the Americans were very concerned by August 1941 that the British might just be heading for an 'equivalent of the agreement between the Allies to redivide Europe' and what was more, as Keynes had informed Acheson, to base themselves on a 'closed economy for Britain and a British group, which would presumably barter with the United States'.[41] This was not acceptable to Roosevelt or virtually any others involved in PWP, but it required American entry into the war to be able to say so publicly. As we saw in Chapter 4, the Atlantic Charter afforded the possibility to do so and firmly established the pecking order for the post-war world. Britain was no longer a 'super-power' but it must be kept powerful in the ultimate interests of the United States. Without it shepherding Europe there would be no Rooseveltian NWO.[42]

The future of Germany and Europe

Germany

During the inter-war period a huge part of the problem in Europe and elsewhere had clearly been over how Germany had been treated. Many references have already been made to this debate, which crystallised around the multi-faceted analysis of the Treaty of Versailles. The historical reputations of the key statesmen at Versailles have since become embroiled in the whole debate about the 'appeasement' of Germany in the 1930s.[43] What this section aims to do is further to show briefly how Germany figured in the thinking of the major players in the PWP process during 1940–45. Germany was discussed at summit level at Conferences at Moscow (1943), Teheran (1943) and Quebec (1944), as well as Yalta and Potsdam (January and July 1945). The debate at these Conferences was clearly long and complex, and all that will be attempted here is to bring out the major strands of the arguments used to justify various options.

Dismemberment?

Treasury Secretary Henry Morgenthau was one powerful voice who felt the United States could not trust Germany at all. He proposed at the Quebec Conference in September 1944 to turn it into a 'country primarily agricultural and pastoral in its character'. The main part of his Plan entailed giving the Saar to France (which was what France wanted) and making the Ruhr into an International Zone, giving Denmark a large area of northern Germany and dividing the rest of Germany into two states. In the post-war period much of the central deindustrialisation idea was shelved (except in the East controlled by the Soviet Union), although Morgenthau always claimed that Roosevelt agreed with it. It should be noted that some parts of the Plan, such as its section 1, on the demilitarisation of Germany, were agreed and implemented by all concerned, as was the 'treatment of special groups', such as the SS and Gestapo. And even Morgenthau did not advocate Versailles-type reparations in cash and kind, as well as agreeing in a conversation with Roosevelt that education of the Germans to democracy would be vital. In effect his 'Plan' can be seen as one end of a spectrum that united Washington, an unsentimental spectrum that dictated radical reform, not the creation of a vacuum at the heart of Europe.[44]

Pasvolsky and the 'Treatment of Enemy States'

The blueprint that most resembles the final treatment of Germany was drawn up by Pasvolsky, with whom Morgenthau had expressed his total disagreement to Roosevelt on 2 September 1944. In a succinct memo on 1 September, before the Quebec Conference, five principles emerged:

> 1) To compel [German] unconditional surrender ... 2) To require them to make just recompense ... 3) To treat them in a manner that will encourage their peoples to develop liberal and peacefully-inclined governments 4) To prevent their economic collapse and ultimately to provide for their participation without discrimination in world economic activities; and 5) To render them eligible, after adequate demonstration of their desire and capacity to live at peace, for eventual participation in international political and economic arrangements.

Roosevelt talked at length to Pasvolsky about his memo on 15 September, and 'thought that it was entirely satisfactory', with a small caveat about the Commanders in the field.[45]

The final version of Allied policy and actions towards Germany is well known, in that there was an attempt to thrash it out in the EAC by the Big Three's representatives in London in 1943–44 and finally after the war a trizonal partition of Germany. This division proved to be permanent until 1989. The 'Treatment of Enemy States' was largely settled by who got there first in the military campaigns, with all of Bullitt's worst fears realised. But it is important to note that the PWP principles of economic reconstruction, international organisation and a form of democratic self-determination were highlighted as the main menu for defeated enemies after a period of atonement had been completed. The final (intended) treatment of Germany can thus be seen as one of the best examples of the NWO putting PWP principles into practice.

The problem of Europe

As with most other areas of concern, the State Department, the President and others in London were thinking about how Europe should be organised even before American entry into the war. Americans again dominated the debate, although we shall consider below the British input, especially as Ellwood claims that '[t]his was practically the only time during the war that the American planners reacted to a proposal from outside', somewhat of an overstatement.[46] In the general mêlée of discussion about 'world order' in 1940–41 it was felt that Europe must bring about its own salvation, and that it must appreciate that 'the greater the surrender of sovereignty, the more health there will be in Europe'. This must be evidenced by more economic unity, but also by guarantees for the sovereignty of small states and for the peaceful settlement of disputes.[47]

The question of European 'union' has exercised a great many minds in Washington over a long period. The security of the entire world has been seen, with some justice, as being linked into that of Europe, probably since the American Revolution. Other ideas, such as the Wilsonian panacea of self-determination, did not seem to have improved matters. Europe was the only place where self-determination had been tried post-Versailles and it had led to the rise of National Socialism.[48] The State Department thus became increasingly keen to see a 'well-rounded union', not just for Western Europe but also for Central Europe. One concern that echoes down the years in the debate stimulated by Samuel P. Huntington's 'spheres of civilisation' was the suggestion that this union would exclude states that were Orthodox Christian, 'thus one potential source of disturbance could be reduced to a minimum'. Such thinking also brought up the related question as to whether Russia was to be considered as 'European' or 'Asiatic'. But the State Department became equally convinced that there was 'undeniably the making of a moral grouping of West European nations' and it was on this that they wished to concentrate.[49]

Kennan and many others in the Department were also very drawn to the idea of the creation of larger multi-state sovereign units, one example being a 'Danubian' federation of some kind. It might be pointed out that discussions of such Danubian unity dated back at least to the early twentieth century. Hankey had made a similar suggestion during the build-up to Versailles, making a case for three 'federated states', one in the North of Europe to include the Benelux countries, Alsace-Lorraine and Switzerland; another in Central and Eastern Europe, including a 'Greater Serbia', Romania, Poland and what we would now call the Baltic states; and a third to include all of Scandinavia (although he seems to count the 'Baltic provinces' in here as well). He also wished to create a 'new colonial power', Switzerland![50] The idea had remained in British thinking in the inter-war period before the rise to power of Hitler, especially the encouragement of a Customs Union linking Paris, Berlin, Rome and the South Danubian states.[51]

Kennan's views on the future of Europe

George Kennan was very well placed to see what the German 'New Order' would mean for Europe and American hopes for peace and democracy. He was an American representative in Prague during the takeover of 1938–39 after Munich, in Norway in 1940 when the Germans took over there and in Berlin when Germany declared war on the United States, after which he and his colleagues were interned for several months. His views about the nature of totalitarian regimes were confirmed after what he had seen of the Soviet

Union in the mid-1930s and his was a conservatism very akin to that of Winston Churchill in these respects. He wanted a Europe that was viable, well run and reasonably democratic to act as a permanent antidote to totalitarian, 'Imperial' expansionism. This would be consonant with American vital interests for a 'zone of liberty' within which Europe could continue to prosper and with what he saw as the necessities of a balance of power, not some vague moral imperative.

From Norway when the Germans invaded in 1940 he reported that the German *Reichskommissar* had told the population that 'nations which persisted in their blindness in crucial moments, and did not find understanding men to take care of their destinies, were apt to be "swamped in the flood of events and buried away for all time" …'. For Kennan this was particularly sad because 'nowhere did the liberal–bourgeois ideals of the nineteenth century reach a healthier and sounder state of development than in Norway'. At least one of his biographers has pointed out that his views on American politics were similar to those of H.L. Mencken and Walter Lippman in their scorn for the excessively democratic politics of the United States. Their collective preference was for a kind of Platonic Republic where the elites would rule in a 'managerial statist' way, but with absolute integrity and intelligence. It is possible to imagine that Kennan thought Norway almost an ideal type of this kind of state.[52] However, he was not a great admirer of small states *per se*, only ones that had stood the test of time. He was also more than aware of their vulnerability to outside interlopers. As Mayer puts it, these states had to be 'compact, well-balanced, neutral … [with] sufficient resources of social cohesion and venerable traditions', which he did not think that the states of the former Hapsburg Empire, such as Czechoslovakia, possessed, for example. Democracy mattered to him, but not at the cost of civilisation.

What he hated most in any regime was 'cruelty, stupidity, ignorance, violence and pretense', factors particularly evident in Nazi Germany and Soviet Russia.[53] He developed his thesis on the nature of German 'imperialism' in a document of April 1941 when he was based in Berlin. Whatever sympathy he may have temporarily harboured for German order in 1939 had evaporated as he saw them fritter away their advantage by their 'clumsiness, stupidity and brutality'. The National Socialist Reich could not cope with non-Germanic peoples, he concluded, precisely because it was pan-German and therefore it had 'nothing to offer them [non-Germans] politically which could conceivably arouse much enthusiasm for German rule'. It did not even have the appeal of the communist Third International as there was 'no universal application of its tenets, as did the Catholic Church of the Middle Ages. Its soldiers cannot march through Europe as the bearers of abstract ideals, applicable to all humanity, as did the soldiers of the French Revolution' and in this situation '[i]t is difficult to believe that this sort of situation could produce a happy Europe', even if Germany could maintain its power for the foreseeable future by force of arms and even be moderately economically successful.[54]

Mayer points out that Kennan has been accused of being against the idea of a federal Europe. Mayer rightly writes that 'practically the exact opposite was true …'. Kennan's opposition to a federal Europe was based almost exclusively on his worries about a renewal of the problems surrounding the Treaty of Versailles, leaving a 'single sovereign entity … [with] a series of permanent grievances and irritations which can only serve to keep alive its discontent and challenge it to greater national unity and effort'. If Germany itself was not made into a federal state it would be the only 'great country of central Europe'. It was thus not a question of breaking it up, but of federalising it internally, 'an intelligent federalism', and then planning the rest of Europe's future.[55]

As Kennan pointed out in 1942, there was very little expertise about Germany in the State Department although he was not entirely right to claim that 'no-one in the Department, to my knowledge, is even endeavoring to follow in detail the developments in this most important of European countries.'[56] Kennan was one of the first to urge against dismembering Germany, and indeed was engaged in secret discussions with aristocratic dissidents of the Nazi regime, such as the Count Helmuth von Moltke and Bismarck's grandson Gottfried, although he never reported these contacts to Hull or the President, whom he did not believe would have appreciated the need to cultivate such suspicious men. Kennan shared a desire to see a renewed Germany within a federal Europe of some kind, as a necessary counter to a future Bolshevik threat.

Other American views on Europe

So how could a happy, or at least a successful, Europe be engineered after the war? Some extremely ambitious plans for the partition of certain states and the unification of others were proposed within the State Department's PWP process in its Sub-Committee for the Organization of Peace, set up in January 1940.[57] Out of this emerged by May 1940 the idea of a series of possible ideal permutations of European states, first tied by economic cooperation, with the hope that this would spill over into political unity. A federal model was suggested, along Swiss lines, with a rotating Presidency, leading to security and legal instruments, all as part of a wider global arrangement. This group therefore saw Europe as the foundation for a renewed LON, although that was still an idea that could not speak its name in the still isolationist period in which it was discussed.[58]

While Russia and Germany were running the whole of mainland Europe, the Department viewed with alarm the vision of a 'German or Russian ideal prevail[ing]'. Just before the United States entered the war, fears were being expressed that if there were not an overall unification of Europe, the continent could well end up being divided between the newly reconciled

British and Russians.[59] Neither prospect appealed in Washington. Once in overt alliance with both after December 1941, this distaste had to be swallowed, but not forgotten. As Berle put it in November 1942, in Europe 'Britain had ... leadership from 1920 to 1939. The results were disastrous not only for her, but also for us.' There might therefore be a 'recognition of the United States and Great Britain as co-equal in continental [European] politics' or even a 'recognition of the United States as a permanent and dominating factor in Western Europe'. This was really thinking the hitherto unthinkable. In one of his admirably succinct memoranda (this time barely a page long), Pasvolsky wrote at the same period that a whole series of projects for Europe had to be considered, but all mentioned regional political and economic 'arrangements' or 'unity'. The net result was the setting up of the machinery in London known as the EAC which was to test these different propositions (see below).[60]

William Bullitt, who had great influence with Roosevelt, put a different twist on the European question in a series of important memoranda just before the major Conferences of 1943. He saw the future peace and stability of a Europe 'integrated and democratic' as 'an essential element for the construction of a durable peace. If such a Europe can be achieved it should become – as a unit – one of the powers which unites with the United States, Great Britain, the Soviet Union, China, etc., in world-wide agreements for the maintenance of peace.' Europe was in effect 'the substructure' on which all else would succeed or fail. The LON had failed because Europe was not at peace, and the new 'super peace organization would suffer the same fate ... [but] if the harness strapped on the nations of the world by the terms of the peace galls too intolerably, the donkey will kick the cart to pieces'.[61]

To find out if the nations of Europe (the most important 'donkey') would be prepared to live in peace with one another, the CFFR was encouraged to take a great deal of evidence from representatives of the different governments in exile in the United States. In line with Mosely's strictures against 'Utopian blueprints' an attempt was also made to get the spokesman for the Central and Eastern European states, as well as the Italians and French, to be realistic in their demands as well as according proper weight to democratic considerations. This was not much in evidence. It had immediately to be acknowledged by the CFFR that many of the demands, on borders especially, 'obviously conflict with each other', most crucially in Central and Eastern Europe and 'the claims of ethnic groups would have to be subordinated to general necessities', although it must have been realised that this had not helped in the elaboration of the Versailles settlement. On a return to, or the emergence of, democracy (e.g. for Italy) optimism was expressed by nearly all Europeans, as it was for the solution of the 'peculiar nationality problems' of such states as Yugoslavia, Czechoslovakia and Belgium.

Outside interference was strenuously rejected by nearly all the representatives, although they also all expressed a conviction 'that his nation would

willingly accept such limitations on its sovereignty as may be necessary to
secure the establishment and maintenance of a system of international military, political and economic collaboration, provided the United States and
Great Britain take a wide measure of responsibility in such a system'. The
only exception to this came from French spokesmen. But when minorities
were considered, Poles, Romanians and Hungarians all expressed themselves as seeing 'compulsory exchange arrangements' of populations as
'entirely admissible', especially of Germans (except in the Czech Sudeten-
land where the Czechs expressed generous feelings), while 'considerable
caution' was expressed towards the safeguarding of other minority rights.
The main worries were of Germany and Russia, with a lot of the East Europeans, including the Ukrainians and White Russians, believing that they
could all group together in a 'buffer zone, or through democratic elements
gaining ascendancy in Russia'. The burden of enforcing all this would fall
entirely on Britain and the United States if they did not want European states
to ensure their own security 'by their own drastic methods', as would the
primary role in economic reconstruction.[62] A similar message came through
in the other meetings of the CFFR War and Peace Studies Group. Roosevelt
and his key advisors feared a re-run of post-Versailles *revanchisme* if such
views were to prevail.

However, such views were not universally held by the governments in
exile. The Dutch, led by Prince Bernhard, provided a key external input into
American thinking on the future of Germany in particular. As a suffering
small state they fitted the Rooseveltian bill for recognising the rights of small
states and they evidently had his ear. They were also among the first
governments to open discussion on the post-war treatment of Germany, as
they were concerned by April 1943 that 'it seems that none of the United
Nations has a clearly defined policy on this score'. Their views were that
'peace-terms dictated by a spirit of vengeance are to be avoided' and that
there was a 'common desire not to repeat past mistakes, but to apply the
lessons learned in the hard school of experience'. However, this did not
mean being kind to Germany, rather that the wildest suggestions, such as the
'extermination of the German race, or the sterilisation of all Germans', were
to be avoided. Here again Versailles was their model of what to avoid.
Germany must be locked into a 'new order' by ensuring its economic and
'co-prosperous and co-peaceful' future. This thinking proved vital in the
creation of an integrated Western Europe after the war, a unification in
which the Benelux countries played a vital role.

British views on European federation, 1939–45

For many Americans British support for a united Europe was essential. As
Bullitt put it, '[i]f you cannot get Churchill to work for an integrated Europe,
there will be no integrated Europe. We are not strong enough in force or
brains to achieve such an aim against the will of the British' (and this from a

man who had long harboured resentment against the British over
Versailles!). To ensure this the United States would have to give Britain
security guarantees against enemy bombers, an idea that Bullitt knew had
long obsessed Roosevelt.[63]

But, as was outlined in Chapter 3, major differences between the British
and United States Governments emerged about the future of Europe. Dulles
had reported back to Sumner Welles in July 1942 that there was likely to be
a distinct difference of views with the United States over the question of
European federation. Given Welles' advocacy of regional post-war security
arrangements (see Chapter 6), this was a severe annoyance. The reasons
behind such British reluctance were, as seen by Dulles, that the problems
that would be faced by Europe were precisely the problems of 'continental'
Europe, not those of the British Isles and its Empire. Dulles found only 'the
possible exception of Mr. Attlee' in favour of a 'general federation in
Europe', although the idea of a 'series of continental federations' had a
limited appeal for the entire Cabinet, mostly without Britain being a
member.[64]

Books such as Clarence Streit's *Union Now* had not been as enthusiastically received in Britain as they had been in the United States. As we saw in
Chapter 4, Chatham House actively considered the idea of a federal Europe
at least from 1939. Federalist thinking of one kind or another had entered
the intellectual discussions of the inter-war years in the writings of Leonard
Woolf, David Davies, James Bryce and others mentioned earlier in this book.
An organisation, 'Federal Union', was set up in January 1939, including
such luminaries as philosopher C.E.M. Joad and Lord Lothian, later British
Ambassador to Washington. But even one of its advocates had to admit that
'federalist practice and federalist theory … were and remain foreign to most
Britons'. However, it is acknowledged that it was Streit's *Union Now* that
really took root in the public imagination.[65]

Churchill is often seen to have been the exception to this cool attitude. He
had lent his name in the 1930s to federalist causes, and he famously acknowledged an unlikely debt to the unusual Count Coudenhove-Kalergi in his
1946 Zurich speech, which called for a 'kind of United States of Europe', a
name he also explicitly evoked in 1943. But Coudenhove-Kalergi had been
seen as a crank by most in Britain in the inter-war years, and Churchill had
of course been firmly in the wilderness until late 1939. Even the much more
respectable ideas of French Foreign Minister, Aristide Briand for some sort
of closer European union in the late 1920s, the 'Briand Plan', had been
rejected as nonsense by both the then Prime Minister Ramsay Macdonald
and by virtually all other British politicians.[66] It was precisely this kind of
'utopian' thinking that Carr was railing against in the *Twenty Years' Crisis*.
It is of course interesting to speculate whether such a plan tried in the early
1920s, bringing in Germany, might have created the necessary spirit of
reconciliation that might have prevented Hitler's rise to power.

So it is misleading, but tempting, to say that Bullitt's prayers were answered with Churchill's speech of 22 May 1943 in Washington about a 'United States of Europe'. There is no evidence that he discussed this speech with his Cabinet, or indeed that they would have agreed with it, and he stressed rather disingenuously that 'he was expressing only personal views'. But he must have known it was a topic that rang well in American ears and one with which he had personal sympathy, perhaps informed by his American genes. What Churchill did achieve by this speech was to highlight the *problematique* that had always simmered not far from the surface in all the discussions about reorganisation – what balance was to be given to global, as against regional, organisation? As will be discussed in the next chapter, this was to be one of the central questions for the implementation of the NWO.

Grand strategy and the NWO

During the war there were many points of continuing disagreement between Britain and the United States over both grand strategy and details of policy, although they did not become really apparent until 1944. Until then Roosevelt essentially went along with Churchill's policy on conducting a 'Mediterranean' war and then insisted on a Second Front to relieve the Russians, with which Churchill was forced to go along in spite of his preference for a Balkan thrust, by which was meant an exploitation of the Italian victories of 1943 and a thrust into Yugoslavia and beyond. But the disagreements became more obvious as the Allies turned the tide of war and started to win. In the case of the Russians it was because of their constant, and understandable, clamour for a 'Second Front'; in the case of Anglo-American relations because of widely differing views over grand strategy and the future of Central and Eastern Europe.

Churchill's main reason for wanting a Mediterranean strategy to predominate was to stop the advance of Soviet troops and influence in Eastern and Central Europe, and to avoid what he saw as the inevitable slaughter attendant on an unprepared and precipitate assault on northern France, one which Roosevelt's Chief of Staff, General Marshall, had advocated from 1942 on. There has been much debate among historians about this disagreement. It has also been said that Roosevelt always professed either not to worry about, or not to be able to affect, Soviet strategy, given the huge numbers of Soviet troops moving from the East and the absence of any other Allied forces. This on occasion led to major rebuffs to Churchill by Roosevelt, on occasion in front of Stalin, and arguably the sacrifice of many British troops in the Eastern Mediterranean (such as in the Dodecanese in 1943). As Roosevelt told Stimson in November 1943, not only did he not agree with Churchill's plan to get US ground troops into the

Balkans, it 'would not be favorably regarded on Main Street'.[67] Churchill was arguably right to worry about the future of Central and Eastern Europe, whereas Roosevelt and the PWP teams in the United States seem to have been unaware of the consequences of Soviet involvement in the area until it was much too late or considered that there was nothing they could do about it.[68]

It was also appreciated in some quarters in Washington that there was a real danger of Churchill drawing the United States into giving a blank cheque for the future security of Europe, or at least for a Churchillian view of it, and a fear among the military side of Roosevelt's Administration that this was not appreciated at all by the State Department. In the immediate future it was a problem of 'whether or not we, the Government of the United States, or Great Britain, our ally, should dominate this military government of Husky [the landings in Sicily] and hereafter probably of Italy', wrote Stimson in his diary in April 1943. In the longer term, '[i]t was a problem which related to the Empire policy of the British Empire and the post-war policy'. Would the British not want to dominate the finances of the continent of Europe, 'while we had no such ambitions ... while she is very much set on it, over an issue which was fraught to us with nothing but possibilities of trouble and no gain'.[69] But it would also be fair to say that even Stimson was very keen on a continuing 'close association between the English speaking countries ... a raft which has just barely saved us from the wreck in the storm ... don't let us abandon that raft for the purpose of trying to construct a new boat which will carry us through the post-war ground swells that are sure to come'.[70] The exact design of the 'boat' was the problem.

Anglo-American differences of emphasis on the economic and political future thus emerged early in the Allied advance and especially over the role of the United States in Europe. Broadly speaking, the British were extremely keen that there be an American presence post-war to prevent a recurrence of the problems of the 1920s, as the State Department, unlike Stimson, realised. But some in the State Department also knew that there were also occasions when '[t]hey [the British] are plainly motivated by a fear lest we assume a leadership which tends to exclude them from the picture. Certain people view the British nervousness as a desire to assume the leadership of all con-tinental political arrangements; others consider that they merely wish to be co-equal with us.' As was mentioned above, Berle suggested that there were various ways to resolve this dilemma: first, by recognising a 'primary interest of Great Britain in continental [European] politics', which he believed 'would be the point of view of the British Foreign Office, were it frankly addressed', or, second, 'recognition of the United States and Great Britain as co-equal in continental politics', or third, a'[r]ecognition of the United States as a permanent and dominating factor in Western Europe'. Berle believed that the first was ruled out by Britain's seemingly incompetent handling of European security between the wars and the third option by a probable refusal of American public opinion to countenance such a huge role. Consequently, he preferred the second and suggested the setting up of a 'joint committee on political planning', based preferably in the United States, to review, country by country, the future of the states of Europe. The military side of this would be supervised by the Combined Chiefs of Staff and the political side by the Foreign Office and State Department.[71]

Thinking on the subject was developed in May and September 1943 when Churchill twice visited Washington and made the famous speech analysed above. To carry on the post-war relationship he, like Berle, wanted to make sure that the United States was involved in the post-war settlement from the beginning of liberation, now going slowly but surely up the leg of Italy. The concern in the State Department and the Roosevelt Administration generally was that this should be a unified approach that saw as its first priority the relief of Europe or, as Stimson put it, 'an association of all the allied powers' which should 'start with an economic association to repair the ravages of war …'. Churchill's worry was that 'we should become the almoners of the other nations' to which Stimson's initial reply was that there was a 'necessity of preparing against a great depression like the last one which is bound to follow after the war and to prepare for it by avoiding tariff barriers and also clearing the currency'. Sumner Welles, and of course Hull, were all in favour of this approach, sharing Roosevelt's prejudices against a reliance on force in international politics. All agreed 'the need for force' but also that it must not be based solely on a treaty, but would have to rely on 'an alliance between the people who are really fighting now and who our people have grown to trust', that is, the United States and Britain in alliance. The implication of a United States leadership for Europe was clear, but at this stage it was a grudging implication.[72] The Americans still hoped that a global solution through the United Nations would avoid a major military commitment by the United States in Europe.

'The Turning Point': Moscow and Teheran, 1943

Keith Sainsbury refers to these series of Conferences at the end of 1943 as being at the 'Turning Point', when it finally looked as though Germany would be defeated and plans would have to be converted into realities. At Moscow in October 1943 the Foreign Ministers of Britain (Eden), the United States (Hull) and the Soviet Union (Molotov) met, and at Teheran in December the Heads of State, Churchill, Roosevelt and Stalin, met together for the first time. The agenda of the three Powers at these meetings was quite different. As Sainsbury says, the Russians wanted simply to agree 'measures to shorten the war'. The Americans wanted to secure commitment to international cooperation after the war that would require membership of powerful international organisations in the security and economic areas, along the lines of the Atlantic Charter, with which the British had some sympathy. The Americans also wanted to see a serious preliminary discussion of the future of Germany, with various different geometries being envisaged. The British also wanted this, but with the wider aim of a general European settlement, including Eastern Europe, which the Americans were anxious to avoid even discussing for fear of upsetting the Russians. British fears were of Russian expansionism after the war, especially in Eastern Europe and the Middle East.[73] For Roosevelt, his worry about creating breaches in the Alliance outweighed all else: as Hopkins reported to Eden and Molotov; '[t]he President feels it essential to world peace that Russia, Great Britain and the United States work out this control question in a manner which will not start each of the three powers arming against the others.'[74] The mistakes of the 1920s must not be repeated.

As a corollary to this conviction, the American desire not to upset Russia lay at least partly in the emphasis that Stimson, Roosevelt and Hull thought should be put on the economic side of a peace settlement, especially their ideas for Central Europe. But Stalin was not really interested in such matters – he wanted a political and military settlement in Central Europe. However, he cleverly made Hull think otherwise by playing to Hull's obsession with trade issues throughout the Moscow Conference in October 1943. Hull was told, for example, that trading with state trading organisations 'would present no difficulties', while Stalin, Molotov and Mikoyan together entertained American businessmen with high hopes of trade in the post-war period, a promise which flew in the face of virtually all previous experience and indeed economic logic. Stettinius informed Stimson of this and he was also delighted. This was the chance not to make the Versailles mistake, of not creating 'self-sustaining states' as had been done with Austria. Without 'proper economic arrangements' to go with the 'political' ones they could 'not make the peace stick'.[75]

The disappointment attendant on this should also figure in an explanation of the post-war American dismay over Soviet behaviour. At this point of the war, and indeed until Roosevelt's death in April 1945, many in his Administration seemed quite happy to give Stalin Central and Eastern Europe 'politically' as long as economic arrangements between the Allies were soundly based. In fact none of the detailed proposals put to the Soviet Union at Moscow, ones suggested moreover after discussions at the highest level in Washington before the Conference on commodity agreements, commercial policy, cartels and other cooperation, were ever implemented. Given Marxist–Leninist views on collaboration with capitalism, this was certainly the greatest naivety of all.

The machinery of Allied consultation, 1943–45

Immediately upon American entry into the war it had become apparent that some sort of machinery was necessary for coordinating Allied policy towards the end of, and after, the conflict. In December 1941 Berle had proposed the setting up of a Supreme War Council, which would also include China and the Soviet Union and even 'possibly Holland,' the only non-power to have been so suggested, as well as a Supreme Economic Council to carry out relief work. Both these ideas were essentially drawn from the experiences of 1917–19, where so many of the PWP personnel had been involved in the process, if at a junior level.[76] But even by the end of 1943 there was no real machinery in place, and all had been decided by the leaders in the Conferences. Most discussion and decisions had of necessity been to do with winning the war.

Walter Lippman's views in the *New York Times* were that the Moscow 'Conference will be successful if it produces organs of consultation and combined action'.[77] Public opinion was now pushing the democracies to give organisational substance to plans for the post-war period. The key area for Roosevelt, Stalin and Churchill was the setting up of a mechanism to decide the fate of Germany, which became the main task of the EAC. London was finally settled on as the venue for this body that determined the immediate tasks of liberation. This and the Tripartite Commission set up to investigate the future of international organisation with UNRRA were the first concrete results along the lines suggested by Lippman.

The EAC

Of the two bodies set up as a result of the Moscow foreign ministers' meeting of 1943, the EAC turned out to be the most disappointing. The British had hoped that its placing in London would give Britain a distinct advantage in the elaboration of plans for Europe in the post-war period. Many Americans hoped that it might be the basis for a new Europe. In fact the EAC turned out to have a very limited policy importance for the Allies, and largely concerned itself with the arrangement of Germany's surrender and the exact zones that should be occupied in Germany after this surrender. The main decisions about the world after the war were in the end taken by the Big Three acting alone and, as we have seen with Teheran and Yalta, largely meant that any dreams of a global NWO had to be postponed to discussions in the United Nations, the establishment of which was also decided in the Conferences.

The delegation was headed by US Ambassador to London Winant, and included George Kennan, who despised Winant, after December 1943[78] and Hamilton Fish Armstrong. Kennan put it succinctly to Harriman: he wanted to be where the action was, to influence 'the type of world in which our children will have to live, which [was] being determined by the actions taken at this time', while the EAC was merely 'executing decisions taken elsewhere'.[79] Armstrong's view was that 'there was not much work for me to do here'. He was disappointed at the very 'military and technical nature' of the discussions which 'neither interest me nor provide much field for me to help even if I were interested'. He was also dismayed that 'the real problem that we talked about in those two years of committee work at the Department are not under discussion'.[80] He went back to Washington in December 1944 as a Special Assistant to Stettinius (now Secretary of State) and was asked if the EAC should be abolished.

Armstrong urged that it should not be, as he perceived there 'was no other forum for negotiation between the three major allies on a tripartite basis'. There have been accusations about Winant's leadership and even Armstrong had to admit, in strictest confidence, that Winant was 'secretive and suspicious'. Armstrong could not fault him, however, for his 'tact and patience in trying circumstances' and his success in putting over the American point of view. The most trying of these circumstances was the distrust of the Russian delegate, Gusev, for virtually every suggestion, even though Winant was able to put the points across in fluent Russian through his Political Advisor, Philip Mosely, a CFFR colleague of Armstrong's whom he held in high regard. The State Department did not escape criticism, for having Winant be both US delegate to the EAC and Ambassador to Britain, and Armstrong also implied that Winant was constantly stymied by 'Washington's omission to take either affirmative or negative action'. The only solution was a greater degree of synchronisation between the EAC and both the War Department (under Stimson) and the State Department in Washington, and a wider brief to consider the 'broader political and psycho-logical aspects' of the technical matters under consideration. As a practical example of this he cited the cases of Bulgaria and Hungary, where coordination had been so slow that the Russians had been able to present the Western Allies with a *fait accompli* in the time taken for London and Washington to take a decision as to how to react.[81]

However, Stimson's resistance to this at a time of great moment for the American armed forces, matched by Roosevelt's desire not to upset the Russians unduly, meant that Armstrong's urgings largely went unheeded. There was thus little chance that the EAC could achieve much that was important in a global sense. Armstrong grew increasingly desperate in his advice to Stettinius as he saw the Americans seemingly acquiescing in the EAC to the Russians arriving first in Berlin on the grounds that they would 'deal with the Germans as they deserve'. The new directive that had been discussed for the partition of Germany after the defeat showed clearly 'the difficulty of divorcing consideration of long term policy from that of policy immediately following the cessation of hostilities'. He realised that this would be discussed by the Big Three at Yalta, but he still feared that without a clear policy for Germany the United States Government would be dismissed by the press as 'weak, indecisive and too tender to the Germans' or consider that the 'Russians are brutal rapacious and imperialistic', not to mention its effects 'on the German public and on Allied solidarity'. Specific policies had to be arrived at, not 'generalities', before it was too late.[82] It very nearly was.

There were several reasons for the failure of the EAC. First, the Soviet Union, which was equally represented with Britain and the United States on the EAC, had no wish to let a body based in London determine anything of its future plans for Central and Eastern Europe. Second, Roosevelt himself had decided that the EAC was not, as he put it, to 'arrogate to itself the general field of postwar organization',[83] which was being dealt with by the committees set up in the State Department and the new Tripartite Commission, which would deal with the central issue of post-war security and economic arrangements, the central planks of his vision of the NWO since 1941. Considerable alarm was expressed in Washington that the EAC might undermine these central discussions, although Hull tried to allay these fears by saying that it 'was a necessary piece of machinery for carrying out the relations with the four powers in between the meetings of the chiefs of state'.[84] As a consequence of this, as Mayers says, 'the American delegation received no leeway to negotiate, but was ordered to follow precise instructions from the State Department'.[85] Harper goes further and accuses Roosevelt of deliberately sabotaging the EAC: 'Roosevelt was more preoccupied with British wiles and with positioning the United States to leave Europe than with Russia.' In the process he was quite prepared to let the Russians have more of Germany on a map he had drawn 'on the back of an envelope', to punish the Germans, a course that Kennan, for one, thought utmost folly.[86] But Kennan was virtually alone in seeing the future of Germany as a major problem. Most of the rest of Washington saw the future as being in the hands of the 'policemen' and the United Nations, the subject of the next chapter.

From Teheran to Yalta

As the war developed into late 1943 and 1944 it became increasingly clear that Russia was not going to agree to a peace without annexations as Roosevelt and Hull and most other Americans wanted. By early 1944, for example, the Russians had made it clear that they were going to shift the borders of Germany and Poland to the 1919 'Curzon Line', which would involve the annexation of large sections of eastern Poland to Russia, and also to give Poland the Polish Corridor around Danzig and East Prussia. The ultimate Faustian bargain struck at Teheran in November 1943 which confirmed most of the agreements at Moscow, was to in effect allow Stalin to determine both the fate of Eastern Europe and the Allied military strategy until the end of the war in return for serious discussions about Germany in the EAC and on the setting up of a world organisation along the lines suggested by Roosevelt and his advisors.[87] By the time of the Yalta Conference in January 1945 the Red Army's advance meant that the military realities on the ground made a nonsense of post-war political planning, at least for Eastern Europe.[88] The results of Yalta, in particular, have exercised historians ever since.

But our concern here is the effect it had on immediate thinking about PWP and Roosevelt's NWO. The 'containment school', represented by Kennan and Harriman, US Ambassador in Moscow, saw the compromises made at Yalta as inevitable given the Russian mind-set. While Roosevelt was insisting at Yalta on free and fair elections in Eastern Europe, Kennan was sure that Russian strategic need 'makes unrealistic the idea of a free and independent Poland'.[89] Equally, some other key figures, such as Stimson, realised by 1944 that there was little that could be done to stop the Russians exercising their options in Eastern Europe and had a certain amount of admiration that they had borne the brunt of the fighting against Germany to that date. It was, said Stimson, 'a hard and an interesting subject and it shows what we've got before us'.[90] Churchill was not pleased with the compromise that Yalta produced over Poland, however much he seemed to support the agreement in Parliament in the interests of the war effort.[91] It is clear that he never believed, even after the infamous 'percentage agreement' of October 1944, when the two men had informally carved Eastern Europe into spheres of influence, that Stalin would be quite so brutal in getting his way in Poland. As Edmonds has pointed out, perhaps he and Roosevelt should have been more suspicious after hearing Stalin referring to Beria as 'our Himmler'. A charitable interpretation is that Stalin took the need for a 'friendly' Government in Warsaw too seriously and that Roosevelt believed that his intentions were basically honourable and that they in any case had no alternative but to trust Russia.[92] Had Stalin not after all signed a 'Declaration on Liberated Europe' that guaranteed free and 'democratic' elections? It should also be noted that Roosevelt was very ill at Yalta and was to die shortly afterwards. The net result was that Poland, the country for which Britain had gone to war, was forced to accept the Lublin Government, that is, Stalin's Moscow-trained placemen, and the 'London Poles' were frozen out.[93]

The treatment of Poland obviously outraged the Poles, but it also left a good deal of distaste among the Western Allies themselves. Although Western public opinion was kept in a state of some euphoria about the relationship with Russia for the obvious reason that the war had to be won, the way the Poles were being treated increasingly damaged the rosy view of 'Uncle Joe' and started to sow the seeds of the post-war conflict well before the end of the fighting in Europe.[94] Many in both the State Department and the Foreign Office were very much against 'selling out the Poles', with Owen O'Malley, British Ambassador to Moscow, being quoted by Churchill's Secretary John Colville as saying that Russia's actions and intentions were bound to lead the Central Europeans in general to put more faith in Germany as 'their only hope of protection against Russia'. Colville further noted that many people he knew saw the treatment of Poland as akin to the Munich sell-out, even though his own view was that they would just 'have to accept what they can while still maintaining their right to further claims'. O'Malley was right to see this logic as flawed and that 'what is morally indefensible is always also politically inept'. Gentlemen such as Colville regretted mainly the 'sad ineptitude' of the Russians – 'a little courtesy and a little generosity could have achieved much. As it is the attainment of really close relations with the USSR looks like being very hard to maintain.'[95] Churchill said he was tempted to tell Stalin '[p]ersonally, I fight tyranny whatever uniform it wears or slogans it utters' – of course he did not actually do so! But he was seriously concerned that Germany would use Yalta to make the same arguments as it had about Versailles.[96]

The Polish case can with hindsight be seen as the key concrete test of the relative weight given by the Allies to moral rights as opposed to *realpolitik*. In the short term Roosevelt may have been right to sweep the problem aside, although in the long run O'Malley's arguments have proved prophetic. Poland (and the rest of Central and Eastern Europe) now does look to (a democratic) Germany as a way of escaping from Russia. It also shows that Churchill and Roosevelt were drawing different conclusions about the likelihood of, and conditions for, a breakdown of the Alliance. Roosevelt hoped that by giving the Russians what they wanted there would be no repeat of the 1930s, because the Alliance would be cemented in the United Nations; Churchill felt that by making public promises about democracy and then breaking them they were storing up the inevitability of a revisionist movement, as had happened in 1919. He preferred to see the world as full of '[Nazi] wolves and [Soviet] *bears*' and he was only prepared to go along with the United States on Poland and Eastern Europe because he believed in the necessity of an Anglo-Saxon Alliance to support him against such 'bears'.[97]

As to Stalin's view, recent scholarship seems to indicate that he really did mean to keep to the letter of the 'Declaration on Liberated Europe', but that his interpretation of the word 'democratic' was different to that of the Western Allies. Kennedy-Pipe quotes a Soviet commentator as saying just after Yalta that '[a]fter the last traces of fascism and Nazism [have been removed] the peoples of liberated Europe will have the possibility of creating democratic institutions according to their choice. They can take as example any form of democracy that has been shaped by history.' She also suggests that Stalin may have expected the peoples of Eastern Europe to vote communist out of gratitude for their liberation.[98] Until the archives are fully opened we shall never know whether either of these hypotheses was honestly believed in the Kremlin. Kennan's cynical realism certainly makes the most intuitive sense.

Conclusions: what was left of the NWO after 1945?

The central practical dilemma for the NWO architects was the future of Germany and of Europe, but there was no real meeting of minds between the Big Three at Yalta or Potsdam. The exclusion of France until Potsdam fuelled an enmity between de Gaulle, Churchill and Roosevelt that was to poison the relations of these countries for years to come. Without agreement on this there could be no real NWO after 1945, only a set of interim decisions within the framework of the United Nations and a set of global aspirations in the Atlantic Charter and in the combined output of the NWO planners from earlier in the war. Does this mean that we should just see the disagreements as destroying any prospect of a truly 'one world' NWO in 1945, much as had happened in 1919?

The evidence in favour of such a view is certainly strong. Neither before nor after Roosevelt's death was there much that could be done to stop Stalin behaving exactly as he wanted in Eastern Europe, and the officials that worked for Roosevelt and Churchill knew this. The United States had no policy to deal with the eventuality that Roosevelt had been wrong to trust Stalin at least to respect the spirit, if not the letter, of the Atlantic Charter after the war ended in Europe. Of course, historians have been arguing ever since about why this was the case. In a classic account of the post-war disagreements about Eastern Europe, Lukács has written that

> it was but the logical consequence of the division of Europe which occurred with the Western and Eastern armies meeting in the center of the continent. The tragic element here was that the Russians regarded this division as permanent and self-explanatory, whereas the Americans originally thought it to be not much more than a temporary demarcation line based on momentary military expediencies.[99]

There is evidence that Stalin even expected the East Europeans to be genuinely enthusiastic about joining with the Soviet Union as allies and partners. As Gaddis has recently pointed out, it was the 'manner' of this partnership that so galled the West. For politicians in the West with public opinion to consider, the way in which the USSR dealt with Eastern Europe was very embarrassing.[100] Far from settling the question of the future of Europe, the division that took place at Yalta condemned it to a conflictual future that we are only now, in 1997, seeing partially resolved.

Kennan's celebrated 'Mr. X' article in *Foreign Affairs* in 1947 was the first official acknowledgement that the Russians had a very different approach to the post-war world, due to the fact that their view of international politics was at radical odds with that of the Western Allies.[101] After 1947 the development of 'containment' based on Kennan's views, and that of 'roll-back' based on the views of Dean Acheson, Secretary of State after 1949, and Paul Nitze, demolished the final residual Rooseveltian hope that the USSR could be brought into full partnership in a 'one world' NWO. The world that developed after 1947 was bipolar, and can be seen as that of the 'Free World', not that united one envisaged in the heady days of 1942–43.[102] The United States had hoped that it could leave Europe to be pacified by a combination of British benevolence and an outbreak of European unity. This was of course not to prove the case, and the institutions of the Free World had to be created, the 'creation' referred to by Acheson in the title of his autobiography. The implications of this will be discussed briefly in the next chapter.

With, as Arthur Sweetzer put it, 'peace disintegrating'[103] after January 1945 what can be said to have remained of the broad ideas of Roosevelt's NWO? Clearly the world was not going to be run by an Alliance of the Big Four. We can nonetheless summarise the main areas where there remained a consensus of sorts and which continued to form global politics for the next fifty years until 1989, after which it could be argued that the Rooseveltian dream was largely realised. One key idea that remained, and that will be the focus of the next thematic chapter, was that of the accepted importance of the principle of international organisation. Although it has been increasingly questioned over recent years, the UN still remains a key factor in global political discourse. The main reason for this is that it has come to be seen as the focus for action by the 'Four Policemen' and lots of other 'smaller police-men' as well. A second idea was that of economics playing an increasing role in the machinery of international relations, and not just, as had been the case, in the domain of private transactions between individuals and firms; this will be dealt with in Chapter 7. Economic statecraft at the disposal of states and international organisations in a surveillance or regulatory mode has become a commonplace, which it was not before the setting up of UNRRA and the Bretton Woods organisations. Finally, the notion of self-determination has become a central part of our thinking about international relations, whether it be to encourage it through decolonisation or to critique it in terms that were perfectly familiar to the thinkers of the first and second NWOs. This is especially the case in the 1990s, and is reflected in a resurgence of thinking about 'normative 'questions in international relations, and particularly what is termed the 'moral standing of the state'.

Roosevelt and Wilson before him, as well as the myriad other thinkers and groups that have been described in this book so far, were thus the clearest architects of a discourse in international relations that still domin-ates the discipline today. They were of course not the only ones to reflect on these matters, but it is the central assertion of this book that the two world wars, and arguably the end of the Cold War, that have most concentrated minds on the fundamental problems of IR. The rest of this book hopes to elucidate further how these major categories of thought and policy have developed.

Notes

1 For good overviews of this see Herbert Feis, *Churchill, Roosevelt, Stalin: The War They Waged and the Peace They Sought* (Princeton University Press, 1957); Christopher Throne, *Allies of a Kind* (London, Hamish Hamilton, 1978); Keith Sainsbury, *The Turning Point* (Oxford University Press, 1985) and *Churchill and Roosevelt at War: The War They Fought and the Peace They Hoped to Make* (London, Macmillan, 1996); Diane Clemens, *Yalta* (Oxford University Press, 1970); and Robin Edmonds, *The Big Three* (London, Penguin, 1992).

2 State Department Memorandum, 28 May 1943, report on luncheon addressed by Churchill at the British Embassy in Washington, attended by Vice-President Wallace, Stimson and Sumner Welles among others; Pasvolsky Papers, Box 7.

3 'Some Preliminary Notes on Preparations for an Armistice', 13 March 1942; Armstrong Papers, Box 78.

4 For an overview of this 1970s and 1980s literature see John Lewis Gaddis, *We Now Know: Rethinking Cold War History* (Oxford, Clarendon Press, 1997), *The United States and the Origins of the Cold War, 1941–1947* (New York, Columbia University Press, 1972) and 'The Emerging Post-Revisionist Thesis on the Origins of the Cold War', *Diplomatic History*, vol. 7, Summer 1983, pp. 171–190, as well as Melvyn F. Leffler and David S. Painter (eds), *Origins of the Cold War: An International History* (London, Routledge, 1994). For a 'traditionalist' view see Herbert Feis, *From Trust to Terror* (New York, Norton, 1970) and Dean Acheson, *Present at the Creation: My Years with the State Department* (New York, Norton, 1969). For a 'revisionist' view see Daniel Yergin, *Shattered Peace: The Origins of the Cold War and the National Security State* (Boston, Houghton Mifflin, 1977). Yergin paints a picture of a clique within the State Department (the 'Riga Axiom') who were ideologically so opposed to the Soviet Union that they would do anything to disrupt good relations with the United States. This group, according to Yergin, included notably George Kennan, Charles Bohlen, Loy Henderson and Robert Kelley (Head of the Department's Eastern European Desk until he was sent to be Ambassador to Ankara in 1936). Called after their main pre-1933 base, the US Embassy in Riga, they are supposed to have poisoned the atmosphere of US–Soviet relations in a systematic way. Roosevelt is portrayed by Yergin as being much more pro-Soviet, as evidenced by his renewal of diplomatic relations in 1933, his sending of a Soviet 'appeaser', Joseph Davies, as Ambassador to Moscow in 1936, and his generally accommodating attitude to Stalin, especially from 1941 on. He is accordingly referred to as cleaving to the 'Yalta Axiom'.

5 Anthony Adamthwaite, *Grandeur and Misery: France's Bid for Power in Europe, 1914–1940* (London, Arnold, 1995), p. 231. *La Décadence* is the sub-title of Jean-Baptiste Duroselle's book on the 1930s: *Politique Etrangère de la*

France: La Décadence (Paris, Imprimerie Nationale, 1979). Other writers agree with Duroselle, Andrew Shennan writing that, 'The catastrophe of May–June 1940 had laid bare a profound national crisis [which] was perceived to permeate every aspect of French life – economic, social, demographic, political, even ethical', Andrew Shennan, *Rethinking France: Plans for Renewal, 1940–1946* (Oxford, Clarendon Press, 1989), p. 9.

6 François Kersaudy, *Churchill and De Gaulle* (London, Collins, 1981). See also Edmonds, *The Big Three*, from whom the 'Joan of Arc' quote is taken, p. 323.

7 Kersaudy, *Churchill and De Gaulle*, Chapters 4 and 5.

8 De Gaulle to Pleven, 18 March 1942; Pleven Papers, A.N. 550 AP 16.

9 Kersaudy, *Churchill and De Gaulle*, pp. 155–160 and 184.

10 Mendès-France to Noel-Baker, 29 January 1944; NBKR 4/261.

11 For Roosevelt's views on de Gaulle, see Robert Dallek, *Franklin D. Roosevelt and American Foreign Policy, 1932–1945* (New York, Oxford University Press, 1979), pp. 376–379.

12 Hopkins to Roosevelt and reply, 15 May 1942; Roosevelt Papers, Secretary's Files, 168, Box 3.

13 File of 2 January 1941, Berle Papers, Box 44. In 1942, Berle to Hull, 18 June 1942; Berle Papers, Box 58. Brinton's comments are in a document by the CFFR 'Peace Aims Group': 'The Political Outlook and the Possibility of Collaborating with Democratic Groups in France and Belgium'; H. Fish Armstrong Papers, Box 73.

14 Shepherd B. Clough (London) to Berle, 13 September 1943; Berle Papers, Box 65.

15 Jean Lacouture, *De Gaulle: The Ruler, 1945–1970* (London, Harvill, 1991), pp. 8–9.

16 Lippman in *The New York Herald Tribune*, 6 June 1942, used in his Preface by Kennan in 'Russia and the Post-War Settlement', written in the Summer of 1942: Kennan Papers, Box 25/4.

17 See my *Trading with the Bolsheviks* (Manchester University Press, 1992), Chapter 5, and Thomas R. Maddux, 'American Diplomats and the Soviet Experiment: The View from the Moscow Embassy, 1934–1939', *South Atlantic Quarterly*, vol. 74, Autumn 1975, pp. 4658–4687.

18 Caroline Kennedy-Pipe, *Stalin's Cold War: Soviet Strategies in Europe, 1943 to 1956* (Manchester University Press, 1995), p. 78.

19 Dallek, *Franklin D. Roosevelt and American Foreign Policy*, p. 533. For another account of Roosevelt's dealings with the Russians see Edward R. Stettinius, *Roosevelt and the Russians: The Yalta Conference* (London, Jonathan Cape, 1950).

20 Roosevelt to William D. Leahy, US Ambassador to Vichy France, 26 June 1941: Roosevelt *F.D.R.: His Personal Letters*, p. 1177.

21 Hopkins Memorandum on meeting Stalin in Moscow, 30 July 1941; Hopkins Papers, File 306.

22 The opinion of Leo Crowley of the State Department as reported to Henry Morgenthau, 7 July 1944; Morgenthau, Diary, Fiche 17.

23 Sainsbury, *Churchill and Roosevelt at War*, Chapter 4, quote on p. 59.

24 Dallek is very clear that Roosevelt had no choice in this matter. He quotes Adam Ulam's dictum that 'Suspicion was built into the Soviet system' and that

whatever the West had done would not have helped them get over it: Dallek, *Franklin D. Roosevelt and American Foreign Policy*, pp. 534–535.

25 Kennan, 'Draft Paper on Russian–American Relations', 1944; Kennan Papers, Box 23/14.

26 'X' [George Kennan], 'The Sources of Soviet Conduct', *Foreign Affairs*, vol. 25, no. 4, 1947, pp. 566–582.

27 Berle, 'Sub-Committee: Organization of Peace', 3 January 1940; Berle Papers, Box 54.

28 'E.R.' [Eleanor Roosevelt] to Roosevelt, 21 August 1941; Roosevelt Secretary's Files, Box 24.

29 The opinion of Leo Crowley of the State Department as reported to Henry Morgenthau, 7 July 1944; Morgenthau, Diary, Fiche 17.

30 Berle, 'Sub-Committee: Organization of Peace', 3 January 1940; Berle Papers, Box 54.

31 William Bullitt to Roosevelt, 29 January 1943; Roosevelt Secretary's Files, Box 24.

32 Winston Churchill, *The Second World War* (6 vols, London, Cassell, 1948–1954).

33 For a clear description of this view see David Reynolds, *The Creation of the Anglo-American Alliance, 1937–1941* (London, Europa, 1981), Chapter 4 *supra*.

34 A good overview of this can be found in Robert M. Hathaway, *Ambiguous Partnership: Britain and America, 1944–1947* (New York, Columbia University Press, 1981) and Sainsbury, *Churchill and Roosevelt at War*.

35 Sainsbury, *Churchill and Roosevelt at War*, pp. 1–16.

36 Edmonds, *The Big Three*, p. 270.

37 See Chapter 4. This was an act described by Kenneth Harris as 'one of the greatest and least defensible mistakes made by a President of the United States in the twentieth century …': Kenneth Harris, *Attlee* (London, Weidenfeld and Nicholson), p. 271.

38 Pasvolsky, Memorandum for Ambassador Winant (London), 15 February 1941; Pasvolsky Papers, Box 7.

39 Berle Papers, Box 54; see Chapter 3, pp. 93–94.

40 Discussion between American officials and the 'Research Committee on International Organization' of the RIIA (Chatham House) at Balliol College, Oxford, 2 May 1941; Welles Papers, Box 192: also quoted in Chapter 4.

41 Berle, Memorandum of 4 August 1941; Berle Papers, Box 58.

42 One interpretation of this can be found in David Reynolds, *Britannia Overruled: British Policy and World Power in the 20th Century* (London, Longman, 1991).

43 A good summary of this can be found in Keith Robbins, *Appeasement* (Oxford, Blackwell/Historical Association, 2nd edn 1997). See also Chapter 4 *infra*.

44 The Morgenthau Memorandum, presented at the Quebec Conference in September 1944, quoted by Harper, *American Visions of Europe* (Cambridge University Press, 1994), which also gives a concise summary of the Plan's reception in the United States (pp. 104–106). The Memorandum on which Morgenthau's intentions were first elaborated and his account of the discussion with Roosevelt and Eleanor Roosevelt about it are to be found in his Diary, entries for 1 and 2 September 1944.

45 Pasvolsky, 'PWP Progress Book 1', that is, summaries of State Department policy on various topics, this one being the 'Treatment of Enemy States', 1 September 1994; Memorandum on the 'Treatment of Germany', 15 November 1944 (present were Stettinius, Pasvolsky, Gene Hackworth and Roosevelt); Pasvolsky Papers, Box 7.

46 David W. Ellwood, *Rebuilding Europe: Western Europe, America and Postwar Reconstruction* (London, Longman, 1992), p. 23.

47 Hugh R. Wilson, 'Memorandum on World Order', 22 January 1940; Berle Papers, Box 54.

48 See Chapter 8 for more discussion of this.

49 See, for example, Memorandum of 7 May 1940, Berle Papers, Box 54. Samuel P. Huntington, *The Clash of Civilisations and the Remaking of World Order* (New York, Simon and Schuster, 1996).

50 Hankey, Manuscript Diary, 26 August 1918; HNKY 1/5.

51 FO 371/15208, 14 January 1932, cited by David E. Kaiser, *Economic Diplomacy and the Origins of the Second World War: Germany, Britain, France and Eastern Europe, 1920–1939* (Princeton University Press, 1980), p. 42.

52 Kennan, 'The Appointment of the New State Council in Norway', 1940, Kennan Papers Box 23/3, and Mayers, *George Kennan and the Dilemmas of US Foreign Policy* (New York, Oxford University Press), pp. 54–55.

53 Mayers, *George Kennan*, pp. 65 and 50.

54 Kennan, 'Technique of German Imperialism in Europe', April 1941; Kennan Papers, 23/4.

55 Mayers, *George Kennan*, pp. 77–85. Mayers also rejects charges that Kennan was in any way anti-Semitic.

56 Kennan (Lisbon) to Shaw (State Department), 18 August 1942. Kennan was chafing that he might be sent into enforced exile in the backwater of Portugal and asking to be allowed at least to stay in Washington, where he was one of the most experienced staffers about both Germany and Russia. Naturally he was sent to Lisbon: Kennan Papers, 23/11.

57 This included Welles, Berle, McMurray, Armstrong of the CFFR, Cohen and Taylor, a very heavy-weight line-up: 3 January 1940, Berle Papers, Box 54.

58 'Memorandum Arising from Conversations in Mr. Welles' Office', 19 and 26 April 1940, dated 1 May 1940; Berle Papers, Box 54.

59 '... these ['tentative commitments'] may be taken as the equivalent of the agreement between the Allies in 1916 to redivide Europe ...'. Berle to Hull, 4 August 1941; Berle Papers, Box 58.

60 Berle to Hull, 'Anglo-American Collaboration, Political and Reoccupation Plans for Europe', 26 November 1942, Berle Papers, Box 58; Pasvolsky memo of 23 November 1943; Pasvolsky Papers, Box 7.

61 William Bullitt to Roosevelt, 29 January 1943; Roosevelt Secretary's Files, Box 24. All of these memoranda are preserved in Roosevelt's papers, and Bullitt certainly had the ear of Roosevelt for much of the war, whatever their occasional contretemps.

62 As previous note and 'Preliminary Peace Aims of Eastern European Nations', n.d.; Armstrong Papers, Box 73.

63 Bullitt to Roosevelt, 29 January 1943; Roosevelt, Secretary's Files, Box 24.

64 Dulles, Document on Trip to England, June–July 1942 (quoted in Chapter 3), p. 3.

65 Richard Mayne and John Pinder, *Federal Union: The Pioneers* (London, Macmillan, 1990), p. 8 and *passim*.

66 Mitrany commented that it 'was both anti-Bolshevik and anti-Anglo-Saxon, but it never had any solid outline or more than a dubious and changeable support': Mitrany, in an article of December 1965 published in the *Journal of Common Market Studies*, reprinted in Mitany, *A Working Peace System* (Chicago, Quadrangle Books, 1966), p. 188. Briand's Plan of 1929 fared slightly better in Mitrany's opinion, but not much.

67 Stimson, Diary, entry for 4 November 1943; Reel 8.

68 For more details on such PWP thinking see the sections on regional security and Europe. For an account of the Anglo-American differences over Balkan, Mediterranean and Northern European (Second Front) strategy, see Sainsbury, *Churchill and Roosevelt at War*, Chapters 2 and 3. Sainsbury points out the 'general US tendency to use "the Balkans" as a cover-all word for all eastward-looking operations...' (p. 53).

69 Stimson, Diary, entry for 6 April 1943; Reel 8.

70 Stimson, Diary, entry for 11 May 1943; Reel 8.

71 Berle to Hull, 'Anglo-American Collaboration, Political and Reoccupation Plans for Europe', 26 November 1942; Berle Papers, Box 58.

72 Stimson, Diary, 22 May, and again 8 September 1943 after a lunch with Churchill at the White House, with Hopkins and Baruch, on the occasion of the Italian surrender; Stimson, Diary, Reel 8.

73 Sainsbury, *The Turning Point*, pp. 12–35.

74 Harry Hopkins, 'Memorandum of Meeting of Big Three at Teheran', 30 November 1943; Hopkins Papers, File 332.

75 Stimson, Diary, 28 October 1943; Reel 8.

76 Berle to Hull, 16 December 1941; Berle Papers, Box 58.

77 See correspondence between Moscow and Washington, especially Hamilton to State Department, 18 October 1943; Robert Kelley (Istanbul, probably the main American expert on Russia and subsequently 'exiled' to Turkey, see *supra*, in the inter-war period), same date; and Lippman's comments in Stettinius (Washington) to Moscow, 19 October 1943, Hull Papers, Microfilm, Reel 23.

78 Roosevelt, in *FRUS, 1944*, vol. 1, p. 12, quoted by Mayers, *George Kennan*, p. 80. Kennan made quite clear that he was chafing at the bit very early in his stay in London and was mercifully (for him) sent to Moscow in September 1944 at Harriman's suggestion, where he commenced the most influential part of his career: Mayers, pp. 95 and 344, fn. 16.

79 Kennan (London) to 'Mr Ambassador' (Harriman in Moscow), April 1944; Kennan Papers, 23/14.

80 Armstrong (London) to James Clement Dunn (Director of the Office of European Affairs State Department), 24 August and (to Isaiah Bowman), 7 December 1944; Armstrong Papers, Box 79.

81 Armstrong to Bowman, 7 December 1944 and to Secretary of State Stettinius, 11 January 1945; Armstrong Papers, Box 79.

82 Armstrong to Stettinius, 26 January 1945; Armstrong Papers, Box 78.

83 Mayers, *George Kennan*, p. 80.

84 Stimson commented that 'we were all very afraid of [the EAC because] ... the British are going to work to build it up, just as I feared they would, into a regular

big institution in London...', Diary, entries for 28 October (during the Moscow Conference) and 8, 9 and 23 November 1943; Reel 8.

85 Mayers, *George Kennan*, p. 80.

86 Harper, *American Visions of Europe*, pp. 181–182.

87 For details of the Teheran meeting, see Sainsbury, *The Turning Point*, Chapter VIII.

88 For further details on Yalta see in particular Feis, *Churchill, Roosvelt, Stalin*, and Edmonds, *The Big Three*.

89 Kennan to Harriman, 18 December 1944; Kennan Papers, 23/19.

90 Stimson, Diary, 11 January 1944; Reel 8.

91 For an analysis of British public opinion towards the USSR during and after Yalta, see Bell, *John Bull and the Bear: British Public Opinion, Foreign Policy and the Soviet Union, 1941–1945* (London, Edward Arnold, 1990), pp. 174–181.

92 Edmonds, *The Big Three*, pp. 416–421; Pierre de Senarclans, *De Yalta au Rideau de Fer: Les Grandes Puissances et les Origines de la Guerre Froide* (Paris, Presses de la Fondation Nationale des Sciences Politiques, 1993), pp. 36–42.

93 Feis, *Churchill, Roosvelt and Stalin*, pp. 518–529.

94 Even during the Yalta debate in Parliament, certain notes of discord were heard about a 'puppet Poland', but only from a few right-wing MPs: Bell, *John Bull and the Bear*, pp. 177–78. The major criticism emerged after the fighting in Europe had ended, as indeed was the case in the United States.

95 Colville, Manuscript Diary, entries of 20 January, and 14 and 29 February 1944; File 1/6.

96 Colville reports this in his Diary, 4 and 13 March 1944; File 1/6.

97 Churchill, speaking to Colville, Macmillan and others, 4 March 1944; Colville, Diary, 1/6.

98 Kennedy-Pipe, *Stalin's Cold War*, pp. 49–51.

99 J.A. Lukács, *The Great Powers and Eastern Europe* (New York, Regnery, 1953), p. 683.

100 Gaddis, *We Now Know*, pp. 16–17.

101 Kennan, 'The Sources of Soviet Conduct': see note 26. For a discussion of this by its author, see Kennan, *Memoirs, 1925–1950* (London, Hutchinson, 1967), especially Chapter 15. For commentary, see Harper, *American Visions of Europe*, Chapter 5 and Gaddis, *Strategies of Containment: A Critical Appraisal of Postwar American Security Policy* (New York, Oxford University Press, 1982), especially Chapter 2.

102 For this transition see Gaddis, *Strategies of Containment*, Chapter 4; Harper, *American Visions of Europe*, Chapter 7; and Acheson, *Present at the Creation*, especially Chapter 41.

103 Sweetzer to Armstrong, 13 January 1945; Armstrong Papers, Box 79.

6

International organisation, global security and the NWO

Introduction

In any discussion about how to achieve an NWO the question of how to implement that order has always been paramount. However, it has often been observed that 'one man's order is another man's repression', in other words, that order is a normative concept. The many different models suggested for achieving it – balance of power, alliance systems, 'concerts' and 'leagues' – are all underpinned by a dialectic between those who see the aim of the order so created as a more 'just' international system, and those who wish merely to see 'disorder' is kept to a minimum compatible with a reasonable functioning of the system of states.[1] The NWO architects that are the prime focus of this book have played a key role in this debate, and this chapter is mainly dedicated to showing how their thinking developed in what might be called the area of 'global security' from the period of the First World War until the present. Again, a primary emphasis will be put on the period between 1914 and 1945.

As we have seen, one of the key Wilsonian principles encapsulated in the Fourteen Points was the creation of an international organisation that would help to solve the problems of what Inis Claude rightly calls an '*interstate*' system. Wilson's thinking had an ancestry dating back to the setting up of the modern state system after Westphalia and was given particular impetus by the perceived need to avoid what Claude calls an 'accidental' war, as had occurred in 1914.[2] As was stressed in Chapters 1 and 2, this was a determinedly 'realist/statist' enterprise, but it also stood in uneasy but linked relation to an emerging belief that an alternative to the sovereign imperative of war as a means of solving international disputes had to be found.

It has consequently often been observed that the origins of international organisation were in response to the phenomenon of war in general, but of the First World War in particular. Men such as Sir Edward Grey, Lord Bryce and the other statesmen described in earlier chapters did not live in any 'idealist' utopia, they were the masters of a great Empire gained through war. They were more than aware that war has provided a source of meaning, of status and of 'identity'[3] for many centuries, and that the call for peace as a rallying cry for the creation of a better world against war was (and remains) a relatively recent phenomenon. For them, international organisation is generally seen as a move towards a change in the way that inter-state relations are conducted, by attempting the provision of a guarantee of three things in one package: the re-direction of the impetus towards war into more peaceful channels; the creation of a system of collective security to counteract naked aggression; and the provision of economic security and disarmament to take away the ability to wage it. The purpose of this chapter is to show how these ideas developed in practice during the periods of most intense NWO thinking this century.

It is worthwhile remembering that although attempts at some sort of regulation of world order date back to the 1648 Treaty of Westphalia, they have really only seen institutional form in this century, first in the LON and then in the UN as international organisations.[4] As to other forms of *global* regulation of economic and functional issues, in what are commonly called 'specialised agencies', these are even more recent, and really only the product of the period since 1960. Before then such organisations as the Universal Postal Union were directed mainly at the regulation of Europe. The NWO projects of the two world wars gave a great impetus to the development of global international organisations, but it was the emergence of decolonised developing countries that has transformed the global organisational picture. and, since the 1980s, the emergence of the global economy (whether this is 'globalisation' or not is a moot point, for a discussion of which see Chapter 7 and the Conclusion).

One major question that this chapter must answer is to what extent we can see the roots of the contemporary system in the NWO ideas of 1914–19 and 1939–45, both on the security and, in the next chapter, on the economic (or what might be termed 'functional') front. These two areas of activity were clearly linked in the minds of nearly all NWO thinkers (a point that will be enlarged upon in Chapter 8), a link that has become entrenched in the post-1989 security debate about 'economic', 'humanitarian' and even 'societal' security.[5] This chapter will concentrate more on what can be seen to be the enduring debates about security in the international organisation context, those on the causes of war and the conditions for peace, as well as those about the relative virtues of different kinds of international organisation (global or regional in particular) and of the possibilities of disarmament. Another focus will be to examine the way that international organisations have emerged and been abolished – after 1919, 1945 and 1989 there has been a significant pattern of both happening. Eric Roll was told by the Professor of Economics at Yale, Dick Bissell, in the 1950s that '[y]ou will end up by leaving the landscape littered with derelict international organizations'.[6]

It is therefore not the aim of this chapter to go into forensic detail about the international organisations that have emerged this century[7] in the context of the NWO, but to try and elucidate the main strands of thinking (both 'intellectual' and policy oriented) that went into them, in the context of their time(s) and using a selection of the private and public musings of some of the key thinkers and policy makers that made a significant input. It must be repeated that it is not the task of this book to reinvent the wheel of current debates, but rather to point to the historical genealogy of these debates. Hence reference will be made throughout to the main literature that describes the mechanisms of the LON and UN agencies that were set up as a result of the discussions in 1914–19 and 1941–45, as well as briefer reference being made to what has happened since 1989, but it will be assumed that the reader has a reasonable knowledge of the institutions themselves.

International organisation as the arbiter of peace and war

The basic dilemma: how can peace be guaranteed?

Even before the First World War had properly got under way, there was a growing feeling among liberal and what Carr terms 'realist' thinkers that the root causes of it could not be undone unless a 'good' peace was arrived at. The question was what this 'good' peace should look like. Hankey, as the British Secretary to the Paris Peace Conference after April 1919 and a key actor in British policy making for most of the first half of this century (cf. Chapters 1 and 2), took Edward Burke as his main text:

> The proposition is peace. Not peace through the medium of war; not peace to be hunted through the labyrinth of intricate and endless negotiations; not peace to depend on the juridical determination of perplexing boundaries of a complex government. It is simple peace, sought in its natural course, and in its ordinary haunts – it is peace sought in the spirit of peace, and laid in principles purely pacific.

But, said Hankey, it is rare that such a peace can be achieved 'in an atmosphere of bitterness, hate, revenge and acute nationalism' such as followed 1914–18, 'especially when a large number of nations is concerned with peacemaking'.[8] In such circumstances, all that might be achieved is to create a peace that would do as much as possible to guarantee 'order', even if that meant a punitive and probably unfair stigmatisation of one side as the loser who has to be blamed and the other as the victor, who is entitled to the spoils.

One of Hankey's natural political adversaries, G. Lowes Dickinson, a prominent liberal and one of Carr's 'idealist' targets, nonetheless agreed with many of Hankey's doubts about the possibilities for a 'good' peace. He wrote to Bryce in October 1914: 'My own view is that what is not done at the peace will hardly have a chance after it, in a fresh era of competition, fear and revenge.' But he also felt, as he expressed it in 1917, that 'war proceeds from wrong ideas and wrong policies', so get these right and peace should be assured. He had a vision of a 'general congress including the neutral powers and of course, in particular, the United States, to settle the whole basis of European relations by general agreement'. Lowes Dickinson summed up the dilemma as being one where either of two kinds of settlement was possible. One way was to 'strengthen the victors and crush the vanquished, arresting, for a time, a practical hegemony of Europe by one group of powers, imposed by force on the others [which would] ... lead eventually to another European war after an arms race', and 'no settlement, but an armed truce'.

The only way Lowes Dickinson could see was to think creatively about the future of international relations, in effect to rip up the rule book of classical political realism and write another. For him, any alternative way 'implies [creating] a new conception and purpose for Europe' which would not give 'a temporary supremacy' to any group of powers, but would 'give a permanent peace to Europe; first, by removing, so far as possible, the more deep-seated causes of war – and these are those connected with oppressed nationalities; secondly, by directing international policy towards building up the machinery whereby all disputes shall be settled by judicial authority'. A third condition was general disarmament. This would prove most difficult as the peace movements of nearly the past hundred years had noted the links between war and the armaments industry and its links in turn to political power structures in all the major states.[9]

These two opposing ideological positions (Hankey and Lowes Dickinson) on the necessary conditions for the conduct of international relations have come to be defined over the intervening period as 'realist' versus 'idealist'. Idealism was essentially a construct developed out of an understanding of how the war had started and what were the root causes of war itself. It derived from a liberal nostalgia not only for peace itself, but for the ordered freedom of the pre-war period. This period was remembered as one where the individual, and not the state, was the main point of reference in international relations, giving a freedom of action economically and politically that many liberals feared would now be destroyed by the increase in state control over many aspects of life.

Idealism thus was, and remains, a complex phenomenon, but can be said to have spawned at least two major sub-sets of ideas, of which 'pacifism' was an absolute form, that is, the rejection of all forms of violence, even in self-defence. A second sub-set can be found in a reformist rejection of war as an efficient and sensible way of solving inter-state differences and a call for alternative modes of directing humankind's energy, especially through economic cooperation and regional integration. We therefore need to 'unpack' the internal logic of, particularly, this reformist idea to see how it influenced the NWO agenda.

Attitudes to war and peace in the major First World War groupings

In trying to elucidate the motives behind the NWO planners of 1919 and 1945 we have to make more than a passing reference to contemporary beliefs about the motives and necessary strategies for the discouragement of war and the encouragement of peace before, during and after the First World War. We also have to ask how this thinking provided some input into policy decisions as to what the new international organs such as the LON were supposed to achieve. Was, for example, 'disarmament', which took up so much of the LON's time and effort in the 1920s and 1930s, in any way a useful aim? In broader terms, what should the LON be aiming to achieve? Should it be creating, through education, a better informed youth, one that understands the equation 'war bad, peace good'?

Science, rationality, peace and war

The age demanded rational explanations for everything, especially among the liberal thinkers that we have described as being appalled by the 'irrational' recourse to violence for political ends. Explanations for such irrationality were often sought in science, or pseudo-science. The use and abuse of socio-biology was a key element in this, continuing a long nineteenth century tradition of eugenics and other forms of Darwinian thinking. Nearly all the thinkers of the period of the First World War make repeated allusion to racial stereotypes of 'warlike' and 'peace-loving' peoples.[10] The British tended to see the Germans (or 'Teutonic races') as being a key member of the former grouping and the English and Americans ('the Anglo-Saxons') as being members of the latter. The Axis Powers, especially the Germans, stressed their cultural superiority on every possible occasion. The new languages of psychoanalysis and the physical sciences were used extensively to denigrate or explain the other side's motives and behaviour.[11] To reformulate the thought of Daniel Pick slightly, the 'canon' of war has been a constant factor in defining and redefining our collective identities as national groupings and in our definition of what we mean by 'civilisation'. It therefore has to play a significant background role in the way that NWO planners saw their primary task, the taming or abolition of war.

'Militarism'

'Militarism' was the disease that 'warlike' peoples were seen as having caught. Attacks on the disease pre-date 1914, and were a key feature of thinking in the socialist Second International.[12] Militarism also became a key target of practically all liberal NWO thinkers of 1914–19. If 'war proceeds from wrong ideas and wrong policies' then 'militarism' was obviously the main problem affecting Germany. The problem was that it could also destroy the rest of the civilised world, as the war had demonstrated. Militarism came to assume in liberal and socialist thinking of the first thirty years of the century a status akin to the influence of the Devil for the Inquisition, 'too complex for definition' – it was seen as lurking in every corner ('a state of mind and a military and political system'), so that 'nothing but a complete and radical reform of international relations can stop its spread'.[13]

On the other hand, many 'realists/statists' took the view that militarism could not be 'cured' and was even a complaint that might be usefully emulated. Hankey was not alone in his Nietzschean belief that 'all through history the advance of civilisation ha[s] proceeded side by side with war and conquest'. The only problem was to make sure that you had the right kind of armaments, not to get rid of them or your martial spirit. 'Neglect of sea power was a frequent cause of disaster', he warned in a volume of reminiscences in 1946, and 'few, if any, civilisations have been able to withstand a prolonged period of peace without degeneracy, often followed by collapse.' His main exemplars for this thesis were drawn from a classical literature with which all of the elite would have then been familiar from their expensive educations in schools wedded to the study of the classics. Hankey's conclusion was that without a military spirit civilisation was doomed, but equally that with too much of one it was also bound to be damaged. We can take this almost as a commonplace view among the British and other elites of the time, and one which would have a certain echo even today.[14]

In any discussion about the future of the international system at the end of the war, the 'mental attitude of the Central Powers' was frequently evoked as being the major obstacle to the success of any League. Hence even the very learned Grotius Society used a language redolent of the pseudo-Freudian: Germany had to be beaten, as '[a]n unchastened Germany could never be a member of such a League'; how could you teach 'the spirit of service to the cause of humanity and justice ... [as] nobler than the lust of conquest ... The curse of our time was the desire of dominance – the lust of selfish aggrandisement among the nations.'[15] Liberals and realists were at one on this, with the former seeing militarism as peculiarly embedded in Germany, the realists seeing this as a threat but also as something to admire and emulate. But their policy suggestions were correspondingly radically different.

The varieties of pacifism

As a counter to militarism, pacifism seemed one logical response to many liberal thinkers before 1914 and, especially, in the inter-war years. The intellectual origins of this are naturally complex, as are its manifestations. Martin Ceadel has convincingly argued that the opposition to war in the nineteenth and twentieth centuries took many and varied forms depending on the national and cultural place of its attempted flowering. He makes the important distinction between 'pacifism' and '*pacificism*', the first meaning an outright opposition to participation in war, a perfectionist 'moral creed'; the second more an 'ethic of responsibility' which 'believes in implementing reforms at the political level – rather than waiting for profound changes in men's consciences'.

Before the First World War this latter essentially meant some form of 'internationalism', of which Ceadel discerns three main strains. The first of these is a mainstream liberal belief in the innate illogicality of war which has its origins in national prejudices. This had to be cured by 'improved international contact', essentially economic and cultural or, if this failed, by diminishing the sovereignty of the state by transferring power to federal or confederal higher bodies. The second puts the causes of war down to capitalism and imperialism and sees some form of socialism as the only answer. A third strand, which Ceadel rightly sees as being strong just before the war, blends the first two strands, seeing war as economically irrational while attributing its encouragement to various capitalist influences, and in particular the arms manufacturers.[16]

Pacificism, says Ceadel, was particularly strong in inter-war Britain, but also a feature of the United States, and in both countries 'was an integral part of its liberal, protestant political culture'. Where nationalism was the dominant feature of political culture, as in Germany, and 'where liberalism was too weak to nourish [any form of] pacifism', or in France where such movements were almost exclusively on the left, there were also 'strategic factors' at play. It was easier to take a 'middle position between submissiveness and Realpolitik', as *pacificists* did in Britain or the USA, when the threat of an expansionist neighbour was not as obvious as it was for France.[17] It could equally be argued that to stand out against the German 'will to power' in 1914 or the late 1930s as any form of pacifist ensured that only the very brave did so. It was not an easy form of intellectual dilettantism.

Perhaps this is one reason why the Nazi hierarchy misjudged British willingness to fight, by judging the essentially *pacificistic* voters in the 1934 Peace Ballot as pacifists in the moral absolutist sense. The British and the Americans would on the whole fight for what they believed in, which was liberal democracy and 'civilisation', even if they would not fight as easily as they had in 1914 for cruder jingoistic slogans. This would also explain, at least partly, the particular appeal of Wilsonian NWO thinking in Britain and the United States as it posited a re-ordering of international relations along lines that were already embedded in a growing liberal consciousness. In order for such ideas to spread, the over-arching liberal ideology had also to take root elsewhere. It duly has in, for example, Germany and the rest of Europe, under the impact of the second and third NWOs, both arguably due to the victory of a militant *pacificistic* liberalism.

The 'failure' of the LON?

As was stressed in Chapter 1, Wilson's crusade incorporated much of the flavour of the liberal aim of transforming the way that international relations were conducted. This in practice meant, in the words of Lowes Dickinson, that 'world peace' depended on 'bring[ing] together nations on substantially the same level of civilisation, and so far as might be capable of being members of the same state'.[18] This is very similar reasoning to that used by Sir Edward Grey in his 1916 Memorandum (also quoted in Chapter 1) or of Clarence Streit in his 1939 *Union Now*, quoted in previous chapters or, indeed, to the drafters of the Charter of the United Nations. The League of Nations was therefore only 'open to all civilised nations … a defensive alliance against such state or states [that challenged it]'. Membership could then be opened to other states, which would solve their problems, such as the disease of militarism as 'the preliminary moral and intellectual conversion [to peace] took place'.[19] Being in the League was thus like being declared 'cured' by Alcoholics Anonymous, a mark of membership of international society, not of a mere system of states, and of, to quote Wilson's speech of 22 January 1917, a 'community of power', not a 'balance of power'.[20]

This vision did not fulfil its promise in the inter-war years. The reasons are at the heart of the entire 'realist/statist' critique of 'utopian' liberal thinkers such as Wilson and Lowes Dickinson. Carr gives us the classic definition of the failure of the LON. For him, 'the dangers of abstract perfection [had led to] … such purely utopian projects as the International Police Force, the Briand–Kellogg Pact [to outlaw war, of 1928] and the United States of Europe'. Among the principal mistakes had been 'purporting to treat' all members as equal, which gave the Great Powers a majority on the LON Council. This was a problem that many liberal thinkers also recognised after the First World War, but they believed, in the words of Salvador de Madariaga, Director of Disarmament at the League between 1924 and 1928, that the 'Master Cook is Time'. Another key criticism by Carr was that the LON did not prohibit war altogether, but showed great vagueness about 'the occasions on which it might be legitimately resorted to' – it assumed that this would be 'obvious'.[21] This emphasis on the membership of an international organisation and the promises that it makes is at the heart of all subsequent NWO thinking on the subject. Is the idea of a security-based international organisation flawed in its essence or merely in its membership or application? The League of Nations provided the first testbed for these questions.

The failure of collective security?

The first ground on which the LON has been faulted by history lies in its non-implementation of the idea of collective security. This half-way house between the balance of power and a global security system has quite rightly been seen as part of a realist world view. It was ultimately tested in the period after the First World War in 1939 and finally made operational in the Grand Alliance that defeated Hitler. But in the period after 1919 and until 1939 it was never properly evoked and certainly not implemented. The history of the 1920s and 1930s has hence been seen by many as the demonstration of the lack of political will to implement it and even of a fatal flaw at its heart, pointed to by Hankey in his 1916 Memorandum (see Chapter 1).

The collective security clauses of the Covenant of the LON were greeted with the most enthusiasm by the smaller states of Europe, which felt that the principles of self-determination and of independence for them were best guaranteed by being under its auspices. The 1920s seemed to prove this a correct assumption – several small-state disputes were worked out within the LON framework, as with the 1925 near-war between Greece and Bulgaria.[22] This may be said to have proved that when the machinery of the LON to settle disputes was actually used, it was successful. But unfortunately this was the exception and not the rule. After 1925 most Great Power discussions on security and other matters took place, more often than not, outside the LON. Hence the Locarno Pacts (between France, Britain and Germany in 1925) and the important discussions on naval disarmament were made multilateral, not LON, concerns. The League was therefore demonstrated to be perceived by the real Powers not to be the place where their security concerns could be addressed. The fig-leaf of the 1927 LON Preliminary Disarmament Conference and the 1930–33 Disarmament Conference (discussed below) could not disguise this fact.

Most importantly, Great Power rivalry could not be discussed within the LON with the absence of arguably the two most powerful states of all, the United States and the USSR (the latter joined in 1933 when it was already too late). The withdrawal of Germany in 1933 and Japan (same date) sealed any hopes that might have existed. The problem was moreover that the negative legacy of Versailles was not worked out in the LON but either unilaterally (as with most of Hitler's reconquests until Poland in 1939) or in secret (as with the Hoare–Laval Pact over Abyssinia in 1935) or ultimately on the battlefield. A more general conclusion has to be that when the real interests of major Powers cannot be solved within an international organisation, those Powers will go outside it for satisfaction.

A key example of the problem: Japan, the United States and Britain

One vital conflict that can be included in this category and that brings together all the failings of the 1919 NWO can be seen in the build-up and resolution of Japanese tensions with the United States in the Pacific. The Japanese nurtured great feelings of hurt pride over the refusal of their Allies to insert a discouragement to racial discrimination into the Treaty of Versailles.[23] They also felt that the lack of any economic settlement had gravely damaged their interests in the Pacific. And lastly they were constantly annoyed at the grudging way that they perceived their presence to be tolerated at the great naval disarmament Conferences of 1921, 1927 and 1930.

As a key Japanese national defence policy document of as early as 1923 put it: 'The longstanding embroilments, rooted in economic problems and racial prejudice, are extremely difficult to solve ... Such being the Asiatic policy of the United States, sooner or later a clash with our Empire will become inevitable.'[24] This attitude, based or baseless as one might think it, epitomises the feeling of exclusion that the Versailles NWO had created among rising and risen Powers. Without a more inclusive and effective machinery for collective security discussions, the LON was bound to fail in its primary task of preventing war. But it can also be said to demonstrate that even before the Second World War, policy makers saw that 'security' was as much economic and normative as it was military. In this sense they were at one with derided 'utopians' such as Norman Angell.

The LON and disarmament[25]

Much of the energy in implementing the liberal cure for the evil of militarism was directed at what was seen as its major symptom, excessive armaments. The great literary defence of this idea can be found in a book by Salvador de Madariaga. His major classical liberal argument against armaments is almost the same one used by Angell (see Chapter 7): that 'the world has reached such a degree of interdependence ... that international cooperation has become essential ... the only self-supporting region of the world is the whole world ... Only one opinion and only one market cover the face of the earth.'[26] Armaments were therefore an economic absurdity, and war a tragic net cost to humanity and only of benefit to arms manufacturers. Armaments also fostered fear, and prevented such projects as the Channel Tunnel from coming to fruition.[27]

The main obstacles to progress on this issue were 'outlived forms of thought', such as that 'in the final analysis the military and naval strength of the Great Powers will be the final guarantee of the peace of the world'. But how could that be, argued Madariaga, when even the great Royal Navy had not ensured British security? For him, the only cure for humankind consisted in accepting 'one general law' of international relations: 'the cause of war is the tendency of life to create a set of conflicts. Such a tendency can only be dealt with by the World–Community organized to that end ....' Even the Covenant of the League, born as it was 'in the original sin' of Allied compromise, had the institutional basis for a peace that would last.[28]

It must nonetheless be admitted that as a cure for war, disarmament has had one of the longest pedigrees and been one of the greatest disappointments. This has not surprised 'realists'. Given his above stated beliefs about the need for martial spirit, it is hardly surprising to learn that, for Hankey, disarmament was a pernicious idea. Rome had apparently collapsed because of it (and more generalised 'decadence' such as the decline of agriculture and divorce). To his support and defence he quoted contemporaries of all political persuasions such as (unsurprisingly) Arthur Balfour and even Lord Bryce.[29]

Others saw practical problems that are as valid now as then: 'What are armaments? ... How do you keep a check on armaments?' What kind of sanctions are appropriate or effective to reduce them? To these questions from Professor J.H. Morgan, during a discussion in 1918 of the Grotius Society, Lord Parmoor rather lamely replied that he 'relied on good faith and on the co-partnership between the nations which would be sufficient without special difficulty to bring force to bear with any recalcitrant member'.[30] H.G. Wells agreed, with the added comment that

> countries contemplating war and having no serious intention of disarming effectively will enter quite readily into conferences upon disarmament, but they will do so partly because of the excellent propaganda value of such a participation and mainly because of the chance it gives them of some restriction which will hamper a possible antagonist more than it will hamper themselves.[31]

This use of disarmament as a propaganda ploy was precisely what happened at the 1932–33 LON Disarmament Conference where the Soviet Union used the proceedings to propose a 'zero arms' option in the certain knowledge that it would be refused.[32] It has happened many times since.

Wells's solution was that disarmament Conferences were bound to be nothing more than ritual nonsense until states themselves had been abolished and a world federal system set up: 'Given stable international relations, the world would put aside its armaments as naturally as a man takes off his coat in winter on entering a warm house.'[33] This idea of a 'merging of sovereignty' was very acceptable to American federalist thinkers such as Streit and British thinkers such as Toynbee with his concept of 'pooled sovereignty'. But it was not the principal aim of the LON, which accepted the principle of the equality and good will of states, and those that put their faith in the other extra-League Conferences that proliferated in the inter-war period. Neither naturally did it appeal to those such as Carr who believed that the nation state was now more firmly entrenched than ever and that only overwhelming power could tame the vile spirits of war.

NWO successes as a result of Versailles?

With such an unremitting catalogue of failure to its credit it is hardly surprising that the Versailles settlement and the LON were deemed at the time, and have been deemed ever since, to have been 'failures'. But are there any grounds for claiming that it was successful, even if only partially, in advancing some of the key ideas of the 1919 NWO? In looking for optimism there are several places that we might search. First, was there any real change to diplomatic practice in the direction of 'Open covenants openly arrived at', the first of the Fourteen Points? We shall also have to ask, in the context of Chapters 7 and 8, whether there was any real progress in the direction of global economic reform or towards human rights and self-determination.

Changes in diplomatic practice

A first major development in international relations that has out-lasted the LON has been the development of what is termed the 'New Diplomacy', the first of Wilson's Fourteen Points – 'Open covenants openly arrived at'. Multilateral diplomacy is as old as the state system itself, with most commentators taking the Treaty of Westphalia of 1648 as its defining moment. Wilson's additional idea was that such bilateral and multilateral diplomacy that had dominated international discourse since 1648 had been a major cause of the First World War through its reliance on a 'secret' diplomacy that fostered fear and suspicion among nations.

The Versailles settlement saw Harold Nicolson, who was part of the Foreign Office delegation to Versailles, sure that '[n]ow ... democracy is sovereign to us all, certain obvious changes in the conduct of diplomacy have been, are being, and will be introduced'. But he also felt that the practical differences had been exaggerated by the time he wrote of these events in 1933 – the 'sovereign' had shifted and was now that of democracy, but states still negotiated with each other, and that had not changed.[34] Hence one indubitably major contribution of the First World War and its aftermath was the sense of a need for a recurrent, even permanent, conference diplomacy. As one of the key drafters of the League Covenant has written: '[T]he recurrent international conference, which was finally the brilliant success of Lord Grey's tragic failure of 1914, has come to stay: the world could now no more do without it than without the wireless; and that recurrent conference is the fundamental fabric of the League.'[35]

This is perhaps scant comfort for those who really believed in the LON, but it is a lasting result. However, every effort to institutionalise collective security and disarmament in the inter-war years foundered on national jealousy, fear and distrust. It is not difficult to agree with its last Secretary General, Joseph Avenol, who wrote to French socialist Leon Blum at the end of the Second World War that the LON was 'l'alibi collectif de ceux qui ont fait la puissance de Hitler', This is all the more poignant in that Avenol is often portrayed as bearing some of the responsibility for the appeasement of Hitler by the League.[36]

Planning the future of international organisation, 1941–45

Given the disasters of the inter-war years, it is not surprising that the Allies of the Second World War felt that they had to go back to the drawing board. As we saw in Chapters 3 and 4, nearly all reflection on the future of world peace during that conflict was prefaced by a discussion about the 'failures of Versailles'. There is no need to revisit that territory except to stress that it gave rise to a deeply felt sense of despair about the prospects for international organisation in general, and also to restress that many of the architects of the United Nations and other institutions had been blooded at Versailles, or at least deeply affected by it. Carr is a good example of this phenomenon.

What is perhaps more surprising is that in the 'realist/statist' backlash that emerged in the late 1930s there was so much revisiting of the 'utopian' ground of the 1920s. However, it is clear that the liberal underpinning of Wilsonian thought was still very present in the thinking of the NWO planners in both Washington and London. There was a desire that this time there must be no excessive reliance on the benevolent side of human nature, or rather the establishment of institutional devices that would encourage this to emerge and channel any negative impulses, ones which were so apparent by 1940. The resultant planning process of 1939–45 for a future international organisation must therefore be seen as one that took what it saw as the best insights of both the liberal internationalist and the realist/statist agenda, not one that took one to the exclusion of the other.

PWP and the idea of international organisation during the Second World War

For the Western Allies of 1941–45 the road to international peace was seen through the twin spurs of a revitalised project of collective security and a much enhanced programme of economic regeneration on a domestic and international level. This was unlike in 1919 when the second of these was not really even considered until after the Treaty had been signed. This second process will be dealt with in some detail in Chapter 7, the former in this chapter, but they are intimately linked. It slowly emerged that a revitalised global international organisation was to play the lead role in this process, although the concept was not publicly discussed until about 1943. It was then introduced only slowly to avoid unduly alarming American (and wider) public opinion, such was the low esteem in which the LON was held by then. As was described in Chapter 3, the State Department was to provide a lead in both these areas and to coordinate these efforts, principally with the British and to a lesser extent with the French and other Allies.

But as is also clear, the thinking emerging from the bureaucracies and even from the Cabinets in Britain and the United States had to be balanced against the views of the main individual protagonists, especially Churchill, Roosevelt and Stalin. What the advisors wanted to happen was not always consonant with the views of these principal actors. So the questions often have to be, 'what did Roosevelt, Stalin and Churchill want' and 'whose views did they listen to?'. Consequently, the next few sections will look at the key ideas of the advisors and how they translated into policy practice.

The State Department on international organisation, 1941–44[37]

As early as April 1940 the State Department had decided that 'some machinery for political decision must exist' and that any international 'political body' would have to involve a 'derogation of the sovereignty of states as will make for quick and decisive action by the body. This involves the abolition of the rule of unanimity ...', thus establishing that the USA would have to drop its objections to the use of force by an international organisation and if necessary the underlying democratic universalism dear to Woodrow Wilson. The big difference with 1919 was that at this stage the body envisaged was 'regional', that is, 'European' in character, as was a complementary 'international force' and a 'Permanent Disarmament Commission'. The only 'worldwide' bodies would be a 'Technical Commission', mainly to encourage commerce and limited disarmament provisions.[38]

Roosevelt was ever concerned to carry public opinion with him on the post-war settlement, and nowhere more keenly than on the issue which he knew had cost Wilson his reputation, that of membership of an international organisation. The United States Office of War Information stated in March 1943 that '[m]ost Americans appear to be persuaded that isolationism is an outmoded formula. But they are far from happy about the alternative of international cooperation.' In 1943, at the height of optimism about post-war cooperation, only 63 per cent favoured US membership of an international organisation.[39] The Atlantic Charter of August 1941 was drafted specifically so as not to offend American prejudices and ideals about foreign relations by stopping short of introducing the idea of a need for an 'effective' international organisation (Churchill's phrasing) and substituting the 'establishment of a wider and permanent system of general security', as well as seemingly forcing a British climb-down on such important principles (for the USA) as free trade, Freedom of the Seas and self-determination. The idea was thus drip-fed to the American public through an appeal to the lofty war aims of the Allies, renamed deliberately the 'United Nations' by Roosevelt and launched as the 'Declaration by the United Nations' on 1 January 1942.[40]

The State Department's ACPWFP set up a subcommittee on international organisation within the Political Subcommittee, which first met in April 1942, with Welles presiding, and featuring Pasvolsky, Bowman, James T. Shotwell, Gene Hackworth, Benjamin Cohen and Harley Notter as its members. It produced a series of reports over the next year or so and helped define the US position on a variety of issues. It began with a review of the lessons of Versailles, as did most of the subcommittees, and had General Smuts' paper of December 1918 as one of its first major points of discussion, many of whose points were seen as 'surprisingly apt today'.

It is obvious that they were not quite sure how, or indeed where, to start and took several months really to get under way, seemingly over-worried about a repeat of the Senate's refusal to ratify the League Covenant, and especially its Article X, in 1919. When elaborating 'Determining Principles' in a vital lengthy 'Preliminary Memorandum', they could see that 'Security, Welfare, Justice and provision for the advancement of Culture' were all vital but that 'no solution is adequate for any one part which does not take the others into account'. Consequently, '[i]t is clear that we are not ready for a full blueprint of an international organization which will adequately deal with all of these elements of international relations.' The main need after the war would be to balance the need for security with 'an overwhelming demand for speedy action to deal with the pressing needs of impoverished peoples ...' with economic and 'domestic as well as international maladjustments'. But the main aim must be 'such a reform of international relations as will lessen and finally end the menace of international war'. In an important discussion of normative principles this document recognised that this last point on the prevention of war 'may seem utterly Utopian at this time ... Nevertheless this is what the American soldiers fought for in the last war and are fighting for in this.' The liberal critique of militarism was thus taken firmly on board, but in the context of what was perceived to be a changed American public expectation of the peace.

This document in effect lays down the groundwork for all the post-war institutions of the UN, with one or two key omissions. The main ones of these are that there is no mention of an 'Assembly', there is no repeat of Article X of the Covenant and, most interestingly, '[t]here should be recognition of the political equality of all races and peoples. This is the article ... which Japan fought for at Paris and, having lost, determined to impose by force of arms ...' Given the state of the war in the Pacific in 1942 this was a bold and telling statement to make. In July, when this and other documents were discussed, there was no major dissension from its con- clusions, only a widely perceived need for some sort of 'safety valve' for world opinion, if not a permanent Assembly, and the need to realise that 'the impact of hard realities cannot be avoided by an appeal to abstract generalities like "justice" and "morality"'. Equally, it was felt that there must be a realisation that other cultures might not feel the same about these concepts as Americans.[41]

When the subcommittee really did start its work in August 1942 it plunged straight into the moral maelstrom in a consideration of 'Trusteeship', the chosen successor to the Mandate system of the LON. This was mainly out of concern about post-war 'communistic propaganda' in the colonial regions, and reflected the simultaneous State Department discussions with the British about the future of the Empire. The United Nations proposal itself was only considered in October 1942. Then, there was a lengthy discussion about the possibilities of an international police force, which was initially considered with some favour but was finally rejected as 'impractical', rather deciding that 'national forces of the major powers' must be relied upon. A 'World Council', that increasingly came to be seen as having universal membership, and an outline of the economic and social agencies was also discussed, with an 'Executive Committee' made up of the four major Powers first being mooted in November 1942.[42]

To put political will behind any of these discussions needed the Executive branch to approve them. Roosevelt has been rightly presented by several authors as wanting to keep all the final decisions for himself, as befitted his role as President and arbiter of the views being expressed by his subordinates. Both he and Churchill were aware that their primary responsibility was to win the war and this explains why the decisions about the future of international organisation, as with many other areas of the NWO, were taken in 1944 and 1945. It is also clear, however, that the exact intentions of Churchill and Roosevelt were often not clear at the time and indeed even since, especially as regards the future of international organisation. Hildebrand, for example, comments that 'Roosevelt may never have believed that a new Wilsonian international body was the best way to maintain order – his own ideas ... always centered on the primacy of the powerful ...' Harper's view, as we have seen, is that Roosevelt's central aim was to settle the problem of Europe and on this '[his] personal political objectives ... were too brutal to be proclaimed. They had to be dressed up as universal war aims and worked toward gradually, using a combination of military and diplomatic means.' A less 'brutal' way of putting it would be to re-state the evident and widespread American distrust of British motives and of the perfectibility of the Hobbesian Europeans.[43]

It might reasonably be asked therefore whether the whole international organisation project of the Second World War was indeed just a way of ensuring a 'realist' peace based on the exigencies and realities of power. Or was Roosevelt's attitude to his Allies and the State Department planners just a recognition that American public opinion had to be carefully nurtured, and that the United States was an introverted country and deeply suspicious of foreign adventures and ideas? To quote the contemporary Carl Becker, 'How much *better* [would] the New World Order be?'[44] To assess which of these interpretations might have the greater ring of truth, we might usefully break down the main features of the international organisation discussions in the period 1942–43 and see how they were resolved at Dumbarton Oaks in 1944, when the final decisions to create the United Nations were taken.

Global or regional organisations?

As was related in Chapter 5, in May 1943 Churchill informed Vice-President Wallace, Stimson, Ickes (Secretary of the Interior), Sumner Welles and the Chairman of the Senate's Foreign Relations Committee, Senator Connally, that he favoured a post-war 'Supreme World Council' to ensure the 'real responsibility for peace' and that this should be made up of the United States, Britain and Russia. In a wide-ranging policy statement Churchill had also touched on the future of Germany and Europe in general and first properly enunciated his view that American troops should stay in Europe, as well as that a strong France should be re-created. His views on the LON were that it 'was wrong to say that the League had failed. It was rather the member states which had failed the League', with which Stimson and Connally vociferously agreed. Churchill said there should also be an 'international police force' responsible to the World and the Regional Councils.[45]

The central focus of this speech has been remembered as being about 'Europe', but it was far more about how 'to prevent further aggression in the future by Germany or Japan', a problem that was also at the heart of the American dilemma about the post-war world. Great Britain, the United States and Russia should assure this said Churchill, with only a grudging reference to China thrown in as an afterthought. Churchill saw Europe's future as lying with a 'Regional European Council' which would mainly be there to provide a 'strong country on the map between England and Russia …'. The premise behind this was that the United States would not continue to leave troops ('indefinitely on guard') in Europe, by which he explicitly meant 'for more than one Presidential election'. Here was a clear echo of Hankey's cynical reflection of 1916, in a memo that Churchill would have read as a member of the Cabinet at the time (see Chapter 1). To fill the gap in Southern Europe, he hoped for a 'Danubian Federation', which had also been discussed in the CFFR and the State Department, as we have seen. Most interestingly though, he foresaw Poland and Czechoslovakia 'stand[ing] together in friendly relations with Russia' and a divided Germany, which would lose all of Prussia but not be further split up. There would also be a 'Regional Council for the Americas', with Canada representing the British Commonwealth, and one for the Pacific, in which Russia would participate. All of these would be 'subordinate … to the World Council', with the whole structure like a 'three-legged stool'.

But most importantly, Churchill saw Britain's future as lying not with the Regional European Council, but with the British Commonwealth and with the United States. He could foresee a 'fraternal association', with common citizenship, freedom of movement and trade, and even the possibility of common voting and eligibility for public office, very similar to Streit's and even Dulles' views of a transatlantic partnership. In this view of the world the bases deal of 1941 had been but a first step. His American guests ('guests' because the speech was made in the British Embassy) 'had been thinking on more or less the lines propounded by the Prime Minister'. They all in particular agreed on the 'regional and world councils' idea as a way of keeping America in Europe after the war. Vice-President Wallace said on leaving that it was 'the most encouraging conversation in which he had taken part in the last two years'.[46]

Churchill's view that regional organisations might be the way forward had powerful support from Sumner Welles and, initially at least, from Roosevelt himself. The great initial exponent of global organisations was Secretary of State Cordell Hull, much of the time Welles' bitter opponent within the State Department, and of whom he finally managed to rid himself in 1943.[47] Hull's reasoning was mainly economic, while Roosevelt could never bring himself to trust such forces to ensure American security interests (for more discussion of which see Chapter 8). However, it was realised by the time of Churchill's speech that the *balance* between regional and international organisation had also to be considered. Should there be a reliance on the global or the regional to keep the peace?

One possibility was to base the new system on Roosevelt's 'neighbour-hood' concept, one that had been developed in the 1930s, particularly by Sumner Welles in the context of Latin America. In the CFFR Armstrong succinctly expressed the problems of this idea. He recognised that selecting a group of states to protect such a 'neighbourhood' or because of their generalised power in the world might well 'decrease the sense of mutual responsibility which we want to build up'. Moreover, what if the greatest powers were not in the neighbourhood and did not live up to their responsibility to defend it, or what if the states that were most 'responsible' were not the greatest powers at all? The old question of the overlap of responsibilities for regional and international organisations or agreements that had bedevilled the inter-war years, as with the Locarno Pacts overlap with the LON, would remain. If it were accepted that balance of power thinking was the cause of war, a strong belief of the liberal internationalists, then 'we need to find some way of directing the necessary power into an overall organization'.[48]

'Common Denominators of Interest'

Churchill's 1943 speech was discussed at some length in the State Depart-ment. The discussion concentrated on what basic aims any new system of regional or global organisation should have. In the first such discussion Bowman said '[w]e are not putting world organization and regional organi-zation into juxtaposition in order to amuse ourselves intellectually. It is Prime Minister Churchill who has introduced the regional concept [not true, as we have seen above], and we are therefore bound to analyze it.' He rightly observed that Churchill's speech, radical though it might appear, in fact 'reflects [a] long-established British policy of cautious and restricted commitment'. Britain had always been extremely suspicious of Leagues of any kind, an attitude reinforced by the experience of the inter-war years.

But, felt Bowman, Churchill had betrayed in all his remarks, in this and other speeches, that Britain had still not sufficiently grasped the nettle of 'freedom, law and morality', however much Churchill personally might wish this to be so. What America had come to put its faith in was the 'good neighbour' policy it had with Latin America, based as it was on 'flexibility' and 'common bases of interest and action', and on a common opposition to fascism after some regrettable pre-Rooseveltian lapses when 'totalitarian forms of government' had been tolerated. But Bowman doubted that even such a wondrous policy could be a model for other regions, given their internal diversity. He preferred a world organisation first, and regional ones second. But Churchill's views were in general agreement with American policy on at least two things: Europe was the cause of most wars and, quoting Schopenhauer, '[l]ife is a "reconciliation of contradictories"'.[49] Harper believes that Roosevelt shared Bowman's doubts that the 'neighbourhood' concept could be transposed to Europe, where what mattered was 'that troublemakers, bullies and "loose cannons" be rendered harmless, using whatever methods might avail'. This was what finally persuaded the President that a global organisation had to be part of the final UN package.[50]

In a second major discussion a week later in June 1943, Bowman elaborated on his remarks to assert that any region was now too small. '[S]wift communications ... and expanding world trade' had now made it 'desirable to attempt an approach towards common standards of ethics in international affairs.' This would not be easy: 'fair trade' had been 'hard to maintain. So-called international law is only "law" by mild united assent ... the deterioration of League strength is filled with deplorably swift recantations. It remains to be seen how far the nations can recover their will to return to a common moral system.'

Furthermore, to accept regional councils would be to accept 'the moral break-up of the world ... that the world has become too complex to manage in the *common* interest'. So it was necessary to find the 'universals of faith, desire, behavior and power which will win support through self-interest'. These, he declared, would have to be found, it was the 'task of statesmanship to find the elements of world cohesion'. Why not start with 'certain *self-evident truths*' based on the United States' Declaration of Independence, the ultimate declaration of 'faith in mankind in general'? And who could disagree with the main elements of the statement of 1776? Were not 'peaceful relations' of self-evident 'mutual advantage'; was not '[l]ove of peace ... a universal of peoples'; were not 'justice' and 'democratic government' usually agreed?

But how could this be brought about? The doctrine of the 'sovereign equality of states' was clearly not true in practice, but it was even less so as part of a regional organisation where one state would inevitably dominate, and the League had failed because most of the discussions had in fact been regional, not in any sense global. But in a world organisation all would find their place, as long as it became the centre of 'discussion and beneficial action', small states allied to great powers, with a really worthwhile system of 'trusteeship' to help the weaker emerging nations, one that would support the *general desires* (universals)' as laid out in the Atlantic Charter and the Four Freedoms. There must be a global rebalancing of the 'individual' and the 'general benefit' in which all would see their interest, their human rights and their desire for prosperity fulfilled. Only a world organisation 'backed by will, unity and power' could achieve this.[51]

Power and membership in a post-war international organisation

Taken purely as a set of ideas, Churchill's ideas on global and regional organisation had thus not only set a lot of hares running in the State Department, they had also produced a blueprint for the use of power to achieve some very clear purposes. Churchill's speech was a major advance on Roosevelt's statements of 1941–42 and showed a commonality of aim in the two Anglo-Saxon Allies, but it was in the way it cemented some already existing discussion in Washington that we should see its main importance. The main turning point intellectually in the debate over the NWO was about how it could unite normative and security concerns. The difficult practical 'turning point' was to be in the area of implementation. How could 'common denominators of interest' be turned into concrete organisational structures?

The Moscow Declaration of October 1943 led to the Four-Nation Declaration establishing a 'general organization for the maintenance of peace and security'. As Europe was liberated, the EAC was set up (as described in Chapter 5), as well as such bodies as the Advisory Council for Italy, which coordinated relief work under the title of UNRRA. Even more significantly there was discussion on the creation of a 'Currency Stabilisation Fund' (eventually the International Monetary Fund; IMF), on an International Investment Agency (eventually the World Bank) and on a means of relaxing trade barriers. There was also discussion not only of 'old' political areas such as trusteeship, and of functional areas such as tele-communications, migration and settlement, but also of new ones such as human rights.[52]

We have seen that out of the discussions of the failure of the LON and the problem of how to solve the security problems of Europe came a renewed belief in the idea of a global organisation. But it was recognised that any attempt in this direction would have to be based on a far more realistic appreciation of the limits of such bodies, particularly as the Alliance looked more and more shaky by the beginning of 1944. The Tripartite Commission, which was established to operationalise the concept of the 'United Nations', did not get off to an auspicious start. However, the first operational result of this Commission was the setting up of UNRRA after a ceremony in the White House in early November 1943 (the results of which are more fully discussed in Chapter 7).

As to UN membership, in the words of an important summary of American views on the future of the United Nations, the organization 'should consist initially of the United Nations (i.e. the Allies), ... and of such other nations as the United Nations may determine'.[53] Secretary of State for War Stimson again struck the most negative initial note about 'a worthy object but whether or not we can accomplish it I have my doubts'. He believed that it had to 'fall on the shoulders of the United States and Great Britain alone'. But he '"had me doubts", so to speak' when he saw that it was to be 'shared out among the whole body of nations', especially when he considered 'the swarthy faces of some of the representatives of countries like Honduras'.[54] There seems no reason to believe that this was not a widely held view. Applications for potential membership of the United Nations (or 'adherences') were treated with casual levity from the first – Berle wrote to Roosevelt in January 1942 as the first such applications came in: 'We have received a huge stack ... from ... the Danish Minister whom we know and trust, to King Carol of Romania whom we won't even let into the country ... Like Barnacle Bill, the Sailor, we "loves 'em all and marries none" for the time being.' In the same letter he says that 'The three Baltic republics want to adhere – the Russians would probably object. De Gaulle has not yet asked to adhere, which is just as well for the time being.'[55] Membership was contingent on American national interest, not on vague aims of 'universality'.

Neither, in early 1944, was Roosevelt seemingly concerned with what might be termed the 'functional' side of the future United Nations structure. He told Clark Eichelberger of the United Nations Association that there need be no central headquarters: '[t]hey could meet in a different place – possibly a different continent each year. All they need is a storage warehouse for records – most of them obsolete ...' – a greatly prophetic statement as regards the 'records'! Practically whenever he referred to the United Nations before Dumbarton Oaks he stressed the warlike function of the Alliance and what it would do to Germany and Japan after their defeat, 'this righteous undertaking', not to what would happen after this was done.[56]

The cornerstone of United Nations membership was to become the 'Four Policemen' and has arguably remained so ever since, certainly in the eyes of those Big Four (and a Fifth with the inclusion of France after 1945). For Roosevelt and Pasvolsky (a great advocate of the 'functional' role) its 'primary objective' was to be 'the maintenance of peace and security', although it did also include efforts to do this 'through fostering cooperative efforts among nations for the progressive improvement of the general welfare'.[57] As if in reply to de Madariaga, the American post-war planners had not entirely put their faith for peace 'in the military and naval strength of the Great Powers' to try and promote a 'World Community', but neither were they putting their faith in a belief that war was a disease that could be easily cured. This was a realism based on the realities of power modified by a belief that liberal internationalism might be a powerful leavening force for an ultimate global interdependence.

The UN as a post-war security organisation

There is no need, or space, to dwell on the detail of the Conferences at Dumbarton Oaks[58] (1944) and San Francisco (1945), which established the machinery of the United Nations, as these have been well described in a number of excellent texts, except to reflect on whether they can be said to have furthered NWO intentions.

San Francisco was '... a meeting that was history's nearest approach to a global constitutional convention'[59] and it produced, in the Charter of the UN, a document of comprehensive importance for the NWO aspiration. The Charter was universal, and it expressed a vocation to cover so many issues of global concern that it has never been seriously challenged as a basic statement of humankind's aspirations for peace and justice. In so becoming it had to fudge many issues, and the whole document is a tissue of redundancy and repetition, but it has the immense virtue of being largely unchallenged since 1945 and of being a Treaty that binds all members of the organisation to respect it.

The Charter differed from the Covenant of the League in two significant respects. As Nicholas has commented, 'San Francisco differed from Versailles in its genuine respect for "open covenants openly arrived at"'.[60] It also tried to avoid association with the mistakes of Versailles. Since the Second World War there have been many who have criticised the UN for never fulfilling its primary role as a collective security organisation. Many more have pointed out that it could not possibly have fulfilled that role in the context of the Cold War. Roosevelt's 'one world' aspiration was wrecked on the rocks of this global conflict. Arguably it was only with the Second Gulf War of 1991 that the UN was able to fulfil its central role in peace and security matters. The partial replacement for Collective Security came, after 1956 and until 1990 at least, to be the *ad hoc* system known as 'peace-keeping', a useful addition to, but a poor substitute for, the NWO ideal of the 'Four Policemen'.[61]

This relative 'failure' led many quickly to write off the UN as a more or less useless agent of benevolent change in world politics, much as had been the case with the LON in the inter-war period. Kennan was not unusual in viewing the UN and the LON as 'vainglorious and pretentious assertions of purpose' that failed to address 'the real substance of international affairs'.[62]

For Kennan the power of the United States towards a 'truly stable world order' lay in its power of example and this example lay precisely in its appreciation of the value of 'order' over that of 'power'. In a document he wrote while head of the Policy Planning Staff in 1949 he urged the United States to show that kind of leadership 'through that combination of political greatness and wise restraint which goes only with a ripe and settled civilisation'.[63] For Kennan that could only be through a targeted and practical programme of political and economic action such as the Marshall Plan, of which he thoroughly approved, and not through the vague debate of the UN.

As for the original regional ideal advocated by Welles and Roosevelt, it was finally included as Chapter VIII of the United Nations Charter, largely on the insistence of the non-European states, most of which were situated in Latin and South America in 1945 and already grouped in the Association of American States, the basis of the 'Good Neighbour' network. It has since resulted in the establishment of the Organisation of African Unity and other regional organisations of an essentially 'containment' character, such as the Association of South East Asian Nations. To enter into too long a discussion of the reasons for the failure of these so far, at least as envisaged by Welles, would be outside the scope of this book, but it would be fair to say that Chapter VIII is only now, after the Cold War, starting to look like a potential solution to the world's security problems.

Challenges to the security element of the NWO post-Cold War[64]

Leadership?

The success of international organisation in promoting security in the inter-war period was recognised by both realists/statists and liberal internationalists as being predicated on the question of leadership. Carr's comments on this were quoted in Chapter 2 in his analysis of the failure of the League of Nations. De Madariaga wanted Britain to assume the role in 1929, one that it was not able to fulfil. Partly he wanted this because the 'British Empire is a wonderful model of how to [promote global organisations, and] is only rivalled by the United States'. Unless the United States got over its 'mental troubles', by which he meant isolationism, it could not be a leader, a pity since '[it] has everything a leader should have: a wide and generous spirit and a big powerful body'.[65]

In order to claim the mantle of leadership, which the United States did in the Second World War, and even more so after 1947, she needed to see her own national interest writ large. This national interest was as much economic as political, so we cannot see leadership from Washington truly emerging until that global economic interest was realised (a process described in Chapter 7). However, this also meant, as Reinhold Niebuhr perceptively noted, that 'the great moral issue [for the United States became]

... how a rich and powerful nation relates to a weak and impoverished world. Not in terms of ultimate constitutional arrangements, but in terms of immediate political policies.'[66] The next chapter has this question of economic leadership as one of its key themes.

However, this process of the assumption of leadership underlines the insight of the PWP planners in the United States that the failures of the first NWO after Versailles were clearly linked to a lack of understanding among the world's political elites about the links between politics and economics. This essentially liberal appreciation seemed, in the 1930s, to be in diametrical opposition to the realities of nationalism and its economic counterpart, autarky. It therefore took a re-think of what was 'realistic' to reincorporate the economic and the political aspects of the NWO project, as Wilson had intended, in order to build an NWO on more solid foundations.

Arguably since 1990 this realisation has taken root and has spread to most of the rest of the planet. As will be argued in the next chapter, liberal capitalism, although not without its critics, is now seen as a basic building block of international order. Security organisations are there mainly to ensure that the benefits of democracy and capitalism are ensured for as many as possible by hopefully laying down norms of conduct and ultimately upholding them if any state performs too much out of line with the basic norms of the UN Charter, either towards other states or towards its own citizens. We are now at a stage of such development where we can cautiously affirm that the UN has fulfilled its economic regulatory role as conceived in 1945, in spite of the obvious problems that this involves, but that it now needs a radical overhaul of its role to suit it better to a globalised economy. Global society is no longer threatened by the prospect of a nuclear war between the United States and the Soviet Union, but it is arguably threatened by the enormous differences of wealth that exist in the world, and by the legitimacy for many of the world's population of the institutions that control their destinies but are beyond their control.

Following some parts of this logic, there are those who would assert that security has changed in its very nature since the end of the Cold War and that the UN has therefore outlived its usefulness as a security institution. There are yet others who claim that the 'timeless wisdom of realism' still holds, that power politics between states is still the guiding principle of international politics.[67] The new approaches to security tend to stress sub-state pressures such as migration, societal upheaval, even crime as the new sources of insecurity. This in turn is usually based on an assertion of the reduction of the power and importance of the state both economically and politically.

Changed circumstances, changed responses?

It is a truism to say that many things have changed since 1990. We have seen the end of the Cold War and the collapse of the USSR, new Balkan conflicts, the seeming 'End of History' and the triumph of liberal capitalism. What, then, remains of the world of 1945? There is no longer a bipolar power structure, but can we really say that we have a uni- or multi-polar replacement? One of the biggest questions for the scholar of the NWO idea in the light of this structural change therefore has to be: is the United States preparing to give up its World Policeman role? We have seen a dramatic reduction of American troops in Germany and in the Pacific, an enhanced role for Japan, a reluctant involvement in the former Yugoslavia, an arguably 'softly-softly' approach in the Gulf, a slow response to Eastern Europe, and so forth. Does this mean we are now entering a scenario that has been termed 'Back to the Future' – a return to weak international leadership? To put the question at its most pessimistic, 'are the 1930s a better gauge of the future than 1945–1990?'.[68]

The Owl of Minerva has by no means flown on this question, as on many other areas of the post-Cold War NWO, but a few responses have come from debates within and about the UN. Much of the debate has centred around the appropriateness of intervention. Under what circumstances should it, or could it, take place, especially in the light of 'norm of non-intervention', the cornerstone of the UN?[69] There is also an awareness that the resolution of conflicts has now become even more complicated. As Secretary General Boutros Boutros-Ghali put it in 1992: '[j]ust as no two conflicts are the same, so the design [of each operation] must be approached with flexibility and creativity adapted to each particular situation'.[70] It was recognised very early in the decade that regional conflicts will undoubtedly rise in number, with the old list of pre-1989 – Cyprus, the Middle East, South Africa, Ethiopia, Somalia and Cambodia – being added to by the former Yugoslavia, Haiti, Liberia, Moldova, Nagorny Karabakh and many others.

A 'cosmopolitan' might take the view that the 'international community' must intervene whenever basic human rights and dignity are not respected. The dangers of using this as an excuse (as the US has arguably often done) are clear. But some of the cases where intervention has been suggested, or even implemented, such as in Somalia (where a UN force was sent in 1992) or the former Yugoslavia (1994–present), have been when the acts of a local government 'shock the moral conscience of mankind' – Walzer says, 'the old fashioned language seems to me exactly right'. The pre-existing 'legalist' view was that (among other things) '[n]othing but aggression [by one state on another] can justify war'.[71] Under this reasoning, which is that of the Powers in 1945, sovereignty cannot be challenged, the so-called 'norm of non-intervention'. But where is the deciding threshold between these two opposing views?

Walzer quotes widely from Mill's nineteenth century dictum that 'peoples get the Governments they deserve'. There are therefore no grounds for intervention on, say, human rights grounds (as in the former Yugoslavia). His view is therefore that prudence has to be balanced by justice, so you cannot, say, overthrow President Saddam Hussein of Iraq on human rights grounds, because you might in the long run cause more suffering. However, since 1990, this prudent approach has given way to definite evidence that 'humanitarian intervention' is becoming a norm, that is, that powerful states now feel they have a new 'right' to intervene whenever they feel that the fundamental liberties of a country are being threatened by that country's own Government. The implications for the norm of sovereignty are naturally grave.[72]

In each of these interventions many problems are apparent. First, who will lead? Unlike in 1945 there is a clear problem of 'weak hegemony', whether it be by Nigeria in Liberia, or elsewhere by the United States, or by the European Union. Second, how do you define the clarity of objective necessary for any such operation? Third, it must be acknowledged that we are now facing conflicts which are often ethnic in origin, as true now of Europe (as in the former Yugoslavia) as it is of Africa (especially in Rwanda). Fourth, this is not 'peacekeeping' (the norm for UN operations since 1956, involving invitation and consent), but rather 'peacemaking', and arguably the old idea of 'overspill' has been replaced by a much looser definition of international organisation power.

So, to return to Walzer's dilemma, how can the UN and, particularly, the Security Council, now decide the thresholds for intervention actions? The main coherent response from the UN has been discussion of the *Agenda for Peace* of February 1992, and subsequent reactions from governments. This twenty-four page report by the Secretary General, prepared in reply to a request from the Heads of Government of the Security Council on 31 January 1992, addresses the questions of how to improve preventive diplomacy, peacemaking and peacekeeping. The main recommendations of this report were, first, that there must be an attempt at making the UN better at identifying potential conflicts, an idea first seriously mooted by then Soviet General Secretary Mikhail Gorbachev in 1988. Second, there were new proposals for short- and long-term resolution of conflicts; and third, it was suggested that there should be a development of 'post conflict measures'.[73]

Reactions to the *Agenda for Peace* were generally positive from the developed states. But one could be cynical, as when George Bush, in his last major speech as President, said to the UN General Assembly on 23 September 1992 that '[w]e must ensure adequate, equitable financing for the UN and associated peacekeeping efforts', when the United States has the worst arrears record of any OECD state. He also added that '[f]or decades, the American military has served as a stabilising presence around the globe. And I want to draw on our extensive experience in winning wars and keeping the peace to support UN peacekeeping' – Americans have never been good at irony! The reaction of the South in particular criticised UN force proposals, and suggested that the UN (i.e. the North) would use this to intervene whenever it didn't like a Third World Government. Many of the poorest states also said they feared that peacemaking would replace development as the main post-1945 activity of the UN.[74] It might be argued that Third World opposition may be more rhetoric than anything else, and the North has never worried about such comments – Third World leaders have often rightly been seen as dictators trying to hold on to power. But it must also be said that there seems to be no really solid commitment from the USA for the new proposals or an ability to pay for it – the true costs are now known to be prodigious.

Conclusion

After at least eighty years of debate this century about the utility of international organisation in ensuring security for humankind we are still left with two diametrically opposed conclusions. One version is still that of Carr, who wrote that '[t]he League of Nations was an attempt to "apply the principles of Lockeian liberalism to the building of a machinery of inter-national order" … But this transplantation of democratic rationalism from the national to the international sphere was full of unforseen difficulties.' Another is that of Hildebrand: '[i]f it is true … that a good way to find out about a people is to study its dreams, then the citizens of all the Great Powers can take a just pride in the very idea of a United Nations.'[75]

There is now an increasing doubt among Western public opinion, and even more among the intellectual classes, that global organisations are the real guarantee of peace. The Gulf War of 1990–91 was fought under the banner of the United Nations, one that gave the biggest collective security operation in history some of its legitimacy, but the most significant war in Europe since 1945, in the former Yugoslavia, was greeted by what was initially a policy of containment, and then by two regional responses, one of which was relatively ineffectual (led by the European Union and the UN) and another, much more effective, led by the United States and the North Atlantic Treaty Organisation (NATO) – known as the Implementation Force (of the Dayton Agreement of 1996). The striking reaction of the West's intelligentsia was that in their discussion of the rights and wrongs of the war, there was a singular lack of real passion, except in France, the home of most intellectual causes.

This could not have happened in the inter-war period. The war in the former Yugoslavia is the post-1990 equivalent of the Spanish Civil War. This was, after all, a war which brought back the concentration camp, mass rape as a weapon of war and ethnic cleansing, among other horrors. It had its almost exact equivalent of Franco in Slobodan Milosevic, its equivalent of the non-Intervention Pact of 1936 in various UN resolutions banning the export of arms, and its happy breachers of these resolutions in the name of 'level killing fields', as the then British Foreign Secretary, Douglas Hurd put it. But no 'International Brigade' was sent to Bosnia, there were no calls for general disarmament, no equivalents of H.G. Wells or Salvador de Madariaga on moral crusades; indeed, there was very little indignation to speak of at all. Boyd Tonkin, a literary journalist on the staff of the *Independent*, wrote that 'the continent's intelligentsia sat firmly on its post-modern posterior as 250,000 corpses piled up on prime time TV.' Another (TV) intellectual, Michael Ignatieff, railed against 'the narcissism of intervention' or 'intervention by proxy', mere moral posturing, or 'accounting' to use his phrase.[76]

In what do they put their faith? The answer seems to be that the pendulum has swung back in favour of a belief that there are in fact no real security problems left. Western democracy and well-being is not seen as being threatened by the war in the former Yugoslavia or the genocide in Rwanda or, now, Algeria. The only possible problem might be the mass migration that such conflicts inevitably produce, but even this is seen as a wider problem of economic migration away from post-communist regimes. There is a culture of contentment that we, in the rest of Europe, will escape unscathed, and little evidence of the doctrine of the 'good neighbour' except in the most elementary human form of tea and sympathy. It has to be concluded that while Spain was seen as the harbinger of a wider conflict about fundamental ideas, the war in the former Yugoslavia is seen as an aberration, some unfinished business after the Cold War. The peace dividend was supposed to follow 1991, and it will, the former Yugoslavia notwithstanding.

The underlying logic seems to be that the political and ideological discourse of security has now been replaced by one that is much more economic. The economic and political system that is liberal capitalism will eventually triumph and do away with tin-pot dictators such as Milosevic and Sadaam Hussein. It has been seriously suggested that flooding the former Yugoslavia and Iraq with businessmen would have far more effect than any number of economic embargoes, sanctions, or even cruise missiles. This has its corollary in the way that international organisations now present their help to developing countries. The key words used in most international organisation missives since 1990 are 'conditionality' and 'governance'. Briefly put, all new loans by the IMF, World Bank, even regional banks such as the European Bank for Reconstruction and Development (EBRD) are dependent for their disbursement on the system of government of the receiving state. This form of conditionality is a new phenomenon,[77] as it implies that it is no longer solely the financial aspects of a loan that have to be approved, but also the 'normative'. Does this not mean that the interpretation of the Charter of the UN has undergone a radical change since 1991 – that international organisations and the UN are in effect saying that 'you are only a full member of International Society if you agree to our *political* conditionality'? To put it another way, are we seeing an extension of the NWO principles of liberal democracy by yet another coercive power measure, or is such pressure merely a good thing for the peoples of the Third World? There will be further discussion of this point in Chapter 7 and in the Conclusion.

The importance of Europe

One main focus of this chapter, indeed of this book, has been on the salience given by all the NWO planners to the question of Europe. It was seen as the key test of any regional or global security arrangement. No other area of the world had the same record of being able to create such global mayhem. Historically, therefore, the ideas of international organisation and its concomitant dream of a possible global peace are closely linked to that of a new Europe. As Peter Stirk has written: 'The idea of Europe has a long pedigree which is often difficult to distinguish from the quest for peace and a league or federation of nations. Indeed the three tended to mean much the same thing as long as European politics could plausibly be regarded as world politics.'[78] The European Union is the latest manifestation of the ambitious social engineering undertaken by American and British, followed by (mainly) French and German, statesmen and women.

Since 1945, this experiment has generated many different organisational structures – NATO of 1949, the Conference on Security and Cooperation in Europe after the Helsinki Final Act of 1975 (CSCE), since 1994 the 'Organisation' (so now OSCE), and a multitude of functional organisations.[79] Europe still has two seats on the Security Council of the United Nations, held by Britain and France. Any possible rearrangement of this would probably involve either a German seat or one for the European Union. Because of its longest ever period of unblemished peace until the war in the former Yugoslavia of 1991–97, Europe seemed to have solved the security dilemma that has dogged it throughout its history. European security arrangements are now often quoted as being the model that might be followed in other potentially troubled areas of the world. Europe has therefore been the key testbed for NWO ideas, and its continued success is the main measure of whether such ideas can last into the twenty-first century.[80]

The 'poverty' of multilateral diplomacy?

Another main area for judging the success or failure of the post-1990 NWO is that of the continued usefulness (or not) of the key Wilsonian idea of the international organisation. Here the cracks are truly showing. Nearly eighty years after Versailles, thinkers such as Susan Strange are still asking 'Cui Bono' [to whose benefit]? do these international organisations operate? She asserts that Conference diplomacy has outlived its usefulness, that experience has quite overwhelmed any of its pretensions to being of universal use to the poor and oppressed or the rich and powerful.[81] She further asserts that the economic practice of late capitalism has made the idea of international organisations acting as mediators between states irrelevant.[82] The United States has seemingly lost its belief that the UN can really play a global role in anything other than as a support role for the occasional American foreign policy enterprise (such as the Gulf War of 1990–91). The UN is being urged to reform or die, and starved of funds to do much that has any real significance – this only a few years after George Bush put the UN at the very heart of his NWO.

Reform is under way.[83] But the UN is no longer the lynchpin of the NWO. Regional arrangements (such as NATO) will continue to reassert themselves; the Powers will revert to *ad hoc* arrangements when they need to (as in the former Yugoslavia). The UN will only have any real security significance when it suits those Powers, so to that extent Carr was correct in his scorn for the idea of a League of Nations. However, the situation is quite different now than it was in 1919 or even in 1945. The rest of the NWO package – economic interdependence and democratic self-determination – have made the adherence to largely peaceful norms and practices by most states a reality. The UN retains its role as a symbolic, and occasionally real, arbiter of these norms and practices. International organisations have become an acknowledged part of the institutionalisation of conflict resolution.

But why should this be done by a global body, when regional groupings have far greater local knowledge? In a very real sense the UN has become, not an irrelevance, but rather a victim of its own success. However, Strange's accusation still holds – 'cui bono?' – the answer must be that of the powerful states of the international system, all of whom largely agree on the basis on which that international society must exist and cooperate. Those who refuse – Libya, Iraq and so on – will find themselves condemned to sniping from the sidelines or occasional major irritant status – increasingly an irrelevance, but being inevitably accorded a moral authority by those who feel excluded in the same way that the underclass look to criminal leadership *faute de mieux*. The UN illustrates more than any other NWO body the basic truth that an NWO cannot be effective if it is not all-inclusive, universal not only in aspiration but also in reality. The UN cannot work as the agent of a sectional interest, that of the West (as it did from 1945 to the mid-1950s) or of the Third World (as it largely did in the 1960s and 1970s). It must now provide real security for all.

Notes

1 I would here refer the reader back to the discussion in the Introduction about the aims of the NWO – 'order', 'balance' and 'stability'.
2 The best description of this ancestry is to be found in F.H. Hinsley, *Power and the Pursuit of Peace* (Cambridge University Press, 1967) and Inis L. Claude, Jr,

Swords into Plowshares: The Problems and Progress of International Organization (New York, Random House, 4th edn, 1964), pp. 21 and 46.

3   One of the main themes of Christopher Coker, *War in the Twentieth Century* (London, Brassey's, 1994).

4   It is recognised that there is a certain amount of discussion about how to define international organisations – here they are taken to mean 'Intergovernmental Organisations' (IGOs), although we have to acknowledge the growing importance of International Non-Governmental Organisations (INGOs) and even Business International Organisations (BINGOs) – see Clive Archer, *International Organisation* (London, Unwin, 2nd edn, 1992), Chapter 1.

5   This is the particular hallmark of the 'Copenhagen School', and will be discussed later in the chapter.

6   Eric Roll, *Crowded Hours* (London, Faber, 1985), p. 77. Bissell was referring to the now little remembered International Materials Conference set up to safeguard commodity supplies to the OEEC during the Korean War.

7   A good introduction to the history of international organisations this century can be found in David Armstrong, Lorna Lloyd and John Redmond, *From Versailles to Maastricht: International Organisation in the Twentieth Century* (Basingstoke, Macmillan, 1996).

8   The quote is from Burke, 'On Conciliation with Colonies' of 22 March 1775; Maurice Hankey, *The Supreme Control at the Paris Peace Conference: A Commentary* (London, G. Allen and Unwin, 1963), p. 11.

9   G. Lowes Dickinson to Bryce, 20 October 1914; Bryce Papers, Reel 8/21, Folio 58. The comment about war and ideas is taken from Lowes Dickinson's, *The Choice Before Us* (London, George Allen and Unwin, 1917), p. v. For the growth of the arms industry before 1914, see David Stevenson, *Armaments and the Coming of War in Europe, 1904–1914* (Oxford, Clarendon Press, 1996).

10 The propaganda machines of both sides in the First World War were keen to emphasise the 'differences' between the races, and the intelligentsia of both sides mobilised in an unprecedented way to create both crude and more subtle representations of these stereotypes for public consumption. One early example of this in the First World War was the appointment of Lord Bryce to head an inquiry in 1914, into the German 'Belgian atrocities' (cf. Chapter 1), one which arguably did a great deal to damage the credibility of the press when dealing with later, far more concrete, horrors such as the Gulag and the Nazi death camps. H.G. Wells was a typical populariser of racial stereotypes in the inter-war period, as was Kipling and a host of other writers.

11 There have been some excellent studies of the relationship between war and scientific thinking about it during this century. One such study can be found in Daniel Pick, *The War Machine: The Rationalization of Slaughter in the Modern Age* (New Haven, Yale University Press, 1993), especially Chapters 12–15. See also Coker, *War in the Twentieth Century*.

12 See, for example, Karl Leibknecht, *Militarism and Anti-Militarism* (Cambridge, Rivers Press, 1973, first published 1907).

13 Lowes Dickinson, *The Choice Before Us*, p. vi.

14 Maurice Hankey, *Diplomacy by Conference*, chapter on 'The Study of Disarmament' (London, Ernest Benn, 1946), pp. 105–119. The upper reaches of British and virtually all other European and American societies were full of classical

scholars. The spirit of the times seems to have dictated an almost obliged need to make reference to the salutary tales of civilisations past, to the point where we might ask if the study of the classics does not encourage warlike patterns of thinking.

15 Transactions of the Grotius Society, *Problems of the War, Volume IV* (London, Sweet and Maxwell, 1918), pp. xxiii–xxiv.

16 Good examples of this can be found in the writings of Brailsford and Angell discussed in the next chapter. Martin Ceadel, *Pacifism in Britain, 1914–1945* (Oxford, Clarendon Press, 1980), pp. 4–7. He stresses that his book is about pacifism, not its twin sister *pacificism*, which he italicises throughout, even though he acknowledges the linguistic similarity and often interchangeability until the 1930s. See also his *The Origins of War Prevention: The British Peace Movement and International Relations, 1730–1854* (Oxford, Clarendon Press, 1996) and *Thinking about Peace and War* (Oxford University Press, 1987).

17 Ceadel, *Pacifism in Britain*, p. 24.

18 Lowes Dickinson, *The Choice Before Us*, p. 171.

19 Lowes Dickinson, *The Choice Before Us*, pp. 173 and 205.

20 Quoted in Chapter 1, p. 35 *supra*.

21 E.H. Carr, *The Twenty Years Crisis: 1919–1939* (London, Macmillan, 1939), p. 28; Salvador de Madariaga, *Disarmament* (Oxford University Press, 1929), p. 14.

22 James Barros, *The League of Nations and the Great Powers: The Greek–Bulgarian Incident, 1925* (Oxford, Clarendon Press, 1970).

23 See Chapter 8 for more on this.

24 Sadao Asada, 'From Washington to London: The Imperial Japanese Navy and the Politics of Naval Limitation, 1921–1930', part of a collection edited by Erik Goldstein and John Maurer, 'The Washington Conference, 1921–22: Naval Rivalry, East Asian Stability and the Road to Pearl Harbour', *Diplomacy and Statecraft*, vol. 4, no. 3, November 1993, p. 157.

25 For some contemporary views see P.J. Noel-Baker, *The Geneva Protocol* (London, King, 1925), *Disarmament* (London, The Hogarth Press, 1926, 2nd edn, 1927) and 'The Geneva Protocol: An Analysis' and 'The British Commonwealth, The Protocol and the Empire', *The Round Table*, December 1924; Arnold Toynbee, *Survey of International Affairs* (London, Oxford University Press, 1926); de Madariaga, *Disarmament*.

26 de Madariaga, *Disarmament*, pp. vi, vii, 6 and 11.

27 This is interestingly a common example used by liberals; see, for example, Angell in Chapter 7.

28 de Madariaga, *Disarmament*, especially Chapters 1 and 2.

29 Hankey, *Diplomacy by Conference*, especially pp. 108–118.

30 Discussion in the Grotius Society *Problems of the War*, pp. xxiii–xxiv.

31 H.G. Wells, *Washington and the Hope of Peace* (London, W. Collins and Co., 1922), p. 18.

32 See my *Labour and Russia* (Manchester University Press, 1989), pp. 218–219 and 225–227 for a brief discussion of this.

33 Wells, *Washington and the Hope of Peace*, p. 19. For Toynbee's views see Chapter 4.

34 Harold Nicolson, *Peacemaking 1919* (London, Constable and Co., 1933) pp. 4–5.

35 David Miller, *The Drafting of the Covenant* (2 vols, New York, David Putnam's and Sons, 1928), p. 549.

36 Avenol to Blum, 2 December 1945; Blum Papers, 4BL 1 Dr2 Sdrd; 'The League of Nations', Chapter 2 in Armstrong, Lloyd and Redmond, *From Versailles to Maastricht*, pp. 59–60.

37 A very detailed description of this process can be found in Harley Notter, *Post-War Foreign Policy Preparation, 1939–1945* (Washington, US Department of State, 1949) and a less developed, but nonetheless reasonably complete, account in Robert C. Hildebrand, *Dumbarton Oaks: The Origins of the United Nations and the Search for Post-War Security* (Chapel Hill, University of North Carolina Press, 1990), Chapter 2.

38 Memorandum by Berle 'arising from conversations in Mr. Welles' office', 24 April 1940; Berle Papers, Box 54 (n.b. this document is dated a year earlier, but this must be a typing error as the war is referred to).

39 Office of War Information, 'Attitudes Towards Peace Planning', 6 March 1943; Roosevelt Official Files, 4351.

40 For more details on different aspects of the Atlantic Charter see Chapters 3 and 4. Robert Dallek has an abbreviated version of the United Nations document: *Franklin D. Roosevelt and American Foreign Policy 1932–1945* (New York, Oxford University Press, 1979), p. 320.

41 ACPWFP Subcommittee on international organisations, Meetings 17 April (P-IO-1) and 31 July 1942 (P-IO-2). Document cited ('Preliminary Memorandum on International Organization') distributed and discussed 31 July 1942, numbered 2; Smuts Memorandum distributed for P-IO-4 of 20 August 1942: Welles Papers, Box 189.

42 P-IO-4, 14 August; P-IO-5, 21 August; P-IO-10, 9 October; P-IO-14, 31 October; P-IO-16, 13 November; P-IO-17, 20 November; P-IO-20, 11 December; P-IO-21, 18 December 1942; P-IO-23, 15 January 1943: all Welles Papers, Box 189.

43 Hence, says Harper, Roosevelt's relationship with Churchill was that of the dominant, even 'older', man (in spite of the fact that Churchill was the eldest), while with Stalin Roosevelt achieved a great degree of understanding, one that Stalin recognised could not be guaranteed by his successor in the White House. And of course in this Stalin was right. Such is Harper's emphasis on Europe as the focus of Roosevelt's thinking that the whole question of the United Nations Conference at Dumbarton Oaks is allocated only a few paragraphs; Hildebrand, *Dumbarton Oaks*, p. 14 and Harper John Lamberton, *American Visions of Europe* (Cambridge University Press, 1994), p. 77 and Chapter 3.

44 I would like to acknowledge my thanks to Professor Ben Rivlin for this reported remark, in a talk at the University of Kent at Canterbury in June 1997: 'The American World View in 1945'.

45 State Department Memorandum, 28 May 1943, report on luncheon addressed by Churchill at the British Embassy in Washington; Pasvolsky Papers, Box 7. See Chapters 5 and 8 for more discussion of Churchill's views on the future of Europe.

46 Churchill's speech as recounted by Pasvolsky in a memorandum, 28 May 1943; Pasvolsky Papers, Box 7.

47 For a discussion of the role this regional/global debate played in the Welles/Hull feud see Hildebrand, *Dumbarton Oaks*, pp. 24–25.

48 Armstrong to Benjamin V. Cohen, State Department, 14 July 1943; Armstrong Papers, Box 78.

49 Isaiah Bowman to Political Committee of PWP, 5 June 1943; Berle Papers, Box 65. When Ellwood talks of Churchill's and Britain's contribution, it is to this that he must be referring.

50 Harper, *American Visions of Europe*, p. 81.

51 'Remarks by Mr. Bowman at a meeting of the Political Committee', 12 June 1943; Berle Papers, Box 65.

52 Pasvolsky, 'Memorandum for the Secretary', 30 November 1943; Pasvolsky Papers, Box 7.

53 Pasvolsky, 'International Organization and Security', 20 March 1944; Pasvolsky Papers, Box 7.

54 Stimson, Diary, 8 November 1943; Reel 8.

55 Berle to Roosevelt, 12 January 1942; Roosevelt Secretary's Files, 4725, Box 1.

56 Roosevelt to Eichelberger, 11 January 1944, in reply to a quite detailed 'Outline of the General International Organization' by Eichelberger of early in the same month. Also 'Statement by the President', Press Release of 24 March 1944; Roosevelt Secretary's Files, 4725, Box 2.

57 Pasvolsky, 'International Organization and Security', 20 March 1944; Pasvolsky Papers, Box 7.

58 Hildebrand, *Dumbarton Oaks* is the best concise description of that Conference.

59 Claude, *Swords into Plowshares*, p. 60.

60 Herbert G. Nicholas, *The United Nations as a Political Institution* (London, Oxford University Press, 1962, 1967), p. 8 (1967).

61 Alan James, 'UN Peacekeeping: New Developments and Current Problems', in D. Bourantsonis and J. Wiener (eds), *The United Nations in the New World Order: The World Organization at Fifty* (London, Macmillan, 1995); Alan James, *Peacekeeping in International Politics* (London, Macmillan, 1990); and Paul Diehl, *International Peacekeeping* (Baltimore, Johns Hopkins Press, 1994).

62 George Kennan, *Memoirs, 1950–1963* (Boston, Little Brown, 1972), pp. 171–173.

63 Kennan to Dean Rusk (then Under-Secretary of State for Political Affairs), 7 September 1949, *FRUS, 1949, Vol. 1* (Washington, DC, Government Printing Office, 1976). I am grateful to Stefan Rossbach for pointing out the existence of this document to me.

64 Recent reviews of international organisations in practice since 1989 are: J. Martin Rochester, *Waiting for the Millennium: The United Nations and the Future of World Order* (University of South Carolina Press, 1993); D. Bourantsonis and J. Wiener (eds), *The United Nations in the New World Order*; and Adam Roberts and B. Kingsbury (eds), *United Nations, Divided World* (Oxford University Press, 2nd edn, 1992).

65 de Madariaga, *Disarmament*, pp. 287 and 292.

66 Quoted by Paul Rich, 'Reinhold Niebuhr and the Ethics of Realism in International Relations', *History of Political Thought*, vol. 13, no. 2, Summer 1992.

67 Some recent literature on this includes: Barry Buzan, 'The Timeless Wisdom of Realism?', in Steve Smith, Ken Booth and Marysia Zalewski (eds), *International Theory: Positivism and Beyond* (Cambridge University Press, 1996), pp. 47–65; Jaap de Wilde and Hakan Wiberg (eds), *Organized Anarchy in Europe: The*

Role of Intergovernmental Organizations (London, I.B. Tauris, 1996); Ole Waever, Barry Buzan, Morten Kelstrup and Pierre Lemaître, *Identity, Migration and the New Security Agenda in Europe* (London, Pinter, 1993); Michael C. Pugh (ed.), *European Security – Towards 2000* (Manchester University Press, 1992); Andrew Williams (ed.), *Reorganising Eastern Europe* (Aldershot, Dartmouth Publishing, 1994); and Pal Dunay, Gabor Kardos and Andrew Williams, *New Forms of Security in Europe* (Aldershot, Dartmouth Publishing, 1995). For a documentary account of the emergence of a post-Cold War security order see Lawrence Freedman (ed.), *Europe Transformed: Documents on the End of the Cold War* (London, Tri-Service Press, 1990), which contains all the key late-Cold War documents, such as the 1975 Helsinki Final Act, the SALT Agreements, Conventional Forces of Europe agreement, Open Skies etc.).

68   The expression is used by John Mearsheimer in his 'Back to the Future', in Sean M. Lynn-Jones (ed.), *The Cold War and After: Prospects for Peace* (Cambridge, Mass., MIT Press, 1991).

69   Boutros Boutros Ghali, UN Press Release, 26 August 1992, SG/SM/4798.

70   Report by Boutros Boutros Ghali on *The Work of the UN* (New York, United Nations, 1992).

71   Michael Walzer, *Just and Unjust Wars* (New York, Basic Books, 2nd edn, 1992), p. 107. There will be further discussion of such normative thinking in international relations in Chapter 8.

72   The following are all useful on this area of post-Cold War activity by international organisations: Oliver Ramsbottom and Tom Woodhouse, *Humanitarian Intervention in Contemporary Conflict* (London, Polity Press, 1996); Paul Diehl, *International Peacekeeping*; Sydney Bailey, *Humanitarian Intervention in the Internal Affairs of States* (Basingstoke, Macmillan, 1996); Marrack Goulding, 'The Evolution of UN Peacekeeping', *International Affairs*, July 1993, pp. 451–464; G. Kostakos, A.J.R. Groom et al., 'Britain and the UN: Towards Global Riot Control', *Review of International Studies*, January 1991, pp. 95–105; William L. Durch and Eric Grove, 'Blue Helmet Blues', two articles in *International Security*, Spring 1993, pp. 151–182; Gareth Evans (Australian Foreign Minister), *Cooperating for Peace: The Global Agenda for the 1990s and Beyond* (London, George Allen and Unwin, 1993); Raoul Jennar, 'UNTAC: "International Triumph" in Cambodia?', *Security Dialogue*, vol. 25, no. 2, June 1994, pp. 145–156; Michael Barnett, 'Partners in Peace? The UN, Regional Organizations, and Peace-keeping', *Review of International Studies*, vol. 21, no. 4, October 1995, pp. 411–434; Adam Roberts, 'Communal Conflict as a Challenge to International Organization: The Case of Former Yugoslavia', *Review of International Studies*, vol. 21, no. 4, October 1995, pp. 389–410; Trevor Findlay (ed.), *Challenges to the New Peacekeepers* (Oxford/SIPRI, 1995); and Rosalyn Higgins, 'The New United Nations and Former Yugoslavia', *International Affairs*, vol. 69, no. 3, July 1993, pp. 465–484.

73   Boutros Boutros Ghali, *Agenda for Peace* (New York, United Nations, 1992).

74   UN Press Release, October 14 1992, United Nations, New York.

75   Carr, *Twenty Years' Crisis*, p. 28; Hildebrand, *Dumbarton Oaks*, p. ix.

76   Boyd Tonkin, *The Independent*, 10 January 1998; Ignatieff, 'Virtue by Proxy', in Alex Danchev and Thomas Halverson (eds), *International Perspectives on the Yugoslav Conflict* (London, Macmillan, 1996), pp. ix–xix.

77 For a discussion of this in the EBRD context, see my chapter in Dunay, Kardos and Williams, *New Forms of Security*, pp. 103–116.

78 M.L. Smith and Peter Stirk, *Making the New Europe: European Unity and the Second World War* (London, Pinter, 1990).

79 In Chapter 8 there will be an examination of more views on Europe.

80 Susan Strange, *The Retreat of the State* (Cambridge University Press, 1996), Chapter 12. Other critical voices on multilateralism include W. Andy Knight, 'Beyond the UN System? Critical Perspectives on Global Governance and Multilateral Evolution', *Global Governance*, vol. 1, no. 2, May–August 1995, pp. 229–253; and Robert W. Cox, 'An Alternative Approach to Multilateralism of the Twenty-First Century', *Global Governance*, vol. 3, no. 1, January–April 1997, pp. 103–116.

81 Susan Strange, 'The Poverty of Multilateral Diplomacy', in G.R. Berridge and A. Jennings (eds), *Diplomacy at the UN* (Basingstoke, Macmillan, 1985). Similar views are expressed by Robert Cox, 'Multilateralism and World Order', *Review of International Studies*, vol. 18, no. 2, April 1992.

82 See Chapter 7 for more exploration of this idea.

83 The literature on this is vast. Some of the best recent contributions are: Paul Taylor, *International Organization in the Modern World* (London, Pinter, 1993), Chapters 5, 6 and 7; Daniele Archibugi, 'The Reform of the UN and Cosmopolitan Democracy', *Journal of Peace Research*, August 1993, pp. 301–316; T. Kanninnen, *Leadership and Reform: The Secretary General and the UN Financial Crisis of the late 1980s* (The Hague, Nijhoff, 1995); and Hans d'Orville and Dragoljjub Najman, 'A New System to Finance the United Nations', *Security Dialogue*, vol. 25, no. 2, June 1994, pp. 135–144.

7

The economic element of the NWO project

Introduction: some parameters for discussion

In looking for central themes in NWO thinking since 1914, the idea that economic forces can be used in the service of a better, more orderly world is pivotal. The continued extension of capitalist economic practices this century has been a key element in the liberal NWO project, explicitly recognised in the Fourteen Points and the Atlantic Charter. By 1939 it had become apparent that no NWO was possible without a more open global economic system, a realisation that was made explicit in the PWP discussions in the United States and Britain. This in turn led to a greatly expanded economic institutionalisation, especially after the Bretton Woods Conference of 1944 and the 'compromise of embedded liberalism'.[1]

The economic ideas of the NWO had their roots in the classical liberal capitalist tradition of the eighteenth and nineteenth centuries. The ideas of the 'harmony of interests' and what came to be called economic 'interdependence' have long been recognised by liberals as the key motor for the reconciliation of nations and peoples in the common pursuit of wealth and prosperity. In the nineteenth century this was the main impulse behind both the political and economic liberalism that came together in the astonishing spread of capitalism across Europe and beyond.[2] Arguably, such a combined liberalism became, and remains, the motor behind a post-Enlightenment cosmopolitanism, one that has brought the world into a modern age in a whirlwind of social engineering and that has swept away traditional structures and, some would argue, virtues.

The NWO project has at its core a liberal internationalist desire to encourage 'interdependence', a situation where states are mutually dependent. We are now arguably entering, or have already entered, a phase of economic development which goes beyond interdependence. This 'globalisation' is seen as having reduced the role of the state and as encouraging private actors (individuals or firms) to take advantage of differences in national regulation and to, in effect, participate in a transnational economic culture, not in what has been, until now, an essentially national one. This phenomenon might be seen as undermining the very essence of the NWO, in that it transfers authority from the state, or a global regulatory system controlled by states, to the individual.[3] Later in the chapter we shall examine whether such fears have any justification.

Many of those who have attacked liberal internationalist thinking as 'idealist' or 'utopian' have been attacking the very idea of any NWO being possible. The problems inherent in putting any faith in liberal capitalist free-market economics as a path to peace after the First World War from a statist (or 'realist') standpoint was most succinctly put by Carr in *The Twenty Years' Crisis*. Other writers have echoed this criticism down the years, notably Alfred Cobban and Karl Polanyi during the Second World War. Marxists have constantly predicted the coming 'crisis' and the 'crash' of capitalism for the last hundred years at least, while cultural conservatives have bemoaned the loss of traditional values inherent in any global economic system. However, since the end of the Cold War others have restated the liberal internationalist faith, most notoriously Francis Fukuyama in *The End of History* (see later).

One of the central themes of this chapter is therefore an examination of the notion that the forces of economics and of economic statecraft can be marshalled in the service of peace and democracy, in the ultimate benign demonstration of the power of liberalism. The ultimate implication of this would be that there is no necessary contradiction between power, politics and interdependence, that growth can ensure prosperity and limitless goods for all. If wars are over resources and shares of the 'cake', then correct economic policies at a global level can deliver peace for all.

This chapter will also examine some of the sub-debates within this general set of propositions. Should the blueprint for an 'economic peace' depend on 'planning' or on an economic liberalism that eschews Government intervention and leaves all to the market? It has been claimed, for example, and not without some justification, that Keynes saved capitalism and liberalism economically, while Roosevelt saved it morally and politically with his emphasis on justice and planning. This chapter will also examine the debates that come out of NWO thinking as to the importance of, especially, American economic leadership, one which paralleled its political leadership. Again this will be done by looking, in parallel with the intellectuals' debate, at the discussions within particularly American and British Governmental circles, using the archival record whenever feasible.

In the Conclusion we shall resume some of this discussion by asking whether we now, after 1990, have an economic NWO that can be said to be inclusive and 'fair' or whether we now have a world that is desperately divided against itself and an NWO only for the rich capitalist nations. We shall also examine the renewed claims since the 1980s that increasing global interdependence can be demonstrated empirically to encourage global peace and that liberal (economic as well as political) democracies do not go to war with each other.

Liberal thinking on the economic causes of war

There were many liberals before 1914 who believed that the causes of war were economic, and that if humankind were to live in peace it must find an alternative to war as a way of both protecting the existing economic power of particular states and of creating an awareness of a global 'harmony of interests'. International trade, negligible in the eighteenth century, had grown at exponential rates in the nineteenth century.[4] This trade was seen by liberals as having created an interdependent world that had reduced the logic of war. This belief was particularly strong in Britain before 1914 (although not, as we shall see, without its detractors) and is most striking in the writings of Norman Angell and G. Lowes Dickinson (see below), important members of such bodies as the Bryce Group and the UDC described in Chapter 1. They were all therefore strong advocates of an economic internationalism, one that has often been stigmatised as 'idealism'.

Detractors of the liberal internationalist faith have asked, as Dulles did in 1939, how the 'have nots' in this emerging global economy might be persuaded that they could become 'haves' without recourse to war? This question is still being asked in the age of 'globalisation'. Another linked angle of assault came from those who believed (and believe) that interdependence weakened the nation state and its ability to make policy in the best interests of its citizens as well as in no way delivering the pretended benefits of peaceful co-existence. Those who believed in national 'planning', were particularly incensed on this score. Carr, who advocated both a strengthening of the nation state and 'planning', can be seen as a prominent member of this school in his suggestion that the liberals were hopelessly wrong in their understanding about both the causes of war and about the links between political stability and economic interdependence.[5] Thus a visceral distrust of liberal economic policies, which are by their very nature internationalist, is a *leitmoitif* of most 'realist' (or rather 'statist') thinking of this century.

The Great Illusion

This bedrock of liberal belief before 1914 in the benefits of economic 'interdependence' is best illustrated by Norman Angell's *The Great Illusion* (1910), a ringing denunciation of the 'futility' of war in a world of trading nations. He did not believe that Germany or any Power would even contemplate war, in the knowledge that such a conflict would destroy its own burgeoning economic growth. This was an early demonstration 'that international finance has become so interdependent and so interwoven with trade' that war cannot result in economic advantage. But he was equally aware that his book was the 'statement of a thesis still revolutionary',[6] one that had to face up to a much stronger and older current still running, that of Hegel's 'will to power'. It was a thesis that launched a national and international debate, especially among those in Britain who were concerned that Britain would have more to lose from a modern conflict and the 'war spirit' abroad in Europe than any other European Power. Paul Kennedy has also demonstrated more recently that Britain's lingering supremacy, especially in finance, was inherently dependent on peace, as was appreciated by the City and the Royal Navy alike before 1914.[7]

A socialist critique: The War of Steel and Gold

One answer to Angell's thesis lay in the twin counter-analyses of G. Lowes Dickinson and Henry Noel Brailsford. The former regretted, but accepted, the essential anarchy of the international system as an antidote to Angell's 'interdependence', in his *The Choice before Us*, published in 1917. In *The Choice Before Us*, he put competition in trade matters as a key cause of war, along with 'militarism' (explored in the previous chapter), population growth and excessive armaments. Until trade could be understood as being not a fight for markets between states, but rather a struggle 'between the rival interests of producers and purchasers in the *home* country', there would be no understanding of the benefits of free trade for ordinary people – once it was so realised, 'the argument for free trade is unassailable'.[8]

Socialists had a dual opposition to Angell's optimism. First, the manufacturers of arms were of course among the first 'multinational companies', a fact much remarked by those British soldiers who found themselves being bombarded by Vickers shells in the trenches. They therefore set a very bad example for advocates of 'interdependence' ('international cartels' was a phrase more commonly used in 1914 and had widely negative connotations, even for liberals). Second, as Brailsford pointed out, there were strong economic arguments *for* war that needed to be addressed. In his *The War of Steel and Gold* (published in early 1914), Brailsford complained that British liberals, Angell included, underestimated the jealousy that British predominance had fostered elsewhere and also the degree to which countries such as Germany had also caught up in economic and industrial terms. Germany felt herself 'penned in' and 'shut out ... from the places in the sun'.[9]

Brailsford also pointed out that the world had not changed quite as much as Angell seemed to hope. Had not a British (and Liberal) Government just refused (again and not for the last time) to allow the construction of a Channel Tunnel? Fear had vetoed the scheme on every occasion, fear of invasion principally. Britain did not live in peace, but in an 'armed peace'. The 'adoption of the group system [such as the Concert of Europe and the

Alliances] has ... brought diplomatists no nearer to the ideal of stability. It has changed the conditions of their problem, but they are still bound at every turn of the wheel to bargain for support and buy off opposition'. As a consequence, states looked still to a 'balance of power' for security as a means to an end, in the case of Britain for the 'preservation of our natural liberties'. Power was now directed to conquer markets and into the economic motive in general – 'predatory appetites have assumed a new form'.

However, Brailsford did not see war as inevitable: 'In Europe the epoch of conquest is over, and save in the Balkans and perhaps on the fringes of the Austrian and Russian Empires, it is as certain as anything in politics can be, that the frontiers of our modern national states are finally drawn. My own belief is that there will be no more wars among the six Great Powers.' In essence he agreed with at least some of Angell's analysis, that of the logic of economic interdependence making war less thinkable. Even those parts of Europe dominated by a Great Power against their will – he cites Alsace-Lorraine and Poland – might want 'autonomy but would regard separation as a disaster'.[10]

The warning note of what we would now call 'realism' was clearly there, an awareness of the exigencies of power, the need for national self-reliance in matters of security, and a need to number 'war and invasion a possibility to be reckoned among everyday perils'. The question was how these different trends could be managed. Brailsford could personally put no hope in alliances to keep the peace, neither could Britain imagine itself immune from European wars, either by acting as 'balancer' or by remaining aloof.[11] As a socialist he saw the forces of class domination, financial speculation and the needs of the armaments industry to sell its wares as likely to foster increasing imaginary terrors. His answer was that the demons of nations would only be 'exorcised ... when clear and negative thinking has dispelled the megalomania that distracts us'. The real enemy for him was 'an imagination too facile, a reverence [for class and nation] too little exacting ... Let a people once perceive for what its patriotism is prostituted, and its resources misused, and the end is already in sight.'[12]

These words were published in March 1914. The subsequent four years of world war destroyed the economic system that had been underpinned by the currency stability provided by the Gold Standard (backed by Sterling) and the steady emergence of a global (or at least European) trading system with free-trade characteristics. It has been suggested that the pre-1914 economy was more fully integrated than the one we have today – 'genuinely international, tied by efficient long-distance communications and industrialized means of transport'.[13] The travels of Finneas Fogg in *Around the World in Eighty Days* might be more difficult today. Norman Angell's memoirs relate how he was able to cross the Atlantic in the 1880s on a cheap passage, spend as much time as he liked working as a cowboy in the American West, and only being asked by United States Customs not to use the revolver he had stuck in his waist-band illegally.[14] The world outside and within Europe was bound by Empires that could be crossed without difficulty.

It might be argued that the Listian economic policies of import substitution followed by many European states (notably Germany) gave writers such as Angell to believe in a 'harmony of interests' that was more apparent than real.[15] But there was a generalised perception in liberal circles before 1914 that this harmony existed and was growing and after 1919 that it had been lost. Hence H.G. Wells was able to say in 1922 that '[t]he catastrophe of 1914 is still going on ... Since 1919 this world has not so much healed its wounds as realised its injuries. Chief among these injuries is the progressive economic breakdown, the magnitude of which we are only beginning to comprehend.'[16]

Economic considerations at Paris, 1919: sanctions, reconstruction and revenge

Wilson professed an enthusiasm for economic solutions to political problems. In his initial musings about the nature of the LON and of the peace in August 1918, Wilson had told Wiseman in Washington that he 'look[ed] to economic pressure to supply the main force which might be used to support a League of Nations'.[17] As was mentioned in Chapter 2, when he went to Paris Wilson took only three Memoranda with him: on the LON, 'An Association of Nations', a 'Declaration on Open Diplomacy' and a third on 'Equality of Trade'.[18] Wilson's Fourteen Points had among them some key economic demands, including Freedom of the Seas for commerce (Point II) and the removal of economic barriers to trade (Point III), with the reduction of armaments and decolonisation (Points IV and V) having a strong economic element. Unfortunately, in the *mêlée* that was the Paris Peace Conference, these intentions seem to have got rather lost. What did emerge in the discussions was the possible use of economic statecraft in the service of the LON, particularly to enforce collective security.

The discussions at Paris gave at least a chance to redress this situation. However, as Robert Skidelsky has aptly put it, '[a]ny chance the world had of regaining political, economic and moral equilibrium [after the Treaty of Versailles] was fatally undermined by the inability of American and European statesmen to liquidate the twin and connected problems of inter-Allied War debts and German reparations.'[19] Once Germany had been blamed for the war and its consequences it became inevitable that the main economic business of Paris would be tied up with assessing the bill with which Germany was to be presented. The main economic questions raised at Paris were therefore to do with the inter-Allied debt and German reparations, questions that were never fully resolved and have spawned a huge critical discussion ever since.[20]

This might not have been so decisive for the future of world peace if all the Allies had stuck to their original commitment to 'squeeze the lemon [Germany] until you can hear the pips squeak',[21] as Sir Eric Geddes put it. But they fell out about both this and who should pay whom back for the loans taken out during the war during the Paris Peace Conference itself. Regardless of whether Britain, France and Russia could, or indeed should, have paid the United States back, as some historians have argued, they were almost terminally split over the questions of how to restructure the ravaged economies of Europe, which Keynes rightly saw as the only long-term solution, and to decide what role economic statecraft might play as 'carrot or stick' in future diplomatic and security crises.[22]

Sanctions

During the war the economic weapon had been seen as very effective. Admiral Lord Fisher claimed that in spite of 'the effete, apathetic, indecisive, vacillating Conduct of the War [it had only been] won by an effective Blockade'.[23] The British delegation at Paris had put great emphasis on a 'Freedom of the Seas', guaranteed by a strong British fleet, as was noted in Chapter 1. They could not see how economic sanctions could guarantee peace or enforce compliance with LON rulings except where blockade was possible. As Balfour put it, the big problem was how to deal with 'our small Allies and our small enemies. The former, one would suppose, would obey us through gratitude; the latter through fear.' But would there ever be an effective back-up of force, and could the economic sanction fill the gap? For him it was 'not very easy to use ... except in the form of blockade, [and] has not, as far as I know, been systematically employed'.[24]

The economic weapon was seen by others either as a club with which to beat Allies and enemies alike, or as a secondary consideration. The Paris Conference set up an EAC (also referred to as the 'European Economic Committee') to supplement the Supreme Economic Council of the Allies, which met for the first time on 10 May 1919. Robert Cecil was asked to chair it, a significant choice as he had been the very effective British Minister for the Blockade during the war and was now a major advocate of economic sanctions being used by the League of Nations. The French were initially opposed to the EAC as they thought it likely to detract from the main business of punishing and containing Germany, but eventually agreed after discussions with Eyre Crowe, Cecil and Philip Kerr (later Lord Lothian).[25]

By April 1919 Cecil had managed to persuade himself that the 'really urgent danger is the economic one', mainly because he was sure that Germany was about to collapse, but he was also in favour of punishing Germany severely, as is evidenced by his reply when he was confronted by Keynes protesting about the excessive reparations bill being heaped upon Germany. Cecil remarked that: 'Keynes thought the whole thing rather disreputable – I could not quite make out why. But apparently he holds the view that you should not use the peace in order to secure economic advantages.' He was later further shaken when Henry Morgenthau, later US Treasury Secretary under Roosevelt, told him that 'America had made a lot of money out of the war; that they did not care very much what happened to their foreign trade … and that they were rapidly becoming in favour of withdrawing altogether from Europe, and letting it shift for itself'. This was confirmed by talking to Norman Davis, the 'financial man' of the American delegation. The disillusionment that gripped this key delegation was clear even before the Treaty was signed.[26]

John Maynard Keynes, as the key representative of the British Treasury at Versailles, was far more bitter. As he told Secretary to the Treasury, Sir John Bradbury on 19 May:

> The events of the last three weeks have filled me with a degree of depression, disgust and dismay which I can hardly express. The terms of the draft Treaty are dishonourable and unjust and not even workable. In the deplorable event of the Germans being compelled to sign under threat of starvation and overwhelming force, public honour will have ceased to exist in Europe and popular trust in Governments will, when the facts become known, be so grievously undermined as to prepare the way for revolutions and unrest every-where. Many persons share my opinions. But unwisdom and opportunism have won the day and nothing else counts.[27]

This extraordinary outburst, in a letter originally intended to be about 'staffing problems at Versailles', shows that Keynes was preparing to resign well before he actually did so (see below).

Economic reconstruction versus revenge

Keynes put his finger on the key problem of Versailles. How was the peace to be kept once the guns were silent, especially if it were couched in terms that were almost calculated to offend the defeated? The British and French Governments wanted to reconstruct their economies. Lloyd George even referred to his post-war Cabinet as the 'Reconstruction Cabinet'. But both were weighed down by huge debts in a complicated arrangement orches-trated by the British Treasury (an arrangement for which Keynes was to some extent responsible), where money borrowed largely from the United States had been used to finance the war effort in France and on the Eastern Front. The Russians never paid their contribution back, the Bolsheviks repudiating their predecessor Governments' debts in one of their first acts after October 1917. By ridiculing Wilson and the entire economic discuss-ions at Versailles in the *Economic Consequences of the Peace* only shortly after the Conference ended, Keynes managed to be blamed by many at the time and since for introducing another major source of tension between the United States, France and Britain.[28]

Keynes was throughout the main critic of the economic clauses of the Treaty. Even though he blamed the Germans for starting the war, he saw that 'the French and British peoples have run the risk of completing the ruin ... by a peace, which if it is carried into effect, must impair yet further, when it might have been restored, the delicate complicated organisation, already shaken by war, through which the European peoples can employ themselves and live.'[29] It later became fashionable for virtually all of British public opinion to agree with Keynes that Germany had been too harshly treated.[30]

The American demand for reparation had always been the least demanding on Germany, 'a fair construction of the agreement with Germany' (in the Armistice, based on the Fourteen Points), as John Foster Dulles (the American chief legal expert at Paris) put it.[31] Keynes' suggestion of 17 April 1919 for 'a grand scheme for the rehabilitation of Europe', which later became the section of the *Economic Consequences of the Peace* entitled 'Remedies', was received sympathetically by the Americans in Paris, but not by the politicians in Washington, conscious that Keynes wanted, as a corollary, a mutual Allied debt cancellation, suggested by him in March 1919. Keynes' reaction was that 'Washington rejects my proposals by reason of their strong desire to clear out of European responsibility ... They would like to help Germany if they could do it without helping our reparation schemes; but France and Italy they would like to see punished.'[32] But unfortunately, as Keynes saw it, although Lloyd George had belatedly realised that this 'Carthaginian peace' would not be supported by a rapidly changing British public opinion, it was by that time too late to explain to Wilson, who had let the Conference work on the basis of the British or French draft on reparations. In consequence, Keynes resigned from the Treasury on 5 June and left Versailles. 'I am slipping away from this vision of nightmare ... The battle is lost. I leave the twins to glare over the devastation of Europe and to assess what remains for the British taxpayer.' He sent a similar message to his American counterpart Norman Davis ('You Americans are broken reeds'), but also characteristically invited him to dinner.[33]

But *French* public opinion could not have been more opposed to Keynes' ideas. As Pierre Miquel has rightly said, 'sur la nécessité de faire payer l'Allemagne, l'opinion française était unanime'. Clemenceau could not have even contemplated being 'fair' to Germany. 'Le Boche paiera,' raged French Finance Minister Klotz, incidentally one of the men Keynes loved to hate. When the Treaty was published a typical comment in the informed French press was that 'la Traité de Paix ne représente que la plus grande approximation possible de l'achevé et du définitif'; in other words, that it was perfectly fair on Germany.[34] Many French writers blamed Keynes and British Governments after Versailles for dragging out the negotiations with Germany, so giving Germany hope that it would eventually be let off a large part of the reparations bill. Etienne Mantoux, in his *The Economic Consequences of Mr. Keynes*,[35] was particularly incensed. So Keynes was

right to say that '[i]nsofar as the main economic lines of the Treaty represents an intellectual idea, it is the idea of France and of Clemenceau'.[36]

Was Keynes correct in his blanket condemnation? One key fact in his
favour is that many of the states of Europe, including Germany, were indeed
in a state of economic collapse in 1919, and this collapse accelerated in the
early 1920s. The LON did try and salvage some of these problems, notably
in Austria, described by one writer as 'an abode of wretchedness',[37] with a
programme of economic help, a process that will be described below. But
this minor LON success was as nothing compared with the collapse of the
German currency in 1923 and the consequent bitterness among the German
petit-bourgeoisie, widely blamed for their support for Hitler in the 1930s.
The collapse of the Mark hurt British and French commerce, and it severely
damaged the Anglo-French Alliance by revealing the different emphases of
the two states on reconstruction versus reparation, forcing Curzon into a
condemnation of the French occupation of the Ruhr in 1923.[38] Nothing was
gained by either of the Allies and it merely served to reinforce the isolationist
tendencies of those Americans who believed the French and British were
incapable of any higher feeling than that which directly affected their wallets
and Imperial designs. Had Wilson exercised real leadership and insisted that
the economic clauses of his Fourteen Points were respected, the outcome
might have been very different, but in the atmosphere of 1919–20 it is still
doubtful that he could have brought American public opinion with him and
stayed in the LON.

More widely, the reparations question served to emphasise the breach
which existed between those who wanted the Treaty to encourage greater
freedom both within and between states, especially the successor states of
the European Empires. The French had won the argument on the question of
reparation and restitution, not Wilson with his ideal of economic openness
allied to self-determination. The importance of these two ideas being linked
in practice became increasingly clear in the inter-war period.

Economic nationalism as a cause of war: thinking in the inter-war period

During the inter-war period liberal internationalism was the main victim of
the disillusionment felt about Versailles. In spite of the attempted 'return to
normalcy' of the 1920s, there was no one state willing or able to underpin a
return to an open economic system such as had existed before 1914, or to
steady international capitalism after such an event as the 1929 Wall Street
Crash. 'Economic nationalism' was the result, with its main landmarks in
the Smoot–Hawley tariff of 1929 and the Ottawa 'Imperial Preference'
arrangements of 1932, which confirmed that both the United States and the
British Empire had lost faith in the concept of free trade. Other major states

followed suit, in the case of Germany developing a system of almost autarkic proportions as occurred, in the USSR. 'National planning' came to replace internationalism as the guiding economic principle.[39] Hence the argument made by Brailsford (or Carr) about the need to accept nationalism as being more powerful than economic motives and 'interdependence' was even more relevant in 1935 than it had been in 1914.

It still remains to be asked why the collapse of liberalism was so sudden and so complete. For Carr, the 'Paradise of Laissez-Faire', which might have had its logic before lots of small nations appeared on the scene, all jostling for their bit of the 'Harmony of Interests' cake, could no longer be said to exist. The 'invisible hand' would not keep the peace. Biologically and economically, the doctrine of the harmony of interests was tenable only if you left out of account the interest of the weak, who must be driven to the wall or called in the next world to redress the balance of the present. 'To make the harmonisation of interests the goal of political action is not the same thing as to postulate that a natural harmony of interests exists; and it is this latter postulate which has caused so much confusion in international thinking.'[40] Carr was explicitly using Darwin and List to outflank Adam Smith and J.S. Mill. The key point for Carr was that self-determination had created too many small and unviable states and this, allied to the nationalism that he saw as inevitable, had brought great instability to the international system. As Carr put it,

> the mirage of the nineteen-twenties was of ... [a] golden age of continuously expanding territories and markets, of a world policed by the self-assured and not too onerous British hegemony ... of the easy assumptions that what was good for one was good for all and that what was economically right could not be morally wrong ... The utopia of 1919 was hollow and without substance.[41]

According to the Van Zeeland Report of the LON Economic Committee in September 1937: '[e]very country seeks, and seeks rightly, to protect its own economy'. Cobban commented in 1944 that '[e]conomic Nationalism ... is merely the contemporary form of a universal phenomenon', dating from the origins of the modern state and Colbert in the seventeenth century.[42] So why was it seen as having caused the Second World War? For Cobban it was because '[t]he triumph of economic nationalism was naturally aided by the idea of national self-determination' and the rise of autarky that that implied as, especially, small states asserted their economic independence along with their new sovereignty. It went along with a renewed belief in the need of the state to prepare itself for war, the German *Wehrwirtschaft* and similar policies pursued by all the Powers, including Britain, in the name of a 'common national interest'. But, asked Cobban, does this actually exist; he argued that in all but the greatest of states 'the common national interest' turns out to be 'the operation of the selfish interests of particular classes or groups'.[43] This was particularly true of the period of the 1930s when selfishness was enhanced by the observation, made in 1937 at a LON

Conference, that 'nations live under the obsession of war ...', without any countervailing international mechanisms to ensure stability '... the exchange and monetary systems are to-day completely disorganized'.[44]

The Grotius Society devoted much of its discussions in 1918 to asking what might happen if the war had damaged free trade irrevocably, and put some faith in Wilson's call for a revitalisation of international law to solve this. International law was based, like his thinking, 'on an appeal to the opinion of the world'.[45] But the Society was well aware that the real challenge was 'how to prevent war occurring' because only this could guarantee Freedom of the Seas and of commerce. The idea (at the time the papers were given) of a League of Nations 'with an international police force' that would be used to keep the peace and reply to aggression was very appealing. But this could only happen when, as Dr Eliot of Harvard had put it, 'British control', benevolent as it had been in protecting all commerce, was replaced by 'international control'. This would require drastic naval disarmament by Britain and its replacement by 'a better instrument of freedom' – 'an international naval police'. The problem was that all mainstream American thinking on the subject downplayed, or indeed eliminated, any such notion. The United States had always been wedded to the simple idea of the freedom of commerce from any interference by any power, and some of Britain's main conflicts with the United States had been over that issue.[46] It therefore desired a reduction of British sea power and a corresponding increase of other navies, a goal achieved at the Washington Naval Conference of 1921, where the 'two power standard' was officially buried.

This difference of opinion and the withdrawal of the Americans from the LON convinced many in Britain that the ideal of a free-trade system guaranteed by some sort of international agreement was illusory. Before the war there had been a growing challenge to the sacrosanct nature of free trade from within the Conservative Party, which had begun to espouse 'Tariff Reform', and this view grew into one proposing 'Imperial Preference'. But as an expedient to maintain British power against other sea-borne powers it was equally doomed to fail, for how could so far flung an Empire stand up to submarine warfare and a war on many fronts? The awful shock of the fall of Singapore was the most eloquent demonstration of this. Imperial Preference was thus a counsel of despair, but it was sincerely believed in by many and saw its albeit reluctant acceptance at the 1932 Ottawa Imperial Conference. It would probably not have appeared seriously on the agenda if it had not been for the breakdown of the wartime cooperation between the Allies.

It was Karl Polanyi who, in *The Great Transformation* of 1944, identified better than anyone else what he considered were the precise links between the international financial system and international power politics. For Polanyi, as for Carr, the nineteenth century had been a successful one for Europe because economy and politics had moved in tandem. He felt that one of the key causes of the First World War had been the progressive dissolution from 1900 onwards of the liberal economic system, and that all attempts to resurrect it in the 1920s were doomed to failure, so that 'by 1940 every vestige of the international system had disappeared'. In this situation no statesman understood what was happening, according to Polanyi, because none of them could liberate themselves from the old-fashioned thinking that had given them a financial system, the Gold Standard, that was no longer appropriate for the twentieth century. He saw the failure of the inter-war period as being due to an excessive faith in liberal free-market capitalism and the Gold Standard. This economic failure brought down with it the balance of power system and the liberal state.[47]

By 1923 (and thus well before Carr and Polanyi) Angell had realised that the private world of trade was being transferred into the public domain of the state – and that therefore the relationship of the individual to the state and of states to each other was fundamentally changed. Trade after the war was, said Angell, 'less a matter of processes maintained by individuals who disregarded their nationality, and more a matter of arrangement between states, in which the non-political individual activity tends to disappear'. This process had been accelerated by state intervention and the organisation of national economies by states during the war, and by the example of the Soviet Union, which had done away with private property altogether.[48] Angell's preference was for a 'transnational individualism' not for a 'militarised Nationalisation', which he correctly foresaw for an economically repressed Germany. But he also recognised that this was not likely, given the realities of the Treaty of Versailles and its 'Balance of Power or preponderance as a political method'. Carr and Angell thus had much the same analysis of the situation, but different solutions.[49]

Liberals never quite gave up the fight. In his two main offerings on the subject, *The Fruits of Victory* (1921) and *The Great Illusion – Now* (1938), Angell was unrepentant in his claims of the 'economic futility of military power'. In parts of these books that now read as quite 'contemporary' in their appreciation, he persisted in his belief that it was state intervention during the war that had created a new situation. This intervention was bound to increase tension and might possibly be damaging to those it most wished to help. One example of this can be found in Angell's 1921 assertion that '[t]he old individualist economy has been largely destroyed by the State Socialism introduced for war purposes ... The economic clauses of the Treaty, if enforced, must prolong this tendency, rendering a large measure of such Socialism permanent.' Although he was able to accept that '[t]he change may be desirable', this would inevitably mean that the 'political emotions of nationalism will play a much larger role in the economic processes of Europe, [thus] we are likely to have not a less but a more quarrelsome world, unless the fact of interdependence is much more vividly realised than in the past.'[50]

What ultimately reinvented free trade, which was, as Angell had correctly seen, essential for an interdependent, 'modern' world, was an alliance of the main commercial powers in a regulatory framework and the imposition of a different hegemony, that of the United States of America, a theme that we shall develop below. Sea power itself became less important but the principle of commercial freedom did not. As Cornelia Navari has pointed out, what Angell was arguing, both before and after 1914, was that interdependence was 'not only a logical category, it was also a historical category'. It needed, in effect, to be protected, as present day 'liberal internationalist' followers of Angell have also asserted.[51]

Economic reconstruction after 1919: policy responses

With these ideas as the intellectual background, it was agreed by the policy makers that Europe was devastated and that 'something' must be done about it. However, unlike in 1945 there was no consensus about what this should be and no state to give a lead in how it must be done. The debate that developed pitted the war-enhanced economic liberalism of the United States against the more *dirigiste* instincts of Lloyd George, who has been characterised as a 'Keynesian before Keynes' in his attempts at Genoa in 1922 to revitalise European trade.[52] Stuck on the sidelines in what became a political and ideological battle between the Big Three was the League of Nations, trying to find a role but not being allowed to have one by any of the major players. This dispute came to a head in 1922 at the Genoa Conference, intended both to find a plan to reconstruct Europe and to bring back into the system the 'pariah states' of Germany and Bolshevik Russia, an effort which failed dismally and contributed to Lloyd George's loss of office later in the year.[53]

But the important fact is that the novel idea of 'reconstruction' had taken root. One of the first Professors of International Relations, Philip Noel-Baker, complained that the expression was 'often used without any clear concept of what is meant. It is a new addition to post-war vocabulary and like many new things it is used indiscriminately and vaguely thought to mean everything that helps the return to the good old days when all were prosperous before the war.' Noel-Baker sought to pin down the concept more clearly to two major elements: the 'restoration of pre-war efficiency [and] … reconstruction of the economic mechanisms of manufacture, credit, purchase and sale [and] transport …'. This translated, he said, into a necessary involvement of '*citizens* of the countries involved … [plus] government action … [plus] international action by governments working together – this is the real experiment'.[54] It cannot be said that the experiment worked, so why was this so?

League of Nations attempts at reconstruction in the 1920s

Most of the economic Conferences organised under or outside League of Nations auspices in the early 1920s were conspicuous for their lack of success. The European Economic Conference at Genoa in April 1922 is a good example, but there were many others. Each failed over an unwilling-ness by individual states to override their individual political obsessions in a wider common good. The League was never properly given the task of economic reconstruction that the United Nations was given during and after the Second World War. (It was, for example, explicitly rejected for any kind of secretariat role at Genoa by Lloyd George.) As we saw in our discussion of the Versailles Treaty, there were few, if any, economic clauses that did not stress punishment. An enormous amount of energy by bankers and govern-ments was then expended on a problem that they themselves had created. This was exacerbated by the break-up of the Empires and the creation of a host of new small and largely economically unviable states, 'unviable' in the circumstances of the 1920s when there was no real economic coordination between states.

Austria's problems illustrated this early on in the 1920s. The war had left Austria bereft of its political and economic hinterland, with Vienna in particular as a huge bureaucratic centre of an Empire that no longer existed. Unemployment and poverty, even starvation, were widespread as it lost its sources of food. The surrounding states initially allied to prevent the restor-ation of a Hapsburg monarchy, thus ensuring quasi isolation. The League attempted to correct this situation by organising a series of economic Conferences to coordinate a resurrection of the economic integration of the area in the interests of all. This effort, directed by Arthur Salter and helped by the young Jean Monnet, implied a measure of political control by the League to ensure the establishment of a more open market.

This was difficult as all the surrounding states feared for their own industries if Austria was allowed to re-start her own, a problem exacerbated by the recent memories of political, even 'psychological' subjugation (in the words of Noel-Baker). Austria itself appealed to the League that '[i]f the League of Nations do not bring us immediate help, the gravest moral responsibility will be theirs for the chaos which will endanger public peace and order, nay even the civilisation of the European Continent.' For the League itself it presented a chance to prove what it could do – in Noel-Baker's words, 'This is a real piece of reconstruction: it is almost the only thing in the world since the war, that is on an important scale, both economically reconstructive and international in character.'[55]

It must be said that the League did pass this test, and Noel-Baker, by 1925 at least, believed that it also passed the test in Germany, Hungary and Greece. In the first of these cases it is difficult to see that the League could do anything to alleviate the hyper-inflation of 1923 or claim any credit for the subsequent parlous stabilisation. The League did not succeed in getting the reparations bill reduced, that was negotiated by American bankers Dawes (in 1924) and Young (in 1929). Hitler finally abolished the problem by refusing to pay any more of the bill in 1933. Perhaps if this ineluctable result had been carried out by a democratic German Government encouraged by the Allies far earlier, Hitler would not have been able to claim the credit for that and much else of the final revision of the Treaty of Versailles. The League did in fact realise that its most important achievements were in the economic and social spheres, as the Bruce Report of 1939 pointed out, but by then such policies alone, even if they had been far more extensive, were not enough to stop the onset of war.

The emergence of American economic leadership

As we have seen, Polanyi's attack on the economic liberal 'idealists' has much in common with Carr's attacks on the political 'utopians'. But, as John Hall points out, Polanyi's additional contribution was to point to the importance of leadership in both the success of the 1945 NWO and its failure in 1919.[56] This theme became a constant of, particularly American political science in the 1970s and 1980s.[57] Polanyi was adamant that British military and financial power was the *sine qua non* of the success of the *Pax Britannica* of the nineteenth century and its absence the guarantee of its demise. Since American leadership had not stepped in to replace the erstwhile British leadership, a descent into economic nationalism and a fragmentation of the global economy was therefore inevitable. However, we now live with the commonplace claim of post-Second World War American economic leadership: 'embedded liberalism'.[58] American leadership has now replaced British, at least since 1945. A pertinent question must therefore be whether this account of an initial reluctance to assume leadership and its subsequent reversal is an accurate description of what actually happened.

A key figure in the move towards global American economic leadership was that of Herbert Hoover, Wilson's 'economic Czar' at Versailles. Hoover's overall strategy was to enlist the forces of American (and indeed also of British) capitalism in forging a benevolent new economic world order, fostered in the words of Michael Hogan, one of the leading American historians of the period, by 'a limited and carefully delineated government action'[59] that would ally the power of the market with a conscious attempt to create a global economy with as few barriers as possible. Hoover tried to implement this from an increasingly secure and expanding power-base in the Department of Commerce in the early 1920s, and from which he was able to climb to the White House in 1928. He recognised what we would now call a growing economic 'interdependence'. Hogan says that his aim was to 'avoid the pitfalls of pre-war imperialism and Bolshevik revolution'.[60] Hoover was thus adapting the Wilsonian agenda at Versailles to a new situation where a more lasting *economic* settlement of the war was to be imposed from outside the League of Nations and Versailles political structure. What sank Hoover's dream was the economic nationalism of the US Congress and the Smoot–Hawley tariff of 1930, one that he vainly opposed.

His successor in office, Roosevelt, accepted the argument that stability had to be brought back to the international economic system and that American leadership had to be developed from the base that Wilson and Hoover had tentatively established. Hogan again is the writer of choice on this. He characterises the American model of economic integration that emerged during the 1920s and 1930s as one

> founded on self-governing economic groups, integrated by institutional coordinators and normal market mechanisms, led by cooperating public and private elites, and geared to an economic growth in which all could share ... The result as it unfolded after the First World War was something of a hybrid economic order: an American brand of corporative neo-capitalism that went beyond the laissez-faire political economy of classical theory but stopped short of a statist syndicalism.[61]

As British liberals looked to their glorious past, American liberals drew on their own experiences of capitalism, ones reinforced by Roosevelt's experimentation during the New Deal era of the 1930s. The eventual resulting economic NWO that emerged from the Second World War was therefore a compromise between the nineteenth century stability of free trade, stable exchange rates and the (new American-ensured) balance of power. It led to the establishment of new global institutions to try and encourage, and if necessary enforce, global compliance.

Therefore it is not strictly true to say, as does Robert Pollard, that '[d]uring the late Hoover and the first Roosevelt administrations, the United States largely spurned international cooperation'.[62] After 1934 the lack of leadership in the world economy, especially through the promotion of multi-lateral trade, was progressively corrected by Roosevelt's Secretary of State, Cordell Hull.[63] Hull nonetheless inherited, in the words of Richard Gardner, 'an unpromising legacy' made up of four factors: political isolation (although, as we have seen and Gardner admits, by no means total isolation); 'potential self sufficiency in nearly all branches of production' given its size and population; considerable local opposition to laissez-faire policies, again linked to isolationist tendencies; and, last but not least, the political system, one 'which tended [and tends] to subordinate national to local interests'.[64]

Hull set about changing this culture with all the fervour of a commercial evangelist. He was totally convinced by the liberal view that trade is the best antidote to war, and thus in agreement with Wilson. As did Wilson, he also 'had a most exaggerated notion of the efficacy of formal statements of general principle'. He made his long tenure at the State Department count by turning it into an extension of his belief, to the point where it seemed that he was almost obsessional, as at the Moscow Conference in 1943 where he spent an inordinate amount of time getting the Russians to agree to multilateral trade reforms, when to most observers he was wasting his time with a country wedded to central planning and autarky. Hull's views were therefore 'idealist' in the sense that he wished to see a universal open multilateral trade regime, whereas in practice it proved difficult to get anything more than Anglo-American agreement to multilateralise trade after the war, a very difficult process in itself, as we saw in Chapter 4.

Gardner takes the view that all the American post-war planners we discussed in Chapter 3 were partners in Hull's universal views, but of course all of them had to compromise down to what in effect was, initially at least, an Anglo-Saxon core that developed the embryonic Rooseveltian NWO in its economic aspects.[65] This was also true of the development of a financial arm of this, with the Russians being largely left in a consultative status. We therefore remember Bretton Woods as essentially a discussion between Harry Dexter White (Secretary of the Treasury, Henry Morgenthau's deputy) and Keynes. However, by providing the necessary economic, as well as political, leadership after 1941 the United States arguably re-created by the 1970s, at least in the West, the essential elements of an international economic system with many of the features of the system of 1914, but with added institutional strength. How this happened will now be explored.

Planning the post-war Economy, 1939–45

'Leadership tantamount to Empire'

It has already been stressed that the demise of the Versailles settlement was seen by many in the State Department and wider American elite as having been for its economic failings. It has also been stressed how much that opinion put the emphasis on a need for a new organisational structure for Europe and a special place for Britain within this reorganisation. This led to a gradual and reluctant appreciation that direct American leadership was necessary. Strong reinforcement was given to this by the economic discussions between Britain and the United States during 1941, 1942 and 1943 described in Chapters 4 and 6. The United States put immense pressure on Britain to renounce 'Imperial Preference' in exchange for Lend–Lease and the promise of post-war help – the 'Consideration' as Keynes put it. After eventually persuading Keynes and the British Cabinet by a combination of Britain's urgent need for help and a resurgence of belief in the benefits of international cooperation after the war, the economic clauses of the Atlantic Charter had been given potential life.

However, before American entry into the war the State Department was pessimistic that the post-war economic regime would be any better than it had been in 1919. It doubted that there would be (in the event of either an Allied or a German victory) 'a far-reaching surrender of national sovereignty ... Indeed it does not seem likely that the principal nations of either the world or even of Europe will be ready for an integration process which will involve a substantial surrender of sovereignty [... in either the political or the economic fields]'. However, it was already accepted, as Berle put it in early 1940, that whatever the future of *political* stability arrangements, which might, as we have seen, be 'regional in character ...[,] *economic* arrangements will be universal, in the sense that they will embrace all or most of the important nations'. At this point Berle could see little hope of 'multilateral action towards elimination or mitigation of trade barriers' and he could see even less point in a 'conference' to encourage this, although he did see the necessity of a 'machinery of international economic cooperation'.[66]

By the end of 1942 this process had matured to the point where Berle was prepared to contemplate what had been impossible in 1940. Would the United Nations now insist on 'economic unification of the European area' as a condition of help in economic reconstruction? Was this organisational task best left to Britain? The aim of all this, as in all American thinking about Europe at this time, was to avoid 'the rise of narrow nationalist economic policies which may lead to future militarism'.[67] This therefore chimed perfectly with the discussion going on simultaneously about what would be the best sort of international organisation for security, a discussion explored in Chapter 6.

But was the United States yet ready at this stage to go the whole way and accept global economic leadership? The first major statement of this comes at the end of 1942 in a memorandum that is well worth quoting. Where it went further than previous statements was in the realisation by the end of 1942 that '[t]he United States now has and proposes to maintain economic leadership in the Western hemisphere.' This was coupled with the knowledge that 'we are about to assume in economics a position analogous to that of Great Britain in politics in the last century – that is we are being asked to assume the responsibilities of leadership tantamount to Empire ... There is thus appearing the vague outline of a real "new order" provided we care to take it on'. This was in the very logic of history, '[e]very element suggests a change of economic center ... and the real center will be in the financial and economic agencies in Washington.'[68] They had proved that they were so prepared in their discussions with Keynes, concluded in 1942, and they were to prove it again in the latter part of the war at Bretton Woods in 1944.

The effort at economic institution building, 1943–44

Once it was reasonably clear that the war was going to be won by the Allies, a phase that we have noted came after the landings in Italy in 1943, that is, the pace of ambitious planning for the economic future under what was in effect American economic leadership, increased. The two main elements that came together were those of international cooperation and the, somewhat contradictory, ideas of 'national planning', very popular in a Britain (see Chapter 4) and France in its liberal capitalist version and the central pillar of the Soviet system in a much more Marxist form. The resulting 'compromise of embedded liberalism', as Ruggie calls it, was driven both by the need to keep Britain involved in the post-war project and by an increasingly acknowledged realisation that Europe and other parts of the world would need reconstruction on a scale to dwarf that of 1919.[69] It was also driven by the desire not to allow a return to economic nationalism and 'the economic warfare, so prevalent in the inter-war years', as Pasvolsky put it in March 1944. This would require a 'gearing together sound domestic and international policies in a large variety of economic fields'. In this the really crucial partner was the British Commonwealth, which with the United States controlled 'well over one-half of the world's total international trade'. Interdependence was being used as the vehicle of lasting peace among nations, but not one which stifled 'the forces of initiative, self-reliance, enterprise and scientific advance'.[70] For the State Department PWP planners it was therefore mainly a case of building on the Atlantic Charter and other agreements with Britain such as Lend–Lease. The result was the Bretton Woods Agreement of 1944.

Bretton Woods[71]

The two major foci of American economic decision were the State Department under Hull and the Treasury under Morgenthau. Morgenthau lacked Hull's evangelical belief in multilateralism, possibly because he had been present at Versailles, but he shared the belief that the economic causes of war were the most intractable and important. Morgenthau was also significant because of his great friendship with Roosevelt, whose views he can be said to have echoed in most respects. Hence Morgenthau was given charge of the financial side of the post-war settlement, which resulted (finally) in the establishment of the Bank for Reconstruction of the United and Associated Nations (now known as the World Bank) and the IMF. Hull's State Department was given control of commercial matters, which eventually resulted in the General Agreement on Tariffs and Trade (GATT) which entered into force in 1948.[72]

Two key questions as to how post-war economic cooperation would work out in practice had to be addressed. First, would the high hopes held out by Roosevelt and Hull of such post-war changes actually see the light, or were they to go the same way as the Covenant of the LON? Second, how would Russia fit into this?

To take the second of these initially, as it is in a sense the easiest to answer, the view taken in 1950 that the USSR was '[l]onely and peculiar in a bourgeois world'[73] has much logic behind it. Whenever the USSR had taken part in inter-war LON economic Conferences it had used them as a propaganda platform. Moreover, given the State Department's insistence on trade as the motor of future peaceful growth, it is not altogether surprising that Russia (and China) were not given the importance they may have desired – by their policies they had effectively excluded themselves from significant international trade. However, there is also the uncomfortable fact that the USSR agreed to the economic and social clauses of the United Nations. As Robert Boardman has pointed out, '[t]he Soviet Union, after all, had a stake in the 1945 deal'.[74]

Kennan's view was far more cynical. For him the Soviet Union would never have allowed any considerations of cooperation to interfere with its much more important strategic goals, especially in Eastern Europe. Both the Bretton Woods organisations and UNRRA were only useful for 'political purposes' and 'it seemed wildly unrealistic to expect that they, with their jealously closed and controlled economy ... would be suitable partners for collaboration in the international monetary field, even if their purposes had been similar to ours, which they were not'. He consequently often expressed contrary views to Hull in State Department memoranda about Russian trade, in one to Harriman saying 'it is not *interested* in trade except' insofar as it hastens 'the achievement of [the] complete military-economic autarchy of the Soviet Union'.[75] Once Soviet interests in Eastern Europe were seen as being put into question by Marshall Aid (as a form of American economic imperialism) and subsequent discussions about how actually to reconstruct Europe, the USSR denounced the Bretton Woods organisations. It can be said that it never again engaged seriously with the economic elements of the UN, even after the United Nations Conference on Trade and Development was set up in 1963, except as a way of scoring points in the Cold War, until its decline in the late 1980s and final demise in 1991.[76]

As to how the Bretton Woods discussions would develop there are several underlying principles that need to be stressed. First, the State Department had been concerned that there should be 'an extension of the Federal Reserve principle to international finance' in 1942. In other words, it was adamant that 'open trade' must be controlled by 'balanced' exchanges so as not to tip the world into another cycle of competitive devaluations, a concern that made for some friction with the Treasury. Morgenthau and White were mainly interested in 'stabilisation'; hence the fund Morgenthau proposed setting up was initially called 'The Stabilization Fund for the United and Associated Nations' with a linked 'Bank for Reconstruction'. The stabilisation aimed at was of the international business cycle, hopefully to eliminate depressions such as that of the 1930s. Second, it was to be explicitly a 'New Deal in International economics'.[77] This implied a great role for Government, and not a blind adherence to free-market economics. However, as Gardner points out, by the time these plans were published in

April 1943, there had been a swing to the right in American political opinion, away from the more ambitious Government intervention of the New Deal, a shift that also affected the international version.[78]

Keynes' views on stabilisation (known as the 'Keynes Plan') were much the same as White's, and the differences should not be exaggerated. Keynes was more than aware who was in charge, and it was not the British. His personal addition had more to do with the suggested creation of a new form of liquidity (known as the 'Bancor') through his 'Clearing Union', in effect giving the world an 'overdraft' upon which it could draw for purposes of domestic expansion.[79] As was noted in Chapter 4, there was a strong desire for 'planning' in British political circles, which implied a large amount of deficit spending. This was a potential flaw, as it could not be known whether such policies would be acceptable after the war ended, especially as the United States swung politically to the right, a fear that proved quite well founded. Another potential flaw was that the overall NWO could not be foreseen in early 1943. As Gardner points out, both the White and the Keynes Plans required 'an entirely new world political order which eliminated the need for special alliances and traditional power politics'. They were assuming 'equilibrium ... on the economic as on the political side'. This they did not get.[80]

UNRRA

This assumption also affected other joint projects, such as Allied efforts at economic reconstruction during the war. Chief among these was UNRRA, an effort on a far larger scale than anything undertaken after the First World War, even by Hoover's ARA in Russia. Plano and Riggs claim that it 'stands as the most impressive intergovernmental relief agency ever established and indeed "the largest non-military intergovernmental organisation in history"'. It operated from November 1943 until 1947, and disbursed the then as now astronomical sum of $3.9 billion in direct aid, averting wide-scale famine in Europe and Asia. It acted as a care and rehabilitation centre for millions of displaced persons and refugees, until the new Truman Administration decided to close it down at a meeting in Geneva in August 1946 with the summarily delivered expression, 'the gravy train has gone around for the last time'.[81] This naturally fuelled the fears of those who believed that American economic (or indeed political) leadership was not going to be forthcoming, a fear only assuaged by the implementation of Marshall Aid in 1947.

Would America assume international economic leadership post-war?

The experience of drafting and implementing the Stabilization Fund, the Bank and UNRRA showed that post-war economic reconstruction was not going to be the easy combination of British, American and French efforts for which Roosevelt had hoped. Kennan rightly predicted that it would be particularly difficult with the Russians. When UNRRA attempted to operate freely in Eastern Europe he commented: 'The Poles [are] totally dependent on the USSR for "reconstruction" – The Russians know this perfectly well' and used it to enforce their desires for border changes.[82] We have already seen the scorn he poured on Hull's desire for open multilateral commerce and on the idea of including Russia in the financial arrangements.

However, it is also easy to forget that, in 1945, there was much suspicion among the other Allies, especially the British, that the United States would not live up to its protestations of belief in international economic management and freer trade after the conflict was over. The memory of American isolationism and economic nationalism before the war was still keen. Those in positions of power and influence over American decision making in this area, such as Keynes, professed to be the least suspicious: he had had discussions in Washington aimed at 'promot[ing] freedom of trade, of travel, and of intercourse between the nationals of all countries and more particularly between the citizens of the United States and of the British Empire'.[83] But others, even those normally well disposed to the United States, doubted that Wallace, Hull or Welles ('the brilliant Wilsonian élite which President Roosevelt has gathered around him') could prevent a Republican protectionist backlash. Had not many American speakers been 'anxious to prove that the United States is not bound *economically* by the Atlantic Charter?', as R.B. McCallum put it.

McCallum, a British supporter of greater Anglo-American ties to create an NWO after the war, concluded that 'It would be wise for this country to prepare in the first place for economic co-operation with America, but not to be taken aback or taken by surprise if it should not be forthcoming.'[84] Eric (now Lord) Roll, a key British member of the negotiating team around Keynes throughout the war years in the United States, has keen memories that whenever discussions with the Americans 'were concerned not with winning the war but with the economic arrangements of the post-war world ... the clash of interests was inevitably deeper and more acute'. Indeed, Roll is convinced that had not Keynes been there to do the bulk of the really difficult negotiating '[i]t is impossible to imagine how the lend–lease or the loan negotiations or the arrangements for the post-war institution would have come out ...'. He also remembers the termination of Lend–Lease on V.J. Day as a significant blow to British belief in American post-war leadership.[85]

The Marshall Plan

Hogan's view is also that the American commitment to European reconstruction was not clear before the end of the war. Certainly, what became the Marshall Plan of 1948[86] was by no means seen as likely until the Cold War began. From his perspective of 1947, before the Marshall Plan was inaugurated by the Foreign Assistance Act in the Spring of 1948, most attention was concentrated on British plans to create a 'Middle Kingdom' made up of Western Europe and the British Commonwealth. The Anglo-French Treaty of Dunkirk of 1947 can be seen in this context, for example. Britain was thereby trying to distance itself and proximate Europe from the United States and the Soviet Union.[87] But from a British point of view, could the United States be trusted not to abandon Europe? Britain had based most of its wartime policy, as in 1914–18, on making sure that America did not leave after the victory parades. Truman's policies of 1945–46 seemed to indicate that this was history happening all over again.

It is thus hardly surprising that Britain was looking to reconstruct some sort of Alliance system that would allow for American absence, even though it was quite clear that this would prove difficult. Hogan is thus right to say that 1947 was the date for real interest being shown in European integration within the American political elite across the board. It is difficult to disagree with his statement that '… the Marshall Plan can be seen as a logical extension of domestic- and foreign-policy developments going back to the first American effort to reconstruct war-torn Europe [in 1919]'.[88] It was the onset of the Cold War that in a real sense 'activated' the thinking on Europe.[89] Kennan put it characteristically – the Marshall Plan 'finally broke through the confusion of wartime pro-Sovietism, wishful thinking, anglophobia and self-righteous punitivism … and placed us on what was, and for six years remained, a constructive and sensible path'.[90]

The lessons of American attempts at NWO economic leadership, 1941–45

Although some of the lessons that might be drawn at this stage are general ones about the American role in NWO planning and attempted execution, they have particular salience in the context of the economic section of this project.

A first and obvious conclusion is that all this elaborate planning and discussion demonstrates yet again the importance of economic power to the United States and the widespread feeling that the economic clauses of Versailles had been the worst damaging to world peace. Second, it demonstrates that Hull's and Roosevelt's desire for a universalism in the application of the NWO was difficult, if not impossible, especially given the refusal of the Soviet Union (and later its 'bloc') to agree to the underlying ideas summed up in the concept of 'embedded liberalism', itself a watered down version of Wilson's original liberal internationalism. Third, it shows that in order to exercise leadership the United States had to have followers who were able to bring in a credible extra amount of global economic activity. Britain was the only state in 1945 that filled that role. Fourth, this experience demonstrates that the atmosphere of ideas that prevailed in the

Western world in the inter-war years had a profound impact on policies, but it also highlights the truism that although ideas and policies have a mutually reinforcing relationship it is often very difficult to show the exact mediation of this relationship. Fifth, it shows once again that the 'apotheosis of public opinion', to use Wilson's phrase, can be as much a hindrance as a help in defining liberal national and international policies. Last, but not least, it shows that the elements contained in the NWO – economic, security and identity (or self-determination) questions – are very intimately linked to each other and that one can overwhelm the others if not thought through properly at any particular attempt (whether this be in 1919, 1945 or 1990).

The post-1989 economic NWO: 'The End of History'?

The triumph of the liberal internationalist agenda?

The single most important summary of the view that the economic aspects of the NWO have triumphed, and that these are essentially of American origin, is of course to be found in Francis Fukuyama's *The End of History and the Last Man*, which has been alluded to in preceding pages on a number of occasions. Fukuyama claims that the basis of Hegel's statement that all men strive for 'recognition', the driving force of history, is no less nor more than a desire for 'self-respect' and that this is at the heart of the American NWO project. Fukuyama also claims that the Lockean ideas that so imbue the American Constitution, which give Americans not only the right to life and 'recognition' but also the right to protect and accumulate material possessions 'without limit', are a deeply liberating agenda that has been willingly embraced since 1990 by most of the planet's population, once they were given the chance to do so.[91]

In other words he would assert that what Carr had disparagingly called the 'harmony of interests' in *The Twenty Years' Crisis* is now seen as an accepted and realisable ideal across all continents. This combination of recognition in a particular version of the notion of civil society is the 'good political order' for which the peoples of the former communist states yearned and now have the chance to realise. So can we say that there is evidence that an American-inspired NWO has in fact triumphed? When examining the lasting impact of the economic elements of the liberal internationalist agenda of the first two NWOs of this century, we have to ask if the end of the Cold War can truly be seen in economic terms as the 'End of History' and the consequent definitive triumph of the NWO project of 'liberal internationalism'. Do we now have common norms and practices of economic behaviour and, if so, what are their main constituent parts? Those current debates that can be readily identified have to do with:

a)   the development after 1945 of American economic (and political) leadership and the eventual emergence of what has come to be known as 'globalisation', but which might also be described as a much extended version of the idea of 'interdependence', a point to which further attention will be given. This can be seen as having been effected through what can be seen as either a 'coercive' use of American hegemonic power or by a 'benevolent' provision of American economic leadership;

b)   the consequent extension through private networks of capitalist activity and the forces of the market of norms and practices of economic behaviour that correspond to the principles of economic liberalism and especially reflect an American view of what this should ideally be;

c)   the reinforcement of these practices by the maintenance and reinforcement of a network of international economic organisations (of which the Bretton Woods institutions are by far the most important), and, to a lesser extent, the enforcement of a system of 'economic containment'[92] against states that refuse to cooperate with these principles and institutions.

After hegemony? American leadership and the 1990 NWO

One of the main arguments of the 1980s and 1990s in international political economy is about whether, unlike in 1945, there has been an end of American 'hegemony' and a consequent weakening of the United States' grip over international economic management. This in turn has led to a huge literature developing about regime theory, an attempt to show how power and institutions interact in given issue areas of international relations, especially economic, over which there is no space to linger here.[93]

The relevance of this for the NWO leadership debate is that the United States, or any other state, is now seen as having lost control of the economic levers. In 1971, many years after the Second World War during the Nixon Presidency, under the financial impact of the Vietnam War and the strains of an increasingly open economic system, the United States abandoned the 'Gold Exchange Standard' that was at the heart of the Bretton Woods regulatory financial system. It became a commonplace to say that '[t]he Bretton Woods international monetary order now lies in ruins'.[94] Did this also mean that, first, it was necessary to have a hegemonic leader and, second, that this in effect must be the United States, if the ideas of the NWO were to prevail and flourish?

The concept of 'order' has been used ever since 1945 to equate the financial and trading power of the United States, its willingness to assert leadership over this 'order' and the possibility of a stable international economic system. Whenever since 1945 the United States has been deemed to 'wobble' in its commitment to free trade or financial stability there has been a crisis of confidence. Fears over the 'new protectionism' of the 1980s were a classic example of this. So is the current (late 1997) flurry of further doubts about the American Congress' commitment to a global liberal economy with the Congressional withdrawal of 'fast-track negotiating capability' from President Clinton and its simultaneous refusal to top up the IMF's quota by $3.5 billion.

'Globalisation' or 'interdependence': the death of international cooperation?

Arguably the most important economic result of the NWOs of this century has been the promotion by political leaders, and especially American leaders, of a transnational capitalist economy. Usually referred to as 'interdependence', it derived its basic institutions and protection from the standard-setting processes incarnate in the Bretton Woods organisations and in the American promotion of the multinational company. It derived its inspiration from the kind of liberal internationalist thinking that has been a particular focus of this chapter. This theme of interdependence has been further promoted with more or less enthusiasm by the other OECD countries since 1949 and with varying degrees of success by virtually the rest of the planet since 1991. There are now very few political entities that do not espouse some form of capitalism and little ideological appetite for a return to the practices of the centrally planned economy on the national level or to a system of protection at the global level.

We now have a sister concept which arose in the mid-1980s known as 'globalisation'. This has been particularly demonstrated by the creation of global capital markets outside the reach of any state or international jurisdiction and by the development of major transnational companies that can locate production and research anywhere on the globe. Many commentators assert that the market is now king, and that states are about to lose all relevance.[95] But the key accusation against globalisation, as compared with interdependence, is that authority is in effect transferred from the state to non-accountable actors, such as the transnational company, and that this can undermine the democratic process.

Hence globalisation is seen with somewhat mitigated enthusiasm even by many liberals and certainly by many on the left and right of the liberal centre. For the left it seems to undermine the fairness of the Rooseveltian New Deal approach to the NWO. For the right it undermines the sovereignty of the nation state, still seen by them as the guarantor of a satisfactory Western 'civilisation'. Liberals fear that it will undermine the global consensus that liberal capitalism provides. There are further fears that globalisation will lead to fragmentation as conflicts emerge both within and between states as political control disappears into the hands of private interests, even into those of crime syndicates.[96] However, maybe the report of the death of the state is premature. Hirst and Thompson, among others, assert that state sovereignty will rather evolve, as there is still no alternative to the stabilising legal framework provided by the state and by states acting in common in some form of 'pooled sovereignty'.[97]

The emergence of globalisation therefore does not mean that the Wilsonian and Rooseveltian ideal of international cooperation at the state level is dead. The Bretton Woods organisations have been greatly reinforced in their powers since 1990. The success in 1995 of the GATT Uruguay Round and the setting up of the World Trade Organisation are eloquent demonstration of this. What do seem to be definitively defunct are such ideas as the 'New International Economic Order' of the 1970s based on an autarkic Third World and an end to 'dependency'. Whether we now have a 'globalised' or merely an 'interdependent' world economy is a matter of appreciation, degree and how relaxed we are about such prospects.

For the globalisation of the 1990s is a multi-faceted phenomenon, of which some aspects would have been familiar to Angell and some would have been entirely alien. The 'interdependence' of which he wrote has been reinstated as a central organising concept after its cruel destruction as a result of the First World War. The economic nationalism and the propensity to put more and more of economic life under the control of governments that he so regretted after that war are (largely) in retreat. The financial liberalism (based before 1914 on the Gold Standard) and now relatively open financial markets have been reinstated and reinforced, on a different basis to be sure. The communications revolution would probably have greatly shocked Angell, not disagreeably, but by its immense and rapid growth since about 1980. He would probably have seen it as a happy accelerator of forces with which he was familiar and in which he had vested much faith.

The basic groundwork for globalisation was laid by an emphasis on free trade, and other multilateral economic practices, institutionalised and later developed through, and underpinned by, the Bretton Woods organisations and the power of American (and other Western) capitalism. The arguments about a 'collapse' of Bretton Woods in 1971 with the abolition of the dollar-based Gold Exchange Standard are in this context an irrelevance. The norms that underpin global capitalism were essentially in place by 1971. Economic developments over the subsequent years until 1990 serve to prove that this was the case. American leadership, especially under President Ronald Reagan, and the reinforcing of the multilateral principles of the founders of the Bretton Woods system, were allied to a staggering growth of multilateral corporate activity. This in turn benefited from a communications revolution born out of the micro-processor technological revolution from which non-capitalist states were effectively barred by the CoCom strategic embargo of the Soviet Union and its allies. Would any of this have happened without American leadership and the embedding of the economic principles of the NWO? – Probably not, although plenty of commentators would argue that this was first and foremost in the interests of an American desire for global economic hegemony in the interests of a capitalist class.[98]

Has economic interdependence through the NWO brought peace?

Many and varied critiques can be made of the economic aspirations and realities of the NWO projects that we have examined. These break down into two major categories: those who believe that what was achieved was a good thing and those who believe it was bad. By 'good' is meant those who have tended to see the world order that was created by the Rooseveltian NWO as tending to increase the moral and physical good of the states, peoples and individuals who won the war. By 'bad' we can incorporate those who feel that the NWO project has led to economic and social results that have tended to aggravate the lot of the poor and oppressed and to enrich those who had been the NWO's architects, loosely speaking the capitalist class, the United States and its multinational companies.

Is it possible that the 'idealists' were right, that planning taken to excess leads to the destruction of individual liberties? Or that the 'realists' were right in seeing that nationalism was the result of unrestrained freedom through political self-determination that led to economic nationalism in the face of an absent 'hegemon'? Britain had fulfilled this role before 1914 and the United States after 1945. Are we now, in terms of the balance of economic power and political will to lead, back in 1919, or rather in an NWO where economic nationalism is effectively dead? Do we have a global civil society with the real possibility of a self-regulating economic and political system, where the logic of economics has defeated the illogic of politics, where the state has given way to the market as the arbiter of the human condition? Or is hegemonic military and economic power vested in a state which increasingly doubts its willingness or ability to act as a leader? Can it cope with the new dangerous states which want, like Brailsford's Germany in 1914, their 'place in the sun'?

Unfortunately, there are no easy conclusions in the debate about whether the NWOs have led to economics being used in the service of peace and the improvement of material welfare, in other words to support the liberal view that economic action can create the basis for a durable peace. There are those whose views of, say, Bretton Woods lead them to a belief that the institutions of 1944 led to a much better chance for parts of the world than they would otherwise have known. To take but one area of the world, the Far East and especially Japan, it could be argued that the agreements encouraged the setting up of a free-trade and free-market system. This was due to the simultaneous granting of large and long duration borrowing facilities from the World Bank (Japan was the largest borrower from the Bank until the 1960s) and access to the all-important American market. This arguably allowed the Japanese economy to 'free-ride' in the liberal trading system while not dismantling its own protectionist mantle until quite recently. To this might well be added the American 'greenhouse effect' that provided a low-cost security umbrella for Japan and also the provision of a 'civil society' through the period of occupation.

The success of Japan and other states would still be at the basis of the logic used by Washington's statesmen and women after the Cold War to justify a continuing American benevolent coercion in pushing the ideas of globalisation and the free market. One recent example of this came with Secretary of State Madeleine Albright stating that the use of a 'fast-track negotiating capacity' was in the interest of all, not just the United States. In this view of world trade, agreements are seen as 'building blocks for peace'. As she also said on the same occasion, '[t]he best course for our country is not to curse globalization but to shape it, to make it work for America'.[99] The clear implication is that what works for the US works for the world ...?

Conclusion: the triumph of 'idealism' over 'realism?'

In the post-Cold War environment where 'globalisation' is seen as the emerging norm of economic behaviour and where individuals are increasingly able to conduct their economic intercourse without undue interference; where states and private networks within states are increasingly seen as facilitators of economic interchange; and where international organisations are seen as global regulators, can we now say that Carr's belief that the nation state is the natural unit of political and especially economic discussion is still true? Or is it more the case that the much derided 'harmony of interests', Angell's and the liberals' belief in a self-regulating economic and political system, is now once more triumphant? Has 'idealism' won, at least in its economic sense?

This chapter has attempted to show that policy can have a strong normative basis and that it can fail to produce all the results required while not necessarily being flawed in itself. The 1920s and 1930s have often been used, unfairly, to show that *all* normative-based policies are doomed to failure. This is E.H. Carr's 'utopianism'. Carr was a clever and subtle thinker, so there should be no counter-reductionist attempt, as his brief was to demand that social purpose has to be tempered with an understanding of the exigencies of power. Clearly, when dealing with a militarily aggressive state such as Nazi Germany, it is not sufficient to have ideals, but it is *necessary* to have them. Hoover and Wilson had a far clearer idea of what they were fighting for in the First World War than did the British, or indeed the French, beyond the dictates of mere survival, and that was a global economic as much as a global political settlement. In the inter-war years Britain and, especially, France, drifted until galvanised by another great idea, that of fighting Nazism in the case of Britain and, arguably at least, that of a united Europe in the case of France.

Meanwhile, the notion of the 'harmony of interests' which seemed 'utopian' to Carr is now bandied around as commonplace; capitalism is portrayed as the 'only game in town' and, moreover, the basis of civil society. We are thus having to redefine what we mean by a lack of 'realism'. If this theory, essentially that of Angell, Brailsford, Wilson, Hoover and others (with minor internal variations such as how exactly you define liberal democracy), is correct, then what was utopian is now eminently 'realist'. In his recent study of the *Twenty Years' Crisis* Peter Wilson has suggested that rather than keeping the 'idealist–realist dichotomy', especially when looking at the inter-war period, we should substitute, as J.D.B. Miller suggests for Angell's thought, a 'short term ... long term' contrast or even reinsert 'the utopian disposition towards normative assertion and enquiry', as Ken Booth suggests in the same volume.[100] As Keynes might have said in reply to his own 'in the long run we are dead': – well, 'in the long run, Angell was right'. Can the 'idealist' liberal economic and political thinking as operationalised in the NWOs now be seen as the centre-piece of a late twentieth century cosmopolitan ethic?

So what was actually happening in 1920–39 was perhaps rather different from what Carr and Polanyi in their different ways thought they were observing. Having rightly noted the destruction of the economic and political world order of 1914 they assumed that it could not be changed again, or even made to revert to a pre-1914 arrangement. For both Carr and Polanyi, laissez-faire and political liberalism had been an aberration. Economic and political nationalism were now reasserting their primary significance; global cooperation to achieve the 'harmony of interests' was a nonsense.

But we can now ask ourselves whether such stark judgements were correct. The pendulum has now swung back, and Polanyi's views are considered old fashioned. The market is back in fashion, enthusiastically embraced from Vancouver to Vladivostok. What was seen as a 'utopian' view by Carr, that the market and free trade were inescapably linked to peaceful behaviour, is now taken for granted by most people again. To re-read Norman Angell's *The Great Illusion* (1910) or H.N. Brailsford's *The War of Steel and Gold* (1914) is to be reminded that in the twentieth century the economic debate has not so much been a battle between the advocates of freedom and markets and the advocates of an intrusive, interventionist and institutional framework, as to what balance should be struck between the two extremes. But we are still left with some stark and difficult questions: How can we legislate for economic freedom at the international level? How can we find appropriate institutions and structures? In other words, *how much* can be left to the market?

Notes

1 The phrase coined by John Gerald Ruggie, 'International Regimes, Transactions and Change: Embedded Liberalism in the Postwar Economic Order', *International Organization*, vol. 36, 1982, pp. 379–415.

2 The classic account of this is F.H. Hinsley, *Power and the Pursuit of Peace* (Cambridge University Press, 1963).

3 The best single summary of the debate about globalisation is Paul Hirst and Grahame Thompson, *Globalization in Question* (Cambridge, Polity, 1996).

4 See Charles P. Kindleberger, 'The Rise of Free Trade in Western Europe', *Journal of Economic History*, vol. 35, no. 1, 1975, pp. 20–25.

5 E.H. Carr, *The Twenty Years' Crisis: 1919–1939* (London, Macmillan, 1939), especially Chapter 4, 'The Harmony of Interests'.

6 Norman Angell, *The Great Illusion: A Study of the Relation of Military Power to National Advantage* (London, William Heinemann, 1910). The quotations here are from the second edition of 1912, pp. v–xi.

7 Paul Kennedy, *The Realities behind Diplomacy: Background Influences on British Foreign Policy, 1865–1980* (London, Fontana, 1981).

8 G. Lowes Dickinson, *The Choice Before Us* (London, George Allen and Unwin, 1917), pp. 122–150. The emphases are mine. See also his *The International Anarchy, 1904–1914* (London, George Allen and Unwin, 1926).

9 H.N. Brailsford, *The War of Steel and Gold: A Study of the Armed Peace* (London, G. Bell and Sons, 1914), p. 43. It might be added that London's financial markets had made a fortune out of financing other peoples' wars: Karl Erich Born, *International Banking in the Nineteenth and Twentieth Centuries* (Oxford, Berg, 1977).

10 Brailsford, *War of Steel and Gold*, pp. 12, 21 and 35.

11 Brailsford, *War of Steel and Gold*, pp. 24–27

12 Brailsford, *War of Steel and Gold*, pp. 315–317. This was also a constant theme of other moderate socialists in the framework of the Second International, notably Jean Jaurès, assassinated the day war was declared.

13 Hirst and Thompson, *Globalization in Question*, p. 9.

14 Norman Angell, *After All* (London, Hamish Hamilton, 1951).

15 The international economy had also been disrupted by tariff increases in Germany (1879 and 1906), and Austria, Russia and Italy in the 1880s. Only Britain, Holland and Denmark were free-trading nations in 1914, and even then their resolve was weakening fast. For an overview of the international economy before 1914 see William Ashworth, *A Short History of the International Economy since 1850* (London, Longman, 1981).

16 H.G. Wells, 'The Immensity of the Issue and the Triviality of Men', in *Washington and the Hope of Peace* (London, W. Collins Sons and Co., 1922), p. 2.

17 Wiseman to Balfour, 16 August 1918; Balfour Papers, Ms. 49741.

18 David Miller, *The Drafting of the Covenant* (New York, Putnam and Sons, 1928), vol. 1, pp. 19–20.

19 Robert Skidelsky, *John Maynard Keynes: The Economist as Saviour, 1920–1937* (London, Macmillan, 1992), p. 31. See also Skidelsky, *John Maynard Keynes, Hopes Betrayed, 1883–1920* (London, Macmillan, 1983).

20 The most complete printed account of the debt and reparations questions is

Philip Mason Burnett, *Reparation at the Paris Peace Conference from the Standpoint of the American Delegation* (2 vols, New York, Columbia University Press, 1940). Some of the best books on the subject are: Marc Trachtenberg, *Reparations in World Politics: France and Economic Diplomacy, 1916–1923* (New York, Columbia University Press, 1980); Denise Artaud, *La question des dettes interalliés et la reconstruction de l'Europe, 1917–1929* (Lille and Paris, Honoré Champion, 1978); Bruce Kent, *The Spoils of War: The Politics, Economics and Diplomacy of Reparations, 1918–1922* (Oxford, Clarendon Press, 1989); and Etienne Weill-Raynal, *Les reparations allemandes et la France, 1918–1936* (Paris, Nouvelles Éditions Latines, 1947). Contemporary accounts include Bernard M. Baruch, *The Making of the Reparation and Economic Sections of the Treaty* (New York, Harper and Brothers, 1920).

21 Quoted by H. Elcock, *Portrait of a Decision: The Council of Four and the Treaty of Versailles* (London, Eyre Methuen, 1972), p. 5.

22 Stephen Shuker, 'American Policy Towards Debts and Reconstruction at Genoa, 1922', in Carole Fink, Axel Frohn and Jurgen Heideking, *Genoa, Rapallo and European Reconstruction in 1922* (Cambridge University Press, 1991), pp. 95–122.

23 Lord Fisher, *Records* (London, Hodder and Stoughton, 1919), p. vii.

24 Balfour, memo on 'Armies and Economics', 27 July 1919; Balfour Papers, Ms. 49750.

25 Cecil, Manuscript Diary of the Peace Conference, entries for 26 and 27 February, 9 and 10 May 1919; Ms. 51131.

26 Cecil, Manuscript Diary of the Peace Conference, entries for 3, 20 and 21 April 191; Ms. 51131. See also Baruch, *The Making of the Reparation*, who was more positive about the reparations clauses and about Wilson's role in framing them.

27 Keynes (at Versailles) to Sir John Bradbury (London), 19 May 1919; Bradbury Papers.

28 Skidelsky, *The Economist as Saviour*, pp. 18–21; John Maynard Keynes, *The Economic Consequences of the Peace* (New York, Harcourt, Brace and Howe, 1920).

29 Keynes, *Economic Consequences*, pp. 3–4 and 29.

30 In 1916 Keynes and Ashley, in a Treasury 'Memorandum on the Effect of an Indemnity', had suggested no total indemnity should be required from Germany: Keynes, *Activities, 1914–1919* (London, Macmillan, 1971), pp. 311–330. In late 1918 Keynes suggested a figure of £1–2,000 million, and with the addition of other German income, 'a grand total not exceeding £3,000 million as a bargaining counter … An actual payment of £2,000 million, if effected without evil consequences, would be a very satisfactory achievement in all the circumstances …': Keynes, 'Memorandum by the Treasury on the Indemnity Payable by the Enemy Powers for Reparation and Other Claims', 2 December 1918 and Keynes, *Activities*, pp. 358, 378. This can be seen as a first draft of the *Economic Consequences of the Peace*, as the 'reparation' section of the memorandum is virtually identical to the relevant sections of the book. Lloyd George and the others of the Big Four actually demanded £24,000 million, near to the actual cost of the war (Keynes' figure in the above cited memorandum had been £25,000 million).

31 John Foster Dulles, statement to the Reparation Commission, 13 February

1919. The French Finance Minister, Klotz, rejected the idea that there was any such 'contract'with Germany, as Dulles had suggested, in a statement in reply to Dulles of 15 February 1919; Dulles Papers, Box 1.

32 Keynes, *Activities*, p. 440.

33 Keynes, *Activities*, p. 471. Harold Nicolson found Keynes' condemnation of Wilson rather simplistic, although he himself wrote that '[h]is [Wilson's] presence at Paris constitutes a historical disaster of the first magnitude'. Nicolson's view is that '[n]othing … was clear cut at Paris'; it was rather a bargaining Conference, 'an adjustment of practical details'. As one of the main 'adjusters' he is entitled to his point of view, but it is also fair to comment that there were basic principles that had to be recognised as vital and that they were not so recognised: Nicolson, *Peacemaking, 1919* (London, Constable and Co., 1933), pp. 71 and 84–85.

34 Pierre Miquel, *La paix de Versailles et l'opinion publique française* (Paris, Flammarion, 1972), p. 424; *L'Europe Nouvelle*, 15 February 1919; *Le Figaro*, 12 May 1919.

35 Etienne Mantoux, *The Carthaginian Peace or: The Economic Consequences of Mr. Keynes* (London, Oxford University Press, 1946).

36 Keynes, *Economic Consequences of the Peace*, p. 29.

37 Byron Dexter, *The Years of Opportunity*, pp. 136–137

38 W.N. Medlicott, Douglas Dakin and M.E. Lambert (eds.), *Documents on British Foreign Policy*, vol. 21, no. 367 (London, HMSO, 1973), pp. 529–535. See also Stanislas Jeannesson, 'Les relations franco–britanniques à l'épreuve de la Ruhr, 1922–1924', paper presented to the Second Pan-European Conference in International Relations, Paris, 1995.

39 For a discussion of this see Charles Kindleberger, *The World in Depression, 1929–1939* (London, Allen Lane, 1973) and (for Ottawa) my *Trading with the Bolsheviks: The Politics of East–West Trade, 1920–1939* (Manchester University Press, 1992). The classic account of the Smoot–Hawley tariff is E.E. Schattschneider, *Politics, Pressure and the Tariff: A Study in Free Private Enterprise in Pressure Politics, as Shown in the 1929–1930 Revision of the Tariff* (New York, Prentice-Hall, 1935).

40 Carr, *Twenty Years' Crisis*, pp. 43–51.

41 Carr, *Twenty Years' Crisis*, p. 224.

42 Van Zeeland, quoted by Cobban from the RIIA's *Survey of International Affairs*, 1937, vol. 1, p. 73, in Alfred Cobban, *National Self-Determination* (Oxford University Press, 1945), p. 157.

43 Cobban, *Self-Determination*, pp. 159–161.

44 Professor Etienne Dennery, Rapporteur, 'Introductory Report on the Study of Raw Materials and Markets: Strategic Aspect of the Problem', in International Institute of Intellectual Cooperation, *Peaceful Change* (Paris, League of Nations, 1938), pp. 88–89.

45 Sanford D. Cole, 'The Highways of the Sea', in the Transactions of the Grotius Society *Volume IV, Papers Read before the Society in the Year 1918: The Problems of the War* (London, Sweet and Maxwell, 1919), p. 17.

46 Cole, pp. 20–23 and reply to Cole by F.W. Hirst, 'What the Americans Mean by Freedom of the Seas', in Grotius Society, *Papers Read before the Society in the Year 1918*, pp. 26–34.

47 Karl Polanyi, *The Great Transformation* (Boston, Beacon Press, 1957), p. 23, Chapters 1 and 2.

48 Norman Angell, *The Fruits of Victory* (London, Collins, 1921), pp. 74–75.

49 Angell, *The Fruits of Victory*, pp. 81–82 and 195.

50 Angell, *The Fruits of Victory* and *The Great Illusion – Now* (London, Penguin Special, 1938, reprinted January 1939). The quotes are taken from *The Fruits of Victory*, p. xii.

51 Cornelia Navari, 'The Great Illusion Revisited: the International Theory of Norman Angell', *Review of International Studies*, vol. 15, 1989, pp. 341–358.

52 See my chapter in Fink, Frohn and Heideking, *Genoa*.

53 On the Genoa Conference see Stephen White, *The Origins of Détente: The Genoa Conference and Soviet–Western Relations, 1920–1924* (Cambridge University Press, 1985) and Carole Fink, *The Genoa Conference* (Chapel Hill, University of North Carolina Press, 1984). The quote about Lloyd George being a 'Keynesian' is from Kenneth Morgan, *Consensus and Disunity: The Lloyd George Coalition Government* (Oxford University Press, 1979).

54 Philip Noel-Baker, Lectures for 1924/25; NBKR 4/33.

55 See Dexter, *The Years of Opportunity*, pp. 136–142; the LON Commission on Austria was headed by Balfour, helped by the Financial Committee of the LON, led by Arthur Salter, on which Monnet served; 'Note on the Austrian Question' by Philip Noel-Baker, 6 September 1922; Letter from G. Dimba to the Executive Committee of the Austrian League of Nations Union, 31 August 1922; Salter to Noel-Baker, 19 March 1923; Noel-Baker, *The Financial Reconstruction of Europe* (Geneva, League of Nations, 1922), all NBKR 4/32. Noel-Baker afterwards presented this reconstruction effort as the great success story for the LON in this area, as in five speeches he gave in 1924–25; NBKR 4/33.

56 John Hall, *International Orders* (Cambridge, Polity, 1996), pp. 22–24.

57 To take the most obvious examples of this debate on 'hegemonic stability': Robert Keohane, *After Hegemony* (Princeton University Press, 1984); Robert Gilpin, *War and Change in World Politics* (Cambridge University Press, 1981). A good survey of hegemonic stability theory can be found in Jarrod Wiener, *Making Rules in the Uruguay Round of the GATT: A Study of International Leadership* (Aldershot, Dartmouth, 1995).

58 See, for example, 'The Contemporary Political Economy', Section III of Jeffrey A. Frieden and David A. Lake, *International Political Economy: Perspectives on Global Power and Wealth* (London, Unwin Hyman, 2nd edn, 1991).

59 Michael J. Hogan, *Informal Entente: The Private Structure of Cooperation in Anglo-American Economic Diplomacy* (New York, Columbia University Press, 1977), p. 1.

60 Hogan, *Informal Entente*, p. 6.

61 Michael Hogan, *The Marshall Plan: America, Britain and the Reconstruction of Europe, 1947–1952* (Cambridge University Press, 1987), p. 3.

62 Robert A. Pollard, *Economic Security and the Origins of the Cold War, 1945–1950* (New York, Columbia University Press, 1985), p. 7.

63 The best description of how this was perceived in Washington, starting with the Reciprocal Trade Act of 1934, is to be found in Cordell Hull, *The Memoirs of Cordell Hull* (2 vols, London, Hodder and Stoughton, 1948).

64 Richard N. Gardner, *Sterling–Dollar Diplomacy: Anglo-American Collaboration*

in the Reconstruction of Multilateral Trade (Oxford, Clarendon Press, 1956), pp. 1–4. See also David A. Lake, 'International Structures and American Foreign Economic Policy, 1887–1934', *World Politics*, vol. 35, no. 4, July 1983, reprinted in Jeffrey A. Frieden and David A. Lake (eds), *International Political Economy*, pp. 120–138.

65 Gardner, *Sterling–Dollar Diplomacy*, pp. 6–8.

66 Berle, 'The Bases of an International Economic Program in Connection with a Possible Conference of Neutrals', 29 January 1940; Berle Papers, Box 56.

67 Berle, 'Economic Policy in Respect of Western Europe', 19 November 1942 and 'The European Economic Policy', 23 November 1942; Berle Papers, Box 58.

68 Berle, Memorandum to the President, 15 December 1942; Berle Papers, Box 65.

69 Ruggie, 'International Regimes'.

70 Leo Pasvolsky, 'International Economic Cooperation', Memorandum of 20 March 1944; Pasvolsky Papers, Box 7.

71 The literature on Bretton Woods is naturally vast. The most useful introduction is still Gardner, *Sterling–Dollar Diplomacy*, and a revised and expanded edition, *Sterling–Dollar Diplomacy in Current Perspective: The Origins and Prospects of Our International Economic Order* (New York, Columbia University Press, 1980).

72 Gardner, *Sterling–Dollar Diplomacy*, pp. 72–73.

73 Rupert Emerson and Inis L. Claude, Jr, 'The Soviet Union and the UN: An Essay in Interpretation', *International Organization*, vol. 6, 1952, pp. 18–19, cited by Robert Boardman, *Post-Socialist World Orders: Russia, China and the UN System* (London, Macmillan, 1994), p. 16.

74 Boardman, *Post-Socialist World Orders*, p. 17.

75 George Kennan, *Memoirs, 1925–1950* (London, Hutchinson, 1968), p. 257: Kennan to Harriman, 3 December 1944; Kennan Papers, 23/19.

76 For more on this see Boardman, *Post-Socialist World Orders*, Chapter 3.

77 Berle to Hull, 28 September 1942, and Berle to Hull, 7 July 1943; Berle Papers, Box 58; Morgenthau Presidential Diaries, entry for 15 May 1942.

78 Gardner, *Sterling–Dollar Diplomacy*, p. 77.

79 This suggestion was not taken up, although it was in the 1970s in the form of the 'Special Drawing Right', a basket of currencies used to create liquidity in much the way that Keynes had proposed.

80 Gardner, *Sterling–Dollar Diplomacy*, pp. 82–95 also has a very detailed account of the technicalities of the discussions, which we have no space to go into here.

81 Jack C. Plano and Robert E. Riggs, *Forging World Order: The Politics of International Organization* (New York, Macmillan, 1967), p. 401.

82 Kennan, Memorandum of 18 December 1944 to Harriman: Kennan Papers, 23/19.

83 Keynes, attachment to letter to Kingsley Wood of 21 June 1941; T 160/110.

84 R.B. McCallum, *Public Opinion and the Last Peace* (Oxford University Press, 1944), pp. 191–2.

85 Eric Roll, *Crowded Hours* (London, Faber, 1985), pp. 42–44.

86 For details of the Marshall Plan, which falls outside the scope of this book, see Hogan, *The Marshall Plan*.

87 See Hogan, *The Marshall Plan*, pp. 88–89.

88 Hogan, *The Marshall Plan*, p. 18.

89 Hogan's view is that: '[s]uch proposals at first received only sporadic consideration in Washington, where officials were preoccupied with the war effort or
otherwise worried that regional blocs might undercut their plans for a world
wide system of multilateral trade. This situation changed in 1947.': Hogan, *The
Marshall Plan*, p. 28.

90 Kennan, *Memoirs*, p. 335: 'for six years ...' refers to the change in American
Soviet policy from 'containment' to Acheson's policies of NSC-68, described in
Chapter 5.

91 Francis Fukuyama, *The End of History and the Last Man* (New York, Free
Press, 1992), especially Chapters 5 and 15.

92 See Michael Mastanduno, *Economic Containment: CoCom and the Politics of
East–West Trade* (Cornell University Press, 1992).

93 For a classic statement of the 'after hegemony' thesis, see Keohane, *After
Hegemony*. The best introduction to 'regime theory' is still Stephen D. Krasner,
International Regimes (Cornell University Press, 1983). See also Robert
Keohane, *International Institutions and State Power* (Boulder, Colorado,
Westview, 1989), especially Chapter 1, and Isabelle Grunberg, 'Exploring the
"Myth" of Hegemonic Stability', *International Organization*, vol. 44, no. 4,
Autumn 1990, pp. 431–477.

94 For a classic treatment of this, see Fred L. Block, *The Origins of International
Economic Disorder* (Berkeley, University of California Press, 1977), p. 1 and
Harold James, *International Monetary Cooperation Since Bretton Woods*
(Washington DC, IMF and Oxford University Press, 1996).

95 One particular advocate of this view is Susan Strange, whose contempt for
multilateralism in recent times has been based on her view that states and
international institutions, including those founded at Bretton Woods, are now
subject to market forces that they can no longer control. See her *States and
Markets* (London, Pinter, 1988), *Rival States, Rival Firms* (Cambridge
University Press, 1991) and *The Retreat of the State* (Cambridge University
Press, 1996).

96 For an excellent discussion of this see Ian Clark, *Globalization and Fragmentation: International Relations in the Twentieth Century* (Oxford University
Press, 1997).

97 Hirst and Thompson, *Globalization in Question*, pp. 170–194.

98 See the Conclusion for more discussion of this point of view.

99 Albright in the *Financial Times* of 19 September 1997, 'Fast Track Key to US
Global Role'.

100 Peter Wilson, 'Introduction', in David Long and Peter Wilson, *Thinkers of the
Twenty Years' Crisis: Internal Idealism Reassessed* (Oxford, Clarendon Press,
1995), pp. 9–11; J.D.B. Miller, *Norman Angell and the Futility of War*
(London, Macmillan, 1986), pp. 9–10.

8

Self-determination and the NWO

Introduction

The construct that is the NWO project does not stand or fall on the idea of self-determination. However, it is the part of that construct that is the most often quoted and the part that has caught the attention of the general public and academe. The reason is that it goes to the heart of the debate about what 'international relations' has been about (at least) this century: the relationship between individual, state and international system, whichever exact definition of these three is used and whatever the preferred permutation is taken to be. This chapter is an attempt to present a genealogy of the idea of self-determination as it is demonstrated in the record of the first and second NWOs. It will also try and show, however briefly, the relationship of those historical musings to the current debate during the third and current NWO.

One aim is to suggest how[1] we can see self-determination as part of a spectrum of ideas for the liberation of individuals, peoples and states. Another is to suggest that we can view it as a flexible concept, even a form of short hand, that sums up the dilemmas of both nations (and nation states) in a global political system and political economy that have themselves been in constant evolution. It is a concept that has had to be re-thought several times this century, most acutely during and just after the First and Second World Wars, during the period of decolonisation, and in the turmoil that has followed 1991 and the collapse of a number of multi-ethnic states in Europe, Africa and Asia. It has always been seen as a problematic concept, even on occasion for those who were its major beneficiaries. As Eduard Beneš, the first President of Czechoslovakia, put it, '[t]he principle of self-determination would need very detailed and precise explanation. It was misused and continues to be misused to an incredible degree ...'[1]

There are constants in this moving picture, although they are not themselves fixed in terms of their extent or importance. The first of these has to be the geometry of power in the international system. If the next century is to be, for example, Chinese, what will be the result for the debate on self-determination? The second of these is the world economy. In 1914 an integrated European financial and, to some extent, commercial system had been torn asunder, although this was not fully realised until the 1930s, as we have seen. In 1945 the United States led a Western system that was to implant the ideas of 'embedded liberalism' firmly into its foundations and practices. In 1990 Francis Fukuyama assured us that this system was the only viable one left. The third, somewhere between the first two, must be said to be the progressive extension of the idea of a localised or global 'civil society', which we can define as the 'realm of rights, exchange and the market'.[2]

The implications of a global, national or individual emphasis on questions such as self-determination and human rights are evident. Without a global political economy the dangers of self-determination becoming translated into economic and political nationalism are evident. To put it in terms of Hirschman's formula, if *homo economicus* has to make his voice heard within a necessarily limited national market-place, he has consequently to be subject to the vagaries of his political masters to whom he is bound to owe 'loyalty', or to exercise his 'exit' option.[3] One of the key reasons for the collapse of communism was that many opted for a physical exit to the West or a sullen internal exit that eventually vitiated the economic and political life of the whole Soviet bloc. In a global political economy these 'risks', if risks they are, are far less pronounced, if only because functional agreements are likely to minimise the differences in the treatment of the individual as all must perceive and obey the rules of a harmonious 'civil society'. Individual freedom, at least to act as *homo economicus*, is essential in such a system, the power of the state to prevent this far less evident, unless that state does not wish to be a full member of the global system, a decision which has evident costs for its overall well-being. State versus individual is thus far more difficult to envisage, as the state has to act as a facilitator of its citizens' economic rights, to preserve its own.

The nexus of problems that will be explored in this chapter thus necessitates a careful analysis that is aware of the shifting sands of political theory and the ever moving background that is 'history'. It also requires a recognition that the authors of the NWO were far from being, to paraphrase the dismissive words of Robert Cox, mere 'problem solvers'.[4] They were self-consciously trying to save what was manageable and, in their eyes, good of the 'old' while grafting on the ideas of the 'new'. They were attempting to deploy a set of new or adapted theories of what the world should be like, not what it actually was like, which they saw as a major disaster. That this was done by members of the 'Establishment' gives power to the feeling that all that is 'conservative' is not necessarily hide-bound, and all that is 'progressive' is not necessarily radical or emancipatory.

Is there a linkage between self-determination and human rights?

The ideas of human rights and self-determination were and are inextricably linked as part of the 'Enlightenment/Romantic Project' to liberate humankind from the fetters of feudalism, ignorance and oppression. This Enlightenment/Romantic dialectic is at the heart of the problem that individuals are supposedly 'free' and yet are constrained by structures, be they religious, philosophical, economic or political. In Western political theory the idea of individual 'rights' arguably pre-dates that of those of the 'community', with the impact of the ideas of Jean-Jacques Rousseau on the French revolutionary struggle as the point of juncture between the two. The Enlightenment had stressed the freedom of the individual, Rousseau now helped give birth to the idea of 'la nation', the modern form of community.[5] The principle of 'popular sovereignty' was increasingly seen as a new standard of international legitimacy and a 'necessary, if not sufficient condition for international peace and security'[6] by the middle of the nineteenth century, for example by John Stuart Mill, thus threatening the dynastic principle, although this was not fully confirmed until Wilson's Fourteen Points in 1918.

The support among radicals for the development of the nation state in Europe in the late eighteenth and early nineteenth centuries came from a belief that it was supposedly to free peoples from tyrannical rulers, rulers who were often not of their own ethnic or cultural disposition. When Shelley urged 'Men of England' to 'Rise like lions after slumber; In unvanquishable number; Shake your chains to earth like dew; Which in sleep had fallen on you; Ye are many – they are few ...',[7] he was equating sovereignty with liberty from internal or external tyrants. The nineteenth century glorification of Garibaldi, Mazzini, even Napoleon, was because self-determination of peoples and their acquisition of the status of 'nation states' was deemed necessarily to lead to a liberty of higher moral worth than mere individual liberty. But it was also seen increasingly from the Treaty of Westphalia of 1648 as being in the natural order of international society, most famously by Hegel in his *Philosophy of Right*.

For the more democratically inclined statesmen of the nineteenth century, even Shelley's hate figure Castlereagh,[8] there was a feeling that the self-determination of peoples would lead to more stability and order in the international system by giving them control over their own destinies through the granting of sovereignty. In his book on Garibaldi of 1911, G.M. Trevelyan summed up its attractions for statesmen wedded to the ideal of international order by calling it *Garibaldi and the Making of Italy, June–November 1860*.[9] Such a tidy settlement of thorny problems has always appealed to both the statesman and exchequers of *status quo* states.

NWOs are essentially gauged by the 'realist' by the extent to which they ensure order. But they are also gauged by whether they seem logically consistent. What Osiander wrote about the 1648 Westphalia settlement was equally applicable to that of 1919 or 1945: '[t]he conviction prevailed among the peacemakers that, provided the rights of each of the participating actors could be established definitively, no source of conflict would remain.'[10] The attraction of self-determination as a policy option after wars was that it came to seem to be legally definable and therefore defendable. When the dynastic principle was seen to be a consensus position in international society, then it too could be incorporated into international agreements, as at Westphalia and Vienna in 1815.

But it was also widely appreciated, at least from the early nineteenth century on, that without the corollaries of a guarantee for minority rights within these nation states and of an international system with reasonably porous borders, especially economically, as well as common norms of the rule of law and democracy, self-determination might well lead to a denial of individual human rights and to potential for conflict. Hence the notions of national and 'individual' sovereignty (through the acceptance of universally recognised principles of human rights) have become inextricably linked and the dialectic of order/justice and duty to community versus rights of the individual has become one of the major philosophical debates of this century, one which has seen a resurgence in international relations theorising since 1989.[11]

The same logic is found in countless documents of the United Nations and other international organisations since 1945: 'The right of self-determination … is an essential condition for the effective guarantee and observance of individual human rights …'[12] The Charter of the UN urges in Article 1 (ii) that member states should 'develop friendly relations among nations based on the respect for the principle of equal rights and self-determination of peoples'. It thus supposedly precedes and guarantees all other rights. The logic post-1945 has been that decolonisation will rid peoples of their colonial 'tyrants' and give them the possibility of full personal and national development, a logic reinforced by subsequent UN pronouncements.

An exploration of the links between the two has been given renewed salience by the post-1989 phenomenon of ethno-national wars, in particular, as it has led to various re-definitions of the relationship between the rights of states and those of individuals, with a corollary debate about the circumstances under which 'intervention' by the United Nations is justifiable on humanitarian grounds. We have arguably come to a point post-1990 where 'settled norms', such as state sovereignty, are being increasingly put into question. Who, in brief, has the right to demand self-determination, and who is supposed to guarantee this right?[13] It is evident that the theory that all peoples should be 'self-determined' is not matched by the existence of many (if not all) multinational or multi-ethnic states. As Mayall says: '[t]he formal order is still defined by the mutual recognition of states; but sovereignty is now said to reside with the people, as a result of an act of national self-determination based on the will of the majority.'[14]

As if that were not enough, allied concepts, such as the 'state', the 'nation' and a 'people', are also, and not surprisingly, the subject of what Walker Connor rightly calls 'terminological chaos',[15] a chaos that goes right to the heart of the project that we glibly call 'international relations'. Post-Cold War 'post-modern' or 'post-positivist' scholars have, in an orgy of demands for an epistemological rethinking of international relations, in many cases suggested that we should simply jettison such expressions as 'nation', 'state', even 'sovereignty', ones that have all been historically linked to the concepts of self-determination and human rights.

The NWO architects of this century have not felt they had that liberty, and most of the pre- (and indeed post-) 1989 writers on self-determination have wrestled purposefully with these definitions. The discourse of Versailles and that of the PWP process in the Second World War is littered with references to these linked ideas, and the main purpose of this chapter is thus to investigate this discourse through a continued examination of contemporary discussions in the NWO 'machinery' and in contemporary literature, from which it is hoped the more significant examples have been taken. It was clearly a complicated debate, and not universally accepted as valid at the time, any more than it is today.

The task facing the NWO architects, as those before them, was to ask 'how can order and stability be enhanced' and 'how could the world be made safer?' These issues were addressed in the ideas of collective and economic security, explored in the previous two chapters. But a third question was linked to them in the liberal internationalist project: 'how can freedom be guaranteed?' To use the language of the current theorist of human rights, where would the limits of the 'public' and the 'private' domain be fixed? What would be the relative rights of the state or of the individual? How important are economic rights for the granting of a necessary 'private' autonomy? To put it into the words of recent normative theorists, can we now say that Hegel's vision of a Civil Society is still only guaranteed as part of a 'fundamental practical association', within the community of a state, and that it starts and ends at the boundaries of the state? Or is it now a global phenomenon that does not depend on the state for its legitimation or reality, as Frost asserts? Or even, like critical theorists, might we affirm that all this discussion about the advance of civil society is merely a smokescreen for the advance of capitalism, to the detraction of all notions of individual, or indeed state, liberty?[16]

The end result of self-determination has frequently led to unforeseen consequences that have led many commentators to doubt the wisdom of such emancipation for all but a small number of peoples, races and nations. Many attempts at self-determination after 1919, 1945 and 1990 have seemed to disintegrate into arguments about minority rights, the collapse of state structures, the mass and usually forced migration of populations and even worse forms of violence, such as the recent ethnic cleansing seen in the former Yugoslavia and Rwanda. Is there a necessary opposition between the 'rights' of the sovereign state and those of the individual?[17] How can you enable peoples to have their independence and dignity, while not denying that to others within the borders occupied by a dominant ethnic or cultural group and while not allowing the granting of that 'right' to damage the cause of international or domestic order? One way to get round this would be to say, with Mill and Michael Walzer, that 'citizens get the government they deserve'.[18]

However, since the Second World War, as Chris Brown says, 'the right to self-determination has taken precedence over all other criteria for member-ship of international society.'[19] Hence no consideration has generally been given to whether a new state can exercise 'negative' sovereignty (i.e. the right to be left alone) or 'positive' sovereignty (an ability to project in the world) or, indeed, have 'real' as opposed to 'legal' status. Others, such as Robert Jackson, have taken the point further and claim that we now have a false debate, an 'incoherence' in our discussions about international relations because the basic assumptions about the nature of the state simply do not apply to most states. Most states are purely 'juridical' in that international society can only 'enfranchise' states, by giving them a vote in the UN, but not 'empower ... [them] to anything like the same extent since this for the most part involves internal relationships. State-building is primarily a domestic process occurring over a long period of time ... The community of states at most can only assist or hinder it.'[20] Equally, the problems of where to put frontiers in order to maximise national inclusion and what to do with minorities that were as a consequence to be doomed to *de facto* exclusion or statelessness (as with the Jews and Gypsies) were there for those with eyes to see them and saw their full realisation in the inter-war period.[21]

Self-determination as an historical idea

Self-determination had not been accepted at Vienna in 1815. It could indeed be argued that the *Sainte Alliance* was set up mainly to prevent small nations becoming small states, as they had been encouraged to do by Napoleon. The Congress of Vienna had deeply conservative intentions. Hence Osiander warns against historians such as Webster who assumed at the beginning of the 1920s that an idea that was by then on everyone's lips had always been so: '[a]t the time of the Vienna congress, national self-determination was present as an idea held by some, but it was not a consensus principle of the international system.'[22] This was because demo-cracy was not a consensus aim of the Powers at Vienna, and why self-determination and its attendant idea of nationalism were seen as a dangerous tendency throughout much of the nineteenth century by the Imperial Powers of Europe, especially Austria-Hungary and Russia. Hence also its romantic attraction, for which many young idealists were prepared to lay down their lives, as they still are today.

The nineteenth century development of these twin ideals and their equally constant repression saw a continual disruption of the politics of the great Powers in Europe and was one of the main reasons why the idea came to be sown that to grant self-determination to these captive peoples would have a calming effect, as John Stuart Mill claimed, for example. However, Mill's views were not universally accepted, then or indeed now, and an observer of the real difficulties involved in such a process might have been led to be rather sympathetic to the rulers of, at least, Austria-Hungary.

The impact of imperialism on the debate about self-determination

The nineteenth century incursions into Africa, Asia and elsewhere by the European imperialist powers had the perverse effect of spreading the ideal of national self-determination while destroying existing communities.[23] The category of the state was a major export of the imperialist Powers. As revolutionaries in Europe had put it at the heart of their agenda, so now colonised peoples put it at the heart of their own. Marx and others of the Historical Materialist School pointed to the modernising effect of colonisation, to the point where it often seems that Marx approved of colonial expansion for its creation of an oppressed class and its attendant spread of educated revolt.[24] This idea that imperialism could spread 'civilisation' was widespread by 1900, with even Americans such as Teddy Roosevelt expressing similar feelings to the British imperialist, Viscount Milner or the German nationalist historian, Treitschke. They were all, in the words of Rebecca West, 'infatuated with the idea of colonial expansion as a means of reforming the world by spreading at gunpoint Western ideals among the backward peoples'.[25]

There were those who could see that this urge would lead to more conflict, both domestically and internationally, and hence its antidote, self-determination, came to constitute a major element in NWO thinking over the next fifty years and more, again from liberal or socialist political economists. For Hobson, the main reason for imperialism was due to the 'financial power' and needs of Britain or, as Lenin put it, a 'stage' of capitalism. It consisted in the export of capital (foreign direct investment), although Hobson criticised this for its necessary detraction from social reform at home. Under-consumption (or over-saving) was for Hobson the basis of social injustice, fostered in order to promote foreign investment and Imperial expansion. The result was an inequitable distribution of wealth at home, aided and abetted by government. If wealth was redistributed ('the false economy of distribution'),[26] there would be no rationale for imperialism. Stopping the export of capital would therefore have the effect of redistributing capital at home and stopping imperialism overseas. But whereas Hobson saw the elimination of Empire as essential to stop revolution and create a more equitable society at home, Lenin wanted to foment revolution by encouraging nationalist insurrection. So before 1914 the battle lines of the links between self-determination and imperialism were already drawn, between a liberal desire to phase out Empire to save capitalism and ensure peace, and an extreme Marxist desire to use it as a lever to bring down capitalism.[27]

Part of the debate also came to be about whether these colonies should benefit from self-determination. For Hobson and others, the climatically 'temperate' areas where 'white colonists carry with them the modes of government, the industrial and other arts of civilisation of the mother country' were different from the later conquests of the nineteenth century. Here there was an 'occupation ... in the presence of a small minority of white men, officials, traders and industrial organisers, exercising political and economic sway over great hordes of population regarded as inferior and as incapable of exercising any considerable rights of self-government, in politics or industry'.[28] A measure of self-government had been extended to the British Imperial 'Dominions' – Australia, Canada, New Zealand and South Africa – as they were safely ruled by white men, but there was no hint of a desire to give such self-rule to other 'native' areas. A deeply ingrained assumption of inferiority of the non-white races was quasi-universal before 1914 and indeed for a long time after it.

This prejudice was largely shared by those who were deliberating the future of the world during the Great War. Although there is virtually no reference in American, British or French sources to the idea of self-determination for non-white races, there was a feeling that it would be of benefit to Europeans, especially those in the Austro-Hungarian Empire. Since Austria-Hungary was also seen as one of the major, if not the major, instigators of the conflict, its obliteration had become a key war aim from 1914 on, and one that is reflected in so many of Wilson's Fourteen Points being directed to the break-up of that Empire. Given its salience in his thinking it is logical that this area of NWO thinking should have been given due weight in the negotiations at the Paris Peace Conference.

Self-determination at the Paris Peace Conference

Nonetheless, the overwhelming impression that one gets from reading the contemporary record of the Versailles Conference is that this was the issue that was dealt with in the most cavalier fashion. What was supposed to be the cornerstone of Wilson's plans for Europe and the rest of the world was in part a major casualty of the compromises made by the Allies in order to ensure a relatively easy passage of the Covenant through the various committees.

American Views

The generally accepted view is that '[t]he leading part in the development of the general ideal of national liberation into an officially recognised Allied policy of self-determination was played by President Wilson, whose ideas on this subject were part of a long considered political philosophy.'[29] However, Derek Heater points out that until 1914 Wilson had 'evinced little interest and little competence in this field'. He also points out that the expression 'national self-determination' does not actually figure in the Fourteen Points Speech but that Wilson was nonetheless 'deeply committed' to it. Indeed, after the Treaty was signed he singled the issue out as a reason for the United States to ratify it: it was 'unique in the history of mankind because the center of it is the redemption of the weak nations'.[30]

What Wilson meant by it in concrete terms became less clear as compromise was heaped upon compromise at the Paris Peace Conference. His best interpreter is probably Colonel House, who continued to preach the Wilsonian gospel long after Wilson's death in 1923. For House the core of the idea was to 'make the world safe for democracy', a mantra repeated throughout the inter-war period. Wilson's model democracy, like that of most American commentators, was one based on republican principles, an absence of monarchy and an emphasis on the 'people' rather than on the military. Such democratic states would also be prepared to cooperate with each other economically and juridically in an intergovernmental framework, which would act as a 'safety valve' for the tensions that would be created by independence. This model new state would also be primarily European, for it was there, as we have noted, that Americans saw the main breeding grounds for war.[31] Later on in the 1930s American commentators such as Streit and Dulles came to see this model as inadequate and started to veer towards an even more American model, based on federalism, as was outlined in Chapter 3.

This emphasis on the export of democracy in the American mould explains, at least in part, why the United States does not see its actions in Europe since 1919 in anything but a benign light. It arguably also explains why they have not seen their activities in the non-European world as 'Imperial'. They have merely, as they see it, tried to give the benefits of their system to the rest of the world.

British and French views

Likewise the British and the French thought they were acting honourably, for they also took it for granted that their model of government was self-evidently the best. Hence the French and the British saw the utility of self-determination as a propaganda weapon of war, but they realised early on that it was a two-edged one, especially when it was also wielded by Lenin to take Russia out of the war. But the Imperial Allies had little real sympathy for the ideal of self-determination even as vaguely expressed by Wilson, largely because of their Imperial presence across the world and their long-standing belief in a balance of power in Europe. Although in his speech of January 1918 Lloyd George had seemed to imply that the peoples of the ex-German colonies would also be given their say, this was watered down when he realised that it would encounter opposition from Britain's largely self-governing Dominions and might encourage the colonies to find a focus for discontent.[32]

During the Paris discussions and immediately after them the concrete example of what might happen to this Empire if self-determination were given came from Ireland. The 1916 Easter Uprising had led to a guerilla war orchestrated by Michael Collins that took great heart from Wilson's declarations on self-determination. The future President of the Irish Free State, Eamon de Valera, thought American opinion so important that he immediately took himself off to the United States after being freed from Lincoln Gaol by Collins in early 1919 to press his people's case. Although this was less successful than he had hoped the episode showed the potential for long-term British discord with America over the Irish question, as was realised by Lloyd George (broadly in favour of Irish Home Rule) and Balfour (himself an ardent Unionist), and as has proved to be the case until the present day.[33]

The British did not accept in 1919, and arguably until after 1945, that self-determination should apply to the Empire as it did to Central Europe. As Cobban wrote, '[i]t did not occur to the Allied Governments that the propaganda they employed against the Central empires would affect their own empires fundamentally, or that by proclaiming the principle of self-determination they had laid the axe at the roots of their own colonial domains.'[34] In 1919 Ireland was offered, and accepted provisionally, a form of it – 'Dominion status'. Canada was the first to be given such status in 1863 and many Imperial believers in Britain continued to put their faith in this model of democratic sovereignty under the Crown. The Statute of Westminster of 1931 that set up the British Commonwealth conceded more in the way of equality, and subsequent developments were seen in London as extending this principle, right up to the 1960s. Churchill was not alone in his indignation when he wrote to Roosevelt in 1944 that some American views on the Commonwealth 'make me rub my eyes. He [in this case American General Hurley] makes out, for example, that there is an irrepressible conflict between imperialism and democracy. I make bold, however, to suggest that British Imperialism has spread and is spreading democracy more widely than any other system of government since the beginning of time.'[35]

Of mandates and 'savages'

Hence no real contradiction was seen by the main decision makers at Paris in giving a measure of 'self-determination' to the Czechs but none at all to those previously dominated by the Ottoman Empire who were clearly not ready for self-government. Smuts squared this with Wilson by suggesting the setting up of 'mandates', nominally set up by, and responsible to, the League of Nations, which effectively divided up German and Ottoman territories among Britain and France. It is a measure of how far Smuts was able to confuse Wilson over the mandate idea that he even persuaded Wilson to take an 'option' on an American mandate over Armenia, and even possibly more of the Anatolian area of Turkey. The ever quotable Hankey remarked to his Diary in May 1919 that 'President Wilson has a very elastic mind, for he has completely shut his eyes to the passage of the ... Covenant which says that the wishes of the inhabitants should be a factor in mandates! He seems willing to have a mandate over Armenia and Constantinople.'[36]

As to the 'savage' peoples of the world, there was no question of giving them any rights at all. Before Versailles there was intensive discussion within the British Imperial War Cabinet about how the question of self-determination should be approached. The main discussion was between the Dominions Prime Ministers (especially Borden of Australia, Smuts of South Africa and Hughes of New Zealand) as to how much should be annexed from previously German colonial possessions. According to Hankey, '[i]t required extraordinarily nice drafting to reconcile Borden, who doesn't want to grab territory and Smuts and Hughes who do.' Although many in the War Cabinet, especially Cecil, disliked this exploitation of the Treaty discussions for the purposes of overt annexation, Lloyd George had to appease his Imperial lobby and did so on a number of key occasions.

One extreme example of the views of this lobby can be found in a conversation between Lord Riddell, one of Lloyd George's closest confidants, and General Botha of South Africa just before Versailles. After discussing the excessively 'humiliating terms' of the Armistice for Germany, Botha spoke approvingly of German actions in Africa, parts of which Britain was to receive as a result of the Treaty:

> German East Africa is an impossible country for white men. West Africa, on the other hand, is a place where whites can live. In East Africa the Germans trained and armed 8,000,000 natives, hoping thereby to dominate South Africa. In the West they exterminated the natives in order to settle the country with Germans. The plan was well thought out ... We must hold East Africa because of its dominating position. The Americans do not understand that. The situation must be explained to Wilson.[37]

The echoes of Cecil Rhodes and his 'Africa made fit for the white man' were clear.

The Imperial Powers at Paris spent a great deal of time arguing with each other about how much of the German and Ottoman 'cake' they were going to give each other. Sometimes this boiled over into 'violent' anger and semi-farce, with Clemenceau once saying to Lloyd George over the border of Syria and Palestine that 'you are the very badest boy [*sic*].'[38] Of course that farce left a very bad odour in the Middle East, in particular. There Britain and France had effectively promised several different groups the same piece of land for their self-determination. In Palestine the Sykes–Picot Agreement of 1916 gave Syria and Lebanon to France, and the Balfour Declaration of 1917 and T.E. Lawrence ('of Arabia') seemingly gave Palestine to both Jews and Arabs. Many in Britain realised that Palestine, in particular, might prove to be 'a thorn in the flesh of whoever is charged with its Mandate'. Only Mesopotamia (modern Iraq) was seen as an unequivocal benefit, almost solely due to its oil. Curzon was not alone in wondering whether the local dangers of tangling with France ('aggressive and imperialist'), or the Zionists, or Arab nationalists were worse than the starry-eyed imperialism of some in the Cabinet.[39] The Ottoman Empire was perhaps the best example of how the principle of self-determination was sacrificed to the interests of the Imperial Powers. It was also one of the best examples of how difficult they found it to agree about the boundaries of these interests and stored up endless trouble for the future.

During the Conference an astonished American delegation, which included William Bullitt, was assured by Lawrence that the United States could have 'the whole of Arabia if the English would not play up about it' until Cecil intervened in the conversation to disabuse them of this. Even Balfour seems to have felt that this carving up of the Ottoman Empire went too far. He complained to Cecil about a 'levity approaching insanity. They have apparently been splitting up the Turkish empire with little regard to any racial or indeed any other considerations except the political convenience of the European Powers, as if they were making a jig-saw puzzle.' Turkey was, he later said, 'The most troublesome of all the troublesome questions with which the Conference has had to deal.'[40] In fact nearly all the questions relating to the Ottoman Empire had not been settled by August 1919, although a treaty was signed with Turkey in August 1920, and had to wait until the signature of the Treaty of Lausanne in 1923 for their final denouement.[41]

Small states, lesser powers and self-determination at Paris

Unsurprisingly, the main support for the Treaty came from the nascent nations of Central and Eastern Europe and, until their hopes were thoroughly dashed, from the nationalist movements of what would later be called the 'Third World' in China and elsewhere. Self-determination was a concept that was recognised, especially by its most stalwart opponents, as a power-fully destabilising idea. The last Foreign Minister of the Austro-Hungarian

Empire, Count Julius Andrassy, wrote in his memoirs that '... [t]he propaganda of Wilson was a more destructive weapon against us than many an army corps ...'.[42] Wilson's 'redemption of weak nations' was useful to break up Central Europe's creaking colossus. But in reality the Powers, on both sides, despised small states. German derision went the deepest – Rebecca West quotes her favourite figure of hate, Treitschke, as writing that small, and therefore weak, states were 'certain to make "in the name of civilisation, demands on the triumphant states which were unnational, unreasonable and improper, in view of the rights of the [powerful] state"'. It might certainly be averred that a very large proportion of British and American elite opinion shared this German historicist view of the superiority of certain races, and saw its logical result in the dominance of certain states. It was a Hegelian view of the world, where civil society, the domain of rights, was subject to the over-arching protection of the 'intelligence' that was the state – 'only to the degree in which the component parts of civil society obeyed the orders of that intelligence had civil society any dignity.'[43] The logical corollary of this had to be that without the state there were no rights, a communitarian view that has many adherents today and a seductive logic.

Most small or aspirant nations had weak state structures, then as now. But whereas now they have a formal and legal equality in all cases and existence in many more, before 1914 whenever they had tried to make their voice heard in international fora, as at the Hague Conference of 1907, they were treated with ill-concealed contempt. As with domestic society the 'global international society' of the period until the First World War had a select membership, almost entirely European. What Gerrit Gong terms the 'standard of civilisation' was a hard-earned international trademark, one that involved the seemingly paradoxical combination of military prowess and 'civilised behaviour' towards one's defeated enemies. Only after the Battle of Tsushima in 1905 was Japan taken even half-seriously as a state, and it took China until 1949 to be universally seen in such a light – Churchill certainly did not, as we have seen.[44]

This was an additional reason for a British, French and even American unwillingness actually to implement self-determination in practice, given its consequences for their interests, even where close allies were concerned. It gave rise to a situation which went a long way to storing up resentment over the next twenty years. China (technically neutral) and Japan (an Allied state) were not given anywhere near the same consideration as the European Allies in the carve-up of German colonies in the Far East, Japan being allocated Shantung and Kioachow in China against China's will. But more seriously, neither was granted effective equality of esteem at Paris. China's position was worst, and subjected to the most abject discrimination. Balfour's reasoning sums this up: 'The proposed transfer [of Shantung from Germany to Japan] ... took nothing from China which China possessed. China was not an ally; she had not spent a shilling or lost a life either in defending her own interest or in supporting ours, and our duties to her were confined to seeing that she lost nothing by her neutrality. This we did.'[45] In spite of this Wellington Koo, China's representative at Paris and in the LON, managed to retain an almost impossible dignity and ended up impressing many, but China's treatment can be said to have precipitated perhaps the most important phase of the Chinese revolution, such was the dismay and anger expressed by the May 4 Movement in the terms of the Treaty.

The Japanese, in spite of receiving some ex-German possessions, were also treated badly. Baron Makino was often excluded from meetings of the Council of Four and made to feel of lesser importance all round, even in ways described as 'industrial' and 'commercial'. Wilson felt he could not accede to Japanese requests for some statement about racial equality, partly to placate the American West Coast, terrified of an 'invasion' of Japanese workers. Australian Prime Minister Hughes also objected on the grounds that he might have to change his country's 'whites only' policy. As a Japanese historian has written of the Genoa Conference, less than three years later 'Japan, an emerging Asian power, enjoyed its status among the Great Powers but was also perplexed and wary at its unaccustomed position. This was not unlike its role at the Paris Peace Conference.'[46] Versailles came to be seen by the Japanese, and even more by the Chinese, as yet another 'unequal treaty' that heaped humiliation on them however much they tried to be 'Western' and 'civilised'.[47] It is little wonder that voices on the left and right in the Far East came to see Western attitudes to self-determination as little more than ill-concealed hypocrisy and the politics of power. Japan in particular found common cause with the revisionist fascist states of Europe in the 1930s to push back the ill-gotten gains of the Americans, British and French. In China the common cause was with America for the right and Soviet Russia for the left, both countries deemed less tainted by the events of 1919 than the old colonial powers.

The treatment of 'minorities' at Paris

Within Europe any 'self-determination' that impinged on the perceived essential interests of the Allies was also rigorously excluded. The Allies considered that historical precedent (the Berlin Conference of 1878 that carved up Africa was a favourite) gave them the right 'when the Powers sanction [...] an increase in territory in the case of any particular state, [that] they [are] justified in imposing conditions on that state in connection with the treatment of minorities.'[48] How exactly this was to be enforced was not properly considered and this again caused intolerable tensions in Central Europe throughout the inter-war period.

The break-up of the Austro-Hungarian Empire left huge numbers of 'minorities' (as they were called from 1920 on). The attempts by Bolshevik Russia to capitalise on the discontent so caused made the Allies even harsher in their pursuit of strategic and economic goals at the expense of the interests of such 'minorities'. This was particulary true in the case of Hungary, which lost 3.5 million Magyars[49] and large areas of territory in the Treaty of Trianon in late 1919, mainly to Czechoslovakia and Romania. The Hungarian Revolution was told in no uncertain terms during the Conference that it would not be allowed to continue, Smuts being sent with Allen Leeper and Harold Nicolson to tell Béla Kun, the Hungarian communist leader, of this decision.[50] Help from Romania in putting down the revolution was actively encouraged by Britain and France. During the Conference Leeper airily dismissed Hungarian allegations of religious persecution (and worse) by Romania in the newly annexed province of Transylvania as 'quite unfounded', although British Government and American Unitiate Church, as well as League of Nations, inquiries of 1920–21 confirmed the truth of the reports. The French, who by this time were endeavouring to build up the '*Petite Entente*', directed against Hungary and Germany, had little sympathy for such claims.[51] This was to develop into one of the longest-lasting 'minority' problems in Eastern Europe, feeding Hungarian anger to the present day, while during the inter-war period it was yet another example of British and French differences and their corrosive effect on peace.

When self-determination affected economic interests it was also sidelined. The Austro-Hungarian border was 'modified', thus cutting Pressburg (now Bratislava) out of Austria in order to give the St Janos railway to Hungary.[52] Balfour, who was the British representative on the Czechoslovak Commission of the Conference, was uncomfortable about this, as the Poles were to lose territory that was theirs by right under the principle of self-determination, but would create strategic difficulties for the new Czech Republic, with which Balfour, like the French and most of the British and American delegates, had enormous sympathy (Benes in particular coming in for regular praise). The railway's route was, wrote Balfour, 'a kind of difficulty which we cannot ignore', and the border was corrected accordingly.[53]

Arguably the most significant departure from the principle was Germany itself. The German population of Bohemia (referred to as the 'Sudeten problem' in the 1930s) was sacrificed to reasons which were, as Balfour put it, 'partly economic; partly what we call geographical – (meaning, I suppose, that the semi-circle of mountains dividing Bohemia from Germany makes a nice looking frontier on the map); partly historic or, as they prefer to call them, political; and partly strategic – i.e. based on considerations of national security.' He was not against any of this in principle, but he worried about the 'adapt[ation of] one set of principles ... for the Germans in Bohemia and another when we take Germans from Poland ... What it all comes to is that we have to guard against the danger of being supposed to use our principles to further our fancies ... we cannot be popular, our only chance is to be just.'[54] The border drawers at Versailles managed to be neither.

Self-determination in the inter-war years

This eliding of principles was at the heart of Treaty revisionism in the inter-war years in all the democracies. It has been rightly said that most of the 'realists' – Carr being an obvious example – of the 1920s and 1930s were critical of the Treaty of Versailles for its mismatching of stated moral principles (of which self-determination was key) and *Realpolitik*. Why should Germany have been satisfied with being a pawn of Great Power infighting and incompetence? The Treaty must be revised and the 'wrongs' done Germany righted. For such realists, the later brow beating about 'appeasement' completely missed the point.[55] This does a great deal to explain why during the Second World War and after it, these same 'realists' saw the problem of how to deal with Germany as a key to preventing another conflict. Their reply was largely to jettison the principle of self-determination in practice – Germany lost a lot more territory and population in 1945 than in 1919 – but to continue with its rhetoric for public consumption. They substituted in effect the idea of a strong and unified Western Europe through NATO and (ultimately) the European Union, which the Russians considerably helped by giving it a sense of a common enemy.

The 1920s and 1930s saw a host of attempted revisions of the issues raised by the issue of self-determination at the Paris Peace Conference. Small states such as Austria were left unable to function as units in a situation of rapidly developing economic nationalism. Attempts to gather several new states to counter Hungarian irredentism and German expansionism in the *Petite Entente* came to little. Germany saw much of its resentment as being due to the inadequacies of the clauses of the Treaty that deprived it of the Saar (given back by plebiscite in and Rhineland (re-occupied in 1936) and, most significantly, the Polish Corridor and Danzig. It is not impossible that Alsace-Lorraine might have voted to remain German had it been given the choice in 1918, giving rise to Hardinge's comment that 'plebiscites taken in countries in our possession ... might be very inconvenient and certainly should not be encouraged'. It was also widely understood that the French wanted the Saar and the Rhineland in order to have a 'buffer' against Germany.[56] In effect the French substituted the principle of 'restitution' for that of self-determination whenever their basic interests were seen as being threatened. Equally, the victors at Paris in Central and Eastern Europe were not too keen to let the population decide on its future state allegiance, thus creating, for example, a substantial Hungarian and German diaspora that was to cause many problems in later years.

So Heater is not wrong in his judgement that the 'several peace treaties were often drafted in conscious violation of the principle of national self-determination' or even that there was, as Cobban puts it, 'a hardly noticed substitution of an allied but different set of ideals for that of self-determination' at Versailles.[57] Its violation after the initial promise that it had held out was to prove in the long run the most corrosive factor in the medium-term collapse of the LON and of the Treaty and in the stability of international order, an instability that was arguably not properly addressed until the Atlantic Charter of 1941 and the Charter of the United Nations in 1945. Both in its promise and in its breach, it is hard to see that the introduction of the notion of self-determination did anything but increase the instability of the international system from 1919 on.

Not everyone was so negative about the idea and practice of self-determination in the inter-war years. It was still possible in 1930 to think that the glass was half full, not half empty, as it appeared only a few years later. William Rappard, Director of the newly established Graduate Institute of International Relations in Geneva and Swiss delegate to the LON, was able to see in the multiplication of independent states in Europe (from twenty-one in 1914 to twenty-seven in 1930, or thirty if Danzig, the Irish Free State and the Saar were included) an increase in democracy and the 'political emancipation of hitherto subject nationalities'. Moreover, fifty per cent (thirteen) were now republics (as opposed to only three pre-war). He also saw a huge increase in international cooperation in the political field. 'Europe has become Americanized in this, as in no other respect, which is saying a great deal.'

What worried him was that this was not yet being translated into the economic field, solely due to poverty and 'the morbid and rather pathetic desire for economic self-sufficiency which has inspired European statesmanship since the War'. When this was rectified, as he did not doubt it would be, it would sound the death-knell for the dictatorships which had been an unhappy, but probably temporary, result of the problems of too rapid a change of system. This had manifested itself in 'rural countries, which, having borrowed political and parliamentary institutions from their more advanced industrial neighbours, found them ill-adapted to their postwar needs'. This was the Achilles' heel of the present situation, not the principle of self-determination itself, which was 'America's greatest contribution to the ideals for which the World War was fought and won'.[58]

It is worthwhile remembering that the beginning of the inter-war period saw a reversal of the long-established trend in Europe towards multinational states. In 1800 there had been over 300 mini-states in what became the German Empire alone. By 1914 there were only twenty-one in the whole of Europe. However, the strains of the reversal of this trend were exacerbated by the factor that Rappard noted, but clearly did not fully understand. These problems lay in the factors identified by Polanyi in *The Great Transformation* mentioned in the previous chapter and in Carr's *Twenty Years' Crisis*. The state did seem to be the irreducible unit of international relations. Moreover, the global economic framework of pre-1914, as epitomised by the self-regulating market and the international Gold Standard, as well as the political concomitant of the balance of power, had been effectively destroyed by the war. The re-establishment of these, thought Polanyi and Carr, was now impossible, with the result ('the snapping of the golden thread') of widespread revolution and the triumph of the strongest states.

All the Conferences of the LON, in which Rappard had put so much hope, had not put Humpty Dumpty together again. Carr and Polanyi could not see any alternative but the reassertion of the nation as the key principle of international politics and the finding of new forms of economic organisation arranged on national lines. So the tentative proliferation of small states in the 1920s reversed in the 1930s now seemed to justify Carr's and Polanyi's pessimism about the likely triumph of self-determination, as first Hitler and then Stalin incorporated the new small states of Europe into their Empires one by one: Austria, Czechoslovakia, Lithuania, Latvia, Estonia, Poland and sections of Romania were all annexed by 1940.

To make a final point about the medium-term results of the Paris Peace Conference, we might assert that self-determination as an idea in fact turned to the benefit of the propaganda of the fascist states of the 1920s and 1930s in ways that would have appalled the liberal democratic Wilson. Wilson had wished to reverse the dynastic settlement of Vienna by giving the oppressed peoples of Europe their communal liberty. He therefore shifted the 'consensus', in Osiander's use of the word, within the framework of the Hegelian ideology of 'community' but not in a progressive liberal way. The 'conservatism' of Vienna, intended to keep the masses in their place, gave way to the 'populism' of Versailles. But when given their freedom the masses misused it, as Ortega y Gasset and many others observed. The 'revolt of the masses' might therefore be seen as having been encouraged by the concentration on self-determination as a norm at Paris. But it gave rise to the populist nationalism of the Fascist states rather than the liberal internationalism for which Wilson had hoped.[59] The states at Paris which had been lukewarm about the idea had every right to feel vindicated in their reluctance. However, it was the successor politicians in Britain, France and the United States who were now in the unenviable position of having to pick up the pieces.

Hitler's New Order and the new small states of Europe

Fascist and Nazi politicians despised Wilson's ideals more than most. They saw themselves as members of the 'trench aristocracy' and endowed with a far stronger mandate for change in Europe than any American politician, a mandate they had won through the shedding of their own and their comrades' blood. Their analysis of the causes of war and defeat lay far away from those of the liberal politicians who had tried to make the peace, and they were prepared to pursue ruthlessly radical policies to undo these politicians' work and substitute their own 'land fit for heroes'. It would be easy to dismiss Hitler's *Mein Kampf* as ranting mystical nonsense, his anti-semitism as obscurantist diatribe. Unfortunately, many agreed with his analysis and were quite prepared to go along with it, becoming, in Daniel Goldhagen's words, 'Hitler's willing executioners'. The very centre of this ideology was one of an expansionist nationalism of a few 'master races', the opposite of self-determination for all.[60]

The centrality of Europe for fascist/Nazi politicians is the key to this. From the beginning of the nineteenth century, arguably from the very inception of the modern nation state, the way that European civilisation would turn has obsessed political philosophers. Hegel's *Geist* moved through European history, not through that of the peoples outside Europe, so for him '[u]niversal history was thus in essence articulated and governed by the concrete destiny of Europe'. As Luis Dìez del Corral pointed out, even the great pessimists, Nietzsche and Spengler saw Europe's destiny as the key to world developments. As Europe declined so did the 'West'.[61] The problem was that Europe had as a result been at war for most of its history. As was suggested in Chapter 5, some European politicians and thinkers had tentatively suggested uniting Europe, but they were seen largely as cranks or visionaries. The name that always crops up in this context is Count Coundenhove-Kalergi, who probably comes into both categories.[62]

But by far the more sinister and important advocate of European Union in the inter-war years was Adolf Hitler. Hitler came progressively to see his view of a mighty Germany as tied up to a Europe that was under German economic, and then military, control. His vision was essentially of a pan-European anti-capitalist coalition of like-minded states which excluded what he saw as the contamination of Bolshevism and Judaism.[63] As insane as this vision now appears, it was not seen as such by many of the bourgeoisie and proletariat of Western Europe in the 1930s and even in the early 1940s. It was also a vision that came close to seeing itself victorious. Ironically, Hitler could probably have had most of the economic gains of nazism without the military expenditure, as several studies of the economy of Eastern Europe in the 1930s have convincingly shown.[64] Nonetheless, Hitler's 'New Order' was essentially a European construct, and some commentators have unfairly criticised all subsequent attempts at unity for being tarred with this brush.[65]

Self-determination and the Rooseveltian NWO

Roosevelt was more aware of this than most and he was determined to try and revise the only seemingly possible viable alternative to the fascist model. This was Wilson's view of the world, with which he essentially agreed, but which he saw had to be built upon more sound foundations. Having encouraged the idea of self-determination, and then not joining the organisation that was supposed to further it, by 1939 the United States stood accused of having abandoned its new creations. As we have seen in previous chapters, the problem lay in the great divisions that existed within the United States about how far it should have got involved in that subsequent development, or to what extent it should now come, once again, to the rescue. Many Americans did not wish to become so involved. Many isolationists, especially those organised in the 'America First Committee' (AFC), considered that the final Treaty of Versailles had been such a distortion of Wilson's original ideas as to have given birth to the dictatorships, a view with which even Roosevelt had some sympathy. The AFC felt that a much better role for America was to stay out of Europe's new war and concentrate on its developing hemispheric experiment, the 'Good Neighbour' policy, leaving an irredeemably lost Europe to its just fate.

This should not be seen as an agreement with Hitler's ideas or methods. It was more of a one with Carr's realism – what cannot be reformed must be abandoned. The resulting logic edged out from certainty into desperation: this war, as that of 1914–18, was one between competing empires. If the United States did not threaten Hitler why should he attack? If he did attack, nonetheless, the United States could survive economically without anyone else. So for the AFC the United States had little to fear from Hitler, even in charge of Europe. Europe needed Latin American produce, while Latin America needed the United States, not Europe. A revitalised Monroe Doctrine which protected self-determination in the Hemisphere was thus a sufficient aim for the concept. As Justus Doenecke has commented, '[i]t is not the least of ironies that an organization [the AFC] backed by believers in capitalism advanced in part a modified Leninist argument ...'.[66] This logic evaporated rapidly with the attack on Pearl Harbor in December 1941, but it had a widespread appeal that Roosevelt could not ignore. The logic re-emerged later in the war, as it had in 1919. Only the creation of a new threat, that of Soviet communism, persuaded the United States to stay in Europe.

Official American thinking on self-determination, 1939–45

In 1941, at the start of the Grand Alliance, perhaps the only area of ideological agreement between the United States and the Soviet Union lay in a commitment to end imperialism and colonialism. As we have seen (especially in Chapters 3 and 4), the main source of friction between Britain, France and the United States was about the British and French Empires. The two main partners in the coalition put immense pressure on Britain and France to decolonise in the post-war era, thus giving an immense boost to the indigenous demands for self-determination and independence in what came to be known as the 'Third World'. It is a matter of record that the British did this with more grace than the French, arguably because the transitional mechanism of the Commonwealth gave the fig-leaf of legitimacy and the impression of British cooperation in the dismantling of its Empire and its transition into a useful international organisation rather than a system of dominance.[67]

The difficulty lies in the gap between American rhetoric and their private doubts that self-determination could really work. As with the public statements of Secretary of State Lansing at the Paris Peace Conference and his subsequent retraction of them, many of the American public statements in 1941–45 on the idea of self-determination were at stark odds with private musings, or at least modified by them considerably. The reason for this is essentially once again tied up with the American obsession over the future of Europe, not the very hypothetical future (during the Second World War) of a decolonised world.

The Atlantic Charter explicitly renewed calls for an extensive revitalisation of the principle in Europe, the area of existing practice after 1919. Yet in private, most American decision makers seem to have favoured some sort of 'federation' for Europe. Roosevelt himself was of the opinion, as we have seen in Chapters 3 and 5, that Europe had to be made to conform to different patterns of behaviour from those of its recent past. He also saw the Soviet Union and Britain as his necessary partners in this enterprise. The reception of Clarence Streit's *Union Now* in the United States showed that there was a counter-force to that of the AFC and isolationism, a space for the creation of a new impulse of thinking about self-determination, one that took into account the problem of small states and the need for economic and political cooperation among them. The AFC's problem with Streit's ideas in general, with which a large section of American informed opinion agreed, was that such cooperation would always prove impossible, as it had in the past. Its particular problems with Streit's ideas were that Britain would never entertain a leading federal role in Europe and that any form of 'Union' would inevitably entail United States involvement in the war.[68] The American Government largely agreed with this analysis, and hence spent much time and effort trying to persuade Britain to act in a more 'European' way, as we saw in Chapter 5.

Others, notably Kennan, one of the key representatives of the geopolitical school of American foreign policy, became keen advocates by 1944 of a Europe divided into American and Soviet spheres of influence with, in Kennan's case, a German counterweight. As he put it in 1942, '[g]ranted moderate and humane regimes in Berlin and Moscow ... I could see no objection to dividing all of eastern Europe (except Finland) up between them; and if only *one* of them, then it could be dominant.'[69] This idea was anathema to many in Washington, most notably Morgenthau, who saw Germany as essentially evil and irredeemable. The essentially dispassionate and deeply conservative Kennan quite simply disliked small states and would have agreed no doubt with Ortega y Gasset, who railed in 1932 against '[t]he smaller nations' which made a 'deplorably frivolous spectacle' where 'every nation and nationlet prances, waves its arms, turns somersaults or struts about pretending to be a grown-up with the right to control its own destiny. Hence the almost bacteriological horde of nationalisms that swarm on all sides.'[70]

Cobban, Carr and the Chatham House view

In Chapter 4 reference was made to the volume edited by E.H. Carr and others in 1939 on the eve of war at Chatham House on *Nationalism*. This volume and the internal polemic it provoked with those in Chatham House who believed that the nation state may have been becoming an obsolete category in international relations, led to a longer-term discussion about the merits of the nation as a political unit and, more particularly, the condition under which self-determination might be a route to nationhood and its corollary of statehood.

In the opening chapter of *Nationalism*, which we can assume was written by Carr, 'The Origins of Nations', he described how the nation and the state had been the natural units of organisation since the dawning of the modern age. He further pointed out that nations were themselves only as strong as their natural inclinations to unity, particularly those that forged a 'national consciousness', as had the rugged individualism of the United States and, embryonically at least, the British Imperial Dominions. There was the possibility that nations could also become states where there was a 'reuniting of a people', as with Poland, but any case of nation building would only happen when there was the creation of a 'common loyalty', not easy to forge and illustrated by the number of states that had not survived the test of history. Carr's aim was to find a definition of what constitutes a nation and to bring acceptance that this category of organisation had to be accepted as the basis of international society, for good or ill.[71]

Alfred Cobban's 1945 volume on *National Self-Determination*, also produced under the auspices of Chatham House, took this discussion further and asked what could be done to alleviate the worst effects of the popular demand for nation and statehood while stressing the positive gains, especially for the democratic ideals that were the basis of Western civilisation. According to Cobban, after the failure of the Versailles Treaty, which had been 'characterized by a failure to apply self-determination logically and systematically ...' and of the LON, the conclusion had been widely drawn that its 'moral basis', the right of peoples to national self-determination, was fatally flawed. However, said Cobban, to blame it for a collapse of the post-war order is illogical since there was no such order to collapse 'as self-determination was not applied in any logical way'. This might lead to an even worse condemnation, because it might mean that it was 'in the nature of things [that self-determination] could not be applied consistently'. If that were so then the entire NWO of 1919 based on 'substantial justice' for the world's populations through the application of the norm of self-determination, especially in Europe, and supposedly implemented by the LON, was based on an assumption that could not be justified. The extension of national sovereignty had not led to a more peaceful international order, '[w]estern civilization became slowly aware that it stood on a quicksand, that it had, not an inadequate basis for its international order, but no basis at all.'[72]

So did it need to be jettisoned entirely as an idea? Cobban rather insisted that it had been wrongly applied. First, self-determination could not be seen as an absolute right, but had to depend on practicalities, not abstractions such as the 'General Will', so that even if it was recognised as a right, it could not always be attributed to 'a collective body such as a nation'. Nations were difficult to define. Were they subjective identity structures, so that 'we can no more choose our *patrie* ... than we choose our father and mother', as the French ideologue of the right, Charles Maurras had put it? Cobban dryly countered that this would rule out any immigrant from nationality of that state. Or should the 'cultural nation' become synonymous with the 'political state', as many had argued? This would tend to exclude cultural minorities and 'multi-national states are ruled out'. But for Cobban this was to put the cart before the horse, as most successful political states (including the United States, Britain and its Dominions, and France) had begun as political units and developed into cultural nations by a 'slow ... natural process' of evolution to a 'common national consciousness'. By replacing this natural process with the idea that the nation had a right to its own state, 'the idea of nationality launches a general offensive all along the line on the world of states'. Nationalism had thus become 'a principle of aggression' and was no longer, as it had been in 1776 and 1789, 'a simple corollary of democracy'. 'National determination' had become substituted for self-determination, with the awful results that had been seen in Central and Eastern Europe and in the German frenzy of annexation since 1871. So what was necessary was to redefine it to stress its positive side and reduce its harmful effects.[73]

Cobban's answer was to stress the values of the Western notion of nationality which fused 'a measure of free individual choice with a consciousness of the inherited traditions and values of communal life', or, as Sir Alfred Zimmern had put it in 1915, 'as an educational creed for the diverse national groups of which the industrialized and largely migratory democracies of our large modern states must be increasingly composed'. For Cobban the nation must be a celebration of difference, not an exclusionary process, and where an attempt had been made 'to force cultural and political nationality to coincide ... the result has usually been disaster'. He later points out that this tolerant view of nationality will always be under constant pressure from the twin forces of sovereignty, which fears secession more than anything else, and self-determination, which can easily degenerate into secession on the basis of race, ethnicity or culture. 'The only hope, it seems, must be in a combination of the two principles, allowing each to operate within its own proper field, and recognizing neither as an absolute right, superior to the rights of individuals, which are the true end of society.'[74]

In his dynamic juxtaposition of nationality, democracy and sovereignty, Cobban summed up the enduring dilemma of the self-determination of peoples better than anyone before or since. His answers were less clear cut as he believed that national sovereignty would not diminish or give way to excessive demands for self-determination. But he did hope that the 'principle of sovereignty [could be] reduced again to reasonable proportions' by the leavening power of economic arrangements across frontiers and even by 'strategic military control being separated from everyday political control ...'. Only in such a balanced world where force would be banned and the 'interdependent conditions of the modern world' fully recognised could there be a 'sane world order'.[75]

Whither self-determination post-1945?

Europe

For the student of international relations the central question continues to be the wider issue of what international system we should try and encourage. In this debate the European example has been seen, again, as emblematic of the wider problem of the importance, or not, of the nation state as the basis for a stable international order. Carr derided the idea of European unity as he derided attempts at global peace through the LON in the inter-war period. The only security for Carr lay in a strong nation state, hence the frequent conflation of 'realism' and 'statism'. But for some the attraction of the idea of some form of united, and even federal, Europe was increasingly perceived as being essential to forestall the recurrent danger of a domineering Germany and a capricious Russia. Set out forcefully by Carr's contemporary, Arnold Toynbee in 1939 as the concept of 'pooled sovereignty',[76] this was also Churchill's logic, elaborated in a celebrated series of speeches between 1946 and 1948 in Zurich, London and the Hague. He chose Zurich and the topic of Europe for his first major speech as Leader of the Opposition. But he had a record of support for what were considered wildly 'idealist' schemes by people such as Carr. His core logic, first concretely expressed in Zurich in September 1946, was for 'a partnership between France and Germany', one that would remove the main source of competing nationalism in Europe.[77]

Since 1945 some 'realist' authors such as Hedley Bull have made the explicit comparison between the project for both a 'world government' and a united (especially 'federal') Europe and that of Napoleon and Hitler.[78] Indeed the recent discussions (during and since the Treaty of Maastricht in 1992) within Britain about the European Union have constantly evoked the role of Germany in the making of this new entity. Bull's reasoning is that the best and main support for the ultimate value in international relations, which for him is order, can only be guaranteed by states. The rights of both peoples and individuals have to lie in the communitarian system of a world of nation states signing treaties that are binding (*Pacta sunt servanda*), not in the 'woolly' recognition of non-binding norms, or so-called 'customary' international law. Against this classical 'legalist' view we have seen many examples of the feeling that the nation state is in many ways an obsolete concept and that other forms of organisation have to be attempted. The ideal of Europe now espoused by those who believe in European Union is that there is no necessary opposition between self-determination and integration, even up to a very high level. The result, they would claim, is 'pooled sovereignty', one which strengthens all. Bull's condemnation of the European project is thus based on the flawed logic that it was somehow the fruit of an 'idealist' vision, whereas in fact it was the opposite. This perhaps demonstrates, if it still needs to be, the difficulties inherent in pigeon holing certain theories as 'idealist' and others as 'realist'. It all depends on the circumstances of their implementation.

Self-determination, decolonisation and the UN

The United Nations was set up to deal with one problem, that of the security of the Powers of 1945, and was immediately asked to deal with another, that of the self-determination of former colonies and their attempted subsequent development into successful nation states. It has arguably failed in both tasks, although we should probably not blame the monkey (the UN) for the failings of the organ grinders (the Great Powers). In the case of self-determination as expressed by decolonisation, the confusion of aim, project and instrumentalities is quite obvious. The key problem is that many of the states that make up the United Nations are severely dysfunctional. Why they are dysfunctional can be laid at two main doors: the super-power conflict that we called the Cold War and with the states themselves.

As stated earlier in the chapter, the UN Charter stressed the sovereign rights of peoples to be self-determined (Article 1(ii)). It also gave them juridical equality and reinforced the duty of other states not to interfere in the internal affairs of their peers. But of course a hierarchy of states still existed after 1945, with the 'super-powers' (the USSR and the USA, with Britain occasionally also included until about 1956) at the summit. Down at the bottom of the pile are small island, land-locked and impoverished entities that are almost totally subject to the domination of their neighbours or of internal splits, Jackson's 'quasi-states'.

Since 1945 the number of member states in the UN has increased from 51 to over 200. This 'revolutionary international change', as Jackson terms it, would have been a surprise to the architects of the NWO had they considered it from the vantage point of 1945. As Jackson points out, no really satisfactory answer exists as to why it took place so fast. He suggests that the war 'certainly was a major cause'; that 'the new post-war rivalry between the United States and the Soviet Union which came to be known as the "cold war" was also a background factor' in hurrying the process of decolonisation. He comes close, but does not actually suggest, that the power of the idea of self-determination was the main impetus, pushed on by the General Assembly of the UN.[79]

In truth the architects of the NWO had found a potent vehicle for their view of the future, but one that they could no longer control once it was released into the UN system. Self-determination was not really envisaged for non-European states until they had a fully operative democratic structure and economy. Neither were these states supposed to exhibit massive ingratitude towards the main architects of this NWO. Yet, until about 1987, egged on by the Soviet Union, the Third World almost consistently outraged Western (for which read especially 'United States') public opinion.[80] In this new situation the powerful have had the constantly galling experience of being expected to help these insignificant entities with their development goals while also having to bear criticism for real or imagined 'colonial' or 'neo-colonial' activities, or be given lessons on human rights by states that are primary violators of the same among their own populations. The US Government now owes $1.3 billion in arrears to the UN because Congress (principally) has expressed its disgust at this *lèse majesté* towards American might. This is a situation not imagined by Churchill, Roosevelt or, indeed, Stalin, in 1945.

The concept was redefined in the 1960 *Declaration of Rights and Duties of States* as self-determination within *existing frontiers*. In fact nearly all these frontiers were imposed, in that they correspond to old colonial administrative boundaries and therefore were usually illogical. In Europe the Hapsburg, and Russian, Empires have fragmented into ever more and smaller states since 1919, encouraged by the Powers. In Africa when this has happened since 1960 it has always been actively discouraged and only happened by war (e.g. Eritrea, 1993) or has been actively discouraged by the local states and Great Powers (e.g. Biafra, 1962). The problem was, as Cirino Hiteng has identified,

> [i]n Africa, the use of concepts of 'nation' and 'state' do not follow their original usages in European politics. In most of Europe, state boundaries often coincided with national ones but during the formative years of the African state-system, the idea that states should coincide with nations was not applied. Thus the search for a coherent theory of the state has remained difficult to establish in Sub-Saharan Africa.[81]

During the Cold War the blame can be laid with equal measure at the feet of the states of Africa themselves and of the super-powers that encouraged such attitudes to strengthen their own positions. Only since the removal of super-power influence have Africans been able to put their own point of view across, which they have done very emphatically across the whole central area of the Continent (see below). Africa is only now being properly decolonised, not from the outside in, but from the inside out. Whether the resulting chaos in the Horn of Africa and in Central Africa, especially in Rwanda and the former Republic of Zaire, will prove in the long run to lead to more stable and democratic states is open to question. These states were not transformed entirely by the sole agency of demand for self-determination, or certainly not by a self-determination that was limited to one tribal or ethnic group. Eritrea (independent in 1993), for example, has at least thirteen linguistic groups in a population of barely 6 million.[82]

Ethnicity and democracy after the Cold War

The Eritreans' demand for secession was based on a desire to run their own affairs, the same desire shown by the southern ('Yugo') Slavs in 1919. Unfortunately, Yugoslavia did not prove to be such a good example to the world.[83] The war in the, now, former Yugoslavia has led many commentators to claim that 'ethnicity' will prove to be the Achilles' heel of the NWO principle of self-determination. Daniel Moynihan voiced the persuasive argument in 1993 that although '[n]ation states no longer seem inclined to go to war with one another, ... ethnic groups fight all the time'. He quoted many commentators who considered the break-up of the Soviet Union, the former Yugoslavia and ethnic clashes elsewhere as harbingers of our collective destiny. At the very moment of the destruction of authoritarianism we were faced with a new heart of darkness, or rather an old one come back to haunt us. Other commentators have seen similar trends, although more recently with less apocalyptic conclusions.[84] The literature on this has certainly grown exponentially since the end of the Cold War. But is not ethnicity but one level of identity among others, such as religion or economic class, and no more worthy of being singled out than any other?[85]

All we can say for certain is that democracy proved to be a difficult concept to implement in economically under-developed post-colonial, or even some European, societies, at least during the Cold War. If we see self-determination as a way of bringing democracy about, then clearly the project has failed. But there is now hope that, at least in Africa, where the evidence for failure is starkest, new states have now embraced a form of democracy and that they have come to terms with a globalising economy.[86] Whether what we now see in these new African states can be called 'multi-party democracy' is doubtful as yet, but it is arguable that this is not necessary if the form of democracy adopted allows for an articulation of individual, ethnic and other forms of difference. In Eritrea specifically, self-determination of the Eritrean people meant not only independence for

Eritrea but also the acceptance of the multi-ethnic nature of the country as a source of strength. In Ethiopia an ambitious new Constitution gives specific regional rights to most ethnic groups and the right of secession, precisely to try and encourage the voluntary maintenance of a unified state. Has the lesson finally been learned that post-colonial, and even some European rulers, such as those in the former Yugoslavia, are not merely the inheritors of absolute power from authoritarian regimes, but have to accept the notion and practice of democratic accountability?

Unless they do then this democratic conception of self-determination will not also bring human rights to the population in the way intended by Woodrow Wilson and Roosevelt. After the decolonisation process the concept got a bad name precisely because, in practice in most parts of the world, it meant its opposite, 'domination'. What will happen now in the new states of Africa once the honeymoon period of national liberation is over? Will the lessons of Europe in the 1920s and 1930s be bitterly relearned in a new context? No country will now claim to be anything but democratic, and few that they are not wedded to the ideas of the free market and therefore to economic interdependence, the absence of which we have noted was a main cause of self-determination being such a force for fragmentation and conflict in the inter-war years. Whether those earlier lessons are indeed learnt is for history to judge.

Conclusion: self-determination after the Cold War

Writing in 1945, Alfred Cobban had attributed the collapse of the inter-war order, as did many of his contemporaries, to the 'balkanization' of Europe. As he points out, this had been translated by those on both ends of the political spectrum into a belief that 'the idea of nationality as a basis for statehood is obsolete' (the words of the British socialist, G.D.H. Cole) and by Hitler and the Nazis into a contempt for 'small nations' (*Kleinstaaterei*). But the Atlantic Charter had implicitly renewed Wilson's pledge of self-determination for all nations, so how could the dilemma be resolved? As Cobban put it, '[t]he real task is to integrate them [the small states] into the fabric of a stable, prosperous, and peaceful world'.[87] This is still the 'real task'. Cobban's strikingly modern view of the problematique of the nation has been dramatically reinforced in its validity by the events since 1989 in Europe, which bear an uncanny resemblance to the problems of the inter-war period and before that, and in the problems encountered and still being faced up to by the emerging nations of the Third World.

A 'realist/statist' view is that the 'anarchical society' is still with us. They would further assert that there are few 'real' democracies and that therefore the Hobbesian struggle for power, influence and order will remain as the guiding logic of international, or intra-national, relations. A 'realist' might also argue that democracy, even in its European heartland, might not survive the onslaught of the East and South Asian economic challenge. How much more is this true of Eastern Europe, where democracy is in its infancy? The example of the former Yugoslavia has many times been used to demonstrate that no amount of UN resolutions or mediated plans brought about democracy, but rather that military logic brought (temporary) settlement.

A pessimistic view of the debate on self-determination as it has developed since the end of the Cold War might thus lead us to believe that Cobban's and Carr's arguments from the 1940s do not seem to have been improved upon. If a state can survive long enough to achieve some sort of historical reality *and* suit the purposes of local powerful states, it can survive. It must then give itself some *raison d'être* in order to continue to flourish. Survival will also depend on whether internal groups also support the state's survival, a support that can be seen to be in some doubt in many of the post-1991 new states.

But it must also be said that to look at self-determination in isolation (no matter how necessary this may be for analytical clarity), is to deny the interpenetration of the other elements of the NWO package, at least since 1990. Without considering the role of the global institutions, formal (such as the UN) and informal (such as civil society), we cannot adequately assess whether self-determination was indeed an effort of 'failed imagination'. We might also be tempted to argue, in considering the example of countries such as Eritrea, Ethiopia and South Africa in the post-Cold War situation, that the concept of self-determination has been given a crucial moral impulse by its success in freeing many of the peoples of Africa from post-colonial tyrants. The state in these cases now, for the first time, represents the people, in all their multi-ethnic and multinational splendour, but also reintegrates the moral and contractual elements of both state and individual rights. This granting of 'moral standing' by and to states is the key idea behind the thinking of new normative theorists of international relations such as Mervyn Frost.[88] It is a new idea in the context of many states that have suffered as badly at the hands of their post-colonial rulers as ever they did when colonised. Arguably, it is also an old idea re-born, as communitarian thinkers of the Hegelian persuasion would also find comfort in the state performing its role as a guardian and support for individual moral worth.[89]

The practical implications of these two kinds of conclusion for a study of self-determination are that either we are seeing the 'withering away of the autocratic state', the triumph of liberal capitalism and a new role for the individual, or we are in fact being deluded if we think that the state is finished or that power is still not essentially vested in successful states. This latter view would in no way deny that *un*-successful states might indeed be doomed, as has proved the repeated case over the past 500 years. The question, then, still has to be 'what constitute the essential elements of successful "stateness" in a post-Cold War world?'

Notes

1 Quoted in Alfred Cobban, *National Self-Determination* (London, Oxford University Press/RIIA, 1945), p. 45.
2 Mervyn Frost, 'Constituting a New World Order', *Paradigms*, vol. 8, no. 1, Summer 1994, p. 20.
3 Alfred O. Hirschman, *Exit, Voice and Loyalty: Responses to Decline in Firms, Organizations and States* (Cambridge, Mass., Harvard University Press, 1970).
4 Robert Cox, 'Social Forces, States and World Order: Beyond International Relations Theory', first published 1981 and reprinted in Robert Cox and Andrew Sinclair, *Approaches to World Order* (Cambridge University Press, 1996), pp. 85–123.
5 As R.J. Vincent has written, 'Rousseau … has been described as a Janus-like figure in the history of natural law, manifesting its individualism and universalism, but looking forward to romantic German thought in his idea of the general will.' Vincent, *Human Rights and International Relations* (Cambridge University Press, 1986), p. 26.
6 For a discussion of this see James Mayall, *Nationalism and International Society* (Cambridge University Press, 1990), pp. 26–28.
7 Percy Bysshe Shelley, 'The Mask of Anarchy', in *Selected Poems of Percy Bysshe Shelley*, edited by John Holbran (London, Heinemann, 1960), p. 23.
8 Also from the 'Mask of Anarchy': 'I met murder on the way; He had a face like Castlereagh', Shelley, *Selected Poems*, p. 18.
9 G.M. Trevelyan, *Garibaldi and the Making of Italy, June–November 1860* (London, Longman, 1911).
10 Andreas Osiander, *The States System of Europe, 1640–1990* (Oxford, Clarendon Press, 1994), p. 48.
11 For a recent discussion of this new, largely post-1989, 'normative' debate see Mervyn Frost, *Ethics in International Relations* (Cambridge University Press, 1996), Chris Brown, *International Relations Theory: New Normative Approaches* (Harvester/Wheatsheaf, 1992) and Michael Walzer, *Just and Unjust Wars* (New York, Basic Books, 2nd edn, 1992).
12 United Nations, Human Rights Committee General Comments, 12 (21) para. 1, *General Assembly Official Records*, Doc A/39/40, pp. 142–143, quoted by Robert McCorquodale, 'Human Rights and Self Determination', in Mortimer Sellers (ed.), *The New World Order: Sovereignty, Human Rights and the Self-Determination of Peoples* (Oxford, Berg, 1996), p. 11.
13 A very useful summary of this debate can be found in Nicholas J. Wheeler, 'Humanitarian Intervention and World Politics', in John Baylis and Steve Smith (eds), *The Globalization of World Politics* (Oxford University Press, 1997) and in Oliver Ramsbottom and Tom Woodhouse, *Humanitarian Intervention in Contemporary Conflict* (Cambridge, Polity Press, 1996). The expression 'settled norms' is explained in Frost, 'Constituting a New World Order'.
14 Mayall, *Nationalism and International Society*, p. 28.
15 Walker Connor, 'A Nation is a Nation, is a State, is an Ethnic Group, is a …', *Ethnic and Racial Studies* 1, October 1975, pp. 377–400, reprinted in Walker Connor (ed.), *Ethnonationalism* (Princeton University Press, 1994), pp. 90–117. Also extremely interesting is Seamus Dunn and T.G. Fraser (eds), *Europe and*

Ethnicity: World War One and Contemporary Ethnic Conflict (London, Routledge, 1996).

16 Brown, *International Relations Theory*; Frost, *Ethics in International Relations*; Terry Nardin, *Law, Morality and the Relations of States* (Princeton University Press, 1983) and Justin Rosenberg, *The Empire of Civil Society* (London, Verso, 1994).

17 This discussion could lead into the important, but complex, area of 'negative' and 'positive' liberty à la Isaiah Berlin, for which I refer the reader to Robert H. Jackson, *Quasi-States, Sovereignty, International Relations and the Third World* (Cambridge University Press, 1990), pp. 26–31.

18 Mill, quoted by Walzer, *Just and Unjust Wars*, p. 88.

19 Brown, *International Relations Theory*, p. 122.

20 Jackson, *Quasi-States*, p. 21.

21 For a detailed recent examination of this, see R.J. Crampton, *Eastern Europe in the Twentieth Century* (London, Routledge, 1994).

22 C.K. Webster, *British Diplomacy 1813–1815: Selected Documents Dealing with the Reconstruction of Europe* (London, Bell, 1921); Osiander, *The States System of Europe*, p. 198.

23 At the turn of the century Hobson defined imperialism as 'the recent expansion of Great Britain and the chief continental Powers' and showed that over 'the last thirty years ... a number of European nations, Great Britain being the first and foremost, have annexed or otherwise asserted political sway over vast portions of Africa and Asia, and over numerous islands in the Pacific and elsewhere'. J.A. Hobson, *Imperialism: A Study* (London, Allen and Unwin, 1902, 1938), p. 25 (1938 edn).

24 For the best exposition of Marx's views on imperialism, see Miklòs Molnàr, *Marx, Lénine at la politique internationale* (Paris, Presses Universitaires de France, 1966).

25 Rebecca West, *1900* (London, Weidenfeld and Nicholson, 1982), p. 86.

26 Hobson, *Imperialism*, pp. 82–83.

27 This is naturally a very schematic overview of the problematique of imperialism. The consensus on imperialism before the Second World War was that it was the product of economic forces in the metropoles. Challenges to this view arose in the 1950s, for example Robinson and Gallagher in 'The Imperialism of Free Trade', in G.H. Nadel and P. Curtis (eds), *Imperialism and Colonisation* (New York, Macmillan, 1966). They developed the concept of 'Informal Empire', so that for them the real heyday of British imperialism was during the period before the Scramble for Africa, with the exercise of economic but not necessarily political control, so that 'Empire' was only one aspect of imperialism, there being many other forms, Robinson and Gallagher being particularly exercised by the rise of US 'imperialism'.

28 Hobson, *Imperialism*, pp. 15–26.

29 Cobban, *National Self-Determination*, p. 13.

30 Derek Heater, *National Self-Determination – Woodrow Wilson and his Legacy* (London, Macmillan, 1994), pp. 18, 43 and 95 (quoting Wilson's speech of 4 September 1919). Point V of the Fourteen Points says that there should be 'A free, open-minded, and absolutely impartial adjustment of all colonial claims, based upon the principle that in determining all such questions of sovereignty

the interest of the populations concerned must be given equal weight with the equitable claims of the government whose title is to be determined.' See also Alan Sharp, 'The Genie that Would Not Go Back in the Bottle: National Self-Determination and the Legacy of the First World War and the Peace Settlement', in Dunn and Fraser, *Europe and Ethnicity*.

31 See, for example, Colonel House's 'Preface' to William Rappard, *Uniting Europe* (New Haven, Yale University Press, 1930).

32 Heater, *National Self-Determination*, p. 37.

33 For an excellent discussion of this see Tim Pat Coogan, *Michael Collins: A Biography* (London, Hutchinson, 1990), especially pp. 109–113. Churchill was quite aware of what the Irish case portended for the clash of British imperialism and Irish aspirations to self-determination as early as 1919: Churchill to Balfour, 5 July 1919; Balfour Papers, Mss. 49741.

34 Cobban, *National Self-Determination*, p. 124.

35 Churchill to Roosevelt, 21 May 1944; Roosevelt Papers, Box 24.

36 Hankey, Diary entry for 8 May 1919; HNKY 1/5.

37 Lloyd George rejected this draft proposal, so as to leave his hands free at the Conference: Hankey, Diary entries for 20 and 23 December 1918; HNKY 1/5; Lord Riddell, *Lord Riddell's Intimate Diary of the Peace Conference and After* (London, Victor Gollanz, 1933), entry for 22 December 1918, p. 5. Hankey was convinced that it was only on Botha's insistence that Smuts agreed to sign the Treaty and on Botha's death in August 1919 said he was 'one of the biggest men in the peace conference. He rarely intervened, but when he did it always produced a good effect': Diary entry for 28 August 1919; HNKY 1/5.

38 Eye-witness account by Hankey, Diary entry of 21 May 1919; HNKY 1/5.

39 Curzon wrote that Geddes (Lloyd George's main confidant in Cabinet) and Walter Long 'revel in the thought of the British flag flying over Constantinople, [and] ... think the Turk is not such a bad fellow after all ... and are firmly convinced that the only people who can solve this or any other problem are the British.' Curzon to Balfour, 20 August 1919; Balfour Papers, Mss. 49734.

40 Cecil, Manuscript Diary of the Peace Conference, entries for 11 January 1919 and 13 May 1919; Cecil Papers, Ms. 51131. Balfour's second comment is in Balfour to Churchill, 17 November 1919; Balfour Papers, Ms. 49694. For a summary of the clauses of Versailles as they applied to the former Ottoman Empire see Michael L. Dockrill and J. Gould, *Peace without Promise: Britain and the Peace Conferences, 1919–23* (London, Batsford, 1981), Chapters 4 and 5.

41 A fact that Balfour bemoaned after his eight months of continual service trying to find an equitable settlement, a list to which he also added Russia, the Adriatic and 'innumerable questions arising in regard to the execution of the Treaty with Germany – plebiscites in particular': Balfour to Curzon, 16 August 1919; Balfour Papers, Mss 49734.

42 Julius Andrassy, *Diplomacy and War* (London, 1921), p. 251, quoted by Rappard, *Uniting Europe*, p. 30.

43 West, *1900*, p. 66.

44 Gerrit Gong, *The Standard of Civilisation in International Society* (Oxford, Clarendon Press, 1984).

45 Balfour to Curzon, 8 September 1919; Balfour Papers, Mss. 49734.

46 Takako Ueta, 'The Genoa Conference and Japan', in Carole Fink, Axel Frohn and Jurgen Heideking (eds), *Genoa, Rapallo, and European Reconstruction in 1922* (Cambridge University Press, 1991), p. 226; Balfour, 'Memorandum on "D" and "C" Mandates, Memorandum on the Present Position', 20 July 1920; Balfour Papers, Mss. 49734.

47 For a very interesting treatment of this attempt at acceptance by China and Japan see Gong, *Standard of Civilisation*, Chapters 5 and 6.

48 Memo by Balfour at the Versailles Peace Conference of 31 May 1919; Balfour Papers, Mss. 49741.

49 If the population of pre-war and post-war Hungary is calculated, it went from 18.2 million to 7.6 million, with 3.425 million of these being Magyar: see Miklós Molnár, *Histoire de la Hongrie* (Paris, Hatier, 1996), especially Chapter 6. See also Raymond Pearson, 'Hungary, a State Threatened, a Nation Dismembered' in Dunn and Fraser, *Europe and Ethnicity*.

50 Allen Leeper, Diary, 1 April 1919: 'sent with Smuts ... to negotiate with Béla Kun and Co ... Crowe awfully nice about letting me go'; LEP 1/2. Leeper was Balfour's main technical assistant on Romania (his was the plan accepted in the definition of the Banat frontier; entry for 28 February 1919), for which Balfour also had a great deal of affection, whereas it is clear that he had none for Hungary.

51 Allen Leeper, Diary, 9 December 1920; LEP 1/3. There is a large amount of material on the Hungarian minorities in Romania which shows the discussion within the Quai d'Orsay about the Hungarian minorities and differences that emerged with Britain and American Church leaders over the issue: MAE, SDN, Secretariat Général/ID. 17. – Optants hongrois, Files 285–286, covering most of the 1920s. The issue was also referred on a number of occasions to the Conference of Ambassadors (which declared itself incompetent) and the Permanent Court of Arbitration of the League (the rulings of which were refused by Romania in 1927). See also C.A. Macartney, *Hungary and Her Successors* (London, Macmillan, 1937) and Raymond Pearson, *National Minorities and Eastern Europe, 1848–1945* (London, Macmillan, 1983).

52 Allen Leeper, Diary, entry for 8 June 1919; LEP 1/2.

53 The Austrian problem was not provisionally solved until after the Conference ended, with the Treaty of St Germain in September 1919.

54 Balfour to Curzon, 1 April 1919; Balfour Papers, Mss. 49734.

55 A.J.P. Taylor, *The Origins of the Second World War* (London, Hamish Hamilton, 1961) and Gordon Martel (ed.), *The Origins of the Second World War Reconsidered: The A.J.P. Taylor Debate after Twenty-five Years* (London, Allen and Unwin, 1986).

56 Hardinge quoted by Heater, *National Self-Determination*, p. 79, in turn quoting Jane Sharp, *The Versailles Settlement* (London, Macmillan, 1991), p. 156; Balfour to Curzon, 2 March 1919 and Curzon to Balfour, 2 March 1919; Balfour Papers, Mss. 49734.

57 Heater, *National Self-Determination*, p. 78; Cobban, *National Self-Determination*, p. 28.

58 Rappard, *Uniting Europe*, pp. 42 and 49.

59 Osiander, *The States System of Europe*, p. 250; Ortega y Gasset, *The Revolt of the Masses* (first published in English, London, Allen and Unwin, 1932).

60 Daniel Goldhagen, *Hitler's Willing Executioners: Ordinary Germans and the*

Holocaust (London, Abacus, 1996). See also Osiander, *The States System of Europe*, pp. 250–251, for some very interesting comments on the appeal of fascism and National Socialism in the context of post-1919 Europe.

61 Luis Dìez del Corral, *The Rape of Europe* (London, George Allen and Unwin, 1959), pp. 9–33.

62 For a discussion of Coundenhove-Kalergi's ideas see Ralph White, 'The Europeanism of Coundenhove-Kalergi', in Peter M.R. Stirk (ed.), *European Unity in Context: The Interwar Period* (London, Pinter, 1989), Chapter 2.

63 The literature on this is of course vast and cannot be given any kind of justice here. The following have been useful for me: Adolf Hitler, *Mein Kampf* (Boston, Houghton-Mifflin, 1943, first published in German in 1925); Robert Erwin Herzstein, *When Nazi Dreams Come True* (London, Abacus, 1982); Klaus Hildebrand, *The Foreign Policy of the Third Reich* (London, Batsford, 1973) and Alan Bullock, *Hitler: A Study in Tyranny* (London, Pelican, 1962).

64 The best of these is David E. Kaiser, *Economic Diplomacy and the Origins of the Second World War: Germany, France and Eastern Europe, 1930–1939* (Princeton University Press, 1980).

65 M.L. Smith, not an advocate of this view, says that we have 'to recognise that the Nazi attempt to shape the destiny of Europe was, in however perverted and unstable a manifestation, a form of European unity': M.L. Smith, 'Introduction: European Unity and the Second World War', in M.L. Smith and Peter Stirk, *Making the New Europe: European Unity and the Second World War* (London, Pinter, 1990), p. 6.

66 See Justus Doenecke (ed.), *In Danger Undaunted: The Anti-Interventionist Movement of 1940–1941 as Revealed in the Papers of the America First Committee* (Stanford, Hoover Institution Press, 1990), p. 18.

67 Peter Lyon, 'The Commonwealth and the Third World', in Robert O'Neill and R.J. Vincent (eds), *The West and the Third World: Essays Presented to J.D.B. Miller* (London, Macmillan, 1990), pp. 173–207.

68 Doenecke, *In Danger Undaunted*, documents produced by the AFC about *Union Now*, pp. 240–248.

69 Kennan, 'Russia and the Post-War Settlement', Summer 1942; Kennan Papers, 25/4.

70 Ortega y Gasset, *Revolt of the Masses*.

71 E.H. Carr *et al.*, *Nationalism: A Report by a Study Group of Members of the Royal Institute of International Affairs* (London, Oxford University Press, 1939).

72 Cobban, *National Self-Determination*, pp. 44–45.

73 Cobban, *National Self-Determination*, pp. 46–55.

74 Cobban, *National Self-Determination*, pp. 57–60 and 69.

75 Cobban, *National Self-Determination*, pp. 73–77.

76 Arnold J. Toynbee, 'First Thoughts on a Peace Settlement', Chatham House World Orders Group, File 9/18f. See also Chapter 4.

77 These three speeches (Zurich, 19 September 1946; London, 14 May 1947; and The Hague, 7 May 1947) have been re-published by the Conservative Group for Europe: *The Cause of a United Europe: Speeches by Winston Churchill on European Unity, 1946–48* (London, Conservative Group for Europe, 1996). Even during the war and after, it could be argued that he was a largely lone voice

in British politics and, of course, 1990s Conservative 'Euro-sceptic' critics of the federal idea tend to dismiss his comments as speculative and to emphasise his imperialism and advocacy of the American Alliance. They also point out that it was never intended that *Britain* should be part of this New Europe. See also Peter Duignan and L.H. Gann, *The United States and the New Europe, 1945–1953* (Oxford, Blackwell, 1994) and Anne Deighton (ed.), *Building Postwar Europe: National Decision-Makers and European Institutions, 1948–1963* (London, Macmillan, 1995).

78 Hedley Bull, *The Anarchical Society: A Study of Order in World Politics* (London, Macmillan, 1977).

79 Jackson, *Quasi-States*, pp. 15–16.

80 Especially during the period of the 'New International Economic Order' of the 1970s and the United Nations Educational, Scientific and Cultural Organisation (UNESCO's) ill-fated 'New International Information Order' in the 1980s, after which both the United States and Britain withdrew from UNESCO. This, of course, also had a 'safety valve' effect, allowing poorer states to vent their spleen about the Great Powers in a safe way.

81 Cirino Hiteng, 'Discourses on Liberation and Democracy in Sub-Saharan Africa: The Cases of Eritrea and Ethiopia', unpublished PhD thesis, University of Kent at Canterbury, 1997, p. 270.

82 Ruth Iyob, *The Eritrean Struggle for Independence: Domination, Resistance, Nationalism, 1941–1993* (Cambridge University Press, 1995).

83 Alex Danchev and Thomas Halverson (eds), *International Perspectives on the Yugoslav Conflict* (London, Macmillan, 1996) is a collection that tells the story from many different ethnic points of view.

84 Daniel Moynihan, *Pandaemonium: Ethnicity in International Politics* (Oxford University Press, 1993), p. 5 and, especially, Chapter 5, 'Order in an Age of Chaos'. On more recent reflections in the same vein see the special issue of *International Security*, 'Ethnic Nationalism, Conflict and War': Fall 1996, vol. 21, no 2. Stuart J. Kaufman's 'Spiraling to Ethnic War: Elites, Masses, and Moscow in Moldova's Civil War', pp. 108–138, concludes, 'it may be easier to maintain inter-ethnic peace than many believe!'.

85 Other recent treatments about the dangers of ethnic conflict since the end of the Cold War can be found in Michael E. Brown (ed.), *Ethnic Conflict and International Security* (Princeton University Press, 1993); Robert Gurr and Barbara Harff, *Ethnic Conflict in World Politics* (Boulder, Colorado, Westview Press, 1994) and Larry Diamond and Marc F. Plattner (eds), *Nationalism, Ethnic Conflict and Democracy* (Baltimore and London, Johns Hopkins University Press, 1994). See the Conclusion below for some comments on this literature.

86 When the present writer went to Eritrea in 1993, a few months after formal independence, I was astonished by how willing the new Government (feared as ultra-Marxist until 1992!) was to accept the rules of an interdependent liberal global economy and the needs of democratic government.

87 Cobban, *National Self-Determination*, pp. 2–3.

88 Mervyn Frost, unpublished manuscript on the 'Moral Standing of States', University of Kent at Canterbury, 1997.

89 Vincent, *Human Rights*, p. 71, and unpublished manuscript by Frost, 1997.

Conclusion

'Failed imagination'?
Has the NWO idea worked?

The main exploration of this book has been into the historical origins and development of the NWO idea, particularly as it applied to the experiences of the First and Second World Wars. In this Conclusion the main aim is to sum up what are seen as the main messages that might be drawn from this material. It is also to ask, at least tentatively, where we might go from here. Are we, in George Bush's words that launched the NWO of 1990, now heading for 'a world where the rule of law supplants the rule of the jungle, a world in which nations respect the shared responsibility for freedom and justice, a world where the strong respect the rights of the weak'?[1] Or can one agree with Daniel Moynihan's warning of only three years later: '[C]onsider that in 1914 the optimists contended it was not 1914. Would it not be at least useful to consider the possibility that the world is in a significant sense back at that juncture in history and that this time we might make a better job of it?'[2] Do the historical lessons of the previous two attempts give us cause for optimism or pessimism?

In the Introduction I asked the question: 'What functions do NWOs perform?' The initial proposal was that they are about the creation of 'balance, order and stability' and the 'defining of an intellectual climate'. I also inferred that the NWO agenda might be seen as one way of helping to create a truly 'international society', where common norms and practices of statecraft and morality are widely accepted by all states in the interests of all individuals within those states. It must, in other words, be seen as an attempt to create an international society that has a truly universal practical and moral basis. The question now has to be whether the third NWO that has now been declared can succeed as the second version did, at least as regards the 'West', or fail as did the first, and whether this will be, to adapt the words of T.S. Eliot, 'with a bang or with a whimper'?

The conclusions that we can draw from the material presented in this book might be summed up by saying that 'there's many a slip twixt cup and lip' for those who try to engineer the future through the pursuit of a global political agenda. The collapse of the Soviet Union and the crushing of Nazi

Germany, both of which promulgated their own version of an NWO, are eloquent testimony to that. But the rapid descent from planned order into unplanned chaos that was clear after both 1919 and 1945 indicates that liberal NWOs can also encounter their problems. And as the crisis in the former Yugoslavia and the break-up of the Soviet Union have shown us, neither of them widely predicted in 1989, we cannot be sure that this NWO will not go the way of the other two this century. This is the logic of those who believe, like John Mearsheimer, that we are now going 'back to the future', or that of Samuel Huntington, who thinks that the most optimistic scenario is one of 'us and them', but more likely ones are either 'sheer chaos' or the 'clash of civilisations'. He, and indeed many others, rejects out of hand the optimistic liberal scenario of Francis Fukuyama that asserts that we are now seing the 'End of History' and the triumph of liberal capitalism that is at the heart of the NWO project.[3]

It is always dangerous to plan the future when the parameters of that future have so many possible ways to evolve. As has been accepted here, the dreams of the Anglo-American NWO architects upon which this book has focused can be easily ridiculed. The belief that Europe could be made to live at peace with itself, that international organisation might provide a functional alternative to war, that self-determination might provide a universal sense of freedom, that there is a 'harmony of interests' that might unite humankind in economic and political harmony, are all ideas that have met their Waterloo at various times since 1914. These beliefs have also aroused enormous hostility because they are seen as being the creation of one civilisation, that of the 'West', or even more narrowly of the 'Anglo-American civilisation'.[4]

This should lead us to two basic observations: first, that any idea we might have harboured about NWOs being successful conspiracies by the rich and powerful against the weak and powerless is slightly preposterous; second, that serendipity can never be seen in advance, no matter how logical and consequential the NWO planners tried to be. The NWO has never been more than an ideal type, and this ideal has often been at clear variance with the historical results. However, this does not mean that we should therefore abandon it as a construct. It is far too potent a vehicle of too many kinds of belief system for that.

We might therefore propose that these ideas have aroused enormous interest and scorn in equal amounts precisely because they are at the very heart of the political, social and economic problematique of humanity. If we could bring together, across the generations, the 'true believers', the architects of the NWOs of this century, they would undoubtedly assert that, in spite of the setbacks, their ideas have provided a clear alternative agenda to the international relations that caused the First World War. They would claim that they have provided a modern, progressive and just aspirational framework for the twentieth century and beyond for the whole of humankind, not just one section of it. They would further assert that NWO ideas are an attempt to create a 'civilised' way for the further progress of the liberal ideal of the Enlightenment. Many other 'non-believers' would and do assert that the NWOs have not delivered a 'fair' or 'just' world, or even that what we now have is an unjust, unequal and divided world masquerading as a unified and contented one.

Are we therefore, as John Kenneth Galbraith once asserted, blinded in the late 1990s by a 'culture of contentment' in our consideration of the fate of the NWO project, or should we not rather consider another of Galbraith's aphorisms: 'Courage is required of the man who, when things are good, says so. Historians rejoice in crucifying the false prophet of the millennium. They never dwell on the mistake of the man who wrongly predicted Armaggedon.'[5] The NWO must be judged on whether it has indeed furthered the ideals that are claimed for it, or whether it has failed in that task. Excessive pessimism is as debilitating as excessive optimism in coming to sensible judgements.

Universality?

One key *leitmotif* of NWO thinking is that it must at least aim to be inclusive for all states and peoples, an idea eventually and slowly expanded after 1945 to include all individual human beings in the notion of universal human rights. In the words of the Fourteen Points, 'open diplomacy' will provide transparency; a global 'League of Nations' of some kind will give every state a voice and a protector through 'collective security'; the unfettering of a benevolent capitalism will give economic opportunity to all; and self-determination will ensure the liberation of enslaved peoples. On at least two occasions in 1919 and 1945 the hopes of those who thought that these ideas could be universalised were dashed. To be more precise, in 1919 these hopes were comprehensively demolished, in 1945 severely modified to apply to the 'Free World' not the whole world.

John Hall seems to argue that this means that 'international orders' have never created 'world orders … that is [,] an arena of justice in which human beings will be welcomed as universal strangers', that the imperatives of power and justice will be for ever separate.[6] Many of the commentators quoted in this book would have agreed, though not out of any great sense of a need for justice for 'all'. For people such as Maurice Hankey, Edward Grey, Winston Churchill and Henry Stimson, 'civilisation' was that of the 'English-speaking peoples'. Others would have to be included as they merited the 'upgrade'. I would put it differently, although without necessarily dis-agreeing with Hall about the ultimate possible futility of a really just 'world order'. The fundamental question has to be about the success of the main elements of NWO thinking in ordering our mental and physical universe and their general acceptability to a wide majority of the world's citizens.

The NWO's success has been not so much due to the universal application of its main tenets as to the quasi-universal acceptance of these tenets as aspirations in what we can describe as a 'holistic package'. It was made clear after 1919 and 1945, and arguably now in the period of the third NWO after 1990, that no one part of the NWO 'package' can be taken in isolation from the others. To attempt to ensure a world that is secure, economically 'porous' (to use Dulles' expression), and where nations and individuals have rights through self-determination in a democratic order, all of these elements have to be fulfilled simultaneously. Eliminate any one of these key elements and the others are in grave peril. The package did not hang together in any way after 1919, and after 1945 it only held together regionally for the 'Free World'. However, if each of these ideas is assessed against the world we now have post-1990, it might be argued that the NWO ideal has indeed come to pass. The end of the Cold War and the proclamation of a 'third' NWO in the wake of the demise of the Soviet Union led, at least initially, to widespread feelings that there would be a significant increase in the number of states in the international system that adhere to NWO principles and a corollary 'third wave' of democratisation.[7]

However, if we can accept that we now have more or less global acceptance of the key ideas of the NWO, we can also admit that the victory is not truly and finally won. There are still major pockets of resistance to liberal capitalism, both within Western societies and outside them. Self-determination has proved a very damaging genie to have unleashed, and it is difficult to say that the ideal Wilsonian variant has been, or will be, triumphant. We could point to the argument that the wars in the former Yugoslavia and Rwanda are severe negations of this rosy picture. Huntington, among others, has voiced his fear that democracy can also bite back at those who spread its word, with the danger that it will create Third World elites hostile to the United States and the West. To this it might be added that the current 'renegade states',[8] as the current regimes in Iran, Iraq, Libya, North Korea and Cuba (for example) might be described, have only scanty claim to being called 'democracies'.

Liberal optimism

Nonetheless, some prominent 'liberals', most famously Francis Fukuyama, have expressed the view that with the end of the Cold War the spread of liberal democracy and its hand-maiden liberal capitalism would most probably ensure the progressive setting up of 'ideal states', as 'the modern liberal democratic state ... is free of contradictions'.[9] These states would not go to war with each other, such would be their commitment to common norms of belief and behaviour. There would be no more 'renegades'. We would therefore achieve the basic ingredients for a lasting 'democratic peace' and the balance, order and stability that are the key aim both of most advocates of an 'international society' and of the NWO architects. In such a world the rule of law would by and large be respected, both for minorities and majorities, as the 'subject' of law would be the individual, and the maximising of his political and economic freedom the aim of political organisation. This would be a self-regulating, non-coercive world order, imbued with its own legitimacy and hence immeasurably strong.

But what would we in fact end up with? The most revealing insights of the 'End of History' debate lie at least partly in the fact that in asking whether we have reached it, as Chris Brown says, Fukuyama has 'ask[ed] the right sort of question'.[10] These questions are to do with what will now happen to the international system that is the product of the period 1914–89. In particular does the 'Worldwide Liberal Revolution' and the triumph of the 'middle class' (in the American sense) mean that the world will become one vast 'universal and homogenous state ... resting on the twin pillars of economics and recognition', as Fukuyama puts it? To be sure, the triumph of liberal democratic ideology and the quasi-total destruction of a socialist alternative is far from complete, says Fukuyama, but the clear advantages of living in a Western consumerist society are now demonstrated, not least because such societies do not tend to go to war with each other.[11]

This is not to deny that the 'liberals' are a category of thinkers that it would be dangerous to conflate too completely. Fukuyama's thesis holds within it some rather dark, Nietzschean, views of the future, ones that carry an explicit warning of not indulging in over-confidence about the liberal 'triumph'.[12] But in support of this optimism we can cite a number of overlapping currents. These mainly have to do with the expansion of what are usually termed the areas of 'democracy' and of 'civil society'.

The democratic peace?

Many commentators in both public and official life now take it as axiomatic that democracies do not go to war with each other, the 'democratic peace thesis', and that therefore a mutually held respect for the rights of states and individuals might well lead to Kant's 'Perpetual Peace'.[13] States that are democracies have to respect the checks and balances of public opinion, and they have to take into account 'net welfare costs' in initiating conflict.[14] This has seemed to be confirmed by empirical studies of which states have started wars. It seemed to follow therefore that an increase in the number of democracies would result in greater peace and stability. This in turn would lead to a reduction of global military tension, which would in turn lead to reduced spending on defence ('the peace dividend') and a more widespread adherence to the norms of international conduct. Such logic was very similar to that espoused by Woodrow Wilson in 1919 and the PWP planners of the

Second World War – a world made safe for, and by, democracy. One aspect of the extension of this debate has led to a huge discussion about the problems of reconciling state, individual and majority/minority interests in the normative discussions outlined in Chapter 8.[15]

One argument that has been evoked in this book, and elsewhere, is that integration into a capitalist world order will ensure norm- and rule-based behaviour. Not only will states behave themselves in a bid to achieve membership of Western institutions that guarantee them security and economic prosperity, but they will be forced to obey the norms and rules that make such security and prosperity possible. The inalienable right to property, and Fukuyama's 'right to consume', swing the balance of power within any state in favour of the individual consumer and producer and against the dark forces of internal repression or of conflict with other states. The transformation of the warring states of Europe of 1914 or 1939 into the European Union is often portrayed as one key evidence of this process in action.

Will the 'ethnic' upheaval in the former Yugoslavia and elsewhere noted in the previous chapter continue and disturb this happy scene? On the positive side we have seen dire warnings of widespread ethnic conflict across Europe of 1990 proven untrue because the Romanian, Hungarian and Slovak states have been forced to come to an agreement of their long-running disputes over Magyar minorities in the region. Regional integration, goes the argument of its promoters, will ensure that this process continues by breaking down barriers between states, creating Dulles' 'structural porosity' and making them all feel citizens of a much larger entity than the state, that of a European, and ultimately of a global, civil society. Similar claims have been made about the likely resolution of intra-European Union disputes, like that over Northern Ireland.[16] Some commentators on the former Yugoslavia have suggested that economic and political reasons are the real cause of the 'ethnic' conflict there, in other words that ethnicity is not the true cause of the problem, and that there are deeper layers of meaning that might be explored such as the needs for old *nomenklatura* elites to keep their jobs.[17] Another argument, as made by Martin Shaw, is that even if states do not wish to adhere to the norms and practices of global civil society, the forces of globalisation and 'people power' will make it inevitable that they do so.[18] Perhaps the conflict in the former Yugoslavia has provided the great service of showing other Europeans what awaits them if they do things the old nationalist way, instead of going along the global, or at least the regional, route.

Thus the main aim of the NWO architects of 1919 and 1945 might be said to have been advanced – the Soviet Union and its satellites and many other states, in Africa, Asia and elsewhere, now proclaim themselves as 'democracies'. Moreover, it might be said that the confusion that existed until 1991 about what might genuinely be called a 'democracy' can be said to have disappeared. Little credence is now given to the idea of 'democratic centralism' as practised by Soviet-style states since 1917, except perhaps in China, Cuba and North Korea, and even there it is subject to attack from within and without.

But it would still be facile to claim that democracy has 'triumphed'. It is still a concept that has seen most of its development as an idea in literate (Western) European societies in a particular brew of cultural interaction, capitalism and state formation over many centuries. How can this be translated without at least some loss of definition to areas of the world where such a brew is either a recent import or an uneasy adjunct to a pre-existing set of historical forms? As Fukuyama himself admits, democracy needs a 'sense of national identity, religion, social equality, the propensity for civil society, and the historical experience of liberal institutions – [which] collectively constitute the culture of a people'.[19] This sounds suspiciously like a concatenation of ideals that only applies to the United States and its Western European Allies since 1945 – in fact to Clarence Streit's 'Fifteen'.

Pessimism

There are dissenting voices, even among the liberals that essentially agree with the above arguments of the 'optimists'. Joanne Gowa takes to task the idea that trade will always tend to bind democracies in non-conflictual relationships, the idea posited powerfully by Norman Angell in 1910. Her warning is that, although this may well be true among 'real' democracies, what about those 'new' democracies, such as those of Eastern Europe, where the rules of the game are not fully understood?[20] It might be added that if this simple rule of trade reciprocity and good behaviour is not understood, how much more so might this be said to apply to human rights behaviour? Not a day goes past without evidence of a political trial or other human rights scandal in one of the former states of the Warsaw Pact. To assume that all these states either understand or want really to play by the rules of the democratic game might be said to be an illusion.

This is also the pessimistic logic inherent in Samuel Huntington's *The Clash of Civilisations*, which seems to contradict (in the mid-1990s) his optimism about democratisation of only a few years before. It is a pessimism that we have seen echoed many times in this book, a disposition to see the difficulties of bringing other (essentially non-European) peoples into the fold of Anglo-American 'civilisation'. From a different (more radical) starting point, Robert Cox also says that the spread of real, as opposed to 'formal', democracy is an essential prerequisite of an NWO, without which it will not even be 'perceived'. His view is that the 'Cold War has not ended [because] [t]he structures of Cold War power continue to exist in the West', now directed against 'Islamic Fundamentalism' or the 'Japan problem' or whatever. His critique is based on a belief that true democratisation requires a 'rebuilding of the structures of social equity and political authority'. By this he means creating a 'coherent global order ... something more than the existing state-centered multilateralism. It would have to be the expression of the cultural diversity of reconstituted civil societies.' Since he rejects the current '[p]olarizing economic globalism' (i.e international capitalism or 'hyper-liberalism') and American leadership, it is not surprising that he feels pessimistic that this can be done.[21]

The horror of living in a kind of permanent Disneyland is of course one of the aspects of a liberal capitalist vision that shocks any thinking human being. Much more seriously, many will feel excluded, those who do not live in Western consumerist societies. Fukuyama looks suspiciously complacent as he stares at us from his book-jacket. This seeming arrogance of the Anglo-American Establishment lies at the root of many of the charges of a unfeeling and Imperialist West made by the critics of the NWO idea. It has certainly resurfaced in the recent crisis over United Nations attempts, backed by United States and British threats of the use of force, to inspect Iraqi weapons sites. It is not so much that anyone doubts that the Iraqis have weapons of mass destruction and that they are trying to conceal them contrary to UN Security Council resolutions, but rather that the world community does not feel that the principles of equity, or indeed democracy, are being respected. It rather looks as though there is one law for the powerful and another for the weak and defenceless. This is the logic of Cox's critique of the current attempts to implement a third NWO and one that cannot be easily countered without a much more transparent system of global accountability.

Is the NWO 'fair'?

So the 'American ideology', that of the innate superiority and eventual triumph of the liberal democratic (or constitutional) state, contested by the Soviet Union and its 'Allies' for many years, is now contested by various kinds of Islamic and other 'fundamentalists', as well as by those who believe that the balance has swung too far from 'recognition' and 'self-respect' to consumerism. Not least it has been attacked by a wide and often incoherent coalition of those who fear that the Americanisation of the globe will result in a destruction of traditional values or lead to a new kind of master–slave relationship becoming the norm, one which values only material accomplishment with a Hollywood accent.

Others predict an 'inevitable' disorder, due to the chaotic nature of the capitalism itself, as it dives into 'hyper-liberalism'.[22] The rosy picture of the benefits of 'embedded liberalism' outlined in Chapter 7 for the Japanese case has also been counterattacked for having simultaneously subjugated the poor of the Third World to the American multinational companies and, moreover, not delivering the goods except to those particularly favoured by the United States (such as Japan). No one could claim that the Philippines, for example, has been able to exploit the existence of a free market, and access to US markets in particular, yet its situation was very similar in other ways to that of Japan in 1945.

One of the most prolific of such critics has been Noam Chomsky, originally a Nobel Prize winner for his work on linguistics, now the main spokesman for what remains of the radical American left. He cleaves to the idea of a military industrial complex in the USA, first properly articulated by C. Wright Mills in the 1950s, one that allegedly created an order designed solely to help American and (to some extent) British capitalist interests.[23] The NWOs of Wilson and Roosevelt, and even more so that of George Bush, are seen by Chomsky as continuing a nefarious control over the inter-national proletariat and the power of the US working class. Wilson is accused, along with many (indeed most) prominent American politicians and capitalists, of engineering the destruction of what was termed 'the enemy within'. Chomsky approvingly quotes Thomas Dewey as saying that '[American] politics is the shadow cast on society by big business'. It does not represent the people, rather the political and economic elites.[24] Chomsky paints a sombre picture of American hegemonic intentions that is in stark contrast to the idea of a benevolent hegemony drawn for the 1920s and 1930s by Hogan or to the ideal of 'embedded liberalism' of such thinkers as Ruggie.

On the right, as on the left, the NWOs have been seen as wanting, often because they are seen as having privileged 'prosperity' of a particular, capitalist, kind over the right of peoples to determine their own economic and political destiny. Some have even asserted that the American NWOs are mainly inspired by a liberal millenerianism, an extension of 'manifest destiny' to the global scale.[25] The United States has consequently been condemned by many that oppose what Juergensmayer calls its 'ideology of order', which he traces back to Alexis de Tocqueville's observation that both the French and American Revolutions had the political attributes of a 'civil religion'.[26] This effective intellectual cooperation of opposites in an anti-liberal coalition has shown itself both in the intellectual motivations of many movements that have had totalitarian leanings with their attacks on the 'failures' of capitalism as well as in the individual humanistic critiques of modern society.

In recent years George Kennan can be seen as one of the most effective conservative critics of these trends from the right, with his *At a Century's Ending* (1988) and *Around the Cragged Hill* (1993).[27] Kennan's conserv-ative views on modernity and its ills are not just based on a nostalgia for a past agricultural lifestyle based on decent folk pursuing God-fearing lives in cooperative harmony. They are also based on an understandable fear for a world of atomised individuals leading essentially meaningless lives. In

France, Zaki Laïdi' s *Un monde privé de sens* (a world without meaning) has made a similar point. With 'hyper-liberalism', the state can no longer perform its protective function, so at the social level individuals see global prosperity but 'individual precarity'. The state is what has given individuals a sense of 'meaning' (*sens*) for generations, globalisation (*mondialization*) leaves both individual people and states with none.[28]

Socialist programmes received a major set-back with the end of the Cold War. But the critique of 'hyper-liberalism' has given them a new lease of life as capitalism continues to experience its periodic catastrophes, even after the 'End of History'. There has also been a reformulation, particularly of the Marxist critique of 'base and superstructure'. For example, Justin Rosenberg's critique in the *Empire of Civil Society* is based on the supposition, one that echoes Chomsky and other 'structuralist' writers such as Cox, that the dominant 'social structures' (such as capitalism) determine the dominant 'political institutions' which in turn results in the dominance of a certain kind of 'geopolitical power'. Hence there has been a direct correspondence of structure, institution and power throughout history. The state and the inter-state system and capitalism are the beneficiaries of this process over many centuries. So is a division of the spoils, with the rich (crudely put) getting richer and the poor getting poorer. In a striking phrase Rosenberg writes that '[t]he community of nations ... thus has its public "heaven" (the sovereign states system) and its private "earth" (the transnational global economy).'[29] For Rosenberg 'civil society', which is often touted as the main beneficiary of an open liberal capitalist system, is in fact a synonym for capitalism itself – freedom for the rich, not for the poor. Indeed, for Rosenberg, 'sovereignty' itself is a 'capitalist political form'.[30] Although not an explicit attack on the NWO project, the criticism is implicit as it makes clear a belief that only the core West that designed the NWO can hope to benefit from it.

The trouble with all such views is that they are very difficult to sustain with hard evidence. In a review of *World Orders, Old and New*, in the *Times Higher Education Supplement* shortly after the book was published, Anthony Giddens commented that '[Chomsky's] west-as-villain, US-as-villain thesis is to my mind so sharply and monolithically drawn as to be quite unpersuasive'. Among his other criticisms Giddens points out that poorer countries' problems cannot be deemed to be merely the responsibility of the 'rich north'. The concerns and interests of states are not just a thin cloak for the power of corporate capital. The expansion of the west, and modernity, more generally, is not just a matter of the spread of free market capitalism; the system of states, and its associated power struggles, has its own autonomy.'[31] All of the opponents of the American NWO would argue that the US has indeed imposed its own *mission civilisatrice* through a mixture of military power and economic muscle. However, would they also disagree with the basic norms of the Atlantic Charter, the Four Freedoms or the Charter of the United Nations? Or could they just denounce these as a smokescreen for some 'real' hidden agenda?

Of 'trust' and 'social capital'

Another, linked, kind of question might nonetheless be, 'what might be said to be the ultimate "glue" that determines the success or failure of the NWO project?' Perhaps the greatest threat to the rosy picture of a triumphant global liberal capitalism has been suggested by Fukuyama himself. In his latest works he suggests that liberal capitalist societies may implode as post-Fordist capitalism destroys our stock of 'social capital', which in turn he sees as the guarantor of a wider civil society, global or national. By 'social capital' he means that 'certain set of informal values and norms shared among members of a group that permit co-operation among them', a kind of capital that exists in, and is created most naturally in, traditional nuclear families and in stable communities that have widespread cooperative networks – based on mutual 'trust'. Hence traditional societies such as China and Japan that stress family ties and social hierarchy and deference might flourish more than those who allow globalisation to put work and productivity before family ties and religious belief. Laïdi takes this view further in his warning that 'globalisation' cannot serve as a focus for global meaning given its vague locus and its consequent inability to evoke trust or loyalty, the very basis of what Fukuyama says makes up the formation of social capital.[32]

Nicholas Rengger also takes up the question of 'trust' and widens it by arguing that no international system can continue in existence without it existing not only within national societies but also *between* them. Rengger's treatment of the idea posits that without a 'presumption of trust' by the main actors in international relations it is 'difficult to sustain at least minimally tolerable conditions for collective social life globally'. We have this problem currently, in our third NWO, 'owing to the growing discrepancy between the legal and institutional forms of world politics', he argues.[33] How much more so was this the case in the inter-war period? Is it now worse? Or perhaps this is Fukuyama's 'Last Man' to which we should pay urgent attention.

Some final remarks

Which of these optimistic or pessimistic scenarios is right may depend on just *how far integrated* our 1990s world, as a result of the latest NWO, actually proves to be. Will we come to see the 'fault lines between civilisations [as] the battle lines of the future', in Huntington's words?[34] The 'civilisation' that was consciously proposed as a universal model by Wilson, Roosevelt, Bush and their advisory teams was one which was first based on a particular interpretation of the nature of the nation state and its problems as a category likely to lead to progress for humankind. It was also, second, a postulation of a set of values, often summed up as 'human rights', which derive their being from a narrowly Western cultural experience that was seen as universalisable. R.J. Vincent, among others, made the case that the notion of human rights is an essentially Western construct.[35] Whether one takes the view that this therefore diminishes the validity of this construct depends on whether one thinks there are alternative viable or morally justifiable constructs that are 'better'. I think not, a personal prejudice based on a belief in the benefits of bourgeois individualism, the relative success of which has helped me in the writing of this book. Third, it was underpinned by the notion of a mode of production, capitalism, which was seen as a better form than that developed in Europe, one that underpins individual initiative in a global market-place. Again, what better system do we have?

NWO ideas may come to be seen by later generations as the last great attempt of global social engineering by Western statesmen and women before the lure of globalisation finally sucked us into ecological and cultural oblivion. They should rather be seen as the last attempt by powerful states to create a world safe for states to flourish globally in a truly international society and that can potentially lead to a global civil society that recognises the right to difference and diversity. Critics of this utopia would assert that it assumes the benevolence of the initiating 'mind', that it assumes that the benefits will be properly distributed and that the results will not be catastrophic in terms of moral equity and justice. This book is not intended to predict either the 'Millennium' or 'Armageddon', but it is cautiously optimistic ...

Notes

1 George Bush, 11 September 1990, *Department of State Dispatch*, 1:3, p. 91, quoted by Molly Cochrane, 'The New World Order and International Political Theory', *Paradigms*, vol. 8, no. 1, Summer 1994, pp. 108–109. As Hall points out, Bush's most complete statement of his NWO idea was to the General Assembly of the UN on 1 October 1990: John Hall, *International Orders* (Cambridge, Polity, 1996), p. xi.

2 Daniel Moynihan, *Pandaemonium: Ethnicity and International Politics*, (Oxford University Press, 1993), pp. 8–9.

3 John Mearsheimer, 'Back to the Future', in Sean M. Lynn-Jones (ed.), *The Cold War and After: Prospects for Peace* (Cambridge, Mass., MIT Press, 1991); Samuel P. Huntington, *The Clash of Civilisations and the Remaking of World Order*, (New York, Simon and Schuster, 1996), pp. 29–39; Francis Fukuyama, *The End of History and the Last Man* (New York, The Free Press, 1992).

4 Cf. Christopher Coker's *The Twilight of the West* (Boulder, Colorado, Westview, 1998). This was published too late for a proper consideration of its contents for this book.

5 John Kenneth Galbraith has often been quoted for his warning about the 'culture of contentment' which blinds the rich to the sufferings of the poor. See, for example, John Burton and Tarja Väyrynen, 'The End of International Relations?', in A.J.R. Groom and Margot Light (eds), *Contemporary International Relations: A Guide to Theory* (London, Pinter, 1994), pp. 69–80; John Kenneth Galbraith, *The Great Crash, 1929* (London, Pelican Books, 1962), p. 30.

6 Hall, *International Orders*, p. 6.

7 Samuel P. Huntington, *The Third Wave: Democratization in the Late Twentieth Century* (Norman, University of Oklahoma Press, 1991).

8 Stephen Chan and Andrew Williams (eds), *Renegade States: The Evolution of Revolutionary Foreign Policy*, (Manchester University Press, 1992). See also David Armstrong, *Revolution and World Order* (Oxford University Press, 1992).

9 Andrew Linklater, 'Liberal Democracy, Constitutions and the New World Order', in Richard Leaver and James L. Richardson (eds), *Charting the Post-Cold War Order* (Boulder, Colorado, Westview, 1993), pp. 29–38; Fukuyama, *End of History*, p. 139.

10 Chris Brown, 'The End of History', in Alex Danchev (ed.), *Fin de Siècle: The Meaning of the Twentieth Century* (London, I.B. Tauris, 1995), p. 2.

11 Fukuyama, *End of History*, p. 204.

12 He has, of course, been criticised for other sins, as in Timothy Burns (ed.), *After History: Francis Fukuyama and His Critics* (London, Littlefield Adams, 1994) and Christopher Bartram and A. Chitty, *Has History Ended?* (Aldershot, Avebury Publishing, 1994).

13 There have been a number of useful summaries of this debate, including Christopher Layne, 'Kant or Cant?: The Myth of Democratic Peace' and replies from John Owen and David Spiro, *International Security*, vol. 19, no. 2, 1994; Raymond Cohen, 'Pacific Unions: A Reappraisal of the Theory that Democracies Do Not Go to War with Each Other', *The Review of International Studies*, vol. 20, 1994, pp. 202–232; and Steve Chan, 'In Search of the Democratic Peace: Problems and Promise', *The Mershon International Studies Review*, vol. 41, Supplement 1, May 1997, pp. 59–91, which has an extensive summary bibliography attached.

14 Joanne Gowa, 'Democratic States and International Disputes', *International Organization*, vol. 49, no. 3, Summer 1995, pp. 511–522.

15 Apart from the readings suggested in the Introduction and in Chapter 8 from the 'normative school' of international relations, the following are also suggestive: Rein Mullerson, *International Law, Rights and Politics* (London, Routledge 1994); Gabor Kardos, 'Can Ethnic Conflicts Ever be Resolved? The Implications of Ethnic Conflicts in Eastern and Central Europe', in Pal Dunay, Gabor Kardos and Andrew Williams (eds), *New Forms of Security: Views from Central, Eastern and Western Europe*, Aldershot, Dartmouth, 1995), pp. 133–149; and Cass R. Sunstein, 'Approaching Democracy: A New Legal Order for Eastern Europe – Constitutionalism and Secession', in Chris Brown (ed.), *Political Restructuring in Europe: Ethical Perspectives* (London, Routledge, 1994), pp. 11–49.

16 Gerard Delanty, 'Negotiating the Peace in Northern Ireland', *Journal of Peace Research*, vol. 32, no. 5, 1995, pp. 257–264.

17 See, for example, Vesna Pesiç in Larry Diamond and Marc. F. Plattner, *Nationalism, Ethnic Conflict and Democracy* (Baltimore and London, Johns Hopkins University Press, 1994).

18 Martin Shaw, *Global Society and International Relations: Sociological Concepts and Political Perspectives*, (Cambridge, Polity, 1996) and Mervyn Frost, *Ethics in International Relations: A Constitutive Theory* (Cambridge University Press, 1996).

19 Fukuyama, *End of History*, p. 219.

20 Gowa, 'Democratic States'.

21 Robert Cox, 'Influences and Commitments', in Robert W. Cox with Timothy J. Sinclair, *Approaches to World Order* (Cambridge University Press, 1996), pp. 30–35.

22 Again, a key point of reference has to be Robert Cox, *Approaches to World Order*. Other critiques can be found in Bjorn Hettne (ed.), *International Political Economy: Understanding Global Disorder* (London, Zed Books, 1995); Robert Cox, 'Structural Issues of Global Governance: Implications for Europe', in Stephen Gill (ed.), *Gramsci, Historical Materialism and International Relations* (Cambridge University Press, 1993); and Roger Burbach, Orlando Núñez and Boris Kagarlitsky, *Globalization and its Discontents: The Rise of Postmodern Socialisms* (London, Pluto, 1997).

23 Chomsky describes Britain as 'America's loyal subsidiary' which can nonetheless at least 'appeal to an imperial tradition of refreshing candour, unlike the United States, which has preferred to don the garb of saintliness as it proceeds to crush anyone in its path, a stance that is called "Wilsonian idealism"': Noam Chomsky, *World Orders, Old and New* (London, Pluto Press, 1994), p. 5.

24 Chomsky, *World Orders*, pp. 84–87.

25 See, for example, Michael H. Hunt, *Ideology and U.S. Foreign Policy* (New Haven, Yale University Press, 1988). See also Stefan Rossbach, 'Gnostic Wars: The Cold War in the Context of a History of Western Spirituality', PhD thesis, European University Institute, Florence, 1997.

26 Mark Juergensmayer, *The New Cold War: Religious Nationalism Confronts the Secular State* (Berkeley, California, University of California Press, 1994), p. 28. For a more sanguine view, see Fred Halliday, *Islam and the Myth of Confrontation* (London, I.B. Tauris, 1995).

27 George Kennan, *At a Century's Ending* (New York, Norton and Co., 1996) and *Around the Cragged Hill* (New York, Norton, 1993). Harper, in *American Visions of Europe: Franklin D. Roosevelt, George F. Kennan and Dean G. Acheson* (Cambridge University Press, 1994 and 1996) also writes brilliantly of Kennan's 'sources of estrangement' in his Chapter 4.

28 Zaki Laïdi, *Un monde privé de sens* (Paris, Fayard, 1994), pp. 15–27.

29 Justin Rosenberg, *The Empire of Civil Society: A Critique of the Realist Theory of International Relations* (London, Verso, 1994), especially Chapter 3 (from which this quote is taken; p. 88).

30 Rosenberg, *Empire of Civil Society*, pp. 126–129.

31 Anthony Giddens, 'Oh, What a Profitable Peace', *Times Higher Education Supplement*, 18 November 1994.

32 Francis Fukuyama, *Trust* (New York, The Free Press, 1995) and *The End of Order* (London, The Social Market Foundation, 1997); Laïdi, *Un monde*.

33 Nicholas Rengger, 'The Ethics of Trust in World Politics', *International Affairs*, vol. 73, no. 3, July 1997.
34 Samuel P. Huntington, 'The Clash of Civilisations?', *Foreign Affairs*, vol. 72, no. 3, Summer 1993, pp. 22–49. In this article he defined 'civilisation' as being made up 'both by common objective elements, such as language, history, religion, customs, institutions, and by the subjective self-identification of peoples.'
35 R.J. Vincent, *Human Rights and International Relations* (Cambridge University Press, 1986).

Select bibliography

Primary sources

Unpublished official sources
Great Britain
All Public Record Office, PRO
Cabinet Conclusions CAB 23/.
Cabinet Committee on Post-War External Economic Problems and Anglo-American Cooperation CAB 87/.
Cabinet Committees CAB 27/.
Cabinet Committees CAB 65/.
Cabinet Committees CAB 66/.
Cabinet Memoranda CAB 24/.
Foreign Office, General Correspondence, FO 371/.
Treasury T160/1105.

France
Ministère des Affaires Etrangères, Quai d'Orsay
Commission Interministérielle d'études pour la Société des Nations, IA. 1–.
Optants Hongrois, ID. 17–.
Société de Nations, SDN 1.
Société des Nations – Sécretariat Général.
Office Universitaire de Recherche Socialiste (OURS)
Commission de la Société des Nations (Commission Bourgeois) – 1918.

Private papers
Great Britain
Individuals
Clement Attlee (Bodleian Library, Oxford).
Arthur Balfour (British Library).
John Bradbury (Private Collection).
James Bryce (Bodleian Library, Oxford).
Robert Cecil (British Library).

John Colville (Churchill College, Cambridge).
Maurice Hankey (Churchill College, Cambridge).
Allen Leeper (Churchill College, Cambridge).
Gilbert Murray (Bodleian Library, Oxford).
Philip Noel-Baker (Churchill College, Cambridge).
Groups
Political and Economic Planning (BLPES).
Royal Institute of International Affairs (Chatham House).

United States
Hamilton Fish Armstrong (Seeley H. Mudd Memorial Library, Princeton University).
Adolf Berle (Roosevelt Presidential Library).
John Foster Dulles (Seeley H. Mudd Memorial Library, Princeton University).
Harry Hopkins (Roosevelt Presidential Library).
Cordell Hull (Library of Congress).
George F. Kennan (Seeley H. Mudd Memorial Library, Princeton University).
Henry Morgenthau (Roosevelt Presidential Library).
Leo Pasvolsky (Library of Congress).
Franklin Delano Roosevelt (Roosevelt Presidential Library).
Henry L. Stimson (Library of Congress).
Sumner Welles (Roosevelt Presidential Library).

France
Léon Blum (Archives d'histoire contemporaines).
René Pleven (Archives Nationales).

Published official sources

Great Britain
A National Health Service (Cmnd 6502, London, HMSO, 1944).
Documents on British Foreign Policy – various volumes.
Educational Reconstruction (Cmnd 6458, London, HMSO, 1943).
Foreign Office Confidential Print – various.
Hansard – various volumes.
Housing Policy (Cmnd. 6609, London, HMSO, 1945).
Principles of Government in Maintained Secondary Schools (Cmnd 6523, London, HMSO, 1944).
Webster, C.K., *British Diplomacy 1813–1815: Selected Documents Dealing with the Reconstruction of Europe* (London, Bell, 1921).

United States
Doenecke, Justus D. (ed.), *In Danger Undaunted: The Anti-Interventionist Movement of 1940–1941, as Revealed in the Papers of the America First Committee* (Stanford, Hoover Institution Press, 1990).
Foreign Relations of the United States (FRUS) – various volumes.
Mantoux, Paul, *The Deliberations of the Council of Four (March 24–June 28, 1919)*, translated and edited by Arthur S. Link (2 vols, Princeton University Press, 1992).

Published unofficial sources

Great Britain

Churchill, Winston; Rhodes James, Robert (ed.), *Churchill Speaks: Winston S. Churchill in Peace and War, Collected Speeches, 1897–1963* (London, Chelsea House, 1980).

Colville, John, *The Fringes of Power, Downing Street Diaries, Volume 1: 1939–October 1941*, and *Volume 2: October 1941–1955* (London, Hodder and Stoughton, 1985 and 1987).

Freedman, Lawrence (ed.), *Europe Transformed: Documents on the End of the Cold War* (London, Tri-Service Press, 1990).

Grotius Society, *Transactions of the Problems of the War, Volume IV* (London, Sweet and Maxwell, 1918).

Keynes, John Maynard, *Collected Writings of … Activities, 1914–19* (London, Macmillan, 1971).

Nicolson, Harold; Nicolson, Nigel (ed.), *Diaries and Letters* (3 vols, London, Collins, 1966–68).

United States

Baker, Mary Stannard (ed.), *Woodrow Wilson: His Life and Letters* (8 vols, London, 1928–29).

Berle, Adolf A. (ed.), *Navigating the Rapids, 1918–1971: From the Diaries of Adolf A. Berle* (New York, Harcourt, Brace, Jovanovich, 1961).

Link, Arthur J. (ed.), *The Papers of Woodrow Wilson* (in 69 vols, Princeton University Press, 1966–194).

O'Brien, Frances William (ed.), *Two Peacemakers at Paris: The Hoover–Wilson Post Armistice Letters, 1918–1920* (College Station and London, Texas A and M University Press, 1978).

Roosevelt, Franklin Delano, F.D.R.: His Personal Letters, 1928–1945 (New York, Duell, Sloan and Pearce, 1950).

Secondary sources

Books

Acheson, Dean, *Present at the Creation: My Years with the State Department* (New York, Norton, 1969).

Adamthwaite, Anthony, *Grandeur and Misery: France's Bid for Power in Europe, 1914–1940* (London, Arnold, 1995).

Angell, Norman, *The Great Illusion: A Study of the Relation of Military Power to National Advantage* (London, William Heinemann, 1910).

— *The Fruits of Victory* (London, Collins, 1921).

— *After All* (London, Hamish Hamilton, 1951).

Archer, Clive, *International Organization* (London, Unwin, 2nd edn, 1992).

Armstrong, David, Lloyd, Lorna and Redmond, John, *From Versailles to Maastricht: International Organization in the Twentieth Century* (London, Macmillan, 1996).

Artaud, Denise, *La question des dettes interalliés et la reconstruction de l'Europe, 1917–1929* (Lille and Paris, Honoré Champion, 1978).

Ashworth, William, *A Short History of the International Economy since 1850* (London, Longman, 1981).

Bailey, Sydney, *Humanitarian Intervention in the Internal Affairs of States* (Basingstoke, Macmillan, 1996).

Baker, Mary Stannard, *Woodrow Wilson and World Settlement* (New York, Doubleday, 1922–23).

Barnett, Correlli, *The Audit of War: The Illusion and Reality of Britain as a Great Nation* (London, Macmillan, 1987).

Barros, James, *The League of Nations and the Great Powers: The Greek–Bulgarian Incident, 1925* (Oxford, Clarendon Press, 1970).

Baruch, Bernard M., *The Making of the Reparation and Economic Sections of the Treaty* (New York, Harper and Brothers, 1920).

Baylis, John and Smith, Steve, *The Globalization of World Politics: An Introduction to International Relations* (Oxford University Press, 1997).

Bell, P.M.H., *John Bull and the Bear: British Public Opinion, Foreign Policy and the Soviet Union, 1941–1945* (London, Edward Arnold, 1990).

Bentley, Michael, *The Liberal Mind, 1914–1929* (Cambridge University Press, 1977).
— *The Climax of Liberal Politics* (London, Edward Arnold, 1987).

Berkowitz, Peter, *Nietzsche: The Ethics of an Immoralist* (Cambridge, Mass., Harvard University Press, 1995).

Berridge, Geoffrey and Jennings, A., *Diplomacy at the UN* (Basingstoke, Macmillan, 1985).

Birn, Donald, *The League of Nations Union* (Oxford, Clarendon Press, 1981).

Block, Fred L., *The Origins of International Economic Disorder* (Berkeley, University of California Press, 1977).

Boardman, Robert, *Post-Socialist World Orders: Russia, China and the UN System* (London, Macmillan, 1994).

Born, Karl Erich, *International Banking in the Nineteenth and Twentieth Centuries* (Oxford, Berg, 1977).

Bourantsonis, D. and Wiener, Jarrod (eds), *The United Nations in the New World Order: The World Organization at Fifty* (London, Macmillan, 1995).

Boutros-Ghali, Boutros, *Agenda for Peace* (New York, United Nations, 1992).

Brailsford, Henry Noel, *The War of Steel and Gold: A Study of the Armed Peace* (London, G. Bell and Sons, 1914).

Brown, Chris, *International Theory: New Normative Approaches* (Hemel Hempstead Harvester, 1992).
— *Political Restructuring in Europe: Ethical Perspectives* (London, Routledge, 1994).
— *Understanding International Relations* (London, Macmillan, 1997).

Bull, Hedley, *The Anarchical Society* (London, Macmillan, 1977, 1995).

Bull, Hedley and Watson, Adam (eds), *The Expansion of International Society* (Oxford, Clarendon Press, 1984).

Bullock, Alan, *Hitler: A Study in Tyranny* (London, Pelican, 1962).

Burbach, Roger, Núñez, Orlando and Kagarlitsky, Boris, *Globalization and its Discontents: The Rise of Postmodern Socialisms* (London, Pluto, 1997).

Burnett, Philip Mason, *Reparation at the Paris Peace Conference from the Standpoint of the American Delegation* (2 vols, New York, Columbia University Press, 1940).

Burns, Timothy (ed.), *After History: Francis Fukuyama and His Critics* (London, Littlefield Adams, 1994).

Burridge, Trevor, *Clement Attlee: A Political Biography* (London, Jonathan Cape, 1985).

Burrin, Philippe, *Hitler and the Jews: The Genesis of the Holocaust* (London, Edward Arnold, 1994).

Calvocorressi, Peter and Wint, Guy, *Total War* (London, Penguin, 1972).

Carr, Edward Hallet, *The Twenty Years' Crisis: 1919–1939* (London, Macmillan, 1939).

— *The Soviet Impact on the Western World* (London, Macmillan, 1946).

Carr, E.H. *et al.*, *Nationalism: A Report by a Study Group of Members of the Royal Institute of International Affairs* (London, Oxford University Press, 1939, reprinted Frank Cass, 2nd edn, 1963).

Ceadel, Martin, *Pacifism in Britain, 1914–1945* (Clarendon Press, Oxford, 1980).

— *Thinking about Peace and War* (Oxford University Press, 1987).

— *The Origins of War Prevention: The British Peace Movement and International Relations, 1730–1854* (Oxford, Clarendon Press, 1996).

Chan, Stephen and Williams, Andrew (eds), *Renegade States: The Evolution of Revolutionary Foreign Policy* (Manchester University Press, 1994).

Chomsky, Noam, *World Orders, Old and New* (London, Pluto Press, 1994).

Churchill, Winston, *The Second World War* (6 vols, London, Cassell, 1948–54).

Clark, Ian, *Reform and Resistance in the International Order* (Cambridge University Press, 1980).

— *The Hierarchy of States: Reform and Resistance in the International Order* (Cambridge University Press, 1989).

— *Globalization and Fragmentation: International Relations in the Twentieth Century* (Oxford University Press, 1997).

Claude, Inis L., Jr, *Swords into Plowshares: The Problems and Progress of International Organization* (New York, Random House, 4th edn, 1964).

Clemenceau, Georges, *Grandeur and Misery of Victory* (London, George Harrap, 1930).

Clemens, Diane, *Yalta* (Oxford University Press, 1970).

Cobban, Alfred, *National Self-determination* (Oxford University Press, 1945).

Coker, Christopher, *War and the 20th Century: The Impact of War on the Modern Consciousness* (London, Brassey's, 1994).

— *The Twilight of the West* (Boulder, Colorado, Westview Press, 1998).

Connor, Walker (ed.), *Ethnonationalism: The Quest for Understanding* (Princeton University Press, 1994).

Conyne, George, *Woodrow Wilson: British Perspectives, 1912–21* (London, Macmillan, 1992).

Coogan, Tim Pat, *Michael Collins: A Biography* (London, Hutchinson, 1990).

Cooper, Duff, *Old Men Forget* (London, Rupert Hart-Davis, 1955).

Cox, Robert W. with Sinclair, Timothy J., *Approaches to World Order* (Cambridge University Press, 1996).

Crampton, R.J., *Eastern Europe in the Twentieth Century* (London, Routledge, 1994).

Dallek, Robert, *Franklin D. Roosevelt and American Foreign Policy, 1932–1945* (New York, Oxford University Press, 1979).

Danchev, Alex (ed.), *Fin de Siècle: The Meaning of the Twentieth Century* (London, I.B. Tauris, 1995).

Danchev, Alex and Halverson, Thomas (eds), *International Perspectives on the Yugoslav Conflict* (London, Macmillan, 1996).

Dangerfield, George, *The Strange Death of Liberal England* (London, Grenada Publishing, 1970) (first published 1935).

Davies, J. Scott (ed.), *Religion and Justice in the War in Bosnia* (London, Routledge, 1996).

Deighton, Anne (ed.), *Building Postwar Europe: National Decision-Makers and European Institutions, 1948–1963* (London, Macmillan, 1995).

Dexter, Byron, *The League of Nations, 1920–1926* (New York, Viking Press, 1967).

Diehl, Paul, *International Peacekeeping* (Baltimore, Johns Hopkins Press, 1994).

Dìez de Corral, Luis, *The Rape of Europe* (London, George Allen and Unwin, 1959).

Dockrill, Michael L. and Gould, J. Douglas, *Peace without Promise: Britain and the Peace Conferences, 1919–23* (London, Batsford, 1981).

Douglas, Roy, *New Alliances, 1940–41* (London, Macmillan, 1982).

Duignan, Peter and Gann, L.H., *The United States and the New Europe, 1945–1953* (Oxford, Blackwell, 1994).

Dunay, Pál, Kardos, Gábor and Williams, Andrew (eds), *New Forms of Security: Views from Central, Eastern and Western Europe* (Aldershot, Dartmouth, 1995).

Dunn, Seamus and Fraser, T.G., *Europe and Ethnicity: World War One and Contemporary Ethnic Conflict* (London, Routledge, 1996).

Duroselle, Jean-Baptiste, *Politique Etrangère de la France: La Décadence* (Paris, Imprimerie Nationale, 1979).

Edmonds, Robin, *The Big Three: Churchill, Roosevelt and Stalin in Peace and War* (London, Penguin, 1991).

Elcock, H., *Portrait of a Decision: The Council of Four and the Treaty of Versailles* (London, Eyre Methuen, 1972).

Ellwood, David R., *Rebuilding Europe: Western Europe, America and Postwar Reconstruction* (London, Longman, 1992).

Evans, Gareth, *Cooperating for Peace: The Global Agenda for the 1990s and Beyond* (London, Allen and Unwin, 1993).

Evans, Martin and Lunn, Ken (eds), *War and Memory in the Twentieth Century* (Oxford, Berg, 1997).

Evans, Richard J., *In Defence of History* (London, Granta, 1997).

Feis, Herbert, *Churchill, Roosevelt, Stalin: The War They Waged and the Peace They Sought* (Princeton University Press, 1957).

— *From Trust to Terror* (New York, Norton, 1970).

Findlay, Trevor (ed.), *Challenges to the New Peacekeepers* (Oxford/SIPRI, 1995).

Fink, Carole, *The Genoa Conference* (Chapel Hill, University of North Carolina Press, 1984).

Fink, Carole, Frohn, Axel and Heideking, Jurgen (eds), *Genoa, Rapallo and European Reconstruction in 1922* (Cambridge University Press, 1991).

Lord Fisher, *Records* (London, Hodder and Stoughton, 1919).

Floto, Inga, *Colonel House in Paris: A Study of American Policy at the Paris Peace Conference* (Princeton University Press, 1973).

Freymond, Jacques, *The Saar Conflict, 1945–1955* (London and New York, Stevens/ Praeger, 1960).

Frieden, Jeffry A. and Lake, David A. (eds), *International Political Economy: Perspectives on Global Power and Wealth* (London, Unwin Hyman, 2nd edn, 1991).

Frost, Mervyn, *Ethics in International Relations: A Constitutive Theory* (Cambridge University Press, 1996).

Fukuyama, Francis, *The End of History and the Last Man* (New York, The Free Press, 1992).

— *Trust* (New York, The Free Press, 1995).

— *The End of Order* (London, The Social Market Foundation, 1997).

Fussell, Robert, *The Great War and Modern Memory* (Oxford University Press, 1975).

Gaddis, John Lewis, *The United States and the Origins of the Cold War, 1941–1947* (New York, Columbia University Press, 1972).

— *We Now Know: Rethinking Cold War History* (Oxford, Clarendon Press, 1997).

Gardner, Richard N., *Sterling–Dollar Diplomacy: Anglo-American Collaboration in the Reconstruction of Multilateral Trade* (Oxford, Clarendon Press, 1956).

— *Sterling–Dollar Diplomacy in Current Perspective: The Origins and Prospects of Our International Economic Order* (New York, Columbia University Press, 1980).

Gelfand, Lawrence (ed.), *The Inquiry: American Preparations for Peace, 1917–1919* (New Haven, Yale University Press, 1963).

— *Herbert Hoover, the Great War and its Aftermath, 1914–1923* (University of Iowa Press, 1979).

Gilbert, Martin, *The Roots of Appeasement* (London, Weidenfeld and Nicholson, 1966).

Gilbert, Martin and Gott, R., *The Appeasers* (London, Weidenfeld and Nicholson, 1963).

Gill, Stephen (ed.), *Gramsci, Historical Materialism and International Relations* (Cambridge University Press, 1993).

Gilpin, Robert, *War and Change in World Politics* (Cambridge University Press, 1981).

Goldhagen, Daniel, *Hitler's Willing Executioners: Ordinary Germans and the Holocaust* (London, Abacus, 1996).

Goldstein, Erik, *Winning the Peace: British Diplomatic Strategy and the Paris Peace Conference, 1916–1920* (Oxford, Clarendon Press, 1991).

Gong, Gerrit, *The Standard of Civilisation in International Society* (Oxford, Clarendon Press, 1984).

Griffiths, Richard, *Fellow Travellers of the Right: British Enthusiasts for Nazi Germany, 1933–9* (Oxford University Press, 1983).

Groom, A.J.R. and Light, Margot (eds), *Contemporary International Relations: A Guide to Theory* (London, Pinter, 1994).

Hall, John, *International Orders* (Cambridge, Polity, 1996).

Hankey, Maurice, *Diplomacy by Conference* (London, Ernest Benn, 1946).

— *The Supreme Control at the Paris Peace Conference: A Commentary* (London, George Allen and Unwin, 1963).

Harper, John Lamberton, *American Visions of Europe: Franklin D. Roosevelt, George F. Kennan and Dean G. Acheson* (Cambridge University Press, 1994 and 1996).

Harris, Kenneth, *Attlee* (London, Weidenfeld and Nicholson, 1982).

Hathaway, Robert M., *Ambiguous Partnership: Britain and America, 1944–1947* (New York, Columbia University Press, 1981).

Headlam-Morley, James, *A Memoir of the Paris Peace Conference, 1919* (London, Methuen, 1982).

Heater, Derek, *National Self-Determination: Woodrow Wilson and His Legacy* (London, Macmillan, 1994).

Henig, R., *The Origins of the Second World War* (London, Methuen, 1985).

Herzstein, Robert Erwin, *When Nazi Dreams Come True* (London, Abacus, 1982).

Hettne, Bjorn (ed.), *International Political Economy: Understanding Global Disorder* (London, Zed Books, 1995).

Hildebrand, Klaus, *The Foreign Policy of the Third Reich* (London, Batsford, 1973).

Hildebrand, Robert C., *Dumbarton Oaks: The Origins of the United Nations and the Search for Post-War Security* (Chapel Hill, University of North Carolina Press, 1990).

Hinsley, F.H., *Power and the Pursuit of Peace* (Cambridge University Press, 1967).

Hirschman, Alfred O., *Exit, Voice and Loyalty: Responses to Decline in Firms, Organizations and States* (Cambridge, Mass., Harvard University Press, 1970).

Hirst, Paul and Thompson, Grahame, *Globalization in Question* (Cambridge, Polity, 1996).

Hitler, Adolf, *Mein Kampf* (Boston, Houghton-Mifflin, 1943, first published in German in 1925).

Hobsbawm, Eric, *The Age of Extremes: The Short Twentieth Century, 1914–1991* (London, Michael Joseph, 1994).

Hobson, J.A., *Imperialism: A Study* (London, G. Allen and Unwin, 1902, 1938).

Hogan, Michael J., *Informal Entente: The Private Structure of Cooperation in Anglo-American Economic Diplomacy* (Columbia, University of Missouri Press, 1977).

— *The Marshall Plan: America, Britain and the Reconstruction of Europe* (Cambridge University Press, 1987).

Hogenhuis-Seliverstoff, Anne, *Les relations franco-soviétiques, 1917–1924* (Paris, Editions de la Sorbonne, 1981).

Hoover, Herbert, *The Ordeal of Woodrow Wilson* (London, Museum Press, 1958).

House, Edward Mandell and Seymour, Charles, *What Really Happened at Paris: The Story of the Peace Conference, 1918–1919, by American Delegates* (London, Hodder and Stoughton, 1921).

Hull, Cordell, *The Memoirs of Cordell Hull* (2 vols, London, Hodder and Stoughton, 1948).

Hunt, Michael H., *Ideology and U.S. Foreign Policy* (New Haven, Yale University Press, 1988).

Huntington, Samuel P., *The Third Wave: Democratization in the Late Twentieth Century* (Norman, University of Oklahoma Press, 1991).

— *The Clash of Civilisations and the Remaking of World Order* (New York, Simon and Schuster, 1996).

International Institute of Intellectual Cooperation, *Peaceful Change* (Paris, League of Nations, 1938).

Jackson, Robert H., *Quasi States, Sovereignty, International Relations and the Third World* (Cambridge University Press, 1990).

Jacobson, Jon, *Locarno Diplomacy: Germany and the West, 1925–1929* (Princeton University Press, 1972).

James, Alan, *Peacekeeping in International Politics* (London, Macmillan, 1990).

James, Harold, *International Monetary Cooperation Since Bretton Woods* (Washington DC, IMF and Oxford University Press, 1996).

Juergensmayer, Mark, *The New Cold War: Religious Nationalism Confronts the Secular State* (Berkeley, Calif., University of California Press, 1994).

Kaiser, David E., *Economic Diplomacy and the Origins of the Second World War: Germany, Britain, France and Eastern Europe, 1920–1939* (Princeton University Press, 1980).

Kanninnen, T., *Leadership and Reform: The Secretary General and the UN Financial Crisis of the late 1980s* (The Hague, Nijhoff, 1995).

Kendall, Walter, *The Revolutionary Movement in Britain, 1900–1921* (London, Weidenfeld and Nicholson, 1968).

Kennan, George, *Memoirs, 1925–1950* (London, Hutchinson, 1968).

— *Memoirs, 1950–1963* (London, Hutchinson, 1973).

— *At a Century's Ending* (New York, Norton and Co., 1996).

— *Around the Cragged Hill* (New York, Norton, 1993).

Kennedy, Paul, *The Realities Behind Diplomacy: Background Influences on British Foreign Policy, 1865–1980* (London, Fontana, 1981).

Kennedy-Pipe, Caroline, *Stalin's Cold War: Soviet Strategies in Europe, 1943 to 1956* (Manchester University Press, 1995).

Kent, Bruce, *The Spoils of War: The Politics, Economics and Diplomacy of Reparations, 1918–1922* (Oxford, Clarendon Press, 1989).

Keohane, Robert, *After Hegemony* (Princeton University Press, 1984).

— *International Institutions and State Power* (Boulder, Colorado, Westview Press, 1989).

Kern, Stephen, *The Culture of Time and Space, 1880–1918* (Cambridge, Mass., Harvard University Press, 1983).

Kersaudy, François, *Churchill and De Gaulle* (London, Collins, 1981).

Keynes, John Maynard, *The Economic Consequences of the Peace* (New York, Harcourt, Brace and Howe, 1920).

Kindleberger, Charles, *The World in Depression, 1929–1939* (London, Allen Lane, 1973).

Kissinger, Henry, *Diplomacy* (New York, Simon and Schuster, 1994).

Knock, Thomas J., *To End All Wars: Woodrow Wilson and the Quest for a New World Order* (New York, Oxford University Press, 1992).

Krasner, Stephen D., *International Regimes* (Cornell University Press, 1983).

Lacouture, Jean, *De Gaulle: The Ruler, 1945–1970* (London, Harvill, 1991).

Laïdi, Zaki, *Un monde privé de sens* (Paris, Fayard, 1994).

Land, Andrew, Lowe, Rodney and Whiteside, Noel, *The Development of the Welfare State, 1939–1951* (London, HMSO, 1992).

Leaver, Richard and Richardson, James L., *Charting the Post-Cold War Order* (Boulder, Colorado, Westview Press, 1993).

Leffler, Melvyn F., *The Elusive Quest: America's Pursuit of European Stability and French Security, 1919–1933* (Chapel Hill, University of North Carolina Press, 1979).

Leffler, Melvyn F. and Painter, David S. (eds), *Origins of the Cold War: An International History* (London, Routledge, 1994).

Leibknecht, Karl, *Militarism and Anti-Militarism* (Cambridge, Rivers Press, 1973, first published 1907).

Lentin, A., *Lloyd George, Woodrow Wilson and the Guilt of Germany: An Essay in the Pre-history of Appeasement* (Leicester University Press, 1984).

Levin, N. Gordon, *Woodrow Wilson and the Paris Peace Conference* (Lexington, Mass., Heath, 1972).

Lloyd George, David, *The Truth About the Peace Treaties* (2 vols, London, Gollancz, 1938).

Long, David and Wilson, Peter, *Thinkers of the Twenty Years' Crisis: Interwar Idealism Reassessed* (Oxford, Clarendon Press, 1995).

Lowes Dickinson, G., *The Choice Before Us* (London, George Allen and Unwin, 1917).

— *The International Anarchy, 1904–1914* (London, George Allen and Unwin, 1926).

Lukàcs, J.A., *The Great Powers and Eastern Europe* (New York, Regnery, 1953).

Lundestad, Geir, *'Empire' by Integration: The United States and European Integration, 1945–1997* (Oxford University Press, 1998).

Lynn-Jones, Sean M. (ed.), *The Cold War and After: Prospects for Peace* (Cambridge, Mass., MIT Press, 1991).

Macartney, C.A., *Hungary and Her Successors* (London, Macmillan, 1937).

Macdonald, Lyn, *Somme* (London, Macmillan, 1983).

Madariaga, Salvador de, *Disarmament* (Oxford University Press, 1929).

Mantoux, Etienne, *The Carthaginian Peace or: The Economic Consequences of Mr. Keynes* (London, Oxford University Press, 1946).

Marks, Sally, *The Illusion of Peace: International Relations in Europe, 1918–1933* (London, Macmillan, 1976).

Martel, Gordon (ed.), *The Origins of the Second World War Reconsidered: The A.J.P. Taylor Debate after Twenty-five Years* (London, Allen and Unwin, 1986).

Marwick, Arthur, *The Deluge: British Society and the First World War* (London, Open University Press/Macmillan, 1973).

Mayall, James, *Nationalism and International Society* (Cambridge University Press, 1990).

Mayer, Arno J., *Political Origins of the New Diplomacy, 1917–18* (New York, Yale University Press, 1959).

— *Politics and Diplomacy of Peacemaking: Containment and Counterrevolution at Versailles, 1918–1919* (New York, Alfred A. Knopf, 1967).

Mayers, David George, *Kennan and the Dilemmas of US Foreign Policy* (New York, Oxford University Press, 1988).

Mayne, Richard and Pinder, John, *Federal Union: the Pioneers* (London, Macmillan, 1990).

McCallum, R.B., *Public Opinion and the Last Peace* (London, Oxford University Press, 1944).

Miller, David, *The Drafting of the Covenant* (2 vols, New York, David Putnam and Sons, 1928).

Miller, J.D.B., *Norman Angell and the Futility of War* (London, Macmillan, 1986).

Miller, J.D.B. and Vincent, R.J., *Order and Violence: Hedley Bull and International Relations* (Oxford, Clarendon Press, 1990).

Miquel, Pierre, *La paix de Versailles et l'opinion publique française* (Paris, Flammarion, 1972).

Miscamble, Wilson D., *George F. Kennan and the Making of American Foreign Policy, 1947–1950* (Princeton University Press, 1982).

Mitrany, David, *A Working Peace System* ((originally published 1943), reprinted with an introduction by Hans J. Morgenthau, Chicago, Quadrangle Books, 1966).

Mitrany, David and Taylor, Paul (eds), *The Functional Theory of Politics* (London, Martin Robertson, 1975).

Molnàr, Miklòs, *Marx, Lénine at la politique internationale* (Paris, Presses Universitaires de France, 1966).

— *Histoire de la Hongrie* (Paris, Hatier, 1996).

Morgan, Kenneth O., *Consensus and Disunity: The Lloyd George Coalition Government, 1918–1922* (Oxford, Clarendon Press, 1979).

Mowat, C.L. (ed.), *New Cambridge History, Vol. XII, 'The Shifting Balance of World Forces, 1898–1945'* (Cambridge University Press, 1968).

Moynihan, Daniel, *Pandaemonium: Ethnicity in International Politics* (Oxford University Press, 1993).

Mullerson, Rein, *International Law, Rights and Politics* (London, Routledge, 1994).

Nadel, G.H. and Curtis P. (eds), *Imperialism and Colonisation* (New York, Macmillan, 1966).

Newton, Verne W. (ed.), *FDR and the Holocaust* (New York, St. Martin's Press, 1996).

Nicholas, Herbert G., *The United Nations as a Political Institution* (London, Oxford University Press, 1962, 1967).

Nicolson, Harold, *Peacemaking 1919* (London, Constable and Co., 1933).

Noel-Baker, Philip J., *The Geneva Protocol* (London, King, 1925).

— *Disarmament* (London, The Hogarth Press, 1926, 2nd edn, 1927).

Notter, Harley, *Post-War Foreign Policy Preparation, 1939–1945* (Washington, US Department of State, 1949).

Osiander, Andreas, *The States System of Europe, 1640–1990: Peacemaking and the Conditions of International Stability* (Oxford, Clarendon Press, 1994).

Pearson, Raymond, *National Minorities and Eastern Europe, 1848–1945* (London, Macmillan, 1983).

Peden, G.C., *Keynes, The Treasury and British Economic Policy* (London, Macmillan/The Economic History Society, 1988).

Petriciolli, Marta (ed.), *A Missed Opportunity? 1922: The Reconstruction of Europe* (Bern, Peter Lang, 1995).

Pick, Daniel, *The War Machine: The Rationalisation of Slaughter in the Modern Age* (New Haven, Yale University Press, 1993).

Plano, Jack C. and Riggs, Robert E., *Forging World Order: The Politics of International Organization* (New York, Macmillan, 1967).

Polanyi, Karl, *The Great Transformation: The Political and Economic Origins of Our Time* (New York, Beacon, 1944).

Pollard, Robert A., *Economic Security and the Origins of the Cold War, 1945–1950* (New York, Columbia University Press, 1985)

Pugh, Michael C. (ed.), *European Security – Towards 2000* (Manchester University Press, 1992).

Ramsbottom, Oliver and Woodhouse, Tom, *Humanitarian Intervention in Contemporary Conflict* (London, Polity Press, 1996).

Rappard, William, *Uniting Europe* (New Haven, Yale University Press, 1930).

Reynolds, David, *The Creation of the Anglo-American Alliance, 1937–41* (London, Europa, 1981).
— *Britannia Overruled: British Policy and World Power in the 20th Century* (London, Longman, 1991).
Lord Riddell, *Lord Riddell's Intimate Diary of the Peace Conference and After* (London, Victor Gollancz, 1933).
Roberts, Adam and Kingsbury, Benedict (eds), *United Nations, Divided World* (Oxford University Press, 2nd edn, 1992).
Rochester, J. Martin, *Waiting for the Millennium: The United Nations and the Future of World Order* (University of South Carolina Press, 1993).
Rock, W., *British Appeasement in the 1930s* (London, Edward Arnold, 1977).
Roll, Eric, *Crowded Hours* (London, Faber, 1985).
Rosenberg, Justin, *The Empire of Civil Society: A Critique of the Realist Theory of International Relations* (London, Verso, 1994).
Sainsbury, Keith, *The Turning Point* (Oxford University Press, 1985).
— *Churchill and Roosevelt at War: The War They Fought and the Peace They Hoped to Make* (London, Macmillan, 1996).
Schattschneider, E.E., *Politics, Pressure and the Tariff: A Study in Free Private Enterprise in Pressure Politics, as Shown in the 1929–1930 Revision of the Tariff* (New York, Prentice-Hall, 1935).
Schulz, Gerhard, *Revolutions and Peace Treaties, 1917–1920* (London, Methuen, 1967).
Sellers, Mortimer (ed.), *The New World Order: Sovereignty, Human Rights and the Self-Determination of Peoples* (Oxford, Berg, 1996).
Senarclans, Pierre de, *De Yalta au Rideau de Fer: Les Grandes Puissances et les Origines de la Guerre Froide* (Paris, Presses de la Fondation Nationale des Sciences Politiques, 1993).
Shaw, Martin, *Global Society and International Relations: Sociological Concepts and Political Perspectives* (Cambridge, Polity, 1996).
Shennan, Andrew, *Rethinking France: Plans for Renewal, 1940–1946* (Oxford, Clarendon Press, 1989).
Simpson, A.W. Brian, *In the Highest Degree Odious: Detention Without Trial in Wartime Britain* (Oxford, Clarendon Press, 1992).
Skidelsky, Robert, *John Maynard Keynes, Hopes Betrayed, 1883–1920* (London, Macmillan, 1983).
— *John Maynard Keynes: The Economist as Saviour, 1920–1937* (London, Macmillan, 1992).
Smith, M.L. and Stirk, Peter, *Making the New Europe: European Unity and the Second World War* (London, Pinter, 1990).
Smith, Steve, Booth, Ken and Zalewski, Marysia (eds), *International Theory: Positivism and Beyond* (Cambridge University Press, 1996).
Sorel, Georges, *Reflections on Violence* (New York, Peter Smith, 1941, first published 1915).
Spengler, Oswald, *The Decline of the West* (2 vols, London, G. Allen and Unwin, 1926).
Stephanson, Anders, *Kennan and the Art of Foreign Policy* (Cambridge, Mass., Harvard University Press, 1989).
Stern, Geoffrey, *The Structure of International Society* (London, Pinter, 1995).

Stettinius, Edward R., *Roosevelt and the Russians: The Yalta Conference* (London, Jonathan Cape, 1950).

Stevenson, David, *French War Aims Against Germany, 1914–1919* (Oxford University Press, 1982).

— *Armaments and the Coming of War in Europe, 1904–1914* (Oxford, Clarendon Press, 1996).

Stirk, Peter M.R. (ed.), *European Unity in Context: The Interwar Period* (London, Pinter, 1989)

Strange, Susan, *States and Markets* (London, Pinter, 1988)

— *Rival States, Rival Firms* (Cambridge University Press, 1991)

— *The Retreat of the State: The Diffusion of Power in the World Economy* (Cambridge University Press, 1996).

Streit, Clarence K., *Union Now* (London, Jonathan Cape, 1939).

Swartz, Marvin, *The Union of Democratic Control in British Politics during the First World War* (Oxford, Clarendon Press, 1971).

Taylor, A.J.P., *The Origins of the Second World War* (London, Penguin, 1960).

Taylor, Paul, *International Organization in the Modern World* (London, Pinter, 1993).

Taylor, Paul and Groom, A.J.R. (eds), *The International Institutions at Work* (London, Pinter, 1990).

Thompson, John M., *Russia, Bolshevism, and the Versailles Peace* (Princeton University Press, 1966).

Thomson, D., Meyer, E. and Briggs, A., *Patterns of Peacemaking* (London, Kegan, Paul, Trench, Trubner and Co., 1945).

Thorne, Christopher, *The Limits of Foreign Policy: The West, the League and the Far Eastern Crisis of 1931–1933* (London, Macmillan, 1973).

— *Allies of a Kind* (London, Hamish Hamilton, 1978).

Toynbee, Arnold, *Survey of International Affairs* (London, Oxford University Press, 1926).

Trachtenberg, Marc, *Reparations in World Politics: France and Economic Diplomacy, 1916–1923* (New York, Columbia University Press, 1980).

Trevelyan, G.M., *Garibaldi and the Making of Italy, June–November 1860* (London, Longman, 1911).

Ullman, Richard H., *Intervention and the War*, volume 1 of his *Anglo-Soviet Relations, 1917–1921* (Princeton University Press, 1961).

Underhill, Geoffrey R.D. (ed.), *The New World Order in International Finance* (London, Macmillan 1997).

Vincent, R.J., *Human Rights and International Relations* (Cambridge University Press, 1986).

Waever, Ole, Buzan, Barry, Kelstrup, Morten and Lemaître, Pierre, *Identity, Migration and the New Security Agenda in Europe* (London, Pinter, 1993).

Walworth, Arthur, *America's Moment: 1918* (New York, Norton and Co., 1963).

Walzer, Michael, *Just and Unjust Wars* (New York, Basic Books, 2nd edn, 1992).

Watson, George, *The English Ideology: Studies in the Language of Victorian Politics* (London, Allen Lane, 1973).

Watt, D.C., *How War Came* (London, Heinemann, 1989).

Weill-Raynal, Etienne, *Les reparations allemandes et la France, 1918–1936* (Paris, Nouvelles éditions latines, 1947).

Weissman, Benjamin, *Herbert Hoover and Famine Relief to Soviet Russia, 1921–1923* (Stanford University Press, 1974).

Wells, Herbert George, *Washington and the Hope of Peace* (London, W. Collins Sons and Co., 1922).

West, Rebecca, *1900* (London, Weidenfeld and Nicholson, 1982).

Wheeler Bennett, J.M., *King George VI: His Life and Reign* (New York, St. Martin's Press, 1958).

White, Stephen, *Britain and the Bolshevik Revolution* (London, Macmillan, 1979).

— *The Origins of Détente; The Genoa Conference and Soviet–Western Relations, 1920–1924* (Cambridge University Press, 1985).

Wiener, Jarrod, *Making Rules in the Uruguay Round of the GATT: A Study of International Leadership* (Aldershot, Dartmouth, 1995).

Wilde, Jaap de and Wiberg, Hakan (eds), *Organized Anarchy in Europe: The Role of Intergovernmental Organizations* (London, I.B. Tauris, 1996).

Williams, Andrew, *Labour and Russia: The Labour Party's Attitude to the Soviet Union, 1924–1934* (Manchester University Press, 1989).

— *Trading with the Bolsheviks* (Manchester University Press, 1992).

— (ed.), *Reorganising Eastern Europe* (Aldershot, Dartmouth, 1994).

Winter, Jay, *Sites of Memory, Sites of Mourning: The Great War in European Cultural History* (Cambridge University Press, 1995).

Wolfers, Arnold, *Britain and France between the Two Wars* (Hamden, Conneticut, Archon Books, 1963).

Yergin, Daniel, *Shattered Peace: The Origins of the Cold War and the National Security State* (Boston, Houghton-Mifflin, 1977).

Articles

Archibugi, Daniele, 'The Reform of the UN and Cosmopolitan Democracy', *Journal of Peace Research*, August 1993, pp. 301–316.

Barnett, Michael, 'Partners in Peace? The UN, Regional Organizations, and Peacekeeping', *Review of International Studies*, vol. 21, no. 4, October 1995, pp. 411–434.

Birn, Donald S., 'The League of Nations Union and Collective Security', *Journal of Contemporary History*, vol. 9, no. 4, July 1974, pp. 131–159.

Chan, Steve, 'In Search of the Democratic Peace: Problems and Promise', *The Mershon International Studies Review*, vol. 41, Supplement 1, May 1997, pp. 59–91.

Cochrane, Molly, 'The New World Order and International Political Theory', *Paradigms*, vol. 8, no. 1, Summer 1994, pp. 108–109.

Cohen, Raymond, 'Multilateralism and World Order', *Review of International Studies*, vol. 18, no. 2, April 1992, pp. 161–180.

— 'Pacific Unions: A Reappraisal of the Theory that Democracies Do Not Go to War with Each Other', *The Review of International Studies*, vol. 20, 1994, pp. 202–232.

Cox, Robert W., 'An Alternative approach to Multilateralism for the Twenty-First Century', *Global Governance*, vol. 3, no. 1, January–April 1997, pp. 103–116.

Delanty, Gerard, 'Negotiating the Peace in Northern Ireland', *Journal of Peace Research*, vol. 32, no. 5, 1995, pp. 257–264.

Durch, William L. and Grove, Eric, 'Blue Helmet Blues', two articles in *International Security*, Spring 1993, pp. 151–182.

Frost, Mervyn, 'Constituting a New World Order', *Paradigms*, vol. 8, no. 1, Summer 1994, pp. 13–22.

Gaddis, John Lewis, 'International Relations Theory and the End of the Cold War', *International Security*, vol. 17, no. 3, Winter 1992/93, pp. 5–58.

— 'The Emerging Post-Revisionist Thesis on the Origins of the Cold War', *Diplomatic History*, vol. 7, Summer 1983, pp. 171–190.

Goldstein, Erik and Maurer, John, 'The Washington Conference, 1921–22: Naval Rivalry, East Asian Stability and the Road to Pearl Harbour', *Diplomacy and Statecraft*, vol. 4, no. 3, November 1993, special issue.

Goulding, Marrack, 'The Evolution of UN Peacekeeping', *International Affairs*, July 1993, pp. 451–464.

Gowa, Joanne, 'Democratic States and International Disputes', *International Organization*, vol. 49, no. 3, Summer 1995, pp. 511–522.

Grunberg, Isabelle, 'Exploring the "Myth" of Hegemonic Stability', *International Organization*, vol. 44, no. 4, Autumn 1990, pp. 431–477.

Higgins, Rosalyn, 'The New United Nations and Former Yugoslavia', *International Affairs*, vol. 69, no. 3, July 1993, pp. 465–484.

Huntington, Samuel P., 'The Clash of Civilisations?', *Foreign Affairs*, vol. 72, no. 3, Summer 1993, pp. 22–49.

Jennar, Raoul, 'UNTAC: "International Triumph" in Cambodia?', *Security Dialogue*, vol. 25, no. 2, June 1994, pp. 145–156.

Kaufman, Stuart J., 'Spiraling to Ethnic War: Elites, Masses, and Moscow in Moldova's Civil War', *International Security*, special issue on 'Ethnic Nationalism, Conflict and War': vol. 21, no. 2, Fall 1996, pp. 108–138.

Kindleberger, Charles P., 'The Rise of Free Trade in Western Europe, 1820–1875', *Journal of Economic History*, vol. 35, no. 1, 1975, pp. 20–55.

Knight, W. Andy, 'Beyond the UN System? Critical Perspectives on Global Governance and Multilateral Evolution', *Global Governance*, vol. 1, no. 2, May–August 1995, pp. 229–253.

Kostakos, Giorgios, Groom, A.J.R., Morphet, Sally and Taylor, Paul, 'Britain and the UN: Towards Global Riot Control', *Review of International Studies*, January 1991, pp. 95–105.

Lake, David A., 'International Economic Structures and American Foreign Economic Policy, 1887–1934', *World Politics*, vol. 35, no. 4, July 1983, 543–577.

Layne, Christopher, 'Kant or Cant?: The Myth of Democratic Peace', in John Owen and David Spiro (eds), *International Security*, vol. 19, 2, 1994, pp. 5–49.

Maddux, Thomas R., 'American Diplomats and the Soviet Experiment: The View from the Moscow Embassy, 1934–1939', *South Atlantic Quarterly*, vol. 74, Autumn 1975, pp. 4658–4687.

Mihalka, Michael, 'Building Consensus: The Security Model in the Light of Previous Security Arrangements in Europe', *Helsinki Monitor*, no. 3, 1996, pp. 20–29.

Navari, Cornelia, 'The Great Illusion Revisited: The International Theory of Norman Angell', *Review of International Studies*, vol. 15, 1989, pp. 341–358.

Noel-Baker, Philip J., 'The Geneva Protocol: An Analysis' and 'The British Commonwealth, The Protocol and the Empire', *The Round Table*, December 1924.

d'Orville, Hans and Najman, Dragoljjub, 'A New System to Finance the United Nations', *Security Dialogue*, vol. 25, no. 2, June 1994, pp. 135–144.

Rengger, Nicholas, 'The Ethics of Trust in World Politics', *International Affairs*, vol. 73, no. 3, July 1997, pp. 469–487.

Rich, Paul, 'Reinhold Niebuhr and the Ethics of Realism in International Relations', *History of Political Thought*, vol. XIII, no. 2, Summer 1992, pp. 281–298.

Robbins, Keith, 'Lord Bryce and the First World War', *The Historical Journal* (X, 2 (1967), pp. 255–277.

Roberts, Adam, 'Communal Conflict as a Challenge to International Organization: The Case of Former Yugoslavia', *Review of International Studies*, vol. 21, no. 4, October 1995, pp. 389–410.

Ruggie, John Gerald, 'International Regimes, Transactions and Change: Embedded Liberalism in the Postwar Economic Order', *International Organization*, vol. 36, 1982, pp. 379–415.

'X' [George Kennan], 'The Sources of Soviet Conduct', *Foreign Affairs*, vol. XXV, no. 4, 1947, pp. 566–582.

Unpublished PhD theses

Hiteng, Cirino, 'Discourses on Liberation and Democracy: The Cases of Eritrea and Ethiopia', PhD thesis, University of Kent at Canterbury, 1997.

Rossbach, Stefan, 'Gnostic Wars: The Cold War in the Context of a History of Western Spirituality', PhD thesis, European University Institute, Florence, 1997.

Index

Note: literary works can be found under authors' names